D1829241

KIN

KIN

A Real People's History of our Nation

NICHOLAS DEAN BRODIE

hardie grant books
MELBOURNE • LONDON

For Duncan, Jacob, and Sophia,
you share this particular heritage with me,
so I dedicate this story to you and your families.

Published in 2015 by Hardie Grant Books

Hardie Grant Books (Australia)
Ground Floor, Building 1
658 Church Street
Richmond, Victoria 3121
www.hardiegrant.com.au

Hardie Grant Books (UK)
5th & 6th Floor
52–54 Southwark Street
London SE1 1UN
www.hardiegrant.co.uk

A Cataloguing-in-Publication entry is available from the catalogue of the National Library of Australia at www.nla.gov.au
Kin: A Real People's History of Our Nation
ISBN 978 1 74270 862 1

Cover design by Nada Backovic
Typeset in 11/14 pt Adobe Garamond by Cannon Typesetting

Printed in Australia by Griffin Press

The paper this book is printed on is certified against the Forest Stewardship Council® Standards. Griffin Press holds FSC chain of custody certification SGS-COC-005088. FSC promotes environmentally responsible, socially beneficial and economically viable management of the world's forests.

CONTENTS

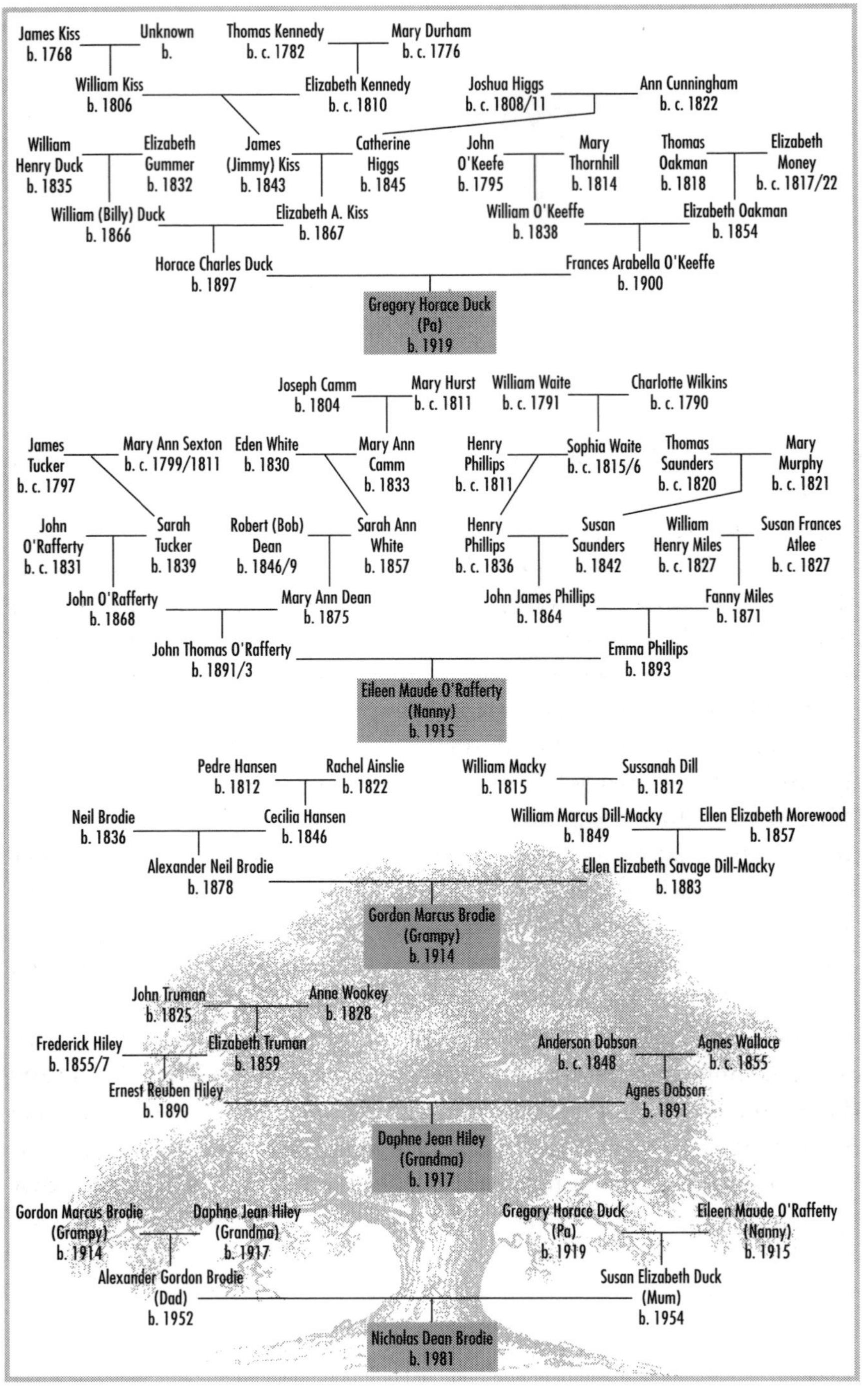
James Kiss b. 1768
Unknown b.
Thomas Kennedy b. c. 1782
Mary Durham b. c. 1776
William Kiss b. 1806
Elizabeth Kennedy b. c. 1810
Joshua Higgs b. c. 1808/11
Ann Cunningham b. c. 1822
William Henry Duck b. 1835
Elizabeth Gummer b. 1832
James (Jimmy) Kiss b. 1843
Catherine Higgs b. 1845
John O'Keefe b. 1795
Mary Thornhill b. 1814
Thomas Oakman b. 1818
Elizabeth Money b. c. 1817/22
William (Billy) Duck b. 1866
Elizabeth A. Kiss b. 1867
William O'Keeffe b. 1838
Elizabeth Oakman b. 1854
Horace Charles Duck b. 1897
Frances Arabella O'Keeffe b. 1900
Gregory Horace Duck (Pa) b. 1919
Joseph Camm b. 1804
Mary Hurst b. c. 1811
William Waite b. c. 1791
Charlotte Wilkins b. c. 1790
James Tucker b. c. 1797
Mary Ann Sexton b. c. 1799/1811
Eden White b. 1830
Mary Ann Camm b. 1833
Henry Phillips b. c. 1811
Sophia Waite b. c. 1815/6
Thomas Saunders b. c. 1820
Mary Murphy b. c. 1821
John O'Rafferty b. c. 1831
Sarah Tucker b. 1839
Robert (Bob) Dean b. 1846/9
Sarah Ann White b. 1857
Henry Phillips b. c. 1836
Susan Saunders b. 1842
William Henry Miles b. c. 1827
Susan Frances Atlee b. c. 1827
John O'Rafferty b. 1868
Mary Ann Dean b. 1875
John James Phillips b. 1864
Fanny Miles b. 1871
John Thomas O'Rafferty b. 1891/3
Emma Phillips b. 1893
Eileen Maude O'Rafferty (Nanny) b. 1915
Pedre Hansen b. 1812
Rachel Ainslie b. 1822
William Macky b. 1815
Sussanah Dill b. 1812
Neil Brodie b. 1836
Cecilia Hansen b. 1846
William Marcus Dill-Macky b. 1849
Ellen Elizabeth Morewood b. 1857
Alexander Neil Brodie b. 1878
Ellen Elizabeth Savage Dill-Macky b. 1883
Gordon Marcus Brodie (Grampy) b. 1914
John Truman b. 1825
Anne Wookey b. 1828
Frederick Hiley b. 1855/7
Elizabeth Truman b. 1859
Anderson Dobson b. c. 1848
Agnes Wallace b. c. 1855
Ernest Reuben Hiley b. 1890
Agnes Dobson b. 1891
Daphne Jean Hiley (Grandma) b. 1917
Gordon Marcus Brodie (Grampy) b. 1914
Daphne Jean Hiley (Grandma) b. 1917
Gregory Horace Duck (Pa) b. 1919
Eileen Maude O'Raffetty (Nanny) b. 1915
Alexander Gordon Brodie (Dad) b. 1952
Susan Elizabeth Duck (Mum) b. 1954
Nicholas Dean Brodie b. 1981

PREFACE

THIS IS THE STORY of how Australia became home. The heroes and heroines of this story are everyday folk who helped people a continent and generate a nation. They are my kin, and I share their stories because their joys and struggles echo millions of others that have been forgotten. This is a history of the land my people settled on, lived in, and knew. Spanning a period from the late eighteenth century into the time of living memory, the documentary trail of my family's experience in Australia reveals a real people's history of our nation.

My connection with this continent and its people stretches back before my birth in Wagga Wagga, or Wagga, as it is often referred to, beside the Murrumbidgee River, over the plains and into the mountains, through the valleys, to the beaches, and beyond the seas. My father's father's grandfather was the first Brodie in my line to arrive in Australia, making landfall in the 1860s. But this is not only the story of the Brodies. Rather, I have pursued every branch, twig, and leaf on my family tree to discover how Australia became home to a diversity of people.

My mother's father's maternal grandmother's people took me back to a penal colony struggling on the edge of empire in the eighteenth century. Many more of my people arrived through the nineteenth century to make this place their home. Their children were born here. Some of my kin saw Australia federate, some fought under its banners. This is a continent that my people helped populate with coachmen, farmers, stockmen, squatters, selectors, nurses, butchers, bakers, waitresses, unknown mothers, and unmarked graves. From Botany Bay to Federation to Gallipoli to Darwin, this is more than the narrative we know of those times. It is the sum of my ancestors' experiences.

Like many of us, I began to wonder about my ancestral past, and set out to recover a sense of what had been lost. But through this journey I also aimed to reclaim my place in Australia's history, to put my people back into the national story. The telling and understanding of Australia's past, in part or whole, has too often been allowed to become both an obscure academic plaything and an argument machine for facile political commentary. There are ideologies of Australian history, both right and left, whose proponents historicise the past to suit their own professional or polemical agendas. Some deny the tragedies of our past, others judge it. Some misunderstand, others misconstrue. Few really learn from it. Australian history has been rendered too political, bizarrely isolated from the rest of the world, overly subjective, and, frankly, often boring. But most of the real stories within our continent are none of these things. We have fascinating and important tales to tell. There have been some excellent exceptions to this trend, but they have generally focused on individual events or issues, and as yet they have not been pulled together. We have not had an honest history of the entire national story for a generation. To restore a true democratic history of this continent and nation requires a new focus on the demos, the people. And so I chose my people, my kin.

My people mainly originated from the British Isles. They were mostly ordinary folk, but their journeys encompass an extraordinary story. Fortunately their interactions with Australia's Indigenous peoples and other settler minorities allow some of the experiences of these groups to unfold through this story as naturally occurring realities, not forced scholarly or politicised impositions. And the same is true of wider political and imperial narratives. My people's stories, documented from the 1790s to the present, reflect the historical record of the period from British colonisation onwards. Major events and historical trends influence them, and are influenced by them, each situation allowing me to see historical agent and historical context interacting through time.

Having begun to discern their tracks, I followed my kin across this land, and allowed Australia's past to reveal itself through them, on its own terms. This is therefore a national history whose structure is entirely the product of original research. It is unburdened by a slavish need to repeat our tired mythologised narratives of memorable events, so some of our 'cosy' stories will be challenged. And this book will not doff its proverbial cap to educational preoccupations and so become another 'short history' or 'concise' volume; it is bigger than that. This charting of my particular crimson thread serves to guide us through that wider set of bonds, the broader kinship network, which make us all a people. It therefore bridges the gaps between memorable events, and can integrate the fruits of scholarly research, without being reduced to a recitation of those events or a summary of scholarship.

What follows is a history of Australia told through overlapping ancestral tales. By the accident of family connection to this historian, me, people otherwise poorly documented have become central to the nation's social history. The past has therefore been populated without some of those prominent biases that strangled a generation of historical discourse. I strive to wear no black armband or white blindfold, or any other metaphorical party clothes. You cannot choose your family, and nor did I. They are here, warts and all: convicts, soldiers, sailors, good wives, bad husbands, the young, the elderly, the famous, the obscure, and many of their animals. I am seeking by this to achieve those simplest of historical objectives: to answer the eternal questions of what happened, why, where, when, how, to whom, and with what effect?

Historians are normally cursed to inhabit worlds in which they do not rightly belong. Spectral observers, they are bound by the real tyrant of distance: time. They can gaze so heavily upon a moment as to take on its attributes, forever lost between the past and the present. Or they can utterly fail, through being bounded to their everyday world, to see another time or place as the different thing it is. But they can never be in that moment they study. Unless, that is, perhaps some small forgotten part of them was there. Could this then become not history, but remembering?

Tales told, documents written, photographs taken, and objects handled all mark the many journeys that carried thousands of people to these shores and across this land. But we are all challenged by the vagaries of memories and evidence. As people disperse, so can memory. As the ground claims our forebears, so too does it claim their footprints. Whether they lived 45,000 years ago or yesterday, our capacity to recall our ancestors comes from recognising those toe marks in the ancient sand, or reading their faded words scratched on parchment and paper.

I have tracked my people through the records of their times in ships and in prisons, their moments of fame in local newspapers, their hardships, their headstones, oral traditions passed down, court transcripts, their letters and photographs, and the many records of their births, deaths, and marriages. I have followed them over the seas to the lands of their birth, and back again as they sailed on creaking and reeking ships to their new homeland, their children's and my birth land. In doing so, I push our understandings of being Australian beyond the academic confines of race, class, and gender, the binaries of invasion or settlement, the politics of left or right, and the great discontinuities of historical treatment between 'over there' and 'over here', 'back then' and 'here now'. Following my kin is not about degenerating into ancestor worship, jingoistic nationalism, or its guilt-ridden antitheses. Rather, it is about overcoming the need to read ideology into the past, and instead to listen to it on its own terms.

Yet paradoxically I have also ended up with what is, by the historical accident that a continent became a nation, a national history drawn wholly from the diversity within my own family tree. Nations were once thought of as naturally occurring ethnic entities, so I am aware of the irony, and do not want to revitalise an outdated and exclusive model of nationality. Nor do I want to affirm the misguided sense of history as a long march of progress. Certainly the charting of the movement of time from the past to the present, and that process whereby disparate peoples came together, has been an unavoidable yet compelling part of this exercise. But that is partly a result of the methodology of working from a particular point—me—into a wider past. And while it reveals the ways in which people make a place their home, and becomes an explanation for why I feel a strong sense of belonging to an entire land, it is not an argument that being Australian is about length of occupation. As far as I am concerned, there is no room for a hierarchy of belonging when it comes to being 'Australian'. That view, I admit, may be a product of the logic of liberal democracy itself, with its balancing of individual rights and government power, but the alternative slope is just too slippery.

In undertaking this journey where the research, and also the writing, has deliberately been done with a twist, I necessarily traverse the realms of popular historical memory, academic research, local histories, my own family's stories, and genealogical research. By this, I can wear down authoritative borders and specialist walls that compartmentalise the past for too easy consumption and often produce attendant intellectual indigestion. Within Australia we have become habituated to thinking of 'the settlers', 'the British', 'the Aborigines', 'the White people', 'the Black people'. And so I am challenging that overconfident and too regular use of a three-lettered determiner, 'the', even while I try to uncover how this diversity of stories and experiences come together to contribute to that thing many people almost instinctively and unthinkingly call 'the Australian people'. What we perceive to be 'the Australian people' is in part a product of our past, yet also a construction of the present moment that is perpetually being renegotiated, and perhaps even a sort of shared fantasy. Aware of the irony, I can only embrace it. That, after all, is what one does with family.

So ignoring the present for the moment, I return to the past. Tracking family has given me a view of the way that individuals and families experienced the processes of settlement, attachment, and community-building. It has ended up less like standard history, and more like a real-life James A Michener or Edward Rutherford novel. But this is not historical fiction. Rather, this is a great Australian historical sweep. It is a true epic. But because it is based on the documented experiences of my identifiable kin, the story starts somewhere else.

CHAPTER ONE

RULE, *BRITANNIA*, AND TRANSPORTATION 1796

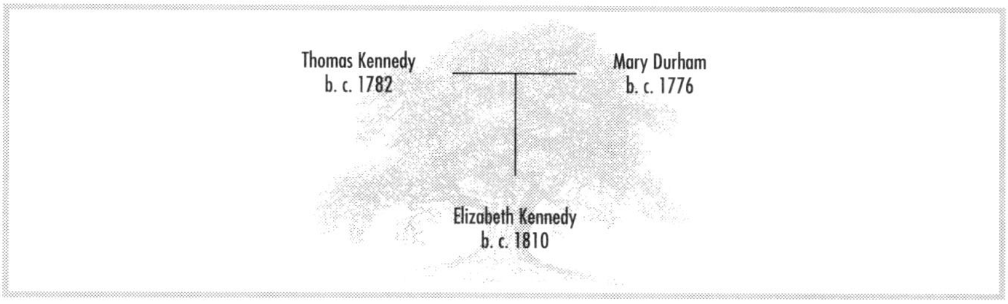

'NOT GUILTY.' With two simple words the young teenage boy challenged the court. His plea was more than a denial of his participation in the crime for which he was charged. The words carried a meaning greater than his innocence. They spoke to Thomas Kennedy's view that he was in the right, and the British government was in the wrong. In this matter he carried no guilt.

The fourteen-year-old apprentice glass-cutter had stood in the dock while the charge was read aloud. Although he had been brought to the court in chains, it was probably a welcome change to be there rather than the dank Dublin gaol where he had been kept waiting for his trial.

Repetitive, wordy, and ominously phrased, the formal indictment denounced Thomas and several codefendants as traitors. He was accused of being a member of 'a party and society formed united and associated for the purpose of subverting and overturning by force of arms the government of our said lord the king of and in this kingdom of Ireland by law established'. He had imagined the death of the King.

Thomas was one of the self-proclaimed 'Defenders' of Ireland. This was a kind of Irishmen's secret society, blending political reading and rhetoric, raids on British military armament stores and the houses of landlords, general rioting, and occasional fistfights against their Protestant equivalents. The society reflected the way some Irish people were becoming increasingly organised in their responses to the British, being one of a number of groups and movements that fed into a wave of resistance, and eventually southern independence. Centuries of aristocratic Protestant British overlordship had led Irish working class interests and Catholic identity to align in the cause of Irish independence. More specifically, in the 1790s, regardless of their actual activities, the formation of the Defenders was clearly a reaction to an increased British military presence and use of troops for domestic policing.

Thomas, although still young, was also a member of the Philanthropic Society, another of the underground political societies. Class resentment and teenage angst might have combined to give him an urgent sense that the world needed changing. In a building in Dublin's High Street several like-minded men and youths regularly met to discuss politics and philosophy. Clearly literate, Thomas was learning a trade that would probably have meant he was engaged in beautifying the houses of the well-to-do English and Anglo-Irish. The wealth he encountered might have angered him, but may also have helped such a young man gain prominence among the Defenders. If they were to attack the big houses, he could very effectively have served as their advance scout.

The formation of the Defenders in the 1790s was not just about getting rid of the British, however. As well as being an anti-colonial movement, it was also a wider reform movement. Defenders took some of their political theorising from writers like Thomas Paine, whose *Rights of Man* of 1791 was quite a hit with Irish agitators. Paine's argument against hereditary aristocratic government was enough to have him tried, in his absence, for seditious libel. Thomas may well have read it secretly by candlelight in his master's house. As an apprentice he was not free to roam wherever and whenever he wanted, but had a strict curfew, and could be punished with a sanctioned beating at his master's discretion within considerable limits. He had to miss some of the Defender meetings for that reason.

Yet unfortunately for Thomas, coinciding as it did with the French Revolution, even a whiff of talk about political reform in the 1790s made the British nervous in a very particular way. Some sectors of the British ruling classes were possibly still smarting from the violent birth of the United States of America, and some may have remembered the last Stuart uprising in Scotland. Certainly the last thing they wanted was a guerrilla insurgency on their doorstep just as they went to war with France. When he and his mates met in a house in Suffolk Street on 20 August 1795, it seems likely that they were either watched, or had a traitor in their midst.

The men ducked in one at a time, at different intervals, no doubt with password at the ready. They would have been trying to avoid notice and remain quiet on the stones and stairway. Unfortunately in a busy city street, it would have been hard to escape notice. Joining him in that room was William Lawler, a man who was there to be sworn in as a new Defender. Thomas opened his fob watch, and pulled out a small piece of paper. He unfolded it, and showed Lawler the oath he was to take. It was a series of questions and answers.

'I am concerned', one of the Defenders started.

'So am I', Lawler read in response.

'With who?' he was asked.

'With the National Convention', he replied.

At least, this was William Lawler's later account of events.

Two days later the authorities pounced. Before the sun had risen on Saturday 22 August 1795, Thomas was a prisoner. In the eighteenth-century Irish equivalent of an anti-terror raid, Dublin's Alderman James had sent men around the city to round up thirteen men suspected of being Defenders. Several of the Defenders reportedly had weapons, and the papers in Thomas's fob watch were discovered. Two captains, two inspectors, and a military guard captured each man, conveying them under armed guard to Dublin Castle. The coordinated raids were a powerful statement about the steady gaze the government was maintaining on malcontents and dissidents. It was meant not simply to nab the Defenders, but to shock the entire movement. And so Thomas, like the others, was subjected to what is euphemistically recorded in the press as 'a long examination'.

Satisfied that they had a case, the authorities put the men and boy in gaol to await trial. They were to be confined separately, and were denied any communication with any other person. No magistrate was present. It must have been a harrowing experience for fourteen-year-old Thomas.

When I first encountered this story, I was not sure what to make of it. On the one hand the records of the prosecution were rather hostile, but on the other I was seemingly able to garner a considerable amount of detail about my ancestor's activities and attitudes. But to what extent the presented 'facts' of the case reflected the actuality is often hard to tell, and I knew that I needed to tread cautiously in my interpretations. Mostly, it depended on what I thought of William Lawler's evidence for the prosecution. The documentary record leaves two interpretive possibilities. Either Lawler was originally a government informant who notified the authorities, or he turned King's evidence and became the star prosecution witness. Either way, the government built its arguments and commenced the prosecutions. The well-publicised 'Proceedings on the Trial of Thomas Kennedy for High Treason; before the Court holden at Dublin under a Commission of Oyer and Terminer, on Monday February 22: 36 George III. A.D. 1796' was, without doubt, something of a show trial.

The facts of the case are a little obscured by a focus on law, because those recording and following the case were most interested in the rare application of the treason statute. Not only that, the recorded details were mostly dependent on a single witness for the prosecution. Lawler had been a member of the London Corresponding Society in 1791 when residing in London, which had introduced him to reform movements. Returning to Dublin he had developed a similar network, but the Irish reformers saw things with greater urgency than their English counterparts. Lawler told of a vague plan to recruit men and then attack Dublin Castle. From the gaze of the twenty-first century, however, the membership expansion plan reads like a dodgy pyramid scheme. Each of the first ten men was supposed to recruit another ten, who were then to each recruit five more. Clearly it did not work out that way, but his association with the developer of that plot first provided Lawler with contacts with the Philanthropic Society and then with a means of entry into the Defenders.

The other key part of the evidence against the Defenders was the oath papers which Thomas Kennedy had kept hidden for the group in his fob watch. The discovery of these papers on his arrest formed the only physical evidence of significance to the trial. Mostly, it was the testimony of Lawler that eventually got Thomas transported to New South Wales. That and the 'court's mercy'. After all, he was an apprentice, still a young man learning his trade. Even though the court found him guilty of high treason, Thomas managed to escape the hangman's rope, unlike two of his codefendants, because he was thought young and impressionable. Yet he was old enough to have written some of the papers in his watch. And, if Lawler's testimony is to be believed, then Thomas was discussing making an attack on the

Chancellor's house during winter 'and to hang him from one of the trees in Stephen's-green'.

The 1795 trial of the Defenders is a good illustration of the forces that were stacked against the Irish in the 1790s. There were multiple elements to Thomas's trial, but it really came down to eight allegations. Thomas and friends were accused of four things: 1, associating with the Defenders; 2, assembling to adhere to France; 3, associating to overturn the British government; and 4, associating to overturn Protestant Religion. Enlisting William Lawler to do the above four things was what made up the eight allegations.

A common thread here is that of association or assembly. The trial does not concern anybody having actually done anything other than hold a little meeting and swear a brief 'oath'. It really was, at law, all about a meeting at a house on 20 August 1795, and the meeting was important for proving 'association', and the talk indicated 'intentions', specifically regarding France and the British government. This accusatory format was designed to make the prosecution's case conform to the requirements of the *Treason Act* by which Thomas was being tried.

The Defenders' oath was a series of challenge questions like, 'Where did the cock crow when the whole world heard him?', which was answered with 'In France', a thinly coded reference to the French Revolution. Thomas, along with many others, was secretly building an organisation designed to oust the British government, and reform the Irish government along more democratic lines. If the British government was considered legitimate, then it was treason. If it was not considered legitimate, then it was not treason. In the same way as the French and American revolutions had, it spoke to new ways of conceiving of the relationship between rulers and ruled. 'What is your designs?' they asked each other in their coded greetings. 'On Freedom', they replied. These were little men in a world of big men, dreaming of a liberty that they saw, perhaps slightly inaccurately, as existing in America and France.

The trial of Thomas Kennedy points to Australia's long and complex legal heritage—it inherited a body of English law that had already been worked out over many generations of colonisation in other parts of the world, including Ireland. As a case in point, the statute under which Thomas was convicted was *23 Edw.3 St 5.c.2*, better known as the *Treason Act* (1351). And the process that sent him there was trial by jury, another medieval English invention brought to Ireland.

About a century after William the Conqueror won England at Hastings the Normans turned their attention towards Ireland. The Norman conquest of Ireland was not the result of a moment, but rather a gradual process of piecemeal acquisition. It is a little like the colonisation of Australia: a chunk of land here or there, some resistance and some collaboration, with some legal niceties being utilised now and then to polish the dirtiness from the prize. In fact, it is a little like the colonisation of any other place: India, New Zealand, Scotland, North America, Germania, and Gaul. One of the legal peculiarities or niceties was the notional Lordship of Ireland. From 1169 the King of England nominally ruled Ireland as feudal lord, with Papal approval. Curiously, the first was King John, generally thought of in popular imagination as a bad king. Legends aside, John was really a weak king, brought to heal at Runnymede by the powerful barons of the realm. *Magna Carta*, literally the 'big charter', placed limits on royal rule (in theory), and mostly those limits benefited barons (again, in theory).

The difference between theoretical and actual authority and power is a running theme of medieval Ireland. Nominally the ruler of Ireland, the King of England really only ruled Dublin and the Pale, the area around it under effective English control. The colloquialism 'beyond the pale' comes from this distinction between reality and actuality, between English perceptions of civilisation and barbarism, divided by a palisade, a fence. But the reality of English rule gradually faded from its Norman beginnings throughout the Middle Ages. The Black Death helped, as did internal English problems, especially the Wars of the Roses. Under the Tudors, however, the autonomy of the Irish lords was curtailed dramatically, as the Tudors feared the use of Ireland as a base for launching Yorkist uprisings against their rule, a trick the Tudors had seen before. Not only had Henry Tudor taken the throne by a French-assisted invasion of England, which probably made him and his descendents acutely aware of the potential dangers of foreign invasion, but Ireland actually *was* used to launch an invasion against him. In 1487 Lambert Simbel was crowned King of England by Burgundian troops brought to Dublin in a failed attempt at foreign-sponsored rebellion.

A Tudor sense of insecurity did a lot to make Ireland subordinate. In 1494 the Irish Parliament was essentially made inferior to its Westminster equivalent, making the English Parliament Ireland's highest law-making authority. Fearing invasion and fretting over the loss of Papal authority for the Lordship of Ireland, because he was now excommunicate and head of his own church, Henry VIII made concerted efforts to bring Ireland to heal, eventually declaring it a kingdom in 1542, with his head naturally wearing the crown. Elizabeth I sent several expeditions to bring the troublesome Irish to obeisance, achieving some success shortly before dying. The reality of English control, and bloodshed, only increased thereafter until the English had successfully brought Ireland to a bloodied state of submission, courtesy of Mr Cromwell and friends in the following century.

Edward III's *Treason Act*, widely known then and after because of features such as hanging, drawing, and quartering, became law in Ireland in 1495 as part of this more active Tudor governance. Imagining the death of the King, or adhering to or aiding his enemies, were among the provisions that 446 years after its passing in England in 1351 got Thomas Kennedy sent from Ireland to Australia in 1797. It is a law replete with irony. Edward III was one of England's stronger kings, a man who was crowned because his mother colluded with Roger Mortimer to depose his father (Edward II) and install Edward III as King. Mortimer was Lord of Ireland at the time, an earlier instance of the use of Ireland as a rebellion or invasion staging ground, although in this case by an English-appointed overlord. Mortimer's influence was widely resented, however, and so Edward III's personal rule was partly established through Mortimer's execution. Edward then asserted his authority by playing the part of a traditional military king. He laid claim to being King of France as well as Lord of Ireland, opening the Hundred Years War, and providing the Irish and French with the potential to hold shared sentiments about the English.

So Thomas was tried against an English law that had been brought to Ireland by a colonising force, just like the Aborigines of New South Wales who were later tried under English law and sentenced to transportation as convicts. As Kristyn Harman's book on *Aboriginal Convicts* shows, the difference between resistance leader and criminal is a matter of perspective. But the historical outcome in both cases reveals the workings of English jurisprudence as a tool of the British Empire, where it was not only English law that saw Thomas transported, but English legal process. The jury trial that King John's *Magna Carta* granted was the right that a man be tried by his peers. But the wording, peers, as in social equals, like Peers of the Realm, spoke to an entrenched notion of legal inequality. A man had to be judged by his equals or betters. The notion of a man's peers passing judgement on the facts of a case was locked in to the *Magna Carta* to ensure that the King would not arbitrarily punish his lords, nor have them tried by commoners. It was never intended as an assertion of universal equality before the law;

in fact, it was proof of the opposite. But gradually the jury trial as we think of it became a useful tool for local governance, essentially allowing a collective of villagers to determine the facts of a case, and the original basis was forgotten. Yet even this early version of the now recognisable form was originally about twelve men good and true who already knew the accused and the facts of the case. It was village justice with a magistrate to authorise the lynching.

That is an oversimplification, naturally, but it points to the ridiculousness of the Defenders' trials, each before twelve men, several generally having very English surnames. Part of the case against James Weldon, another of the Defenders, revolved around the question of whether he was considered a 'yeoman' or not, with advocates quoting Shakespeare's *Henry V* as supporting evidence for their argument. In other words, the case overwhelmingly and almost flippantly focused on issues of English culture, law, and authority, not pre-colonial Irish laws and traditions or current Irish political and social realities. This was how English law worked in Ireland. Weldon's jury of esquires and merchants found him guilty and he was executed in front of Newgate, the prison in which Thomas and the others were being held. In all likelihood they saw or heard him drop from the scaffold and twitch at the end of the rope.

But Thomas probably gained a sense of hope from another of the preceding trials. John Leary's advocate demanded 'was there any evidence to support that overt act', 'any proof' of the events described by Lawler? Unsatisfied that the prosecution had provided such evidence, his jury actually found him not guilty. Six other Defenders were released following Leary's trial. Each Defender who walked out of Newgate must have given Thomas hope that he too might soon have walked out into the sunshine in the streets of Dublin, rather than wasting his time in a dark prison, cold, overcrowded, and notorious for its poor sanitation, even by the standards of the eighteenth century.

When Thomas saw the main part of his trial commence in February 1796 he was probably anxious, but optimistic. He must have had high hopes of freedom, as the balance seemed to have shifted in the defendants' favour. But it was still a serious situation. Walking into the courtroom with his chains clinking he was accused of imagining the King's death and colluding with the King's enemies. According to one witness, whose evidence had helped one man hang and whose untrustworthiness had seen seven men freed, Thomas was said to have sworn an oath and carried copies of that oath in his fob watch. He was not peripheral to the case. His trial, his evidence, and his actions, were central to the matter.

Two members of Thomas's jury had already been jurors for the trial that had freed Leary, and so Thomas's attorney recognised an opportunity. Each was sworn in as witnesses by the defence regarding Lawler's testimony in that previous trial. It was part of the defence's plan to obliterate the reliability of Lawler's account once and for all, and the carry-over jurors allowed the attorney to bring the details of Leary's successful defence to the aid of Thomas. Witness after witness was sworn in, asserting that Lawler was not a trustworthy man. But it was to no avail. Thomas's lawyer did his best, arguing into the night. Eventually, however, he had to stop and let the jury decide. About two in the morning, tired of the trial, the jury retired to consider the case. After Thomas having endured several days of trial, months in prison, and the ups and downs of the previous trials, it took the jury twenty minutes to decide that he was guilty.

And no doubt he returned to Newgate to await his fate.

Thomas and Patrick Hart, another of the accused, had the opportunity to plead for mercy before the court on 27 February 1796. It is poignant to read Thomas's words. 'I hope from the recommendation from the jury', he told the judge, 'that you will have compassion upon me, and I hope for a long day.' The jurors had at least recommended that the court show mercy because of his age, even if they had considered Thomas guilty. He reminded the Bench that 'A man who was not recommended had twelve weeks', effectively proposing that he be given a short sentence. It did not work. Knowing his age, knowing what his 'crime' actually entailed, I could not help but feel revolted by the judge's decision as I read the sad conclusion, even though by then I already knew the result. As he summarised the case, the judge's condemnation and disgust flowed in legalese prose, directed at my ancestor, a boy. Page after page it went on, until, at last, the sentence of death was pronounced.

Both Thomas and Hart were appointed to be executed on 12 March. Both were reprieved until 19 March. Hart, unfortunately, failed to receive further mercy and was hanged. Thomas, luckily, received further respite. He would get his 'long day'. And so, several months later, on 10 December 1796, the convict ship *Britannia* sailed from Cork, bound for Sydney, with Thomas Kennedy on board.

As well as reflecting the experiences of the British and Irish past, Thomas's case usefully serves to highlight the danger of projecting the height of British imperial might back onto the period at the beginning of Britain's Australian enterprise. The British government's actions at this time were often directed at securing the empire in the face of threats at home and abroad, whether ideological, cultural, strategic, or economic. The treatment of Ireland and the initial colonisation of Australia both need to be seen in this light, and are actually linked to each other. Spooked by the recent loss of the American colonies, some in Britain feared losing another colony in Ireland. Britain's main rival, France, soon became belligerent in revolutionary ways, much more threatening to the comfortable British establishment than more traditional and familiar kingly and mercantile forms of imperial competition. There were even murmurs that slavery would not last, reducing the profits derived from Caribbean colonial consumer products like tobacco and sugar, threatening many a gentleman's investments. At the moment of inception of the colony in Australia, the whole British imperial project seemed about to unravel. It was not a good time to imagine the death of the English King.

Certainly the New South Wales settlement established on the east coast of Australia in Sydney Cove in January 1788 with a 'First Fleet' of convicts and their military guards was in part prompted by a need to deal with overcrowded hulks. But so too was it a geopolitical assertion of Britain's confidence that it still had an imperial destiny. The company of exiles that struggled to survive adapting to a new and harsh environment were making good on Captain James Cook's claiming of New South Wales for the British sovereign in 1770 during his expedition to locate and chart New Zealand and the east coast of New Holland. The appointment of the naval officer Arthur Phillip to lead the First Fleet and administer the early settlement pointedly illustrates that it was a military base supported by convict labour, as much as a convict establishment overseen by the military. As Michael Pembroke's biography *Arthur Phillip: Sailor, Mercenary, Governor, Spy* reveals, Phillip had been used for sensitive missions in the past, and was a practised diplomat. The new settlement was designed to project power out over the ocean, by clinging to a suitable anchorage on a convenient spot of land. An Australian colony, however small at first, asserted the projection of British naval power ahead of Britain's rivals. By effectively controlling a new sea, at least cartographically, a new route to the riches of the East Asian trade was secured.

And it was all done utilising a legal nicety, the notion that New South Wales was *terra nullius*, basically not owner-occupied. Cook was not unusual in claiming lands he 'discovered' for his monarch. Whether already occupied or not, or even whether claimed by earlier European explorers, Europe's maritime powers asserted claims to territory with formal flag raisings, gun salutes, and other ceremonies and festivities, which were the imperial equivalent of dogs raising their hind legs. These were shows for later negotiation of disputes between rival imperial claimants. Given that this period was witnessing dramatic changes in international relationships and concepts of international and natural law, focusing on the strict historical legality of such actions becomes a form of misplaced retrospection. The goalposts were shifting and the players were, often as not, making it up as they went along. The ultimate proof of ownership often came down to the fact of occupation, but a documentable record of prior discovery, conquest, cession by treaty or agreement, or simple assertions of ownership, could at least give subsequent arguments a veneer of substance.

Where local peoples were not engaged in working the land by agriculture, urban living, or some other sign of 'civilisation', they were deemed not to effectively occupy it in any proprietary sense. In effect, the land, *terra*, was un-owned, *nullius*. But Cook's 'legal' nicety held relatively little significance for the overall fact of British settlement of Australia anyway. Rather than focusing on *terra nullius* as a matter of international law between 'the British' and 'the Aborigines', the moment of Australian colonisation is better understood through reference to some key chronological facts and connections, leading to a much more interesting conclusion. The penal settlement at New South Wales was established in the wake of the American Revolution, and was contemporaneous with the French Revolution. Arguments regarding the doctrine of *terra nullius* aside, it was not just a space for excess criminals, not simply a possible realm for loyal ex-Americans, not just a pointed flaunting of prior Dutch claims or Papal decrees about the Portuguese and Spanish spheres of global influence, and not simply a thumbing of the British imperial nose to France. As well as all these, it made a bigger philosophical point. The little settlement at Sydney Cove was ruled on the King's behalf by a supposedly benignly despotic Governor. It was a powerful assertion to the world that despite what international jurists claimed and revolutionaries asserted: sovereignty over land was rightly vested only in sovereigns.

Thomas Kennedy was moved from one part of the King's domains to another, not only because he challenged that king's claim, but because he was deemed to threaten the very divine rights invested in the King. And, almost as if to further the argument, the ship they decided to send him on was called the *Britannia*.

Originally, carrying tea was one of the *Britannia*'s main roles. In 1774, the year it was launched, it famously brought tea into Charleston Harbour in South Carolina. Following the Boston Tea Party of the previous year, the lesser-known Charleston Tea Party similarly saw British tea dumped from the *Britannia* into the harbour. It was done as a mock offering to Poseidon, or rather, a giant 'up yours' to the British. The name of the ship probably helped fuel the mood.

It is not terribly surprising that a tea ship would convey convicts. There was really no such thing as a 'convict ship'. Rather, the British government employed merchant ships to convey convicts, and the holds were generally temporarily modified to become prisons. The ship would arrive at a British port, would have cells and bunks built below decks, would board the crew, surgeon, guard, and then convicts, and sometimes free passengers, and then the human cargo would be transported like any other. Generally provision was made to exercise the prisoners on deck for a period each day. A regimen of cleaning and washing, and sometimes religious or educational instruction, helped to structure the voyage and keep the prisoners occupied. Once discharged of its prisoners, the ship would then generally head off to another destination to collect a cargo, and so continue its perpetual round of conveyance around the globe. Eventually they would be wrecked, or become dilapidated beyond repair.

Nominally, convicts were in the custody of the captain of the ship or some other appointed person. They were human cargo in legality as well as effect. The parallels with slavery are fairly obvious, but a crucial difference was that convict ships generally had a surgeon appointed to supervise the health of the cargo and ensure it was landed safely. In typically capitalist fashion, the surgeon's pay was linked to his success rate. But while often compared with the slave trade, there is a better English legal parallel, which again has particularly Irish connections. The basic concepts and legal structures of transportation have their origins, in no small part, in the vagrancy laws of medieval England. These provided a set of legal precedents for passing a person through a series of custodies, casting them beyond a set jurisdiction, and then compelling them to work as a form of punishment. In some of these laws, the Irish were particularly singled out for return to Ireland. Even the word historians usually use to describe people transported to Australia, 'convict', is in a sense a misnomer, a catch-all for what they really were: prisoner-transportees. Like the medieval vagrancy laws, the legal structures and administrative apparatus of transportation focused more on the question of custody than conviction. And the transportation system was not fully developed in 1788 by any means. Rather, it went through a series of changes based on wider political situations, reform movements, and local agitation, which changed the nature of the experience over time. When the first transportees arrived in New South Wales there were some unheeded suggestions that the transportees' punishment of transportation had been effectively completed once the transportation part was over. But as the colony developed, clearer rules were developed about putting convicts into the service of free settlers or the government.

But in some cases, the voyage should have been punishment enough, and the *Britannia*'s 1796–97 run was one such trip.

Being transferred to a freshly built ship prison may have been a relief for prisoners, after what was often several months in a local gaol, city prison, or floating hulk. Thomas was most likely conveyed from imprisonment in Dublin to a prison-ship in August 1796, five months after being sentenced to death. This then sailed to Cork for embarkation on the *Britannia*. Even when the prisoners boarded their 'convict ship' this did not necessarily mean an imminent departure. Officially, the *Britannia*'s voyage began on 10 December 1796, but the ship only actually sailed from the British Isles in March the following year. Such delays were not untypical. The 169 days on board were not all necessarily 'at sea'.

Transportees did not always meekly acquiesce in their sentence, and frequently sought out opportunities for freeing themselves. The *Britannia* carried 144 male prisoners and forty-four female prisoners. Of the men, more than ninety were Defenders or had Defender associations, their crimes being recorded as things like 'Administering unlawful oaths', or simply 'Defenderism'. Thomas Kennedy was not the only prisoner there for high treason, although at fourteen years of age he was certainly one of the youngest. So it is not at all surprising to learn that there were plans to effect a mutiny on the ship. If they could overpower the guard and the crew, the transportees could gain their liberty. From there, they could either return to Ireland, or sail to an enemy of England. France or a French colony might have seemed an obvious choice.

There were reports in the English press that before the *Britannia* had even departed Cork there was an attempted mutiny. Supposedly the prisoners 'had found means to disengage themselves from their irons, and were on the point of rising' when the plot was discovered. It was said that 'Kennedy, who was some time since sentenced to be hanged in Dublin for High Treason, but who was respited through the lenity [leniency] of Government, and his punishment commuted for transportation, was the leader of the mutiny'.

Charles Bateson, author of *The Convict Ships 1787–1868*, referred to the particular voyage that took Thomas from Ireland to Australia, as 'one of the worst in the history of transportation'. Bateson calculated that one out of every seventeen prisoners died. Many of these deaths were from mistreatment and excessive punishment, some of which was ostensibly in reaction to mutinous intent by the transportees. The prisoners were over-frequently chained, punished as groups for individual 'infractions', and deprived of rations. Women had their heads shaved, and were chained and beaten. One woman suicided. This barbaric treatment was meted out by the order of the ship's captain, Thomas Dennott, and was not effectively challenged by the surgeon, Augustus Beyer, whose role it more properly was to oversee the administration of punishment. Beyer seems to have been unable to cope with the situation and was reported to have only entered the prison decks on a few occasions, and always carried a stick. Transportees later stated that they feared his treatments more than their wounds.

So bad was the state of the prisoners on their arrival in New South Wales that Governor Hunter convened an enquiry. From testimony given to this it is possible to get multiple perspectives on the voyage. Apparently, it was said, the would-be mutineers had sworn oaths amongst themselves to kill the officers, take the ship, and 'effectuate their liberty'. This was typical Defender behaviour and planning of the sort that had got a number of them, including Thomas, on the ship in the first place, so the fact of mutinous designs and attempts seems more than plausible. To what degree Thomas was actually involved is unknown. The English reports may not even relate to the same event as that raised at the enquiry, and it seems a little suspect as such rumoured events were often nothing more than that—rumour. Thomas was, after all, only fourteen years old.

But all accounts agree that when a plot was discovered during the voyage, the main ringleaders were severely punished. Most also agreed that the punishment was excessive, and that the captain clearly overstepped the line from punishment to sadism. One convict was ordered to receive three hundred lashes one day, to be followed by a further five hundred the next day when his back was still bloodied and raw. Some of these prisoners died after their floggings. Even if the full complement of strokes had not been given, the decks would still have been awash with blood. Afterwards, infection, dehydration, and loss of blood took a toll on the damaged bodies of the lead mutineers. On the captain's orders, the convicts were kept in chains for the duration of the voyage.

The ship continued west for Rio de Janiero, where it stopped to replenish the food and water supplies. Here, too, the convicts suffered maltreatment: undue confinement, heavy rationing, and harsh physical punishments. Then, leaving South America behind, the *Britannia* turned south to catch the winds of the Southern Ocean's 'roaring forties' and race eastwards. As a final insult, the ship leaked, and many convicts were drenched in their bunks in the lower decks, with fetid water pooling on the floor. There were suggestions that some had made themselves sick by resorting to drinking urine because adequate fresh water had not been provided.

The *Britannia* arrived in Port Jackson, Sydney, on 27 May 1797. It was immediately obvious to observers that something had gone awry. The prisoners were in a horrific state of emaciation. They were likely grateful to disembark, but the Governor was unimpressed that they were not in a fit state to be put to work. As already mentioned, he instigated an enquiry, and both the captain and surgeon were found to have been culpable of gross misconduct. But other than denying the captain and surgeon future employment with the convict service, no punishment was forthcoming. The legal framework that had punished Thomas could not protect him. The problem was that there was no court in New South Wales with the legal competence to try the offenders, and holding the trials in Britain would necessitate the return of convicts to serve as witnesses. So, having left its damaged cargo, the *Britannia* sailed from Sydney for China, to collect a cargo of tea.

More than two and a half years later, in January 1800, yet another boatload of convicts arrived, in the *Minerva*. One of the convicts on board was Mary Durham, who had been sentenced to seven years transportation in May 1798. The precise crime is obscure, but the context is clear. The timing matches riots in Dublin that were, in part, inspired by the Treason Trials of 1796. The British government had failed to smash Irish rebelliousness, and so the colony of New South Wales proved a means to continue to try to placate a restless Ireland.

Mary also had a difficult voyage out, albeit not so notorious as that of Thomas. The surgeon appointed to oversee the convicts on the *Minerva*, John Washington Price, kept a journal of the voyage. This, rather fortunately, provides some interesting insights into the whole process of transportation at this time. Mary was transferred onto the *Minerva* in Cork from the brig *Lively*, which had carried the bulk of the convicts from Dublin. Price went aboard the *Lively* to examine the convicts and 'found them indeed in the most wretched, cruel & pitiable condition I ever saw human being in'. Wet, cold, cramped and 'half naked', the ghostly figures in the prison-ship's hold clearly shocked the surgeon.

Between that February boarding, and the eventual August departure, there were some events of note aboard the *Minerva*. More transportees were taken on in small groups, at times without proper papers regarding their convictions or punishments. Others died. And some even had the good fortune to have letters of pardon arrive. Indeed, on the day the *Minerva* finally sailed out of Cork in convoy a fast ship was sent hurrying after it with good news for a convict, who as it turned out was not aboard anyway. As this highlights, the whole system was far from running smoothly, and the early settlement of Australia needs to be seen in this light.

One September day, shortly into the voyage, the weather was so calm that Price and the *Minerva*'s captain were being dined on the *Friendship*, another ship in their little convoy about two miles away. Upon his return, Price discovered that 'the sailors were claiming a wife each from amongst the female convicts, and in a little time sixteen of the women got husbands for the voyage amongst the sailors and soldiers'. Whether he read the situation correctly, however, is a different matter.

After getting underway again with better winds, the *Minerva* had an exchange of cannon fire with what appeared to be a Portuguese ship flying English colours. In all fairness, the *Minerva* had first raised the Danish flag, a typical exchange of flag-based deception on the high seas. Price lamented not having letters of Marque, a sort of government sanction to attack and plunder the King's enemies, that would allow the *Minerva* to play pirate properly. There were also rumours of a convict uprising on the ship, an ever-present fear, especially on ships laden with known and notorious rebels against the British crown.

Like the *Britannia*, the *Minerva* restocked in Rio de Janiero, where Price commented particularly on the slaves he saw there. And while the convicts were suitably restrained from gaining any freedom in South America, a number of sailors took the opportunity to desert, successfully avoiding being returned to the ship before the *Minerva* had to depart.

Eventually, the Southern Ocean was crossed, and part of Van Diemen's Land sighted. The *Minerva* sailed up the east coast of Australia, entered Port Jackson, and dumped its human cargo onto a foreign land. But not, it seems, without at least one familiar face to greet some of them. It just so happened that Thomas Kennedy was employed assisting the new arrivals to come ashore, and as the disembarkation of the convicts proceeded, the Irish rebel Joseph Holt recognised him. Young Thomas was known to Holt from his days as an apprentice with Holt's uncle back in Dublin. And although I cannot be sure, I like to think that Mary Durham and Thomas might already have known each other, too, given Mary's likely connection to the Treason Trial riots.

After Thomas Kennedy stepped on shore in Sydney Cove I lost him for a while. He entered a young colony that was less than a decade old. To the people of this early European settlement Australia was still a relatively unknown land. At the time Thomas landed at Sydney it had not yet been established that Tasmania was an island, for instance. His name, his position in the society, and the patchiness of survival of some of the early records all make following his life in detail over two centuries later rather difficult beyond the barest outline. Often the historian faces this dilemma where a disproportional amount of effort would be required to elicit a small gain in knowledge. There are only so many muster records, lists of convicts, settlers, and their children counted and recorded by the government, that a person can take. It was, really, only the fluke of Joseph Holt having mentioned seeing him that put Thomas in such proximity to Mary Durham at the very moment of her arrival in the colony.

Unlike Thomas, however, Mary's sentence was finite. Her situation was similar to many, in that by the time of her arrival in 1800 a goodly proportion of her sentence was already completed. Within two years she was giving birth to babies surnamed Kennedy, and not too long afterwards she was free. It seems likely that Thomas was granted a ticket of leave. This allowed him some freedoms, including to work, albeit while still under technical sentence. As was common, he may even have been appointed servant to his then wife, Mary Kennedy, formerly of the *Minerva*. They settled in an area west of Sydney.

They lived out the remainder of their lives as farmers in the district known as Liberty Plains. There is no suggestion that they participated in the short-lived and abortive Castle Hill rebellion, when Irish convicts fought their captors, but had to surrender in the face of the overwhelming obstacles stacked against them. And they watched from the sidelines as the penal system proved triumphant again, surviving the destabilising effects of the more successful Rum Rebellion, in which Governor William Bligh was deposed by members of the New South Wales Corps. In this army takeover of a naval base, a run of naval officer governors came to an end and army officer Lachlan Macquarie was appointed as Governor in Bligh's stead.

To what extent any of this affected Thomas and Mary is difficult to say. For these ex-convicts and landowners, there were certainly administrative annoyances, however. Their legal status is reflected in documents certifying their freedom, and their occupation of a little part of Australia is recorded in land grants and musters records, and notes about the numbers of cows they had received from the government herd. The apprentice glass-cutter-turned-revolutionary had become a cattleman and was living in a colony that was nominally an autocracy, but looks suspiciously like rule-by-administration: a bureaucracy.

Their family struggled to grow in the face of severe childhood mortality, which struck them repeatedly, but not so completely as to stop Thomas from bequeathing his forty acres at Liberty Plains jointly to his daughters Rebecca and Elizabeth, who both went on to have large families. Rather appropriately, it was the land itself that made me so certain I had correctly tracked my way back to Thomas, the first of my ancestors to arrive in Australia by ship from Europe. In tracing a family line, I had found a newspaper account of a fairly long-running court case, which was only settled in 1915. In the few minutes it took to read the old typescript, the details of the trial took me back three generations, all the way to 1841.

The trial concerned a squabble over that land at Liberty Plains near Sydney, bequeathed by a Thomas Kennedy of Bankstown. He had died in 1841 and left the forty acres jointly to his two daughters. Between them there had been eighteen children. By the time the case was resolved in 1915 Elizabeth and Rebecca had also died, but their children's families were divided about how the land should be split up, considering that some of Thomas's grandchildren had predeceased their respective mothers. Being worth at least £1400, a considerable sum, one side proposed selling the property and dividing the money. The other side agreed, but argued over how the money was to be split. Was the share divided among the surviving children of Elizabeth and Rebecca only, or divided on the basis of all their children, living and dead? The court decided in favour of the living children having the only property right in Thomas's land.

It was not so much the case itself that interested me. Rather, its particulars provided me with an immediate and extended family tree, right back to this Thomas Kennedy, which satisfyingly corroborated my research.

And through the land at Liberty Plains I was once again able to hear Thomas's own words, which hark back to the 'Not Guilty' he had declared in Dublin fifteen years before. In 1810 Governor Macquarie's arrival prompted a reorganisation of the system of administering freedom and landholding, and as a result Thomas had to surrender his documents and re-petition the Governor. Thomas's petition survives. In it he referred to how 'at the early age of 14 Years I was by improper companions seduced to those inclinations which often are fatal to youth'. He then begged (in the third person as was the usual format for petitions) for his freedom because 'he has a Wife to whom he is Married, had Four Children to succour and provide for solely by the efforts of his personal labour'. This was a far cry from planning to depose the King and aid a French invasion of Ireland. If nothing else, it speaks to the effectiveness of the convict system in elucidating deference and docility, at least on paper.

I wonder if he really felt this way. The format of a petition required the petitioner to recognise their guilt and accept they had been justly punished. A successful petition was not based on saying what a person really felt, even if Thomas had wanted to scrawl 'NOT GUILTY' in giant letters across the page. The assertion of a history of 'propriety and industry' was to show that he was a productive member of his new society. If nothing else, he had at least learned to play the game. And this crushing sense of powerlessness in the face of government, administrators, and moneyed power, seems to me to be one of the key features of colonial Australia's documented youth. While convict experiences have sometimes been re-written as positive opportunities to escape from urban slums, or the birthplace of Australian egalitarianism, the reality was always one of an utterly asymmetrical power relationship between the state and its subjects. A distinctly Australian sense of humour, I suspect, developed fairly early to ease this burden of oppression. One might 'own' forty acres of land at a place called Liberty Plains, but this just meant that leave was granted to occupy it. The land, according to the King's law, was really the property of the King of Britain.

That there were already people in Australia whose understanding of relationships between land and people was fundamentally different from the new interlopers was a theoretical irrelevancy to the British colonial establishment. Gradually the practicalities of colonial expansion brought this issue into greater relief for jurists and administrators, who were less concerned with the totality of empire than with their little but growing section of it. Meanwhile, thwarting easy characterisation of the early colonial period and processes by jurists, governors, or historians, a complex range of interactions played out on the advancing colonial frontiers.

CHAPTER TWO

CONVICTS AND COLONIAL EXPANSION 1826

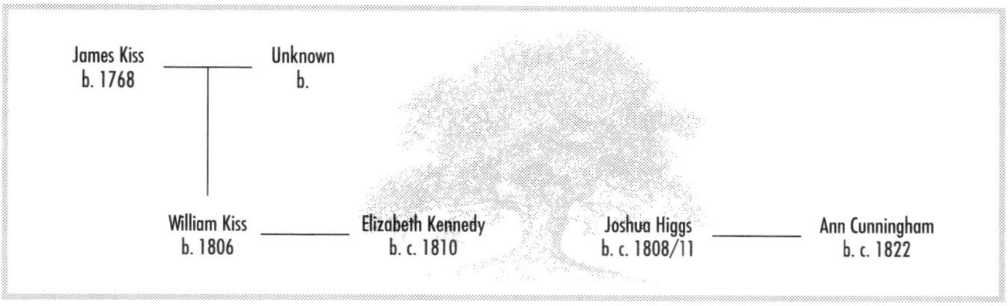

THE YEAR 1826 in Sydney must have been a worrying time for James Kiss, who had arrived in the colony some twenty-nine years previously. His son, William, was running into trouble with the law and was twice charged with offences. Both times the charge was assault, and both times he was found guilty.

An average-sized youth of twenty, with grey eyes and brown hair, William's complexion has been frustratingly difficult to read from the records of the gaols he sometimes inhabited. It seems to have been 'dark'. Certainly, he was unusually skinned for the gaol houses, which were generally filled with convicts and ex-convicts from Britain. In musters and census records William was recorded as 'bc'—born in the colony—in the column where the ship of origin was recorded for his father and other inhabitants of the settlement. When it came to the gaol records, 'A Native' was written beside William's name. It was an administrative abbreviation that could simply mean 'a native of the colony', but, in William's case, whether intentionally or not, it seems to have also pointed to something else.

William's first offence was barely recorded. A newspaper reported the scant details of how in the Windsor Quarter Sessions of March 1826 'William Kiss and Ann Hanshard, were fined one shilling and discharged'. The report indicated that somewhere in the western districts of Sydney's agricultural and pastoral outer zone a minor violent exchange had occurred involving these two people. Apparently, whatever they did, they were caught and found guilty. It could not have been too significant or William would likely have ended up in chains. Yet the fact of having had a female accomplice may have echoed particularly uncomfortably with James, whose own course to New South Wales had started in not dissimilar circumstances.

William's second affray was more serious. He had allegedly committed 'an assault on the person of Patrick McSherry'. This fight had started, the prosecution asserted, because William had struck a dog that was in McSherry's care. Why he did so, whether in self defence, through malice, or by accident, was not detailed. But, as McSherry was a servant of William Cox, one of the magistrates, and there was another Cox on the jury, things did not bode well for William. The whole affair had a smooth veneer of propriety which is recognisable in the better-paid upper echelons of many a community or workplace, with magistrate Cox absenting himself from the judgement. However, it was his servant and his dog on the receiving end of William's alleged assault, and so his colleagues on the bench would have ensured that William was duly punished. He was sentenced 'to be worked in irons for three calendar months'.

By 1826 James Kiss was an ex-convict and William had grown into adulthood. James had originally been transported by the *Ganges* in 1797, arriving in Sydney in June 1797, the month following the *Britannia*. Nearly three decades after James's arrival, both father and son were labourers, supporting the growing colonial economy by working hard for their sustenance. In this, the Kiss line of my family highlights the sweaty end of the British Empire's mercantile frontier.

On board the *Ganges* were at least eleven highway robbers, seven burglars, and a range of other men convicted for crimes like assault, theft, and forgery. Apart from a number of the arrivals having severe scurvy, there were no major issues with the voyage. The *Ganges* had come from Portsmouth in England, bringing both fresh soldiers for the settlement and salted meat. Each was welcomed by Governor Hunter, and probably helped mitigate concerns the authorities had about the recently arrived shipload of Irish rebels. In the wake of the *Britannia*'s arrival Hunter had written to his superiors that the Irish convicts were 'a very turbulent description of transports' who had 'more than once threatened opposition to all authority'. Of those on the *Ganges*, he had simply commented on their better health, despite the scurvy. But this distinction between the Irish and the English convicts is not just a matter of health or national predisposition to rebelliousness. The rationale behind the transportation of each group was vastly different. The *Britannia* was loaded with Defender rebels, whereas the *Ganges* was full of convicts more recognisable in the Australian popular psyche.

In *Australia's Birthstain* Babette Smith argued that sweeping Australian historical narratives have often tended to treat convicts, if they have been included at all, by type or as a group rather than individual people with their own complex lives. Often convictism was a subject that had just been discreetly glossed over in national histories, until a wave of family history research revealed the true scale and diversity of the 'convict' phenomenon. Yet ironically, some academic mass-data analyses of convict records, seeking a wider social context in response to growing public interest, has obscured the importance of individuality. While certainly interesting, this sort of research can tacitly and unconsciously reinforce older prejudices of convicts as constituting a criminal class, defined primarily by their crime and punishment. Similarly, the modern capacity for mass-data research sometimes means that the records of convicts' lives reduce them to economic agents or mere biological data-points for the study of labour and capital, and for retrospective surveys of human health, height, and longevity. And through this the convicts can unwittingly be dehumanised once again.

On first observation James neatly fits the stereotype of a poorer man convicted of a petty property crime—the theft of a hat—who was shipped to the other side of the world in a momentary flash of British justice. But, as James's story reveals, even the most seemingly stereotypical convict record is but shadowy evidence of a real person being punished.

James was born in Birmingham in 1768 when the Industrial Revolution was underway and overpopulation was starting to become a significant urban issue. The parish register of St Phillip's Church records his christening: 'James son of William & Mary Kiss'. These parish registers give a good sense of how the population was shifting. In one of the copies of these records the monthly baptisms were written by hand down one side of a page and burials on the other. Mostly the baptisms far outstripped the burials. So at the time of James's birth Birmingham was a rapidly growing and industrialising city.

The population quadrupled in the fifty years before he was born, largely through the drift of migrant workers from the countryside. James had several siblings, and the Kisses were lucky not to lose any of them to the burial lists, where the annotation 'child of' was sadly appended to many names of the people swelling the industrial town and its suburbs.

The potential for property crime in this particular city was very high, not just because of the poverty, but because of the increase in chattels, moveable property. It was a city populated not only by textile workers, but also those employed making the small mechanical and technical industrial products of the age: buttons, belts, jewellery, and guns. It was the kind of place that produced many of the items which would later appear on television programs like *Antiques Roadshow*. The Industrial Revolution was about more than steam trains, textile mills, and pottery. The factory production method, as well as new mechanical production techniques, changed the whole material fabric of the British world. An age of mass consumption had arrived. And with that, there was simply more stuff to steal, were one so inclined.

But gazing suspiciously at the labouring classes were the thinking men and their families who also filled Birmingham. These relatively wealthy people perhaps provided easy marks for thieves. Clubs and societies, teahouses and coffeehouses, all fostered a public sphere that attracted attention to Birmingham as an 'enlightenment' centre. Adam Smith, Thomas Jefferson, and other luminaries of the age visited the city in these decades and marvelled at its productive capacity. And therein lay the seed of discontent and misery. While working wages could be high, the pull of the city drew immigrants at a greater rate than the factories went up, so unemployment, underemployment, and insecure employment were all problems the working classes faced, while opulent wealth was right there to taunt them with its very inaccessibility. So while I would not like to necessarily accept the judgement of English law on the matter of James Kiss's alleged crime, the fact remains that there was a growing number of poor people swelling a city increasingly famous for well-to-do or entrepreneurial people. As Charles Dickens's well-known stories impress upon readers even so much later, some poorer people could be enterprising too. Unfortunately for them, that often meant criminality.

Rather than stealing a hat for money, however, the twenty-five-year-old James seems to have been caught up in a little vendetta of some sort. On 8 June 1793 he and Mary Howarth assaulted Benjamin Jones in one of the churchyards in Birmingham and took Jones's hat. They were caught and tried for assault and theft, and sentenced to death. Almost certainly it was the assault that got James in trouble, with the hat theft written up as an additional charge to facilitate the prosecution's success by increasing the odds. But it turns out that James had an influential patron. It was not uncommon for people to find an important patron to advocate for them, and this system was rather feudal. Your family found a local gentleman, who would then find an aristocrat, who would then do the petitioning. The higher the class of help you got, the better your chances were. Vagrants, orphans, widows, and widowers were seriously disadvantaged in such a setting. It was proof that the class structure and the feudal system were still thriving in late eighteenth century England. James was luckier than some, because the Earl of Warwick petitioned the court on his behalf.

The Earl pointed out that James's parents had died when he was young, and that he had been acting under the influence of a 'bad woman'. The woman who was charged with James was a few years older, and it is possible that they had a relationship of some sort, and that perhaps she somehow prompted the assault. The Earl noted that James had been an honest boy who had been entrusted with valuables in the past, which suggests a reasonable employment history. There was also another petition on James's behalf, signed by a number of Birmingham residents and some character witnesses, which all suggests he was fairly well networked within his immediate community. Fortunately for him this circle of friends and web of patronage saved James from the hangman's noose, but that was the limit of their success. His sentence was instead commuted to transportation.

James's crime, trial, and sentencing are the kinds of experiences which nicely illuminate the dangers of simplistic analyses of the past, because James's recorded crime seems to have little bearing on the key incident instigating the sequence of events leading to his transportation. His was not a poverty-driven property crime, although the formal conviction suggests this. And perhaps counter-intuitively, his transportation was a direct result of being relatively well networked within his community—without a network of support, he would more likely have been hanged. So James was not necessarily a sample of Birmingham's downtrodden refuse, but a well-regarded young man known to the Earl of Warwick. The politics of his transportation may have been very different from that of Thomas Kennedy, but it was political nonetheless.

In August 1796 James boarded the *Ganges* along with three other men tried in the same July 1793 sessions of the Warwick Assizes. The missing years suggest that they had waited three years in holding cells and prison hulks when they were finally transferred onto the ship that would sail to New South Wales. But convicts were not its only cargo. That month the *Ganges* was supplied with barrels of salted beef and pork for the convicts during the voyage. It was also carrying excess meat from two other ships. But the settlement of New South Wales needed more supplies, and the *Ganges* had to wait for them. Only in late December 1796, with convicts and colonial supplies both on board, did the *Ganges* sail from British waters for New South Wales. Although he never returned to England, there is evidence that letters were sent to him in Australia, suggesting that he maintained some connections with his former home.

After that relatively uneventful voyage and a few years of obscurity in the historical record, James Kiss ended up in the Hawkesbury River district. This region, north and west of Sydney, is one of those areas where the small colony pushed its frontier outwards into the great continent. Governor Hunter intended that the convicts of the *Britannia* and the *Ganges* were mostly to clear and prepare ground for cultivation, so Thomas Kennedy and James Kiss may have crossed paths at this early stage. But whereas Thomas Kennedy's farm is no doubt now a suburban or industrial portion of the suburb of Liverpool, parts of the territory to which James Kiss was sent are still bushland. After generations of settlement it is an odd mixture of beautiful agricultural and pastoral enclaves separated by rugged and hilly terrain. When James first arrived, it was just rugged, and the convicts worked hard to eke out farming plots among the expansive bush, scrubby hills, deep ravines, and unfamiliar rivers.

James was appointed as a servant to the Surveyor General Charles Grimes, who, among other things, charted the Hunter River and King Island, and identified the mouth of the Yarra River, highlighting how Sydney proved a base for wider regional exploration. Working out James's story involved a great deal of fiddly comparative research just to identify some scant details such as where he was and how employed. But this is usual for those below a certain class of settler who were not consistent trouble-makers. By 1801 James was living at the Hawkesbury settlement. In 1806 he had a ticket of leave, and was renting a farm. He grew two acres of wheat, three acres of maize, a quarter acre of potatoes, three and three quarter acres of pasture, and had one acre lying fallow. If it were not for the gum trees, the Australian wildlife, and the peregrinations and visits of the local Aborigines, it would be easy to mistake this for a farm anywhere in some timeless agricultural moment. He had ten acres all to himself. No animals, wife, or children were listed as present.

But this was not arcadia. Firstly, the settlers struggled to cope with the way these rivers flooded. In 1806 the floods caused catastrophic damage, threatening the colony with famine because of the loss of crops. The fluid dynamics of these ravine-dominated rivers, the different soil conditions in Australia, the new weather patterns, and even the fact that many of the farmers had never farmed before, all made the experience a difficult one. The region was also on the very fringes of the frontier of settlement, and the isolation must have taken an emotional toll of which historical records leave no real trace. This decade was also dotted with conflict with Aborigines in the Hawkesbury and Nepean districts. In part this is a response to the arrival of Europeans and the transformation of the landscape, but that explanation is only part of the story.

Governor Hunter had earlier insisted that Europeans discourage Aborigines from visiting their farms, and Governor King did likewise in 1805. These prescriptions, regardless of how obeyed, point to a reality that became increasingly complicated. As Grace Karskens wryly noted in *The Colony*, such acts of banishment 'would have been meaningless if Aboriginal people were not already living within the settler landscapes'. We know a lot about when things went badly, which often enough they did, but there is a fundamental source bias which means we can know relatively little about when things may have gone well. While it was once thought Europeans simply pushed Aborigines aside, it is now recognised that Aborigines continued to live in the same area as the settlers, even to the extent of some considerable cohabitation. But more than that, it is important to see that Aborigines could and did subsume Europeans into their own cultural worlds.

There is an existential documentary bias from this period towards convicts, land settlement, and criminality, which in some ways obscures the great complexity of human relationship existing at the intersections of empire. The colonial expansion into the Hawkesbury from Sydney Cove, in which James Kiss was taking part, occurred about a generation after the first Europeans had permanently arrived in New South Wales. The Aborigines had more time to adjust than is sometimes allowed them. In turn, the framework of social interactions, kin networks, and tribal affiliations and retributions all became further intertwined and complicated over time.

But Hunter's edict also probably had the effect of ensuring that Aborigines were not recorded even if they were present, excepting when, for the purposes of administering criminal justice, Aborigines seem to suddenly appear in a 'settled' area. This exacerbates the general difficulties with interpreting the historical sources available for examining this district and similar frontiers at this time.

By the 1820s James Kiss had two adult children, William and Ann. Their births were unrecorded and the first clear indication of their existence comes when their names appeared in muster lists from 1822 onwards. It is significant that they were not listed prior to this, as applicable documentation survives through 1806, 1811, 1816, and 1817 which all record James, but not his children. Many later records corroborate that William was born in 1806. His age can be calculated from records like his adult baptism and the 1826 census, and he clearly told his sometime gaolers that 1806 was the year of his birth.

But in 1806, when James Kiss was renting a farm, a detailed survey was conducted that seems to show James living alone. He had two acres growing wheat, three growing maize, and a quarter of an acre with potatoes. The remainder of his little ten-acre farm was given over to pasture or lying fallow. Ostensibly, he was all alone, no wife, no children, no convict servants, and no animals having been recorded. This was curious, because he already had a daughter, and sometime during that year he gained a son.

William's sister Ann complicates this story slightly, because she was sometimes recorded as Ann Ruse, in ways that make it clear she was Ann Kiss, James's daughter. It seems that she at least, and possibly William also, spent some time in the care of the family of James Ruse, whose 'experimental farm' was later lauded as the first successful Australian farm. Such informal adoption of children was not uncommon, especially in a frontier situation, but this does nothing to remedy the complete lack of documentary evidence of William and Ann's mother.

If the mother had been a convict woman, then she and James would have been required to formally request permission to marry, and these records survive in relative abundance. If she and James had married, some sort of documentary mention would most likely have survived. It is very unusual to have several corroborating references to a person, as I do for William Kiss, and no mother recorded. Perhaps more strangely, when James petitioned Governor Macquarie in 1820 as so many did, he made no mention of having a wife or family, which would be usual in a petition of this sort. Petitioners wanted to prove they had reformed their character, that they had a need for help, and that they had settled down to a respectable existence. A family would help point to respectability and to his being in a state of need. Even if the wife had died, then being a widower would also help the argument. The problem of having children to support would be just the kind of point worth mentioning.

So the most likely explanation is the least provable. William was born at the time that James was living in the Hawkesbury region, with no wife or children listed. It was the fringes of settlement, and men were known to cohabit with Aboriginal women at that time, in that place, despite having been told not to. It therefore seems a likely explanation that James was one such man, and thus his family remained unofficial. Although known to be present, Aborigines were generally not recorded in the muster lists, a fact which is in part the basis for early historians' assumptions about colonists simply pushing them aside. It helps clarify the oddness of no family being recorded for James at the time William was born. It makes sense of James's lack of any mention of family in his petition. Annoyingly it is a puzzle for which, unfortunately, there is unlikely to ever be a perfect documentary resolution, but it is an illustration of the very complexity of human relationships formed on the frontiers that can only ever be imperfectly captured by the historian. It is no exaggeration to say that it is my one ancestral connection with this land which stretches beyond the reach of memory.

Friendly relations with Aborigines could mean the difference between life and death, as well as offering the warmth of companionship, or simply satisfying the urges of the body. I suspect that James Kiss was, for a time, integrated into an Aboriginal kinship network he may not have fully understood. The absence of his children William and Ann from formal records of the colony until their early adulthood points to their ambiguous status. But colonial officialdom's eventual embrace of them as fully fledged members of the labouring classes, perhaps facilitated by semi-adoption within a more established colonial family setting, illustrates the fact that there was not necessarily an unbridgeable cultural divide.

But frontier relations between convicts, settlers, and Aborigines were not the only things James Kiss had to navigate. As the penal colony shifted towards a settler colony, the dynamics of internal politics shifted accordingly. James farmed in the Hawkesbury district throughout the period of the Rum Rebellion and Governor Bligh's ignominious arrest, which James almost certainly only heard of after the fact, even though he seemed to know some of the men involved. When James later petitioned Governor Macquarie in 1820 the document was supported by a note from Simeon Lord, one of those who had advocated Bligh's arrest. Lord wrote that he had 'known the petitioner many years, and believe him to be an honest, industrious man'. By then James was possibly uncertain of his precise age. He simply described himself at that time as 'about fifty years of age'. The purpose of his petition was to ask for 'an allotment of ground in Sydney, to build himself a small cottage upon'.

This petition to Macquarie contributes to a sense that the difficulties of life on the Hawkesbury may have been too much for this would-be farmer. By 1816 the colonial muster records place James as a 'Labourer' living somewhere in Sydney. This move came in the wake of a conditional pardon he had gained in 1812. His short petition indicates that this was granted 'on the recommendation' of the evangelical Anglican chaplain William Cox, whose dog James's son later struck. Cox had also supported the petition by noting, like Lord, that James was 'an industrious man'. Subsequent records essentially reveal snapshots of working life for an ex-convict, and the petition supports this. James described how since his emancipation he had 'been for most part of his time employed in the service of different individuals'. He described himself as 'an industrious and sober man'. Relatively soon after his petition, during 1822, he was clearly a 'Horse Dealer'. But James was thereafter generally identified simply as a labourer.

By the time William was getting into trouble with the law, James appears to have worked for a Mr Underwood of Sydney, as indicated by records of 1825 and 1828. But there is a problem in identifying which one, because there were two. Like James's former patron Lord, James Underwood was a successful merchant and trader, and his brother Joseph also travelled to Sydney, working in the same industries. In 1830 a panorama painting of a view of Sydney by Robert Burford was displayed for the London public, which had been painted the year before when James Kiss was likely still working for Underwood. A printed pamphlet for the exhibition notes that the 'elegant building' numbered 36 was 'the residence of Mr. Underwood, a rich merchant, who has been very successful in the oil and seal-skin trade'. It can be seen sitting near the water at Sydney Cove, near the middle of the picture where the expanse of the houses of Sydney gradually gives way to a view of the harbour, dotted with several ships. The farmland on the far right is in striking contrast to the Aborigines on the left, one of whom is throwing a boomerang in the foreground, with St James' Church prominently behind them. James will likely have lived in a nondescript and unmarked building of the sort barely drawn in for the London public.

James may have left the agricultural frontier for the town, but it is possible he ended up working in support of the whaling and sealing frontiers. Whale oil provided a range of products from soap to lantern oil, and sealskin was highly valued for warm and fashionable clothing. These products were among New South Wales's first successful exports. The industry was expanding coastal settlement and exploration, particularly around the south-east and southern coast of mainland Australia, and into the islands in Bass Strait and New Zealand. Depending on which particular Mr Underwood employed James, and what task they put him to, he may have worked in a supporting role in the warehouses of the Sydney merchant. Alternatively, there is the possibility that he was working in the Underwood-owned George Street Coffee Lounge, or at least a brewery and distillery which was attached.

James's story was a microcosm of early Australian settlement and expansion. Transported, he entered a colony struggling to feed itself, and then within a few years was involved in either an ambitious sub-colonial expansion, or in support of an urban consumer economy. Gradually his hard life may have taken a toll, and he seems to slip quietly from the records.

Unlike his father, William followed the frontier as it expanded beyond the area of his birth. Following his bad year of 1826, and three months of hard labour in chains as punishment for the incident with a servant and a dog, William may have tempered a bit. At least, he was no longer getting caught for doing anything wrong.

In fact, the next key colonial documentation of his life concerned a spiritual turn. In 1834 the now twenty-eight-year-old William was baptised into the Catholic Church at St Mary's in Sydney. The record did not give much information beyond his age and suggesting he was resident at Lower Minto. But the context seemed significant. The baptism was a precursor to a wedding, because William Kiss soon thereafter married Elizabeth Kennedy.

Elizabeth had lived with her father Thomas in the late 1820s, apparently the last of his children to leave home, and beyond this it is really hard to get much sense of her early life.

The young family took up cattle farming, perhaps with help from Thomas Kennedy. The colony's demand for meat and leather products made this a sensible option. William's later legal history reveals the family's movements west and south from Sydney. In 1838 he was accused of stealing cattle at Campbelltown, a common accusation among pastoralists. Fortunately, through the assistance of David Noonan, a settler, and a publican named Michael Ryan, he was granted bail. When finally tried, he was found not guilty.

In 1844 William also gave evidence for a trial, perhaps for the first time not his own, concerning a forgery at Goulburn. This placed him further into the Southern Highlands south of Sydney. These short court reports and the other brief records of William's life reveal two things. Firstly, his career highlights a very successful movement from labourer to groomsman to cattleman, which to some extent allowed that generation to escape the confines of class. Secondly, it reveals a process of movement and an explosive widening of the colonial frontier.

William did not live much longer, dying at Liverpool in 1853. But the family continued to advance southwards. Following William's death Elizabeth took her children further into the cattlescape of colonial New South Wales, and she eventually remarried in Cooma in 1861. The family had left the districts immediately surrounding Sydney and, before two decades were complete, were poised by the Snowy Mountains. A unique piece of family history recorded in 1933 placed the sixteen-year-old Jimmy Kiss, one of William's sons, 'cattle dealing on Monaro on the country around Coolringdon'. This puts them in the region before Elizabeth's second marriage, suggesting that colonial expansion from the Sydney region to the High Country may have been even faster than the traditional documentary sources of the period reveal. Unlike the initial Sydney Cove settlement, with its documentary plans and prescriptions, this wider expansion ran ahead of the main keepers of records.

Rapid pastoral expansion is also highlighted by Jimmy Kiss's eventual father-in-law, Joshua Higgs, who arrived in Sydney in 1826 on the *Marquis of Huntly*. This ship had spent late 1825 and the earlier part of 1826 carrying British troops to African ports, yet another illustration of the interconnected global empire that was being carved out at this time. And underscoring one of the reasons Australia was chosen over Africa for a convict establishment, probably half of those troops died of fever at Sierra Leone. The Australian climate could be harsh, but it was not as lethal as some other places.

Between May and September 1826 the *Marquis of Huntly* did what was an increasingly familiar convict run, with 197 male prisoners on board, including Joshua Higgs. Emptied of convicts in Sydney, it filled its holds with wool at Sydney, made for Broken Bay to get some timber, and headed back to London.

By 1840 thirty-two-year-old Joshua Higgs was at Goulburn, and wanted to marry eighteen-year-old Ann Cunningham. Being a convict, Joshua had to apply to the convict department for permission. Notations regarding their application survive, showing their ages and names. It confirms that Joshua was a convict, and also revealed that Ann was a free emigrant. She had arrived in the colony on the *Margaret* in 1839, which had sailed from Dublin and stopped at the Cape of Good Hope on the way to Australia. A voluntary emigrant, Ann was one of fifty-seven free females aboard a convict ship carrying 166 unfree women and their forty-four children. It has been hard to trace details of her life and the reasons for her voyage. There might be one clue, however, because on board the *Margaret* there was also a Bridget Cunningham, a convict girl two years older than Ann. Possibly she was a relative with whom Ann had decided to travel to Australia.

When the *Margaret* arrived, its human cargo quickly disappeared into a poorly documented world of female servitude. After the ship docked, the free immigrants would have been allowed to disembark practically immediately, but the convicts would have had to wait to be processed. If Ann and Bridget were travelling together, then their joint voyage to the new world was about to end in separation as Bridget was pulled into the machinery of the convict system. Only days after the *Margaret*'s arrival advertisements were printed in the Sydney papers advertising how settlers 'in want of Female Servants' could be 'supplied from the Prisoners arrived by the *Margaret*'. Ann, however, would have had to find her own employment. Unburdened of women, the *Margaret* was moored in Sydney Harbour and was used as a marker for a regatta of boat racing before eventually departing.

Within a year, Ann had somehow crossed paths with Joshua Higgs, and the two had formed enough of a relationship to wish to marry. This they did. One of their children, Catherine Higgs, went on to marry the son of William and Elizabeth Kiss, Jimmy—clearly named for his paternal grandfather—in Cooma in 1861, the year Elizabeth herself remarried, wedding William Tandy.

But whereas Ann Cunningham's life was poorly recorded, Joshua Higgs's activities can be charted in detail. His story reveals multiple aspects of the rapid colonial expansion from the 1820s into the 1840s. And it is unlike the more common perspectives of the moneyed men who established large pastoral stations. Nor was Joshua part of the well-reported and lauded traditions of the early 'explorers' who generally discovered lands that Aborigines had pointed out to them, or followed rivers already populated with Aboriginal people, and wrote up their findings for government and public consumption. Instead, Joshua's frontier life started off involuntarily, and it proved to be rough and ready stuff.

As with James and William Kiss, the time Joshua spent under the gaze of the apparatus of British justice makes him easier to trace in documentary records. In the 1828 census he was living in Camden as a servant of Thomas Cowper. He had a ticket of leave by 1837 and received a conditional pardon in 1843. In fact the documentation for the pardon is particularly illuminating. From the scratchy nineteenth-century script I could learn that he was born in 1808 and was a native of Salisbury. When convicted to death, which was commuted to transportation, he was a farm labourer. His crime: cattle stealing.

Because the convict department was so meticulous about tracing its prisoners, they recorded detailed physical descriptions of each prisoner. This meant that if they absconded they could be more easily identified. The ritual of being recorded was also part of the mind game of the transportation system. It was a way of reminding each and every prisoner that they were effectively powerless against the government, that they were the property of the state. Not all of these records have survived, but I was fortunate to be able to find one for Joshua. Our genetic ties are not in any way evidenced by our physical appearances. Joshua was short, at 4 feet 11 inches; I am practically 6 foot. His complexion was described as 'ruddy'; mine has seasonal shades, but I have never been called or thought of myself as ruddy. His eyes were hazel; mine are brown. At least we have the same hair colour: brown.

Joshua also sported tattoos. Although a farmhand originally, by the time of his pardon he had a ship drawn on his right arm. It was likely to have been made during or in response to his voyage on the *Marquis of Huntly*, illicitly done below deck out of the sight of the guards, and probably quite crude because of the darkness and the rolling of the wooden sailing ship. He also had 'JH' on the left arm, presumably for Joshua Higgs—or maybe Josiah Higgs, which is what the convict department tended to call him. Names were a little more flexible in the past.

By the time he was an old man, though, he was definitely Joshua. I know this because on Wednesday 4 July 1883 he marched into the office of the *Bega Gazette and Eden District or Southern Coast Advertiser*. Bega was a good-sized town by then, nestled in the rolling hills of the green Bega Valley. Joshua told the editor that he 'was the oldest living pioneer white man of the district'. It seems that conveying that fact was his primary intention for the visit. He had been to another newspaper with this piece of news, but they had wanted to charge him to print it, so he had walked to the *Bega Gazette* office instead, a little old man determinedly marching up the sloped streets of Bega. Fortunately for me, the editor must have sniffed a story over the fumes of the ink and presses. He reproduced their conversation in the newspaper, and it sheds amazing light on old Joshua's story. As well as neatly confirming details garnered from the less poetical convict sources it also helps reveal the development of the wider district through the eyes of the old ex-convict. It also reveals him to have been quite a character. When I first read it, I could not help but like the old fellow.

'I came to this country in 1826, in the ship *Marquis of Huntly* the First', Joshua said. He explained how he came to be transported. 'Did I have a free passage? Yes, but I got into trouble in a simple way. My father was a small farmer and dealer near Salisbury, not far from Stonehenge. One night as I was going home from market I met a man driving some three or four head of cattle. The man said he would give me a shilling if I would help him. I went with him, glad enough, like most boys at home, to earn a little money. But, before we had gone far the constables took us in charge for cattle-stealing. I and the man were sent to Winchester gaol and cast for death, but our sentence was commuted, and I was sent out here.'

Joshua was transported from a profoundly inhabited landscape, and the physical remains of past peoples were everywhere. Winchester, for instance, has several claims to fame. It has a wonderful example of the medieval High Street, city walls, tower, and Cathedral, and it even lays claim to having King Arthur's Round Table. The table is a fake, but at least it is a medieval fake, which still makes it interesting. And Salisbury Cathedral, with the highest medieval cathedral tower in England and bending pillars inside struggling against gravity to support it, is instantly recognisable. Certainly one of the best-loved English paintings of all time is John Constable's view of *Salisbury Cathedral from the Bishop's Gardens*. The gentle pastoral beauty conveyed in the painting is a striking contrast to the oppressiveness of a legal system that could send a boy away from his parents and home to the other side of the world. It was painted in 1826, the same year that Joshua was transported to New South Wales.

Old Joshua Higgs told the Bega newspaper editor how after arriving in New South Wales he was sent to live on Thomas Cowper's Braidwood property. Given that Joshua Higgs was recorded as being at Camden in 1928, this suggests that he was only at Camden for a short period, or happened to be visiting at the time of the census, or was simply recorded as nominally there. Camden is just outside of Sydney, a part of the colony then known as the Cowpastures for the obvious reason that cows were pastured there. Cowper's expansion into Braidwood, much further south, and Higgs's work in aiding that, shows how the convict servants assisted the squatters to expand their empires, and also shows how important cattle were in driving that expansion, especially into the highlands.

'I was about Braidwood for over 20 years', he said. These days Braidwood is a pretty little town with wide verandahs, one that I know extremely well. My paternal grandparents have a holiday house on the South Coast just south of Bateman's Bay. When travelling to the nearby coast, Braidwood is the last town before one crosses Clyde Mountain and descends the Great Dividing Range to the coast. It is a place where many people stop to do a wee and give the children travel sickness medicine before the steep and bendy bit. The street tends to be either empty or full of Canberran and New South Welsh travellers, depending on the time of year. It was a famous gold rush town, which Joshua would have seen grow rapidly during the time of his long association with it. It once had a significant Chinese presence, brought by the prospect of gold. In fact I had the good fortune many years ago to help do a surface survey of an old Chinese mining settlement in the nearby hills. It was scrubby terrain with little in the way of built remains, which reminded me that most of the accommodation was of wood and other temporary materials and has left little trace on the landscape. Australia has deserted villages, just as other places do, but they can be hard to spot. In this one there was glass, pottery, tools, and even a sawn-off shotgun. This weapon is a pointed testament to the need some Chinese person may have felt for protection. I later learned that when cleaned in the lab, the gun was found to be still loaded.

Chinese men were a significant feature of Australia's gold rush period, but there was also a significant Chinese presence in the pastoral industry, particularly after the transportation of convicts ceased and landlords looked for new sources of cheap labour. Joshua Higgs's first forays in the Monaro district were a little early for this phenomenon, but had he travelled east towards the Murrumbidgee river valley then he may have encountered the occasional Chinese man tending a flock of sheep.

As already seen, the multicultural and complex nature of the Australian frontier also applies to the relationships formed with Aborigines. For Joshua, this is illuminated by his recollection of how 'we went out together for mutual protection' when running herds of cattle in the hills and plains. He told the Bega editor how one hutkeeper 'seemed not to fear the Blacks', but came to a bad end. This hutkeeper disappeared, and was only found when Joshua and his team 'caught' two Aboriginal boys who were able to direct them to the location of a body at a waterhole. Rightly or wrongly, the suspicion was, of course, that Aborigines had killed the hutkeeper, but Joshua says nothing beyond the fact that they buried the corpse. This is a reminder of the fraught nature of the frontier. This was a big country, sparsely inhabited, and conflicts were short, sharp, and easily left unrecorded. But the settlers did not always have it their way. Joshua recalled the early settlers of Brogo, near Bega, having 'made yards, and put up a hut, but', he said, 'the blacks hunted them and the cattle away'.

Yet, as William Kiss's likely parentage suggests, the frontier was not always a place of conflict or murder. 'I am the man who gave the name to Taraganda', Joshua informed the Bega editor. 'We asked the blacks what they called that spot and in their quick way they said what I took to be Taraganda.' This tiny line, loaded with the terminology of the time, nonetheless points to dialogue. It was an important marker for Joshua of his engagement with the Indigenous inhabitants of the land he was opening up to settlement. The many Aboriginal names of Australian places derive from short conversations just like this. There are many silences in Australia's history, but the land is full of words that at least recognise some communication.

Joshua won the first Braidwood horserace in 1843, and I am not surprised to learn that he tried his luck as a jockey, considering his small stature. This small fact shows the early development of a communal sporting culture. All those years later in the Bega newspaper office he could still recall the name of the horse, Miss Phantom, and those of the competitors. For these men, each horse had a unique personality and was remembered fondly.

Of wider historical interest and importance, Joshua and a few other men commenced the successful settlement on the Brogo River, having come down from the mountains with a herd of 300 cattle and taken over the area where the earlier settlers had previously been chased away. He and three men cleared an acre of land, 'sowed wheat, reaped it, and ground it in a steel mill'. Again, a short line reveals a lengthy process. Clearing thick bush was not a job for a day or two. Moreover, the period from sowing to reaping was a matter of months. Months that took him at least one mountainside away from the main frontier of settlement, with only his immediate companions, and two similar groups nearby, to provide the 'mutual protection' he mentioned, in what may at times have seemed like a hostile forest. The Brogo River is a windy little thing and rather sandy, and today is still thickly wooded along its banks, including pine trees grown from cones that have washed down from the higher country. It is one of a number of tributary rivers that run through the district. The area is hilly and hard to traverse. Certainly, it was a far cry from the open plains of Salisbury, or the pastoral idealism depicted in the foreground of Constable's Salisbury Cathedral.

Paralleling the settlement of the interior, the coast also had an increasing European presence during the first half of the nineteenth century. In yet another illustration of a wider process, Joshua described the arrival of the Imlay brothers in Twofold Bay. These men were whalers, and Joshua's time in the region can therefore be dated to 1831, the time of their arrival on the South Coast. Some of the sailors worked their way inland to the cattle station, so Joshua 'drove some fat cows down to the Bay, made a yard, and killed the first fresh beef' the whalers had had for a while. This meeting of the cattlemen and the whalers must have proved a success, because by late 1835 Twofold Bay was known to be exporting cattle.

But the Imlays were not there for cows. *Moby Dick* is one of the great American novels, but it also has a strong Australian connection, in the sense of being set in the Pacific. Australia was not just a giant sheep station, the seas around it were the site of a number of sea-based industries, most notably sealing and whaling. James Kiss may well have worked supporting this 'oil industry' in Sydney, but one of the frontline outposts was at Twofold Bay, where another of my ancestors probably saw the whalers boiling down the blubber in a series of pots.

Twofold Bay was a perfect site for whaling, but, as I learned upon visiting, it was not only men who did the hunting. Standing at the lookout from the little town of Eden, Twofold Bay opens up before you as one of the world's most magnificent harbours: deep, blue, and wide. The site is a part of a strategic environment for killer whales, which, as winter approaches, move up from the Antarctic waters to ambush migrating baleen whales. Amazingly, at this place humans and whales eventually worked together to hunt other whales, but this was far in the future from the time when Joshua Higgs drove some cattle down to feed the hungry sailors.

However, he probably did see the local Aborigines helping with the shore-based whaling. In one of the earliest and most extensive economic collaborations, the Imlays employed Aborigines on their whaling expeditions, reportedly at the same rates as white employees. The Aborigines adapted their seasonal movements to live in houses during the whaling season and then returned to the bush as the season shifted. Aborigines to the east of the mountains were also reportedly regularly employed in the washing of sheep.

For the first few years after his marriage, Joshua continued to work in the wider Monaro district. About mid century, however, he turned to work shepherding for Henry Wallace 'at Dandenong', working in that other great pastoral industry, sheep farming. This area, which is now on Melbourne's south-eastern edges, is almost 600 kilometres by road from Bega. It was a considerable journey to make, a greater distance than that which separated Bega from Sydney. Whether his young family travelled with him or not, I do not know and probably never will. It points to another stage of Australia's colonial expansion, the settlement of the Port Philip District and Victoria, but Joshua's story does not seem to have involved a great amount of time on the southern side of the Snowy Mountains.

Joshua was certainly a frontier man, if ever there was, but even these men cannot go on forever. Unfortunately for him, he claims to have 'went blind' in 1877, and had to return to Sydney. Incredibly, considering how long a distance it is, he had walked from Sydney to Cooma and found employment there, and was in Bega 'for the doctor's help' when he spoke to the newspaper man. It was only the fact that he made a point of recording his story that allowed me to see Joshua's experiences through his eyes. It was an unusual record of a convict's experience of the frontier. Perhaps he was in some way challenging the fairly triumphal narratives of gentry settlement beginning to gain traction by that time, making a point that convict labour had fertilised squatter wealth. Perhaps he felt that they made him do it and then took all the credit. His hard labour had grown Thomas Cowper's wealth, while Joshua remained a labouring man into his darkening old age. He had strode the length of the colony, yet he and his efforts would remain unknown but for the attentiveness of a newspaper editor in a country town.

And this is the story of our convict past. It was a brutal system, which punished people, often young victims of circumstance, and used them as labour in dangerous situations to make other people rich. There was a deliberate use of convict labour to facilitate a military outpost and drive and sustain colonial and economic growth, which once achieved, resulted in a strong anti-transportation movement pressuring the imperial government. Free settlers, even ex-convicts, did not want their reputations blemished by the taint of criminality or the accusation of having engaged in something akin to slavery. In a weird historical moment, attitudes within the British government shifted firmly against slavery, even as some perceptions hardened against the poor and criminal 'classes'. The Australian colonies were not immune to these wider cultural movements and contradictions, but perhaps the unrecorded sentiments of men like Joshua also played a part. Whatever arguments commentators used, there may have been a widespread and guttural sense that transportation was wrong. But the system only died slowly. The cessation of transportation to New South Wales simply transferred the transportation of convicts to other colonies, and while later revision of the system saw it focused on reforming criminals into productive members of the labouring classes, this was still largely just a more sanitised and less blatantly capitalist version of the same thing.

It is from this levelling phenomenon of a convict society that many Australian commentators popularly believe an Australian sense of egalitarianism has developed. Yet I suggest the evidence given for this was largely the product of aspiration, reflecting a sense of longing for the *liberté, égalité, fraternité* that some non-British possessions like republican France and an independent America ostensibly promised, and from which the very word egalitarianism derives. Australia was not, has never been, and is yet to be, a fully equal society, even though it aspires to it and many people have rejected the old strictures of class. But when foreign visitors in the later nineteenth century commented on the sense that each Australian felt as good as the next person, they were expressing surprise that the working classes did not keep their place and peace. And while Joshua Higgs could march into a newspaper office and have his story recorded, it is worth remembering that the first newspaper he approached ignored him.

Although Joshua lived for another fourteen years after striding in to tell his story, it was the early part of his life that is best recorded, thanks principally to his own effort. 'I was born on December 11, and I am 72 years of age', he told the newspaperman in summary. 'You may rely upon all this being true', he insisted. 'All I want is to have it printed that I am the oldest resident about these parts.' And then, with a final 'Good Morning', he walked back out onto the street.

CHAPTER THREE

THE MASSES MIGRATE 1833

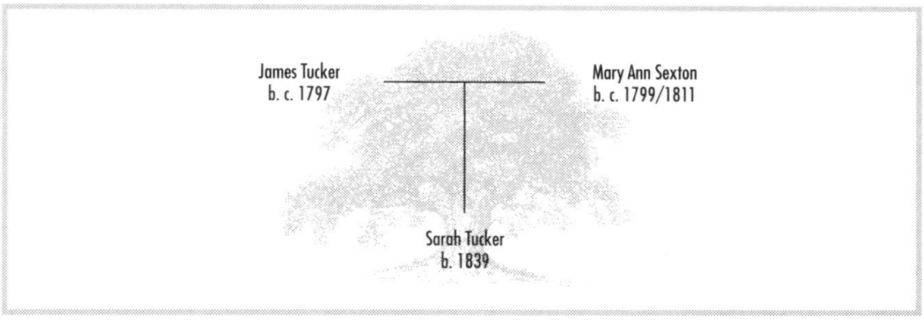

ON WEDNESDAY 9 October 1833, with a south-westerly wind blowing against it, the *Edward Coulston* sailed up the Derwent Estuary. The Tuckers were going to enjoy a few weeks rest on land, breaking their journey from Britain to Sydney. And so my ancestral brush with Van Diemen's Land was about to begin. It was a poignant moment for the family to arrive in Hobart.

The 340 ton ship had left the British Isles in the summer, bringing to the colonies a boatload of free immigrants. James Tucker was a 'painter and glazier'. He had married a minister's daughter named Mary Ann Sexton in St John the Baptist's church in Bristol in 1830, only a few years before emigrating for the Australian colonies. James's five-year-old son William from an earlier marriage was also with them. Although many such British folk were destined for Sydney, including the Tuckers, the *Edward Coulston* was also carrying a specific cargo for the island of Van Diemen's Land. This was a scheduled stop. Thirty women had been selected from Ireland by 'ladies of distinction' to fill the need for female servants in Van Diemen's

Land. These girls had boarded at Liverpool and were girls who 'have never wandered from the paths of virtue'. At least, this is what prospective employers or partners in Van Diemen's Land were assured by advertisements announcing their arrival.

The problem of gender imbalance in the colonies was one that the authorities were understandably interested in redressing. More men had arrived than women, either as convicts or free. As Ann Cunningham's relatively rapid marriage to Joshua Higgs highlights, available women were not short on marriage proposals once they arrived in the very manly Australian colonies. Sometimes historians have queried Australia's own strange bush machismo, and there have rightly been plenty of studies of women and men that aim to remedy this gendered bias, but there can be little doubt that its early development relates to a distinctly male environment. And as well as the blatant desires of working men for suitable partners, there were also demands for female employees to act as domestic servants, a lacuna fuelled by the frenzied marriage market. But, under the watchful gaze of the captain and fellow passengers, these girls were reportedly very well behaved en route to Hobart.

Van Diemen's Land, later renamed Tasmania, had been settled in 1803 shortly after the British realised it was definitely an island. The logic applied to their understandings of international law was that as it was not connected to mainland Australia, it was therefore not subject to the British claim of settlement made in 1788. That Able Tasman had earlier claimed the territory for the Dutch did not seem to trouble the British authorities, who promptly ensured the island was occupied and claimed. Although initially a military–convict outpost, the island quickly became a thriving colonial economy, and then a colony in its own right. Free settlers and freed convicts settled the interior, particularly the fertile midlands between the major towns of Hobart and Launceston. A cheap convict labour force enabled a mixed agricultural and pastoral economy to thrive, and the island's new landlords produced wool for British textile mills, but also meat and grains for Sydney.

Van Diemen's Land's coastal zones were also brought within Britain's colonial economy. Around the coasts of south-eastern Australia, especially northern Van Diemen's Land and the islands in Bass Strait, many men turned to sealing. Hundreds of seals were clubbed to death for their fur. Whales similarly bled for economic gain. Many whalers operating in the Southern Ocean made Hobart their major stopping spot, and shore-based whaling also developed rapidly to exploit the international demand for oil.

The landscape may have been taken and settled on, but the seascape was predated upon.

These country and coastal frontier economies brought men to Van Diemen's Land and its outliers from around the world. Hobart, a thriving port town, was a surprisingly international place. The pubs on the waterfront serviced sailors from all parts of the globe: Americans, British, French, and the south-east Asian sailors known widely at the time as Lascars. Māori, Samoans, and other Pacific Ocean indigenous people were also familiar. The shorefront was filled not only with white Christian people, as popularly mythologised, but also people of various hues who were Muslim, Pagan, Hindu, Buddhist, Daoist, and much else besides.

With a busy port and a growing population, Hobart had an active local press scene. In the 1830s there were two local weekly newspapers, the *Hobart Town Courier*, published on Fridays, and the *Colonial Times* published on Tuesdays. There was also the monthly *Hobart Town Magazine*, which printed a range of fictional, factual, and poetic pieces, addressing a range of historical, literary, and geographical matters. On their arrival, desperate perhaps for fresh news, the Tuckers may have read that a continent had been sighted in the Southern Ocean by Captain John Biscoe, who had recently explored and visited the southern polar regions.

This sense of potentially reading the same papers, and learning of events through the same channels, inspired me to further explore the physicality of the Tuckers' stay in the city that I had for a time made my own. So I decided to go down to Hobart's waterfront and explore some material relics of their time there.

Antiquity and relative penury combined to leave Hobart with an abundance of original colonial buildings into the twenty-first century, so I was not short of interesting sights. St David's Park, the settlement's original cemetery, had been tidied up many years ago. Some of the great men's headstones still occupied places of prominence, and the commoners' headstones were relegated to a few walls behind the Supreme Court.

Coming out on the famous Salamanca Place, I walked along the rows of warehouses. These were very old, and at the time of the Tuckers' visit would have been bustling with activity. The *Edward Coulston* may even have moored almost alongside, because much of the present waterfront area is reclaimed land.

From the waterside, Mount Wellington dominates the horizon. This was something they too would have noticed. Bristol is hilly, but not quite like this. And after weeks as sea, the sight of anything other than water was probably welcome. They would have seen the mountain as they came up the coast and then turned into the estuary, and only gradually would the small settlement nestled in its foothills have come into view.

My objective was in the old Bond Store, the commissariat office which supplied the penal colony, now part of the Tasmanian Museum and Art Gallery. It was an old hand-worked printing press. This was the machinery of mass information of its day, and the means by which much of what we know about the past has come down to us. The mechanical ingenuity of the printing press greatly appeals to me. The typeface would be methodically set by hand, letter by letter. Then, in a flurry of ink and activity, page after page was printed, each probably having its own slight variations in inking, scorning, almost, the whole process of bulk production.

But it was not only a general love of old printing technology that had brought me to risk the noise and bustle of a museum gallery during a school holiday season. I knew from a previous visit that it had originally belonged to the proprietor of the *Colonial Times*. If it had been passed to the subsequent owner of the paper, it may have been used to print the papers that allowed me to gain some little insight into the Tuckers' sojourn in Hobart in late 1833.

The *Colonial Times* detailed a bit about the female immigrants that were on board. An electronic search of Trove, the online repository of Australian newspapers, had identified the particular article for me, but I also wondered about what else was going in Hobart at the time. Glancing over the page, I started perusing the articles that preceded the one about the female immigrants. Mary Ann could not write, but it seems James could, so he would be the more likely to have read the papers. We historians sometimes focus so much on what is recorded in the newspapers that we forget the most common of daily experiences in the colonies may have been the very act of reading them.

And it was heavy going. The dense text had few headings to separate one item of news from another. If reading it, James would, like me, have simply absorbed large sections of news, perhaps passing on the essentials or reading bits out to his wife and child. One of the first stories on this page reported a plan to settle New Zealand. This puts in context how early this still was in the scheme of the European settlement of the wider region. Although the papers reported the recent arrival of whaling ships from New Zealand, that archipelago was still really a Māori domain, with a few

Europeans on the fringes. This, however, was in striking contrast to the story revealed through the following article.

'Mr. Robinson has lately arrived in Hobart Town, after a most successful expedition in search of the few remaining Aborigines now wandering over the island.' Whatever our understanding today of the events of that time, that sentence alone may have assuaged any fears the Tuckers had if they read it. The case of the Black War in Van Diemen's Land that had raged through the late 1820s and early 1830s was notorious. Years of pastoral expansion had set the scene for an increase in hostilities between Aborigines and the settlers, as sheep pushed kangaroo off the grasslands. A tense half-decade of guerrilla conflict and cycles of savage tit-for-tat violence had wracked the island, and the effects would shock the globe. Ultimately, having failed to capture the Aborigines by a series of lines of soldiers and settlers walking the densely settled portion of the island, a series of expeditions to 'conciliate' them was undertaken by an ex-bricklayer named George Augustus Robinson.

But in that mid October report Robinson had recently returned to Hobart from one of his 'friendly missions', as they were called, to the west coast of Van Diemen's Land. He had, the paper reported, 'opened a teraty with the last tribe alluded to, and the tribe was willing to join him; but when he went to the place where he considered they were, he found they had migrated to some other part of the island'. An obvious printer's mistake, 'teraty' should of course have read 'treaty'.

Robinson's mission involved convincing the island's Aboriginal groups to place themselves under government protection, which ultimately became exile on islands in Bass Strait. The Tuckers arrived in Hobart near the end of this process, when Robinson was asserting 'that there are only seventeen Aborigines now at large in the bush' and he was confident that with one more expedition, he would 'bring in the last black native'. But it was, the newspaper enthused, a cause of thanks that Robinson had 'ridded us of enemies of the very worst description'. Although there is good evidence that the process of removal was part of a negotiated settlement between some Aborigines and the government, conciliation turned out to become a euphemism for confinement, whatever the terms of the original 'teraty' may have been.

The Tuckers may have seen Robinson wandering the streets. He would have been quite distinct in a very stylish hat, which over a century and a half later looks decidedly like a train driver's cap. This statement of fashion was made famous by Benjamin Duterrau's painting of Robinson with a group of Aborigines in a work called *The Conciliation*, which depicted the great bulking figure of Robinson surrounded by pacified Aborigines. Duterrau's Campbell Street gallery was being advertised in the papers in early November. Supposedly it was well worth a look and the Tuckers may well have peered through the windows or even ventured inside to see the paintings of the colonial scenery. They may even have chanced upon Duterrau working on *The Conciliation*, which by then was almost certainly underway, because it was viewed in December by members of the press. Perhaps they even saw Robinson striking a pose, fresh back from his 'successful expedition', or one of the Aborigines, who, it was noted, had dutifully come 'and stood still till he took their likeness'. The Tuckers had arrived at a moment when the people of Van Diemen's Land seemed very satisfied to be nearly rid of their Indigenous population and were busily trying to capture what was thought to be an important marker of colonial progress.

In November, before either the painting depicting the 'conciliation' or the process itself was completed, the *Edward Coulston* sailed for Sydney with the Tuckers on board. The ship passed east of the islands where many of the Aborigines of Van Diemen's Land were being held by the government, waiting for a post-war settlement that never exactly panned out as either side had hoped.

When the *Edward Coulston* arrived in Sydney on a cloudy day, as well as passengers from Britain it brought oats from Van Diemen's Land as a supplement to Sydney's food supply. It almost certainly also had copies of the latest Hobart papers on board. This shuttling of publications across the oceans explains why early newspapers devoted so much of their space to reporting the news of other colonies. As a result, however, old newspapers can prove very tantalising when it comes to working out the details of a family's experience upon disembarkation. Fortunately, the shipping reports would often print names of people, so the Sydney *Herald* confirmed that 'James Tucker, Painter, Mary Ann Tucker, and William Henry Tucker' had arrived safely. There was also a suggestion of Sydney's waterside district's rough drinking culture, because the captain of the ship took out an advertisement warning that he would not be responsible for any debts his crew made while in port, putting publicans on guard against the fast talk of the thirsty sailors.

But more intriguingly the *Herald* had a letter of thanks to the captain, co-signed by the Tuckers and other passengers on the ship. They were thankful for the captain's kindness on what had been a 'long and rather tedious voyage'. Immediately below this was an advertisement. 'Employers Wanted', it said, and listed a range of occupations including 'Painters and Glaziers'. Published by the Emigrant's Friend Society, it was a sign that people like the Tuckers did not necessarily walk off the boat into immediate employment.

At that time Sydney was a city rapidly in the process of becoming a bricked one, however, so it probably did not take long for James to find work. Being able to market himself as either a painter or a glazier, he is likely to have found regular work adding the finishing touches to new buildings, or restoring older ones. There were a few James Tuckers around, so working out whether he was any of these is virtually impossible, and the details are of minimal interest anyway. It is possible that he was the James Tucker appointed overseer of improvements to the Government Domain in Sydney in 1837, where the erection and painting of fences was one of the major duties during that year. Even then, the green space above the town was a pleasant spot for walks.

As the city grew, changed, and urbanised, parts of the Sydney environment would therefore have been quite familiar to the former residents of industrial Bristol. Visitors sometimes recorded their perceptions of the city. One such person was Charles Darwin, who visited Sydney in January 1836 while on his voyage around the globe on the *Beagle*. He was on his way back to Britain after visiting the Galapagos Islands, which so profoundly marked his mind and facilitated his later thinking about natural selection as an explanation for the evolution of species. 'At last we anchored within Sydney Cove', he noted, perhaps a little sick of sailing. 'We found the little basin occupied by many large ships, and surrounded by warehouses. In the evening I walked through the town, and returned full of admiration for the whole scene. It is a most magnificent testimony to the power of the British nation.' With its broad and clean streets, and fine big houses, Sydney, he observed, compared to suburban London—only it was faster-growing. But not fast enough. He noted that 'every one complained of the high rents and difficulty in procuring a house'.

The Tuckers eventually settled in the city's densely populated central district. In 1839, when Sarah, their third Australian daughter, was born, they were recorded as living in Phillip Street. Running back up the hill from the original Government House, which was still in use when they arrived, it was a real inner-city suburb, populated with tenements of brick. During winter, hundreds of chimneys would send a thick cloud of smoke above the city. When it rained, the water ran down the street, creating a muddy mess. Living there, the sight of foreign sailors exploring the city would have been familiar, especially as the street was extended to Circular Quay from 1837.

While James Tucker helped build Sydney, colonial expansion continued. Only a few years after their arrival in Sydney, the settlement of the Port Phillip District was well underway, and the township of Melbourne had been founded. Similarly, that talk about the British settlement of New Zealand was set in motion, famously marked by the Treaty of Waitangi of 1840. Within a few years of the Tucker's arrival various plans and schemes for settlements within the wider region had become realities.

Two events led the Tuckers to join the colonial expansion and leave Sydney. The first was revealed by that rare thing for a historian: evidence of absence. It is a favourite phrase of mine—a logical truism that serves to temper some of the outlandish claims historians and archaeologists can be prone to making—'Absence of evidence is not evidence of absence.' Simply failing to find evidence of something is not a proof that it was never there. But sometimes it is possible to find evidence of absence, like a fossil cavity, and in this case it was another advertisement in a Sydney newspaper, which mentioned James Tucker.

William Townsend, 'plasterer & painter', wrote that 'I hereby give notice to James Tucker, Painter, &c. that unless he returns to my employment before Tuesday the 29th of June, 1841, I will have a warrant issued for his apprehension'. James, it turned out, was contracted to work for Townsend, who was rightly irritated at his absence from work. But there are two peculiar aspects to this advertisement. The first is that it was actually published on 29 June 1841, making the notice obsolete. The second reason was that he seems to have already been dead. He was not going back to work anytime soon.

No record appears to survive recording his death, but Mary Ann Tucker remarried in 1841, suggesting her husband had died. For a single woman from the working classes with young children to support, marriage was as much a survival strategy as a romantic attachment, although that should not necessarily be discounted altogether. Mary Ann's new spouse was Richard Curd, an ex-convict Kentish gardener who had been transported for life for 'beef stealing'. He arrived in Sydney in 1830, and had a conditional pardon by the late 1840s. After he and Mary Ann married, the family was soon on the move, and Mary Ann had three more children by Curd. Perhaps Richard had returned to gardening, or more likely was working as a pastoral labourer in the rapidly expanding settled districts of the south-eastern portion of the continent. The registrations of the births of Mary Ann Curd's children mapped out elements of the family's movement throughout lower New South Wales, including places in what was soon to become the colony of Victoria. Meanwhile, other relatives of mine were arriving directly in the south.

1851

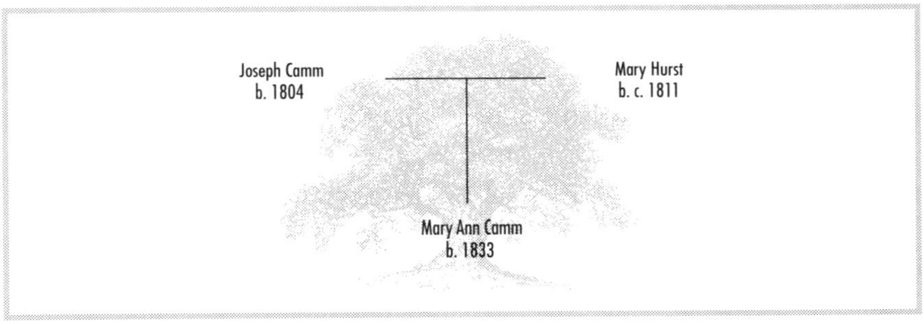

In the year that Victoria became a separate colony from New South Wales, the Camm family—like the Tuckers, one of the upper branches of Nanny's family—were farmers in the rural fringes of the township of Melbourne, battling against their neighbours' animals. Throughout 1851 there were a string of advertisements in the Melbourne *Argus* that attest to Joseph Camm impounding animals that had strayed on to his property at Boorondara, which illustrate the successful plantation of a settler community by Port Phillip Bay. Because the local poundkeeper responded to these bovine intrusions by publishing the infractions in the newspaper, it is possible to follow in some detail this obscure yet telling aspect of the Camm's day-to-day existence. There was the 'red cow' and 'yellow sided cow' of May 1851 that strayed onto the farm and were both detained by Joseph. August was a busy month; two bullocks, four cows, one bull, and a steer made nuisances of themselves. There were nine more animals later that same month, five more in early September and another five by mid September. Each animal could represent fences damaged, crops or vegetables eaten, or stock animals illicitly impregnated. The problem with meandering cattle was surprisingly serious.

Other newspaper advertisements in the *Argus* chronicled a wider set of social relations concerning the constant negotiations between neighbouring settlers. It seems that Joseph might have had an agreement to keep a Mr Pollack's grey pony in exchange for a fee. Such an arrangement would be a good way of earning a little extra income for a family with a small farm. In June 1851 Mr Pollack had failed to pay for the pasturage and Joseph had taken out an advertisement demanding payment. This likely shamed Pollack and points to a raising of the stakes in a neighbourly quarrel. Historians have tended to focus their attentions on the naturally much bigger social relations of the frontiers between the settlers and the Aborigines. However, in reality, for those people who came after the first wave of pastoral exploration and expansion had taken place, it was the everyday relationships between neighbours that would have been of most immediate and constant significance to them. Fortunately for the Camms, they at least had some experience of countryside politics before they came to the colony.

Each immigrant's decision to try their luck in the colonies was different, but was likely to have been influenced by reports of the opportunities for economic betterment. Booster literature abounded, which purported to tell prospective emigrants and investors about the prospects of any given colonial settlement or scheme. Broadly contemporary with the Camm's arrival in Port Phillip was John Dunmore Lang's *Phillipsland; or the country hitherto designated Port Phillip: its present condition and prospects, as a highly eligible field for emigration*. It was the kind of thing that may have circulated among intending emigrants, and provides some information about the given destination. There were also small pamphlets or advertisements targeted at particular classes or professions, and there were agents in Britain that arranged travel and assisted immigrants in finding employment. Britain, at this time, had emigration fever.

Of Melbourne, Lang said that it had a 'number and variety of respectable buildings', shops that could 'disgrace any of the fashionable places of business in London', and 'churches of respectable appearance'. Lang described the transition of a wooden town to a brick and stone one—in other words, a town of nearly 11,000 people passing from frontier town to a respectable colonial civic domain. This change was taking place as the Camms arrived. As James Boyce suggested in *1835: The Founding of*

Melbourne and the Conquest of Australia, the occupation of the Port Phillip District and the establishment of Melbourne in the middle of the 1830s marks a turning point in colonial history, where the momentum of settler expansion tipped past any semblance of government restraint. By the time the Camms were in Melbourne, men like Joshua Higgs had already opened up the Gippsland area and other surrounding southern districts. Even before gold rush money gave it a boost, the settlement had come a long way from being the outpost of a bunch of Vandemonian sheep farmers. 'The situation of Melbourne', Lang wrote, 'is decidedly good'.

The prospect of making good, acquiring land, and either gaining, restoring, or extending a family's prosperity certainly had sufficient pull for thousands of people to emigrate for foreign shores, including Australia. The guidebooks for emigrants they might have read remain useful sources of historical information. Their descriptions of the environment, towns, facilities, and opportunities provide much information of use to the historian. But they still need to be read with a touch of cynicism. Their primary purposes were to draw in hopeful labouring immigrants and capital investment.

Somehow, a report of Port Phillip managed to convince Joseph Camm, a farmer from the village of Kirton in Nottinghamshire, to sail for Port Phillip with his family in 1844. The Camm family left England and came directly to the Port Phillip district as part of an assisted immigration scheme. These were basically managed migration packages, and came in a variety of forms. On board the *Lord William Bentick* were Joseph's wife, Mary, and their four children. One of these was an infant. They were one of the thirty-five families and sixty-one unmarried individuals on board. While the Tuckers travelled to Sydney to help provide the colony with at least one more skilled worker, the Camms travelled to Melbourne to provide the colony, still New South Wales at that time, with a greater capacity to feed itself and a more certain demographic control of the landscape.

Almost certainly their incentive to migrate was part financial, whatever other factors may have been involved. The bounty system saw people like the Camms paid to come to the colonies, and promised a voyage and a fee on arrival, which helped allay the costs of migration and establishing themselves in a new situation. Even their eleven-year-old daughter, Mary Ann, earned the family a respectable £9 7s simply for being on board and surviving the journey. So I suspect it might have been this incentive which prompted the family to leave the village they had occupied for more than two centuries, but, as with most past immigrants, we will probably never really know.

The *Lord William Bentick* was fitted out in London, sailed to Plymouth, and then to Cork, before departing British waters for Australia. How the Camms boarded the ship, and precisely where and when, remains obscure. Before the ship's final departure the emigration agent, William Besnard, gave a speech to the passengers. He wished to give the assembled emigrants a little pep talk about good behaviour and a realistic assessment of their prospects. His speech, reprinted for public consumption as an illustration of his philanthropy, was loaded with class prejudices and Victorian moralising: 'prove that you have the true certificate of character, by faithfully fulfilling your engagements, and conducting yourselves honestly, industriously, and soberly', he said. Then he reiterated that they 'mark well the word soberly', and should 'shun all temptation to drink'. The emigrants were all given a printed copy of the same speech, this lesson on character a final gift from their homeland.

The voyage took 113 days. There were five recorded deaths on board, all of which were infants. The Camms were fortunate. Only four years previously another *Lord William Bentick* had been wrecked off the Indian Coast, running aground on rocks. Men were washed overboard by the pounding sea, and all of the women, sent out on the raft as the first priority to be saved, were drowned when the raft was swamped. A rescue steamship was sent, which managed to save some people, but bystanders watched helplessly from the coast as the disaster unfolded in the middle of the night. The weather was so atrocious that when rescue longboats were sent from shore the next day in search of more survivors, another ship was found grounded on the rocks only 600 yards away, the *Lord Castlereagh*. The voyages of my ancestors to Australia were by default all successful, but not all journeys were.

Safely walking off the later and safer *Lord William Bentick*, the Camms entered a historical grey zone. It is possible to get glimpses of their lives, but only a broad and basic picture can really be charted. Despite having a relatively unusual family name, which normally makes searching for particular people easier, the Camms do not frequently appear in any records. Joseph was charged with drunkenness on 21 April 1852, suggesting that on at least one occasion he ignored the emigration agent's advice. Other than this, I have to rely on a bit of supposition to work out what they did. Most likely they initially found accommodation in the small settlement of Melbourne itself. An agent may have helped Joseph find employment, but unfortunately for newly arrived immigrants the promise of opportunities for work did not always align with the reality. When the *Lord William Bentick*'s passengers disembarked in Port Phillip, commentators in the press noticed that the unmarried immigrants found it easiest to find work, noting that 'few of the married men have as yet met with employment'. So the early months may have proved a bit difficult for the Camms.

But, having been farmers already, the Camms were partly prepared for colonial settler life when their opportunity finally came. Even young Mary Ann, for instance, is likely to have been involved in the usual round of farmyard tasks that could be safely entrusted to children, like gathering eggs and carrying buckets. But given his forty years of age, it is perhaps strange that Joseph would have entertained the idea of relocating his family to the antipodes, especially considering the risks of a long sea voyage both to his children and his pregnant wife. Such, perhaps, was the pull of opportunity.

Throughout my research into family migrations to Australia, I was interested in the wider migration experience, not just the fact of arrival. The arriving generations had to have been affected in some way by their notions of home and their connections with particular landscapes, even if they rejected that connection in some way. Convicts had been torn away, but voluntary migrants were different. Perhaps some were torn away as well, due to economic forces out of their control. Some possibly fled situations or circumstances of which no trace has been left. Some of my ancestors had migrated within the British Isles before leaving the security of a familiar landscape. Some travelled as families, others as individuals. None of them, however, simply abandoned the land of their childhood, and perhaps a wider family, and replaced it with a new place without the experience leaving its mark.

And the Camms, it turned out, came from a particular place to which they were deeply connected. As part of an upsurge in popular antiquarian research across England, the original parish register of Nottinghamshire's Walesby, a village adjacent to Kirton with which the Camms had a long-standing family connection, was printed in the late nineteenth century. It is fascinating to think that local historical consciousness reached new levels just as families and individuals were so definitively leaving material associations with their pasts behind. The parish register listed burials from 1680 onwards, and the first Camm recorded as buried there was in April 1681:

James. He was a 'husbandmen', a farmer. It turns out that the family had been farming in that part of Nottinghamshire for a long time.

Rather unhappily, I noticed that a few names further down the list was 'Elizabeth Camm, wid.', who was buried in October 1681. In February 1682 'Mary wife of James Cam' was buried, a little under a year after her probable husband—it gets hard to be sure sometimes. From perusing the register I gained a vague sense of how the Camm family was profoundly connected to this place I had never previously heard of. And that serves, I think, to give pause for thought about just how complex a thing it was for subsequent generations to shift their sense of selves from being British to being Australian. Perhaps generations carried a feeling of duty to remain connected to lands where their people were buried.

Among the earliest baptisms was a John Camm, son of Richard Camm, baptised in 1611. I could also see some of the Camm's hardships, such as when in 1699 the normal list of christenings was interrupted by the annotation that 'James Cam Child was born Feb. 14, which died before it had a name given'.

The editor of the printed volume provided an annotation to this sad story. The lack of a name might, he suggested, have been because the child's parents were Quakers. The editor cross-referenced another unusual annotation, where it was recorded that in 1764 'Jonathan Cam the son of Jonathan Cam renounced Quarerism [Quakerism] in this church openly and was then Baptised … in the 29th Year of his Age'. A similar annotation survived for his brother William, who renounced the sect and was baptised in 1782 'in the 40th Year of his Age'. Being nonconformists may have created difficulties for the family within the small village community, but these seem to have been resolved a good generation before my Camms left their ancestors, and mine, to repose eternally in the churchyard beside the ancient medieval churches of Walesby and Kirton. No wonder the Australian colonies proved so fond of the neo-gothic movement when it came, and populated the landscape with churches that aspired to echo the styles of their deeper medieval past.

But fleeting references to this particular family's long occupation in an English parish also has an interesting documentary parallel. Written evidence of the Camms in Walesby roughly approximates the length of time their descendants have now lived in Australia. They have *literally* been in Australia for at least as long as they were in Nottinghamshire. So perhaps it was with this wider sense of the future prospects of their progeny in mind that couples like the Tuckers and the Camms boarded wooden ships and left their former homelands behind.

And while commentators have become used to talk of Europeans taking away Aborigines' lands, and words like invasion and dispossession tend to dominate discourse on this subject, this really speaks to present-day perspectives and the wider acceptance that colonisation had dramatic and often negative effects on Indigenous peoples. But the little people of Europe who came did not have that benefit of hindsight or even necessarily a strong sense of their role in a bigger settler–colonial whole. Booster literature generally assured immigrants that Aborigines were either docile, friendly, absent, or soon-to-be one of those things. Once here, many settlers recognised the impact of colonialism on Aborigines, but opting out of their new situation was prohibitively expensive and most settlers entered into already seemingly 'settled' territories where their greatest daily concern was ensuring the integrity of the fences they shared with immediate neighbours, or providing for their own and their children's futures.

So while governments and gentlemen in London and Sydney devised settlements and mapped out plans for colonial expansion and its attendant wealth-producing capacities, the majority of the actual settlers battled to establish secure futures. Many immigrants were assisted along the way, selected on the basis of offering something to the colonies, be they skilled labourers or experienced and morally sound smallholder farmers. Others came of their own accord despite the obstacles. And then, just as the orderly settlement of the colonies seemed to be underway, a metallurgical revolution seemed to shake the earth itself.

CHAPTER FOUR

THE MINERS AND THEIR FEVER 1852

'HE CAME TO Sydney when very young, and travelled overland from that city to Bendigo, in 1852, shortly after the breaking out of the gold fever.' So ran part of John O'Rafferty's obituary.

In a newspaper, words cost money. Hence O'Rafferty's obituary was written with that particular efficiency that marks out a balance between respect, detail, and brevity. One sentence reiterated his foreign birth and pointed out his port of arrival. O'Rafferty was Irish, the son of Dominick and Mary O'Rafferty of County Galway. Details of his arrival in Sydney proved both suitably vague and precise. Perhaps no one remembered exactly when, how, and why he came, but he was young—that was the key bit—and he was already in Sydney when the rush started. Three facts then ended this line with more pointed precision: 1852, Bendigo, gold fever. He had caught this unusual ailment, which was an Australian outbreak of a global pandemic.

The fact of gold was not new. But the 'gold fever', as contemporaries called it, was. The California gold rush, generally dated from 1848–49, was rightly famous, and it is no accident that it was a miner with experience of the American goldfields, Edward Hargraves, who in May 1851 publicised the discovery of gold near Bathurst in western New South Wales. Over the following months goldfields bloomed throughout the eastern colonies like explosive little flowers, attracting covetous human-bees who sought their fortunes. By the end of 1851 several of the major goldfields near Ballarat and Bendigo had been identified in the infant colony of Victoria.

News spread by word of mouth, correspondence, and newspaper. In the usual way, the *Sydney Morning Herald* printed information of the Bathurst discovery directly from a copy of the *Bathurst Free Press* which had been passed on. The *Herald* provided its own commentary under a headline sure to capture the attention of readers: 'GOLD'.

If a young John O'Rafferty was reading the *Herald* in Sydney, then he may have noticed subsequent commentary about 'hundreds of the miserable dupes who have proceeded, and are proceeding, to the mines without adequate means'. He probably also noticed the rapid change in the advertisements on the newspaper's front page. Merchandisers helpfully advised people heading to the diggings to equip themselves carefully. All of a sudden 'Gold Diggers or Miners' Boots' appeared as items for sale advertised in the papers, as did other useful items like the 'Patent Portable Tents' that could be bought at David Jones and Co. on George and Barrack Streets.

Some merchants even offered discounts, as they announced they were selling out of Sydney themselves and moving to the goldfields. By 20 May 1851, only five days after the *Herald* had publicised the Bathurst discovery, one enterprising fellow was selling maps of the new goldfield. As the hopefuls trudged westwards, carrying their maps, boots, special clothing, tents, and 'steam manufactured biscuits', wholesalers of liquor rushed to transport enough alcohol in advance of the buzzing swarms. O'Rafferty may have been tempted to join them, but it seems that he deliberated for a few months. Finally, he headed south, on foot, to one of the next big discoveries: the Bendigo Diggings.

The town of Bendigo was ultimately named for an English championship boxer, famous in the 1840s. By way of a shepherd nicknamed for the pugilist, a hut for the shepherd, a creek for the two, and a goldfield and town for the creek, the place went from obscurity to busy fame proverbially overnight. Contemporary drawings and paintings show huts, dirty hills, and many men hunched over as they busied themselves in and with the ground. Into this mix stepped O'Rafferty at some point in the digging's early days.

But more than just a place of gold mining, the location was early identified as a place where miners collectively resisted what they saw as government greed. On 9 December 1851, only two weeks into the commencement of major operations at Bendigo, about 250 miners gathered for a public meeting. The Governor of Victoria had issued a proclamation that would double the licensing fees for the miners, and the miners wished to discuss how they might protest against and resist this arbitrary financial impost.

It showered in the afternoon, but eventually the clouds cleared and, under a bright moon, beside a large fire, the proceedings commenced. A miner named Henry Frencham, dressed in his mining clothes for effect, addressed the crowd. He spoke well and was cheered loudly by the assembled men. Then he read out a resolution that articulated their collective concerns. It referred to the government proclamation, and asserted that 'we, the goldminers assembled on Bendigo Creek ... considering that it is unjust and extremely oppressive, are, to a man, determined not to submit to the wholesale robbery which is contemplated by such proclamation, and to the uttermost will withstand its imposition. We, therefore, solemnly pledge ourselves to resist it in every shape and form, and will aid by all means in our power those who will do the same elsewhere'.

The meeting, and the miners' resolutions, were widely reported.

In hindsight, it is tempting to see this as prefacing one of Australia's great cultural reference points, the Eureka Stockade, and certainly an argument could be carried to that effect. But it is also hard not to hear other echoes within the Bendigo meeting itself. The formal oath-taking and collective resistance is reminiscent of the Irish Defenders. One of the subsequent resolutions was about courting the newspapers and journalists in their struggle, which perhaps hinted at longstanding concerns about the freedom of the press. There were insinuations about the arbitrariness of absolutist government, subtly undermining the dominant English narrative of a beneficent constitutional monarchy poised protectively against Europe's continental kings and emperors. And then, seemingly dangling beyond the careful protestations of the miners' loyalty to Queen Victoria, was the unspoken American catchcry of 'no taxation without representation'.

In some ways the publicity of this meeting had a different effect on members of the wider public than that intended. Rather than seeing an oppressive system of government, many people simply took two words from reports of the miners' moonlight meeting: 'Bendigo' and 'gold'.

So a rush started. Hundreds and then thousands of people poured into the district, and it is probable that John O'Rafferty was one of these. Bendigo had suddenly become a busy place. Such was the result of the dramatic influx of prospectors and their economic train—food and liquor suppliers, tool salesmen, clothing merchants, gold assayers, bankers, and the many faces of officialdom—by mid 1852 the wider Victorian diggings held a population not far off double that of Melbourne.

O'Rafferty may not have stayed long at Bendigo, heading instead towards another localised gold rush near Beechworth, perhaps as one of the precipitating prospectors of that locale. 'He is said to have been one of the party who discovered the Ovens goldfields,' his obituary mentioned, 'of which he certainly was an early resident.'

There had been a European settlement on the Ovens River since 1839, founded by a man, rather curiously known as John Rattray, later sometimes identified as John O'Rafferty, but my ancestor had not arrived there until some ten years later, so it was not him. This fact, which proved a red herring for an hour or so of my research, was an indicator of how confused the situation was in many ways with people flocking to the goldfields. Tent cities seemed to spring up overnight. Newly arrived migrants from the British Isles, young and older men and women born in the colonies, professional miners from America, and soon enough large numbers of Chinese from the pastoral districts and overseas all headed to find gold. Many went to whatever new diggings seemed to provide the next big haul.

But not all gold mining was mining in the true sense of the word. Although the odd nugget could be dug up, and many miners sunk shafts in their plots to try to hit leads of gold beneath, the reality of a lot of gold extraction was in the form of small specks or flakes, or very small nuggets, which were washed out of the dirt. Some of the large operations involved digging the earth and feeding water through an excavated channel called a 'race', which was used to wash away the lightest dirt and let the heavier gold settle to the bottom in large, especially built wooden contraptions. These involved major engineering works and collective enterprise. But the same principle that gold was heavier than earth was behind the much lower-tech panning, whereby men scooped riverside earth, the river's bottom, or the dirt from their holes in the ground, and swished it around to locate the gold in little pans. It was a time-consuming process, but for the determined and lucky 'miner', a quantity of gold could be extracted gradually, tiny bit by tiny bit.

So while many prospective miners converged on the main goldfields and goldfield towns, other true prospectors investigated the creeks and rivers of the ancient continent for the next spot. And so, probably as a small party of men exploring new waterways, stopping every few miles to try out a new place, John O'Rafferty was supposedly one of the men to find a concentration of ancient alluvial gold which for millennia had been making its way gradually from the mountains to the Ovens River. This places him in the Beechworth area by February 1852, further up into the hills from the old Ovens Crossing, which was later known as Wangaratta. If the later report of his leaving Sydney in 1852 and heading to Bendigo was correct, it only gave him two summer months to travel from Sydney to south of the Murray River, down to Bendigo and then back up to the Ovens.

Even if he was later confused with that other John Rattray, O'Rafferty was certainly experiencing an Australian part of a global cultural revolution. Whereas the working classes had previously mostly worked as agricultural, pastoral, artisanal, domestic, or straightforward labourers, at the diggings they could, by their own industry and luck, theoretically leave the working classes behind. It was a dream rarely fulfilled, of course, but the peculiar form of betterment migration that the gold rush was, in essence, helped ordinary people to become pioneers on a scale previously unseen. Little creeks and rivulets adopted names that spoke to their cultural world, whereas beforehand waterways had tended to be named for gentlemen, squatters, politicians, governors, aristocrats, royals, and their spouses. Now they could be named for stockmen, workingmen's huts, and boxers. Almost as an extension of Joshua Higgs having learned Aboriginal placenames, the peripheral geographies of the mining towns became permanent markers of a certain democratisation of the landscape, in which ordinary folk named places for ordinary things, beyond the full control of government.

And while migration had certainly helped to mobilise the working and middle classes of the British Isles and the Australian colonies, the gold fever seemed to speed up that process. What had seemed at times like an orderly and practically unidirectional flocking became frenetic, like animals evading a predator, or like an ants' nest that has been stirred up. Moreover, it destabilised comfortable local economies, as the working classes simply left their employers behind. And all this movement, and the sudden concentrations of people it produced, facilitated the sharing of information and grievances. In a reaction to government taxes which felt like predation on their attempts to escape drudgery, rough handling by authorities, and also agitating against other groups of 'alien' miners like the Chinese, meetings abounded as the mining folk sought by weight of numbers to protect their interests and advance their causes.

Bendigo had its share of further meetings, including a massive march of miners in 1853. It also proved to be the origin of one of Australia's great early documents, a petition by the Bendigo miners. Having professed their loyalty, the petitioners pointed out that thirty shillings per month for each licensing fee was too burdensome. But they also spoke of the ill effects on their health from mining, the difficulties in using their money to buy land monopolised by squatters, how it took time to get established as a miner, and how many of them were being threatened by armed men extracting the government's taxes, including specifically singling out the way some people were chained to trees and put to hard labour. O'Rafferty did not sign it. By then he had already left the Bendigo district to fossick in the Ovens River region. I suspect he would have signed it if he could. After all, the document expressed views that seemed to be increasingly common, and tens of thousands of signatories agreed.

O'Rafferty wasn't the only member of my family to suffer from the gold fever. Many seem to have tried their hands at it for a time. But one other particularly stands out, illustrating as he does the internationalism of the gold rush, including those elements of political reform that it borrowed, facilitated, and heralded.

William Macky had been a farmer in Ireland before leaving its green fields for Australia's golden and gold-filled slopes and plains. His son later related the core elements of his story, saying that Macky was 'caught with the gold fever, [and] migrated to Victoria' in the early 1850s. This recollection, however, proved to be quite a sanitised one. The son was only born in 1849, so his father's absence came when he was still very young, and rather unfortunately became permanent. Although Macky left 'intending that after a time his family should follow him', 'within a year his letters suddenly ceased', and he was never heard from again. The last letter was written from Buninyong, an area just south of Ballarat where gold was discovered. Thereafter the family was left to struggle on a small pension, wondering if the breadwinner lay at the bottom of a collapsed mine in distant Australia. Ever afterwards Macky's son would only ever speak of his mother 'with a reverence and affection that is unbounded', detailing how she 'bravely faced the battle of life'. But his father's story was reduced to this sad little tale of goldfield absence.

William Macky's real story, I rather suspect, helps explain why two of the Macky boys, William Marcus and Richard, both later hyphenated their surnames as Dill-Macky, taking their mother's name in addition to their father's to attach themselves more firmly to the Dill side. In part this was because they both became ministers of religion and hers was a clerical family, but it also seems that they disapproved of their father. Indeed Macky, it turns out, was the subject of much worry and gossip within the wider family.

It was the diligence of a distant relation, and a bit of good luck, that enabled me to see there was more to Macky's story. Barry Nesbitt, who is descended from James Macky, a different one of William Macky's sons to the one from whom I am descended, compiled an extensive family history in *The Dr James Macky Story*. In this, he printed copies of letters written by cousins of William Macky in the 1840s and 1850s from Ireland to New Zealand, which still survive across the Tasman Sea. Through these, I learned that his in-laws may have considered poor William Macky a bit of a black sheep. The letters also gave a good sense of the conditions of Ireland at the time and helped me build up a brief yet good picture of the farmer turned would-be goldminer.

The surviving correspondence started in January 1849, and it is immediately apparent there is much more to the story and that this had been left out of Dill-Macky's later brief synopsis of his father's disappearance on the Victorian goldfields. The letter's New Zealand recipient was informed that 'your Cousin William Macky of Lisfannen has started off to America. He sailed from Liverpool for New York the day before Christmas. Mrs Macky and children are still in Lisfannen and what they mean to do I cannot say.' A few months later, in May, there was a tiny bit more: 'William Macky was going away and leaving Susan behind. So much for marrying for the sake of some paltry gold.' Perhaps these Macky cousins had not entirely approved of the marriage.

'William Macky of Lisfannen has been in America since January last', another letter detailed in July, 'but I hear he is coming home again.' This was the immediate period after the Californian gold rush, so it suggests

William may have been rather impetuous, but also not terribly tenacious. This opinion was clearly shared by his cousins, who wrote with what seems rather like a touch of irony that 'He is a most extraordinary genius. He will never go mad (he is not long in one mind).' They also seemed to feel a bit of sympathy with his family, because 'Mrs Macky and family were not with him'.

But it wasn't just the pull factor of the goldfields that prompted William's short American adventure—there was a sad push factor as well. 'Another year of famine is, I am afraid, about to visit poor Ireland', the Irish Mackys informed their New Zealand relatives in November 1849. 'The prospect is also very bad for farmers for every article of produce is at a very low price, and taxes are getting higher.' And it was to this sorry land that William returned. 'William Macky is home from America', they wrote. 'He has got quite a republican spirit home with him.' The writer detailed how 'I wanted him to go to New Zealand but he would go nowhere that was under British government'.

Almost a year passed without major news. Then, in October 1850, word was that 'William is about to leave Lisfannen. He was ejected for non-payment of rent'. Once again there was an added comment, seemingly an ironic barb: 'I don't know where he intends going—he is a wonderful genius.' There were slightly more details in the following month: 'Your cousin, William Macky, of Lisfannen has given up his farm to Lord Templemore for, I may say, nothing. He gets no money for it. He has gone at present time to Derry but intends going to America in the spring.' The same letter also revealed rather bluntly that 'William Macky's father is dead'.

And, like other letters, it also contextualised William Macky's Ireland, even as it queried the man's behaviour: 'There is no change for the better in this country. The failure of the potato crop is worse this year than it has been yet. The blight came on early before the potatoes got any size and they are very few in this country … High rents are still kept up, but they will soon get a great deal of the land to themselves as the people are emigrating rapidly—but there will soon be few able to do so.'

Another year passed. 'William Macky has quit farming and turned auctioneer', the cousins wrote in October 1851. 'He is doing very little and I am afraid he will never do very well in business. James McMillan is occupying his farm in Lisfannan.'

By the middle of 1852 William had decided to leave. In fact it seems he actually carried one of the cousins' letters a part of the way. 'I write to you by this opportunity by your cousin William Macky', the writer detailed, 'who is leaving this now for Port Phillip and Melbourne and leaving Mrs Macky and his five children behind. He has been unfortunate and is going to try his fortune in that country among the gold.'

Several interesting things aligned in this correspondence. Firstly, the situation in Ireland was producing a push factor, just as news of the gold rush was providing a suitable pull. Then, there was the American adventure, short-lived, certainly, but clearly sufficient to affect Macky's political attitudes, helping both to harden his views on British government and perhaps to better articulate an alternative model. The weight of emigration traffic had gone to America, but the relative proximity to Western Europe also facilitated return traffic. People could experience America before migrating to Australia. The American presence on Australia's goldfields has been noted, but the extent of other people's prior experiences in America, or their understandings of it, might have been underappreciated. And finally, these letters highlight the intense maintenance of wider familial networks. Ireland, England, America, New Zealand, Australia. The Mackys were spreading out, and Australia was but one part of a much wider story.

In Victoria Macky did well enough, although seemingly not principally as a miner. Two more letters gave information about his activities, at least based on what William himself wrote to his family in Ireland. Apparently by April 1853 'there is one [letter] from William Macky who has begun carpenter work at Geelong and gets a pound a day'. In September the cousins could report that William's family 'are all well, they have letters frequently from William. He is still with the same person near Geelong at £6 per week. He has purchased two lots of building ground and is building a house. He has sent home £30 to Mrs Macky'.

The sudden cessation of William's letters is a bit of a mystery. Because his last letter was from Buninyong, it suggests he might have travelled to the Ballarat goldfields. Sadly there is a record of a coronial inquest in Ballarat in May 1853 for one 'William Mackey', which could well be him. This fellow had died 'from the effects of injuries received by deceased during a quarrel, which originated in an aggravated assault'. As an Irishman with republican sympathies, experience of America, and hostility to British Rule, he was precisely the sort of fellow likely to have participated in the Eureka Stockade in Ballarat the following year. Ironically, when his sons later migrated to Australia, they came to serve and encourage British imperial sentiments.

The increasingly democratic sentiments being expressed in the goldfields of Australia, typified by events at Bendigo in 1852 and 1853, bore elements of a number of global struggles. There was the example of the 1848 popular uprisings throughout Europe, where various outposts of the ancien regime were threatened by commoners. Although these were effectively undone or brutally squashed, they had a different flavour to peasant revolts of the past. The would-be revolutionaries looked to the examples of the French and American revolutions, perhaps mythologised, but potent nonetheless. And there was the Chartist movement in Britain, a workers' movement which advocated political reform, including universal manhood suffrage. A heady mix of ideas coalesced as working people took up Christ's assertion that the humble people would 'inherit the earth'; Jean-Jacques Rousseau's catchcry that 'Man is born free, and everywhere he is in chains'; and the new world order outlined in Karl Marx's 1848 *The Communist Manifesto*.

In Ireland, agitation for political reform continued, and actual hunger fed resentment. And it was increasingly clear to a literate public that political Britain's ideological attachments to key enlightenment ideas were naive and contrary to Christian charity or common decency. Adam Smith's benign hand hovered over the marketplace with greater benefit to the capitalists and monopolists than the hungry poor. And Thomas Malthus's scientific 'proof' that famines were natural population checks was little more than a paradigm for denigrating and ignoring the pleas of the poor—particularly those ignorant masses of superstitious Catholics, pagans, and infidels who wilfully overpopulated the planet. Yet even while these ideologies maintained their hold, some of the repressive aspects of Great Britain's economic and ideological underpinnings had been chipped away from the imperial edifice, which seemed tacit acknowledgement that past ways were flawed. By the middle of the nineteenth century the British slave trade had been abolished, convict transportation was in its dotage, and Catholics had been freed to practice their religion without penalty, meaning they acquired rights to own land and potentially vote. And because the right to vote was based on an income threshold, Catholic emancipation encouraged a greater discussion of voting qualifications, such that the notions advocated by the Chartist movement seemed realistic possibilities. Revolutions in Continental Europe contributed to the mid nineteenth century being a time when serious agitation for voting rights and democratic government awakened in many parts of the world. Australia was no exception.

So the sequence of events at the Eureka Stockade at Ballarat, later treasured as a major national historic–cultural reference point, is not as unique as many Australians would like to admit. The mining folk who burned their licences, built a protective stockade, stitched a new flag, swore allegiance to it, and support for each other in their struggle, were the pointy antipodean end of a global trend, part of an almost worldwide phenomenon. Rather than being essentially Australian, the stockaders were decidedly cosmopolitan. And like the participants in the revolutions of 1848, they were crushed brutally, with a police and military assault in the early hours of a Sunday morning. This was not the storming of the Bastille, it was more like the time a Corsican general named Napoleon fired cannon on rioters in the streets of Paris.

But symbolically it is easy to see how a flag was better than any petition. A context of wider violence and savage reprisal helped add revolutionary flavour to a story that really should start with meetings and petitions that protested loyalty to Queen Victoria. Oaths and professions of mutual solidarity again echoed Defender behaviour, as had previous efforts at rebellion like the Castle Hill uprising. But these elements also followed naturally from prior goldfield behaviours. With a heady mix of traditions and mythologies, the swarming people re-appropriated and re-packaged the struggles of the past, ostensibly over particular resentments of the present. So when the Australian and British ancien regime swatted at the problem, it doomed itself to be perpetually remembered as the old regime. It gave the reformers their greatest symbol: martyrs, a useful ingredient for any hagiography.

The event was certainly invested with a pseudo-religious status by some. When the Italian Carboni Raffaello published his account of *The Eureka Stockade* in 1855, a year after he participated in the event, his lacing of the story with Latin references was a deliberate if at times cheeky near-sacralisation of the passion of the men. Chapter titles like *vox populi, vox Dei*, 'the voice of the people is the voice of God', quoting an ancient saying, is perhaps one of the more blatant examples. But it is also interesting how Raffaello used the word 'vandemonian' as a derogative adjective for unsavoury characters, hinting at their being either ex-convicts or their guards, either way tainted by a brutal system. He was not just focused on the events at Eureka, but a wider fudging of the old and the new, typified by the ex-penal colony that renamed itself Tasmania to help blot out the bad old days. His account of the stockade was a pointed reminder to his readers that Eureka was a failure. In one way the message was that the bad old ways were still with us. If Australians should take anything from Eureka, it should be that the fight for equality and equity never ends.

While I may not buy into a mythical narrative that says Australian democracy was born at Ballarat, it is true that adult manhood suffrage did soon follow from the wider agitation, trends, and movements of which Eureka was a prominent part. The saintly stockaders certainly appeared to have interceded on men's behalf with success. Universal male suffrage was granted in South Australia in 1856, in Victoria in 1857, in New South Wales in 1858, in Queensland in 1872, and in Western Australia in 1893. In 1895 South Australian women were granted the right to vote, and by 1896 Tasmanian men finally achieved voting rights. Admittedly, however, these were all for 'British' subjects over twenty-one years of age, which excluded parts of the population. Nonetheless, the wider context suggests that John O'Rafferty probably spoke with other mining folk in tones part reverential, part conspiratorial, as he worked the land of his adopted home and thought of how he might one day own his own part of it.

Several of my female ancestors were also present in the wider Victorian goldfield areas, generally revealed only by the terse records of officialdom. They have not been captured by the sorts of voluminous records informing Clare Wright's *Forgotten Rebels*, an exhaustive study of women on the Australian goldfields. But there are snippets of information, allowing me to chart their progress and some of their activities, even if they are dreadfully stereotyped as wives and mothers. For instance, in 1852 Mary Ann Curd, formerly Tucker, was with her husband Richard and family in Kilmore, apparently a wild and rollicking community of largely Irish miners. Having tracked south from Sydney, they had a daughter, and the following year, still in Kilmore, Mary Ann's older daughter, Sarah Tucker, married John O'Rafferty.

This deceptively simple record of one person marrying another reveals the potential the gold rush has to confound historians, who struggle with the way that effective recordkeeping often lagged behind major demographic shifts, a fact made worse by the dramatic increase of people generally and the duplication of often common names. Moreover, even on an individual level, each person's records often had their own idiosyncrasies, adding another layer of interpretive difficulty. For instance, O'Rafferty signed himself into marriage as John Monroe. Yet his death certificate, his children's birth and marriage certificates, and other official documentation all make it clear this was O'Rafferty marrying Sarah Tucker at this time and place. Every other particular was correct, even to the extent that Richard Curd was listed as giving consent to the marriage. Frustratingly for historians, it was not uncommon for people to have aliases like this in the past. I may never know for sure why John lied about his name, but to be 'John Monroe' suggested deliberate obfuscation in the face of officialdom. It was possible that he was running from the law somehow. Perhaps it was a joke that I will never now get. It certainly fitted with his rather mysterious origins and his quite spectral existence in the goldfields, living just beyond the government's effective gaze, and leaving little trace of his passing. There were so many O'Raffertys about I was not even quite sure on precisely when and how he got to the colonies, and had great difficulty being sure when I was following his trail. But while his marriage illustrates the potential people had during the 1850s to thwart officialdom, it also gives me the uncomfortable feeling that giving men the vote was a way colonial governments had of tracking people. Family histories are greatly facilitated by the advent of the electoral register.

The obituary outline of O'Rafferty's life said that 'For a considerable time he carried on the occupation of a practical miner in various parts of Victoria with a fair amount of success'. He was demonstrably a miner in the Ovens district in the mid 1860s, because he transferred a licence at Hurdle Flat near Beechworth in 1865 to two of his brothers-in-law. I rather suspect that he and his new-found in-laws moved to the Beechworth district as a group. There, Mary Ann married one last time, having buried yet another husband. She did not outlast the final one, however, and was buried at Beechworth.

Yet there is a little hiccup to O'Rafferty's later story. Searching the newspapers, trying to sift the right John O'Rafferty from the seemingly hundreds of wrong ones, I found what proved to be a little nugget. It was in the 20 October 1857 edition of Beechworth's *Ovens and Murray Advertiser*, one of the many local newspapers rapidly appearing across the country. I could see the crucial text sticking out, even before I clicked to open the page, in the automatically generated results preview: 'John Rafferty, alias John Munro'.

He 'was placed in the dock and pleaded Not Guilty to the charge of stealing a mare'. This was a report of the General Sessions. It was a rather strange trial, at least insofar as the account given in the paper reported things. It concerned a horse, which disappeared from James Trigger's stable sometime in June, and, he alleged, was the same horse that he saw in Euroa one day, a town south-west of Beechworth where the country starts to flatten out. He got the local constable to repossess the horse for him, and O'Rafferty was taken into custody for trial. The judge was informed that the horse in question was outside the court, acting as some kind of bizarre living evidence.

The details of this O'Rafferty bothered me, because they seemed a little out of touch with what I knew of him and his family. The 'prisoner', as the court referred to the not-so-presumptively innocent Irishman, 'has land at Euroa and lives there'. He was apparently using the horse to move bricks when spotted. If this was my O'Rafferty, which the alias seemed to make very likely, then it suggested he might have turned to farming or some other trade. There were goldfields in the general area, but not for another decade would there be a specific site of much significance at Euroa.

As I read the account of the trial, starting with O'Rafferty's assertion of innocence, the prosecutor's admission that 'the evidence was of a circumstantial nature', and the lack of any witnesses of the alleged theft, I thought this all seemed rather farcical. When O'Rafferty's lawyer pointed out 'the improbability of the prisoner bringing the horse to Euroa and working it in a public place if it had been stolen by him', I assumed O'Rafferty would be fine. But this was not how things worked in the colonies. Not for the first time was an Irish ancestor of mine trumped by British justice. The jury found him guilty, and he was sentenced to '7 years on the roads'.

He was given the prison number 3671. O'Rafferty's prison record captured his physical details. He had brown hair and grey eyes, bushy eyebrows and an oval face, and bore a series of scars. Three were former head wounds, scars over his 'left temple'. There were other notable marks in evidence of former injuries on the thumb and little finger of his right hand. Whether from mining or fighting, they showed some hardness during his life. The single sheet of the prison record also told its own tale. In the section for 'previous history', it mentioned that he arrived in the Australian colonies 'per "Hamilton" 1844'. It also said simply: 'Wife and boy residing in Beechworth'.

O'Rafferty was in 'irons' by March 1858, engaged in hard labour. But his conduct was noted as 'good', and he was 'taken out of chains' by June. He still had to work on the roads, but his conduct stayed reasonable enough to mostly steer clear of further leg irons. Twice during 1860 he was caught indulging himself with tobacco and was detained for seven days each offence. Then again, in November 1860, he was detained for another week for the elusively rendered 'Improper behaviour'.

By 1862 he was out with a 'free Certificate'. Post-convict Victoria, O'Rafferty shows, is a historical construct and a popular fabrication. The transportation era had ended for the eastern Australian colonies, but the convict era had not.

When released, O'Rafferty almost certainly returned to Sarah, who had continued to live at Hurdle Swamp in the Beechworth area, and therefore he likely also returned to mining.

Although his obituary glossed over his time contributing to the steady growth of Victoria's roads, it did at least record his next major step. 'Finally, getting tired of mining, he took up land at Tarramia'. I suspect this definitive shift from miner to farmer was the reason for the transfer of a mining claim in 1865. After a little over a decade of intermittent mining he had earned enough to buy a farm, it seems, perhaps his second attempt to settle down, achieving one of the key aims of the miners' meeting from Bendigo, back in 1852.

And as if to confirm the move, O'Rafferty's son John was born at Tarramia in 1868.

Tarramia was near Corowa on the Murray River, in New South Wales, west of Albury. The flat floodplains had been opened up for greater settlement in this period, and John and Sarah O'Rafferty seem to have been among the many who looked to a future as small homestead farmers. The mining folk often had this goal in their mind, so when colonial governments finally started to stop renewing squatters' leases and opened up land for the 'selection' of small farms, many took their chance.

The Western Riverina is an amazingly fertile area, but is also prone to the vagaries of climate and weather. Facing drought and floods, as well as tornados, many of the small farmers did not last, and the O'Raffertys were among them. Inexperience was probably the most likely contributing factor, but many elements must have come together. 'The speculation', it was said, 'was a bad one for him.' He tried valiantly for a number of years, but, 'after exhausting all his savings he at length had to abandon his farm'. This was 'in or about the year 1877'.

But not before making a go of it to the best of his abilities. This appears to have involved distilling, probably drinking—and certainly selling—hard spirits, possibly a skill learned on the goldfields. Across outback Australia the production and sale of alcohol was a common phenomenon, part business, part hobby, part social activity. I was alerted to O'Rafferty's involvement by a notice in a *New South Wales Police Gazette* from March 1868. This was a paper printed specially for law enforcement agencies, a way of sharing information throughout the colony. It was a brief notice, and told a common story: 'John O'Rafferty, summoned by Senior-Constable Fullerton, Corowa Police, for selling spirits without a license, has been fined £30; in default of payment, three months imprisonment in Albury Gaol. Fine not paid.'

I searched the Albury gaol entry books, and sure enough managed to find O'Rafferty in the gaol logs. He was there by the end of March for 'sly grog selling'. He was thirty-seven years old and 'Strong & in Sound health'; his occupation was listed as 'gardener'; he could 'Read & Write'; and his conduct, up to that point at least, had been 'good'. Curiously, it was also noted: 'No previous corrections known'. The New South Welsh police did not know about O'Rafferty's hard labour on Victoria's roads.

Albury gaol provided a tiny snapshot of the social problems of the age. Fourteen other people occupied the cells, five from England, seven from Ireland, and two from New South Wales. These last two had the unusual occupation of 'child'. They were eight and two-and-a-half years old respectively, in gaol as 'Vagrants'. Two women were each there for being 'Drunk disorderly & using obscene language'. One was Irish, the other English, and had perhaps been using that language against each other. The Englishwoman was the mother of the two vagrant children. There was one debtor, and several thieves. At least O'Rafferty was the most enterprising of the crooks in Albury gaol that March.

As I looked around the old registers for Albury gaol, I found another more detailed entry register about a John O'Rafferty which was roughly in the right period, but was not dated precisely. I knew it was after 1867, and suspected it was the right one, a duplicate copy of some sort, but I was not sure. I kept flipping about the pages, until I noticed a familiar name. It was one of the other prisoners in Albury gaol with him in March. I realised

I could use the other prisoners to date this register more precisely. If the names all matched up, then I had the right one.

And they did match. This was brilliant, because it seemed to confirm some of the details of O'Rafferty's arrival. He came from 'Dunmore Ireland', which was County Galway, so it matched the other records I had. He arrived in 1845 on the 'Brig Hamilton', and was 'R.C', Roman Catholic. He was of slight build, fair-skinned, 5 feet 6 inches high, and had a tattoo on his arm. His eyes, this time, were recorded as light hazel. Minor differences in the arrival year, height, and eye colour reflect different life phases and recording practices, but they generally align in ways that enable me to be confident this is the same person.

Another record corroborated that he was 'discharged' on 10 June 1868, and it was probably just as well. In the three months that he was in prison Sarah's belly would have begun to show signs of a growing John Jr, who arrived safely in August.

O'Rafferty continued to try and farm for another decade after his run-in with the law, before 'he lost his holding' about 1877 and moved to the nearby town of Yarrawonga, once again crossing the Murray River into Victoria, although still west of Corowa and Albury. There, I learned, 'with his wife and young family' he struggled. Apparently 'he earned a somewhat precarious living'. Some fleeting local records suggested to me what he was doing. He won a prize at the Yarrawonga show in 1887 for 'Poultry', indicating he was rearing chickens.

It seems he also had another legal hiccup at Corowa in 1878, which may have prompted, or been in response to, the loss of his property. A John O'Rafferty was accused of trying to forge and steal documents from the Crown Lands Office. Acquitted and released, he once again passed through the gaol records, giving me another view of him. This time his occupation was listed as 'Farmer', but he was three inches shorter. Such discrepancies could be because of slightly different recorders or recording procedures, and his now grey hair and shorter stature could be products of the passing of ten years with a young family.

But he recorded the ship and year of his arrival as 1846 by the *Thames*. Previously he had given the *Hamilton*, firstly 1844, then 1845. Curiously, there was a brig named *Hamilton* trading to and from the colonies, but it sank in 1843 off Britain. And there is no *Thames* that arrived in Sydney at the right time. Although his name, age, overseas origin, family details, some physical descriptions, and so on all enabled me to be sure this was the same O'Rafferty, the variations of his story of arriving in the colonies was certainly odd. While sloppy recording could explain these anomalies, it is also possibly what O'Rafferty did say when quizzed each time he was gaoled, meaning his story might have drifted about a bit. Wherever and whenever he did arrive, he seemed either a bit forgetful, or perhaps he was concerned to keep it secret. I wondered if he was not a sailor or soldier who had deserted. It seemed a likely explanation which would account for him having arrived in the colonies in his mid-to-late teens, without any apparent documentation, and then to obfuscate this one detail of his life habitually for the rest of his life.

And that murky past seems an apt assessment of the gold rush period. We can be quick to see it as a heady and dramatic thing, heralding great and lasting changes, but for each person affected the gold helped them leverage themselves out of their individual pasts, as well as helping society move out of its structural past. Some like William Macky left families for the prospects of brighter futures of wealth and liberty, leaving lasting resentment and difficulty. Some like Mary Ann Tucker–Curd–Lunn were drawn by circumstance and necessity to the tent cities that for a time acted rather as cities always have—as sites of hope, opportunity, and culture. Some like John O'Rafferty seemed to simply appear.

But the lure of gold itself should not be downplayed. If this second imprisoned John O'Rafferty was my John Rafferty, then the physical description of an aged and stooping man is rather pitch perfect. He sported a grey beard and had 'two front upper teeth wanting'. He must have looked the part of an old miner.

And when O'Rafferty died, that is how the people of Yarrawonga remembered him. 'While in Yarrawonga', his obituary closed, 'he spent a good deal of his time in prospecting the quartz deposits around the town, and on one occasion he sank a shaft in the police reserve from which he secured a prospect of payable gold.' I can see the grey old miner stooped by a lifetime of looking at the ground, hoping, quite literally, for paydirt.

As the heyday of the gold rush drew to a close, gold mining still continued for many years in the colonies, but was generally pushed further from the settlements, or was a more machinery-dependent sort like quartz mining, which involved crushing the white mineral so as to extract veins of gold. The age of men with gold pans and wooden cradles rocking the gold from its slumber in the earth was gradually passing away. So too were the old-timer miners. And I empathise with poor O'Rafferty, who found a good prospect in his later years of chickens and stills and gaol houses, yet, 'having no capital … and being old and feeble at the time … could not work the claim.'

But this was not the end. He left Yarrawonga as the nineteenth century drew to its end, and 'went to Beechworth to engage in a mining venture'.

He died in Beechworth, and Sarah lived on for another twenty years, before dying in Sydney. Her life had, geographically speaking, gone full circle. Like many of the women in my family tree, their lives were extremely poorly documented. The men, simply put, were much easier to follow. And I even wondered as I searched the records if O'Rafferty was partly the model for a fictionalised story that was serialised in newspapers in 1897, about the time he returned to mining at Beechworth. It was called 'The Haunted Mine'. The author suggested that some readers may 'readily recall when and where the circumstances attendant on the original were enacted'. It was fiction, but with some factual basis, apparently.

Set in the hills far south and east of Beechworth, in a mine that followed a seam that meandered along the bed of 'an old Silurian river' and had been abandoned after being extensively worked in the late 1850s at the height of the gold rush, the premise of the tale was that, although deserted, 'memory of the fabulous yields of the abandoned claim' were still recalled by 'several aged individuals'. And so in 1890 'a syndicate was formed' to work the site. 'Accordingly, John O'Rafferty, a man possessing considerable practical experience in mining, was deputed by the Get All You Can Company, to go to Mount Berrigum and open up the long abandoned Wombat mine.'

This fictional O'Rafferty then disappears in the depths of the dark mine. When, after weeks, his party went into the mine to investigate, every appearance was given that O'Rafferty haunted it. And so the mine was once again abandoned. And 'O'Rafferty still held potent sway among the dark and gloomy drives'.

This story points to a strong sense of the working folk's knowledge of their wider country, and a democratisation of the named landscape. And it reveals a deep sense of connection with the very depths of the continent's rocky foundations. Suffrage and political reform were aspects of a drive to modernity that the Australian colonies reflected, and in some ways led, but partly by the accident of having less of an old regime to overcome. The gold rush facilitated discussion of global issues and concerns, but it definitely needs to be seen as part of a wider global phenomenon: a chronological coincidence does not necessarily a causal argument make. And discussion about the effects of the gold rush needs to include the darker sides as well as the saintly narratives of sacrifice and salvation. Just as the flag of Eureka has its global companions, so to the flag raised at Lambing Flat near Young in 1860 and 1861 needs to be seen as the close relative that it is. The site of a notorious riot against Chinese miners, Lambing Flat is part of the wider story of goldfield agitation and collective protesting which helped facilitate the colonial antecedents of the White Australia Policy. Just as I cannot place my ancestors specifically at Ballarat on that day, nor can I necessarily be sure none were at Lambing Flat only six years later. They were out there in the flats, gullies, creeks, rivers, and hills somewhere, looking for the best opportunity for themselves, their families, and their friends. And if parts of their lives were hard, and some of their actions harsh, it was with their futures, and their children's prospects in mind, that they battled to leave old world poverty and subordination behind.

CHAPTER FIVE

LADS, LASSES, AND LADIES 1853

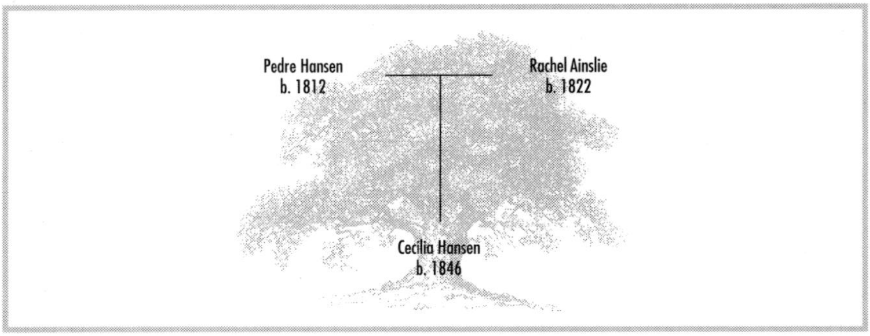

NOTHING QUITE CAPTURES the spirited tensions of the colonial mid-nineteenth century like the Mayor of Sydney's 'Fancy Dress Ball'. The 1853 ball was described afterwards as reflecting 'warm and friendly greetings of the representatives of almost all the nations of the world'. It was like a prototype for the United Nations in fancy dresses. At least, that is how it was presented. But the running of the event reveals a growing sense that colonials shared in and contributed to British supremacy, reflecting a sort of imperial self-satisfaction that was coming to mark many parts of the Australian colonies. It conveyed a strikingly different image from the digger-collective, man-versus-government narrative that too often seems to dominate our national histories. The colonial ball-goers professed a decidedly optimistic view of New South Wales, and it was to what the ball represented that most of the successful gold-diggers aspired. Taking place one year before the Eureka Stockade, it tells a story of a confident colonial society in its cosy urban centre, hopeful for the future, and proud of its collective achievements.

Considerably more than a thousand people were jammed into the Royal Victoria Theatre when the Governor-General arrived with his wife and 'their suite'. They were greeted at the door by the Mayor, and Her Majesty's 11th Regimental band played 'the National Anthem', 'God Save The Queen'. It was a staged meeting, full of pomp and ceremony. When the formalities concluded, the dancing began. On the wooden floors men and women daintily and gracefully as possible turned, chatted, and exerted themselves under admiring, judgemental, predatory, and protective gazes. It was all rather self-consciously Jane Austen and was in fact magnificently populated with costumes derived from British history. There were knights, Shakespearean characters, nobility, royalty, allegories like the 'Spirit of Terra Australis', Indians, Russians, great politicians, and so on. Most men, whether actually soldiers or not, arrived dressed as soldiery of some sort. A few fellows broke the military mould, like the 'Californian gold-digger', but even this example helps illustrate the range of countries represented and points out how much it was a self-consciously international affair. There were Spaniards, Swiss, even a 'Gipsy Girl'.

Yet it is what was not there that is perhaps the most telling. There were several Indians, mostly of the American sort, a handful of Chinese costumes, but no Aborigines. The one fellow dressed as an officer of the 'Native Police' was almost certainly the Indian version, who famously mutinied a few years later. While Aborigines participated more readily in rural social activities like horseracing, their exclusion from the society activities of the capital was a given.

These more troubling thoughts aside, I was pleased to find among the long list of names and costumes printed for the readers of the *Sydney Morning Herald* a 'Miss C. Hanson'. She had chosen to come in costume as an 'Australian girl'.

Whether this 'Australian girl' was intended to be an Aborigine or a typical colonial girl, I will never know, but it was unusual. Cecilia Hansen's siblings' costumes are clearer, being little coded revelations of the family background. Cecilia's sister dressed as a 'Scotch girl', probably because their mother, Rachel, was originally from Scotland. And their brother came as a 'midshipman', which was a very likely costume for the son of a boat builder.

Rachel Ainslie, Cecilia's mother, was one of 205 immigrants that had arrived in Sydney in July 1839 on the barque *Strathfieldsaye*. A bounty emigrant, she had departed Britain from Plymouth at a far and diagonal opposite end of the island from her original home in Dysart, Fifeshire, north and east of Edinburgh. Her father was a pensioner, so she was not leaving a wealthy position in society. Her brother would become a ship's carpenter and another brother was enrolled in the Greenwich naval school, so Rachel came from a very seafaring branch of my family tree.

The colonial press welcomed the fact that in 1839 the 'whole of the emigrants have arrived in excellent health' and also noted the arrival of 'pure bred blood hounds'. While there is sometimes a strong belief that there was always a strong egalitarian sense in Australia, or that this was rapidly developing, the shipping of servants and hounds to a landed economic-aristocracy, the squatters, really shows this to be simply a misreading of the past, or perhaps, as noted in a previous chapter, an over-reading. What sense of egalitarianism Australia now holds has in part developed in response to the classed nature of its colonial past.

Upon arrival in Sydney Rachel was eighteen years old. Her occupation was listed as 'House Servant', she could read and write, and her religion was 'Church of Scotland'. Two years later, in 1841, she married Pedre Hansen in the thriving little port town of Port Macquarie, much further up the New South Wales coast from Sydney. Presumably she somehow found employment in that district as a domestic servant. I can also really only surmise that Pedre was employed in a shipbuilding capacity, perhaps as a ship's carpenter, which would explain his presence in Port Macquarie in the 1840s. How and when he arrived there remains unclear, because his name was very common, especially amongst seamen, and there were several different spelling variations. Moreover, these were almost always anglicised versions of what was originally a Danish name. Pedre was born in Bornholm, Denmark, an island near Copenhagen. Almost certainly he came to the colonies as a sailor, probably with that specialised role as a ship's carpenter.

Visiting Port Macquarie about the time Rachel and Pedre married, the surveyor Clement Hodgkinson described it as 'a well built little town, the houses being of brick, and generally surrounded by neat verandahs, and trellis work'. It was an image of a pretty little river-town by the sea, although the wider region was suffering from an extended drought about the time Rachel and Pedre married there. Port Macquarie's name gives away its approximate age, the area having been surveyed in the late 1810s during the governorship of Lachlan Macquarie. But it was in 1821 that the town was first established, originally a secondary punishment penal station like the more famous Port Arthur in Van Diemen's Land. It was intended to be an isolated and harsh experience, a replacement for Newcastle, which had become too close to the growing settled districts around Sydney.

From the 1830s, however, the region was part of the growing pastoral colonialism of the age, and the town lost some of its strong convict associations. Joseph Backler's painting of St Thomas's Church highlights the shift nicely. Originally built by convict labour, the church, as depicted about the time Rachel and Pedre married there, is surrounded by well-dressed people, presumably congregating on their way to attend a service. There were men in top hats and coats, women in bonnets and colourful dresses, children holding their parents' hands, and a handful of horses, including two horse-drawn carriages. Only the prominent red earth, the deep red stone of the church, and the small glimpse of another building show this as an Australian setting.

The family's gravitation towards this established port centre is in part, therefore, an accident of career. But it is also part of the phenomenon of continued coastal expansion and development that had been a key process of colonial advancement since the earliest days of the colonies. Some settlers moved inland, whether for pastureland, agriculture, or gold, but others followed the easier route of the coast, populating the one-time convict outposts that had grown into thriving townships and cities. And pastoral expansion encouraged the development of nearby ports, and the establishment of ports facilitated the ready settlement and 'development' of local hinterlands.

Within a few years of their marriage, though, the couple had moved to Sydney, and Pedre went on to establish himself as a prominent local boat builder. Perhaps Port Macquarie was not yet quite big enough. Certainly Sydney provided more entertainment options, of which the Mayor's Fancy Ball was a prominent example, and which the Hansens seem to have attended from the late 1840s onwards.

The family, thus, seem to have embedded themselves in the social life of their adoptive city. As a further instance of this, Pedre and Rachel were sufficiently active members of the Sydney Presbyterian Church to sign an extended notice repudiating the actions of a would-be minister. Fancy balls, the politics of church congregations, and the daily provision of the necessities and comforts of life, were the issues that colonial settlers looked forward to, regretted, experienced, and generally failed to leave good records of.

In the heady absorption of narratives of displacement, life-changing experiences, broad cultural shifts, and that old historian's standby, 'difference', we sometimes run the risk of exaggerating the disjunctions between new and old worlds, failing to see the wider everyday world of which the Australian colonies were a part. Certainly there had been obvious tensions, most famously expressed in the label of 'currency' lads and lasses, colonially born children, the derogatory nature of which term could perhaps be over-read into the historical record. Irony is often context-dependent, and a wry joke is easily misinterpreted by a historian a century and a half later. A bit like the later term 'wog', it is a quick shift from offensive, to self-adopted, to badge of honour. Besides, this issue had largely dissipated by the 1850s.

And while the gold fever and continuing frontier wars provided contextual elements relatively lacking in Britain, European unrest, the Irish problem, the potato famine, and many other issues provided their own dangers and insecurities. In the towns of England, Denmark, and New South Wales, the balls still went on.

Australian histories are generally written by Australians for an Australian audience, and have traditionally not strayed far beyond relatively simple geographical parameters, the broad relationship with the British Isles, or large ethnic minorities. Fortunately, this is changing with a new generation of Australian researchers, but in our region it is New Zealand historians that have led the way in situating their one-time colony in a wider imperial setting. Tony Ballantyne's *Webs of Empire*, for instance, highlighted the importance of seeing colonies 'as part of the larger dynamics of British empire-building'. And explicitly addressing Australia as part of a bigger global picture, James Belich's large comparative study of the English-speaking settler-world, *Replenishing the Earth*, revealed many similarities of processes and features in seemingly diverse settler societies and economies.

But while my ancestors were part of an English-speaking world and an interconnected British Empire, they were not simply part of a global march of British-born people. Pedre Hansen, native of Denmark, who had to anglicise his name to Peter for convenience in his new homeland, and joined his wife's Scottish Presbyterian Church, complicates the one-time Anglo-Saxon master-race narrative that was itself a product of the later nineteenth century. Not all migrants were British, and while certain groups like Chinese and Jews could attract press attention, prejudice, and often social exclusion, that in part reflected the fact of ethnic diversity. Pedre was Danish before he became a member of the British Empire. The question of whether, to what extent, and how that shift occurred is complicated even on an individual or familial level, so to posit a simple Australianising narrative on the basis of his daughter's costume, for example, could be a step too far. But perhaps it is still a little step in a pretty dress. And while it is tempting to look for signs of Australian identity-formation, it needs to be recognised how colonial Australians in the mid nineteenth century often saw themselves as Colonial-British, and looked to their place in the wider political and cultural entity that was the British Empire. Even the immigration into Australia of many non-British people during the colonial period illustrates this bigger-than-Australia phenomenon. This branch of my family serves to illustrate that rather than immigrants moving directly into Australia's interior, the first stages of immigration were largely an urban and suburban phenomena, even if only the first part of a longer journey. The story of colonial growth is more urban than often imagined. In fact, while many immigrants may have ultimately sought the opportunity for land, not all were necessarily migrating to the Australian outback. Rather, they were moving to thriving British-style towns and cities, many with sizable ethnic sub-populations. Therefore many immigrants were drawn into the British Empire itself, where the Australian colonies acted as entry points for becoming British.

1854

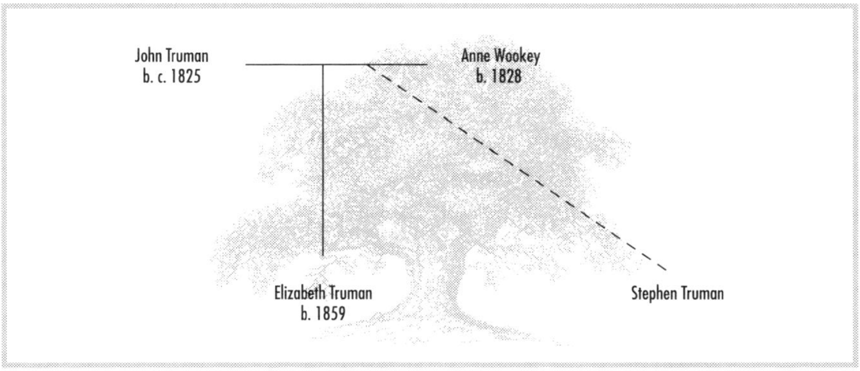

Far to Sydney's north, in another of those coastal settlements, another family lived out the common experience of being colonial suburbanites. They lived in a settlement of small agricultural acreages of the sort familiar in many colonial Australian cities. The presence of often grand houses much older than others in their respective street or block in Australia's major cities reflect this phenomenon. And like the Hansens, the Truman family's experiences reveal the interconnections between everyday people and wider events and trends, sometimes distant, sometimes uncomfortably close.

Living as he did in a landscape slowly changing from semi-rural to suburban, John Truman had his family's proximity to neighbours and wider events brutally impressed on him on a Saturday night in January 1854. The Trumans lived in Kangaroo Point, part of the Moreton Bay settlement, a slither of land formed by a river bend just across the water from the little town of Brisbane. Their night was disturbed by a group of three men employed at the nearby boiling-down works, who took relief from the heat by drinking the evening away.

These workmen, tired and sweaty, were enjoying a languid summer's night, having earlier patronised Mercer's pub. It was observed of two of the drinkers that 'neither of them was sober' when they were at the pub. They all left together, 'singing and making a noise all night'. But it is likely that the community was used to this disturbance, and did not find anything unusual about it, however irritating it may have been. This revelry continued into Sunday morning. Yet as that Sunday morning turned to afternoon, the camaraderie took on a decidedly different tone, and another man ended up dead.

John Truman gave evidence at the coronial inquiry. Reading his words recorded in the thick newspaper print, I can picture the scene, both of the agricultural labourer giving his account, and of the events that he had witnessed.

'I was standing at the door of my house', he said, 'when I saw the deceased standing outside the hut in Mr. Douglas's paddock.'

The Trumans lived a fraction over a hundred metres from the hut, so John had a good view across the paddocks. Even in the dusty noonday haze he could see clearly.

He pointed to one of the prisoners in the dock at the trial, and continued.

'I saw him come out of the hut, with a large piece of wood like a slab, and with this he struck the deceased a blow which knocked him down. He took both hands to the stick, and struck him several blows after he was down.'

'I did not see the deceased arise again', he added.

RIGHT: A list of convicts, including Thomas Kennedy, transported to New South Wales on the *Britannia* in 1796–97. (State Records Authority of NSW, NRS 1150)

BELOW: Part of Robert Burford's 'Panorama of Sydney in the year 1829' showing the district where James Kiss worked. (State Library of New South Wales, a266300)

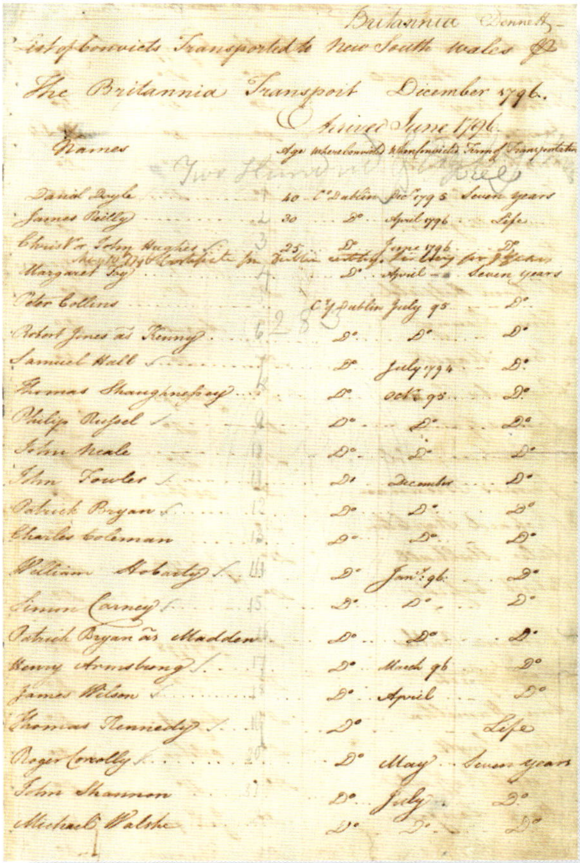

Britannia

List of Convicts Transported to New South Wales by The Britannia Transport December 1796.

Arrived June 1797

Names	Age	where convicted	When convicted	Term of Transportation
Daniel Doyle	40	Cy Dublin	Dec. 1795	Seven years
James Reilly	30	Do	April 1796	Life
Christr John Hughes	25	Do	June 1796	Do
Margaret Fay		Do	April	Seven years
Peter Collins		Cy Dublin	July 95	Do
Robert Jones as Kenny		Do	Do	Do
Samuel Hall		Do	July 1794	Do
Thomas Shaughnessy		Do	Octr 95	Do
Philip Russel		Do	Do	Do
John Neale		Do	Do	Do
John Fowler		Do	December	Do
Patrick Bryan		Do	Do	Do
Charles Coleman		Do	Do	Do
William Hobarty		Do	Jany 96	Do
Simon Carney		Do	Do	Do
Patrick Bryan as Madden		Do	Do	Do
Henry Armstrong		Do	March 96	Do
James Wilson		Do	April	Do
Thomas Kennedy		Do		Life
Roger Conolly		Do	May	Seven years
John Shannon		Do	July	Do
Michael Walshe		Do	Do	Do

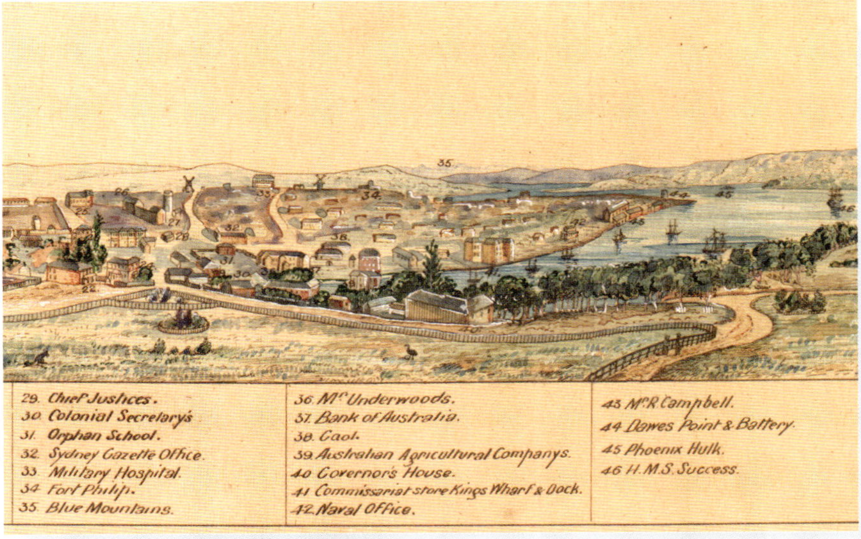

ABOVE: A sketch by John Glover of the Hobart waterfront about the time the Tucker family arrived. (State Library of New South Wales, a3175027)

BELOW: One of Benjamin Duterrau's images depicting Aborigines submitting to George Augustus Robinson. The Tuckers briefly visited Van Diemen's Land as both Duterrau's composition and Robinson's 'friendly' missions were underway. (State Library of New South Wales, a928352)

ABOVE: 'The valley of the Ovens River in Victoria' by Eugene Von Guérard. John O'Rafferty was supposedly among the first gold miners to work this area in the early 1850s. (State Library of Victoria, H25839)

BELOW: St. Thomas' Church, Port Macquarie, by Joseph Backler. The scene captures a sense of colonial aspirations to propriety, and is where Rachel Ainslie and Pedre Hansen were married. (State Library of New South Wales, a7469001)

ABOVE: 'Kangaroo Point, Brisbane', painted by Conrad Martens in 1852. The Truman family settled here in that year. Elizabeth Hiley (née Truman) later reminisced about the lush landscape. (State Library of New South Wales, a9740001)

RIGHT: Agnes Dobson arrived in Queensland in 1879 with her husband and family. A label on the back of this framed photograph confirms her identity, but many working people left relatively little documentary evidence of their lives. (Private collection)

ABOVE: A Cobb & Co. Coach at Hay, a stop on one of Bob Dean's many routes. (State Library of Victoria, H83.429)

BELOW: Part of the mate's log of the *Lavinia*'s voyage to the Solomon Islands in 1872–3. On the last day an entry was made, the ship was attacked, the mate was killed, and the remaining pages are blank. (Royal Society of Tasmania, University of Tasmania Library Special and Rare Collections, RS 84)

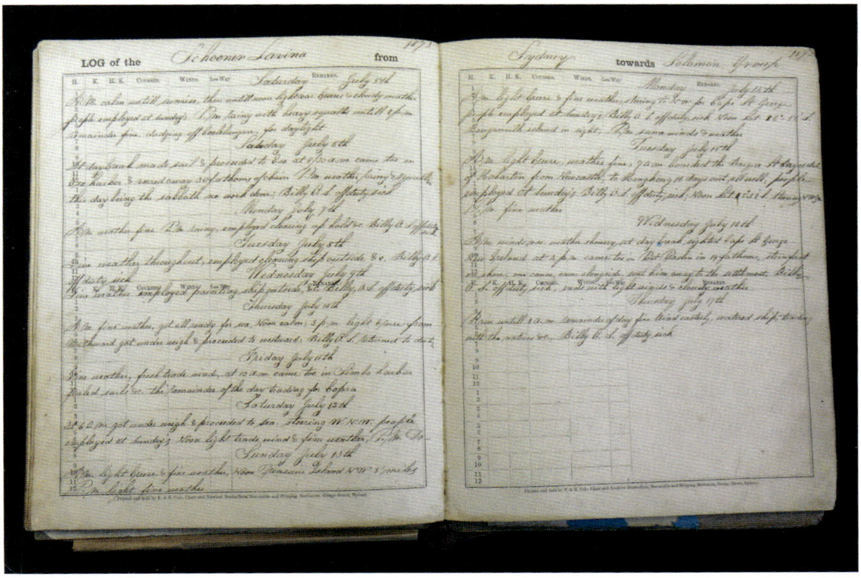

RIGHT: Captain Neil Brodie. (Private collection)

BELOW: William Marcus Dill-Macky and Ellen Elizabeth Morewood during their engagement. Soon afterwards they migrated to NSW. (State Library of New South Wales, MLMSS 1385)

ABOVE: Alexander Brodie's squadron prior to deployment to South Africa in 1901. Alexander is third from the left at the back (*Australian Town and Country Journal,* 9 March 1901, courtesy of Trove, National Library of Australia)

RIGHT: Alexander and Ellen Brodie (née Dill-Macky). (Private collection)

ABOVE (LEFT TO RIGHT): William (Billy) and Elizabeth Duck (née Kiss). (Private collection)

BELOW: Billy Duck's butchery in Junee. (Private collection)

The wounds were horrific. The post mortem examination showed skull injuries 'penetrating to the brain'. This resulted in the victim's death after a few lingering hours in the steamy January afternoon.

John told the inquiry that attacker and victim had appeared to be talking, that the victim had tried to avoid the blows, and that the perpetrator had then left the scene, going first to the pub, then to a shoemaker, and then to the constable where he actually accused one of the other two men. This other man could not have done it, however, because he was apparently insensibly drunk at the time.

John Hanley, the attacker, was sent to the Brisbane Assizes for trial. Curiously, he pleaded guilty, but the judge 'strongly advised him to retract this plea, which he did'. But with John Truman's eyewitness testimony, as well as that of others, plus the fact of a blood-stained plank of wood, Hanley's fate was judicially sealed. He was sentenced to death.

Yet, remarkably for so apparently clear-cut a case, Hanley's punishment was changed to five years of hard labour. There were suggestions that he could have made an insanity defence, or that the assault was in part culturally constructed (because apparently Irishmen resolved disputes with sticks, his lawyer claimed). But what prompted the sentence review remains unclear. Nonetheless, it elicited a blast of editorial rage in *The Moreton Bay Courier*, which criticised what it called a 'mistaken act of clemency'. The editor felt that 'if ever the Gibbet was cheated of its due, it has been so defrauded on this occasion'. The murder, the trial, and the cheated hangman all entered the collective memory of Kangaroo Point. The murder was widely recounted in later reminiscences of the early days of the suburb as an illustration of the violent old days. Its notoriousness was why John Truman's son Stephen long remembered the 'murder that took place at the boiling-down establishment'.

A childhood in the early years of a colony in the antipodes must have been vastly different yet remarkably similar from that of the long-settled landscapes of the British Isles. Fortunately, two of the Truman's children later wrote down some of their recollections. There were those of Stephen, son, and also their daughter Elizabeth, one of my great-great-grandmothers. Although refracted through time, experience, and hopefully some maturity, these reminiscences capture not just the essentials of events, like the fact of a murder, but sometimes also the emotional essence of the experience, or at least its shadowy afterlife as memory.

Elizabeth's reflections on her early life were mostly fairly brief. She recalled the family moving to another part of Kangaroo Point, where John Truman built his family a home near the big 'Shafton house', the only other house in the immediate area. This captures that sense of moving into a landscape of bigger houses and smaller houses. A class system was in place, at least economically. And there were built vestiges of an earlier phase of settlement. Colonially born children like Elizabeth often had the experience of growing up in a land with its own visible architectural history. With the benefit and distortion of distant hindsight, it is easy to miss such nuances of experience, and to be too readily duped by later simplistic narratives of Australia as a youthful land. In the 1850s and 1860s, for a child, it was not.

Elizabeth was born in 1859, the same year that Queensland became an independent colony. But the family had been there since July 1852 when the *Maria Somes* emigrant ship carried 281 immigrants from Britain to the Moreton Bay Settlement in New South Wales, far to the north of Sydney. This ship had famously faced a hurricane when carrying convicts a few years beforehand and was a regular on the Britain to Australia run. John and Anne Truman, and their four boys, were somewhere on the crowded decks during the four-month sailing. John, like so many immigrants, was originally an agricultural labourer. He was born in the village of Clutton in Somerset. He married Anne in the same village and may never have expected to leave until the opportunity presented itself. He almost certainly met his wife at the Clutton 'Church Farm' estate, where she worked as a servant. She had worked there since at least 1841, when she was aged thirteen.

Anne was born in the nearby village of Temple Cloud. Clutton was as old as the great Domesday Book, but Temple Cloud did not date back quite so far, perhaps only to the Templar Knights from whom it derived its name. Whatever encouraged Anne to leave the village of her birth, she did it alone. Her surname was Wookey, named for a little village, but she was not Anne Wookey for terribly long in the documentary record. In 1844 she married John Truman. They had three boys in rural Somerset before departing for Australia. When the ship arrived everyone's health was recorded as 'good', except for Anne, who was 'convalescent'. She was nursing the infant George, who had been born just before the voyage. Anne nursed him safely across three oceans.

Like other immigrants John signed a letter of thanks related to the voyage. This was to Thomas Ness, 'for his kind and active attendance as assistant to George Coward, Esq., the Surgeon Superintendant', possibly because of his help with their infant. Finding brief records like this can be tantalising, because they are little relics of relationships and friendships that would otherwise be unknown, but are nonetheless sadly exasperating, because the details remain unknowable. Various families of mine had signed such letters, but in each case the circumstances must have been different, and the particularities now lost.

The timing of the Trumans' arrival was good. They took up residence in Kangaroo Point, on the opposite bank of the river to Brisbane, about a decade after it had first been opened to free settlement, and over two decades since the bush had first been cleared by convicts in the mid 1820s. Although Elizabeth later said of this landscape that it was 'in its native state', this was not strictly true. Not only had Aborigines long managed their territories, particularly with fire, convicts and settlers had certainly changed Kangaroo Point before the Trumans encountered it. She spoke, it seems, more to the changes witnessed during her own lifetime.

Even the name of the settlement could be misconstrued. Rather than referencing grassland marsupials, which also had their own impact on Australia's landscape, it was probably derived from Kangaroo Point in Van Diemen's Land because of its similar siting across a river from a city, in that case Hobart. Nonetheless, kangaroos were a common sight grazing in the lowlands, and the site was later thought to have been a place where Aborigines herded kangaroo for hunting, so the duplication of name could be a coincidence. If so, the selection of this site paralleled the processes and effects in other colonies, where the best hunting grounds, or landscapes that had been carefully managed by Aborigines, often proved the most attractive sites for colonial settlements.

By the time the Trumans arrived, prior colonists had already altered the immediate landscape considerably. Although John and Anna's situation on arrival remains a bit unclear, there were reports that within a month two-thirds of the immigrants from the *Maria Somes* had found employment at reasonable wages. The family arrived just as investors and prospectors were expressing interest in the mineral potential of Brisbane and the Darling Downs. Coal had been found on the Brisbane River and was being exploited, and, in line with other developments in the Australian colonies, there were great exertions made to discover gold in the area. And, of course, there was also considerable agricultural and pastoral potential in the region that was attracting colonial attention. The immigrants benefited from the rapid pace of development of this region.

Elizabeth's older brother Stephen became a more prolific writer of memories than she, and from his accounts I could piece together a better picture of the Truman children's early years in the decade after their arrival, as well as some of the major events that were memorable for them. He wrote regularly to newspapers in his old age, almost invariably starting with some version of a statement that he was a resident of Brisbane in the 'early fifties'. He described a world of few buildings, steadily increasing. It must have been a noisy place much of the time, with the hammering of builders, and the creaking of cartloads of timber and other building materials.

Of particular fascination for him were the brick buildings, and the way that bricks lined a deep well. In contrast to the images of a new world being made, it is another good reminder that the Trumans had moved into a partly established colonial setting. The vast majority of immigrants entered the Australian colonies though established ports, and so their first views of their 'new' world already had its clear reference points and signs of prior 'European' human habitation.

Curiously, Stephen did not comment on the way that Kangaroo Point smelled, which must have been awesome in its awfulness. At the nearby boiling-down works, a geographical reference point for the murder, large vats boiled bullocks and sheep for oil to make tallow and soap. The smell apparently greatly annoyed persons in the district. Although not commenting on the stench, Stephen certainly had a mind for the less savoury side of his colonial youth. While the murder at the boiling-down works may have been particularly noteworthy because his father witnessed the deed, Stephen remembered other killings which might have related to the boiling-down works in different ways.

Elizabeth did not later recite any tales of murder. In fact, she was yet to be born at the time of Hanley's trial. But she did explicitly mention that her parents were early subscribers to the *Courier*. That being the case, it would have been likely that reading the account of the trial, and seeing his own name in print, John Truman may have perused the edition of Saturday 27 May 1854. And following his own small appearance was a heading concerning a story he is likely to have followed with some interest: 'Apprehension of the notorious Dundalli'.

In the same week that Hanley was tried in Brisbane, this man, 'one of the most audacious criminals ever heard of amongst the aboriginal natives', a 'hero and leader of a host of outrages', had been 'captured by the Brisbane Police, with the assistance of some well disposed native blacks'. The paper described his actions against stations in Brisbane and its suburbs as 'predatory'.

Dundalli was tried in November 1854 for two murders, which had been committed in 1846 and 1847. He was first convicted of the latter, and then tried again on the same day for the former. During this trial he was 'placed in the dock in irons', having earlier been found guilty of the other murder. His lawyer objected to this obvious breach of the presumption of innocence, but the prosecution pointed out that he was 'of great strength and daring … not considered safe to leave unshackled'. The gaoler pointed out that Dundalli had already attempted to escape custody. In both cases several witnesses built up a picture of a strong and dynamic man, prone to violence, whose favourite weapon was the waddy, a wooden club. The cattleman Mason's testimony that Dundalli was involved in 'depredations' on cattle, however, suggests the likelihood that Dundalli was one of the many Aboriginal men throughout the colonies who, acting on the fringes of settlement, were engaged in resistance against the steady invasion of their traditional territory.

Regardless of how he is characterised, having been eventually caught up in the hands of the British justice system, Dundalli was tried as a criminal. British law could not admit of war between its subjects, so frontier war was criminalised. Dundalli was sentenced to death, twice.

He apparently remained relatively unconcerned until the actual day of the execution, supposedly because he expected to be sentenced to transportation as previous Aboriginal men had been. Although Kristyn Harman's book *Aboriginal Convicts* has only recently made historians aware of the use of the convict system to punish Aborigines, it was clearly a relatively well-known phenomenon of the period. So when the executioner came to get Dundalli, he 'cried and wailed piteously, appealing to all near for their help to save him'. The newspaper descriptions of the event highlight the aspirations and complex actualities of frontier justice. It was reported that 'more than the usual precautions were taken to prevent an escape'. Fear of escape was certainly real, but this definitely had a show-trial element. But when taken to the gallows in front of the Brisbane prison, Dundalli's execution was 'bungled', seemingly mocking the system's ineptitude at the moment of its hoped-for triumph. Then, confounding the polar representations of racial warfare too popular today, there were armed guards on site including, very prominently, a number of 'Native Policemen'. Traditional inter- and intra-tribal enmities and the limitations for social advancement for young men in a cultural context dominated by elders were exploited by colonial authorities to recruit 'Native Police'. By enabling access to horses, guns, money, women, and power, these positions offered opportunities that many Aboriginal men used for their own interests, traditional or otherwise, and the 'Native Police' were often also deployed by colonial authorities with brutal effect.

While his body dropped, a knot in the rope slipped. Dundalli's feet landed on his own coffin, which had been placed below the scaffold with a strange mix of symbolism and convenience. It was kicked away, but still his feet touched the earth. His legs were hastily tied back, and the poor man, no doubt twitching and panicking, eventually expired. Although thinking him deserving of death, *The Moreton Bay Courier*'s reporter expressed disgust at the incompetence of the hangman and the 'most sickening sight' produced by the botched execution. More distressingly, there were reported to be 'large numbers of women, many of whom had brought their children with them' attending the hanging.

It was hoped that the execution would teach the Aborigines 'that our laws may overtake the guilty', but was also widely thought to have had the opposite effect. A small group of Aborigines were watching the events from a forested hill nearby. Dundalli had called out in his own language to people he knew as he ascended the scaffold. It was later thought that he had called out to his kinsmen telling them 'to be sure to revenge his death'. By some reports he was demanding vengeance against the 'traitor' Woomboongoroo. There are later stories about a man of that name being killed by Dundalli's relatives, a possible testament to the persistence of tribal enmities into the colonial period, or perhaps the continuation of traditional Aboriginal law, either way a further illustration of a complicated past.

This sense of past violence witnessed at the judicial frontier is also reflected in one of Stephen Truman's other remembrances. He pointed out that he could also remember 'the hanging of two blackfellows at the spot where the General Post Office now stands in Queen-street'. He was probably referring to the execution of Dick and Chamery. They were both hanged on Thursday 4 August 1859 for having raped 'Mary Treatroff, a German shepherd's wife'. In contrast to the case of Dundalli, however, these men had lived with and been employed by European settlers for quite some time.

So my family's connection with Queensland's violent frontier was as suburban spectators of a sort of common law colonialism. It is a reminder that beyond the confines of the smelly boiled-sheep stained air of Kangaroo Point some truly horrible things were happening, assisted with the dreadfully effective aid of the Native Police, and driven in part by the pastoral expansion that was sending sheep to be boiled not far from the Truman residence. The economic whole, of which they were a part, was continuing to impact on the traditional occupants of the land. And this, it is worth remembering, was happening after the height of the gold rush, and would continue to happen for a long time afterwards. It was a dreadful series of waves that crossed the continent, like ripples from stones in a pond. Most of my ancestors, however, were like the Trumans. They were not the stones, nor the front ripple, but lived in the bobbing complexity of the 'settled districts'.

What precisely took the Trumans into Brisbane that day in August 1859, enabling Stephen to witness a double hanging, remains unknown. It is possible that the spectacle of an execution drew them, but it was just as likely to have been a visit to the doctor with their two-month-old daughter Elizabeth. It could, therefore, have been coincidence. Or perhaps it drew young Stephen particularly, and not necessarily the rest of his family. He seemed to have a fixation with murders, later recalling his childhood belief that there was a body at the bottom of a particular well, with a ghost that haunted the pump nearby. He must have been utterly delighted to land one of his first jobs. It was 'in Mr. Ebenstein's cabinet-making and undertaking business'.

But Stephen's recollections of 'plenty of blackfellows about' is suggestive that not all was as violent as his pre-occupation with murders, hangings, and ghosts might first suggest, at least in the immediate vicinity of Kangaroo Point and the growing Brisbane township. In fact, he recalled himself and other boys deliberately seeking out gore, to sate their boyish curiosity, so his stories are in part inflected with his own perhaps slightly gendered preoccupations. 'I remember Joe Darragh's property,' he wrote, 'and his slaughter yard on the bank of Norman Creek.' The boys were naturally drawn to the place. Cows were guided by wooden fences to their doom, and at the site the earth may have been muddy with blood, as a trickle of red joined the water of the Brisbane River. 'We boys', he recalled, 'used to go the yard and watch the sharks fighting for the entrails and other matter that was shot into the creek from the killing houses.' 'Yes, those were the good old days', he concluded in another of his ruminations upon his childhood.

Any sense of the 'good old days' is predicated on perceptions of change. And Elizabeth and Stephen certainly lived in a changing world. While Stephen seemed preoccupied with boyish things macabre, Elizabeth's terse reminiscences convey a better sense of the experience of discord in her immediate locality. She wrote of 'a large number' of the local Aborigines being 'intoxicated', a loaded term when used by the prominent Methodist she was at the time of writing. 'The few residents were very thankful', she recalled, 'to hear the last yell' as the inebriated Aborigines moved away into the bush. Although a description of a regular event, probably part of the traditional patterns of movement meshing with the new colonial landscape, it spoke to the sense of relief many colonists had that the bad old days of warfare and conflict seemed over.

But the Trumans' childhoods were not all hangings and gore. In fact many of their reminiscences concerned the everyday of life, and had quite a pleasant air about them. The Truman children were schooled in a 'small wooden building', later identified as 'in the bush somewhere near where the central railway station is now'. The classes were conducted in a church on a hill, when the district was still thick with scrub. They played cricket with bark wickets, 'an oak paling' serving as a bat. Come springtime, the air was thick with the scent of the wattle, which was remembered fondly as the years passed and it disappeared. The children played and swam at a tidal waterhole, 'girls too', Stephen remembered, so it is likely that young Elizabeth Truman was there as well. I could picture them watching the movements of the tides, so they could know when to head to their muddy pool.

Elizabeth's reminiscences, particularly, provide me with an interesting alternate perspective to the boyish Stephen's. His are tales of derring-do and disasters, but hers are more scenic. People set their watches by the mail coach driver's bugle, she remembered, and her parents read the newspaper. There was a 'Curfew Bell', by which people would 'set their timepieces going'. Such domestic routines come out a little more than Stephen's almost exclusive focus on the world outside.

But Elizabeth had her escapades as well. She told of a past schoolmaster's house of which 'the goats took charge', leaving the children with a daily game of 'hide and seek with the goats'. The rusticity of the landscape comes through in her few published writings, in which she notes how she had 'waded through lobster waterholes, and along winding cattle tracks in the ti-tree scrub'.

For many years childhood memories of 'a variety of trees bearing luscious fruits' stayed with this later holder of garden parties. Elizabeth also described 'a dense forest of large majestic gum and box trees, towering up to a great height. The native sarsaparilla vine entwined itself with its lovely purple hue on to the branches on these magnificent trees. There were smaller trees, such as wattles, with their golden bloom, and the wild raspberry bushes and the great scrub vines like great ropes, beautifying the banks of the Brisbane River'. She was clearly entranced by the landscape of the country of her birth. And unusually, although expressing some fear, she noted that it was not uncommon for hundreds of Aborigines to pass through, or for some 'to camp in the forest'. It was a memory that suggested that as a little girl she had watched them, even if only from a distance.

No one could convince me that this colonially born girl saw this landscape as an unworked landscape that was some sort of geographical canvas for the schemes of empire and colonisation. She was too young for all that. Instead, it is clear that she saw its beauty, and that she saw it as what it was: home.

Elizabeth's was the new generation that felt, quite naturally, that this was their homeland. As with any immigrant community, cultural traits variously continue or adapt, and a sense of origins often persists. Both Elizabeth Truman and Cecilia Hansen each revealed a strong sense of being Australian, even if that had settler, colonist, imperial, Scottish, Danish, British, or other inflections. National history is by its nature anachronistic, because to record the origins and development of the nation means making selections based on the end point. A continental nation makes this easier, but a family history helps bring out more of the nuances. Historians often point to the relative youthfulness of immigrants as a feature of the colonial landscape and focus on identity-making moments and events held as determinants of some pseudo-mythical national archetype or set of characteristics. But the starting point for thinking about being Australian should probably be the youth themselves. The immigrant adults could think of themselves as British, and fit themselves into the wider politico-cultural entity, even if modified as colonial-British. Or they could maintain a strong national tradition: English, Scottish, Irish, Welsh, or a modified colonial-hybrid form. Or perhaps even a purely colonial form as New South Welshman/woman, Victorian, Vandemonian/Tasmanian, South Australian, Western Australian, or Queenslander. But kids, with the benefit of experiencing the obvious, could, at least for a while, uncomplicatedly see themselves as what they were: Australian. When they were older, some could look back and see in themselves and their families their own journeys, but also some echoes of a legendary past, and landscapes infused with memories.

CHAPTER SIX

PIONEERING MEMORIES 1861

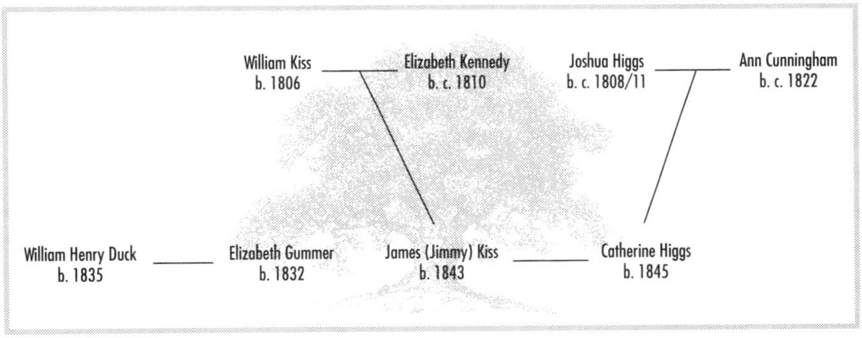

STORIES SITUATE PEOPLE within landscapes. It is a constant of human societies. We tell and record our journeys and actions, and they are remembered after we have returned to the dust. From Abraham's journey westward, to the twists and turns of the Rainbow Serpent, we so often tell each other stories of where we came from, and of how our landscape came to be. And so fully understanding the history of the settlement of the Australian colonies means not just tracking people's comings and goings, but following their storied afterlives. Sometimes historians can focus too much on 'Odysseus' at the expense of understanding the real significance of '*The Odyssey*'. Attempting to uncover the 'original' actions concerned, it is easy to get lost struggling against the limitations imposed by the documentation of the moment, constructing hierarchies of source reliability and authenticity. This is an understandable framework. But sometimes, by letting go of this purist urge and following stories told about people and events as they are passed down through generations, we can open up broader vistas that allow us to glimpse our own heroic ancestral pasts.

In tracing my people I had encountered a bit of this through obituaries and personal reminiscences. But there was one particular event and association which captivated me, and speaks to the way we are all connected to myth and legend. And if we are lucky, sometimes we encounter a story that ripples through time, and we can track it back to a moment where it intersected with historical actualities and people.

One such moment was the most innocuous of events, at least from an historical standpoint. In 1861 Jimmy Kiss married Catherine Higgs in Cooma, in the highlands of New South Wales, just below the Snowy Mountains. Jimmy was the son of William Kiss, and was named for his hat-stealing convict grandfather James. Catherine was the daughter of Joshua Higgs, who at the time was yet to march into a Bega newspaper office and tell his story.

And again it was newspapers that played a strong recording role. In this case they captured a strong family tale, which demonstrates the power of oral traditions in colonial-era families. Two of Jimmy and Catherine's children later recorded details about their parents, quite independently of each other. They were not there to see their own parents' wedding, so these are not eyewitness accounts. Rather, they record the stories they learned of, and probably from, the participants concerned. Apparently, both versions recall, when Jimmy Kiss married Catherine Higgs in Cooma in 1861, he gave her a horse named Robin as a gift.

When he was a seventy-nine-year-old man, James Junior, Jimmy and Catherine's son, actually remembered riding Robin. His recollection of Robin was published in *The Richmond River Herald and Northern Districts Advertiser* in 1940. One of his younger sisters also remembered the story of Robin being given as a wedding present, and her recollection was printed in *The Picton Post* in 1933. The family had become geographically disparate, and time had marched on, but the story of Robin remained clear for both children. Separated by several years, these reports nicely corroborate each other, at least to the extent of showing a commonly held family story.

The Picton version shows the story was told across three generations. It was apparently based on memories of 'the late Mrs C. Duck', conveyed to the newspaper by her children, and concerning events before she was born that a parent had clearly related to her directly. While the event was being recorded almost a century after it occurred, the story of it has a simple line of provenance through that time: grandparent, to parent, to child. And, like studying the copying of medieval manuscripts, by looking at how stories differ and align over time, it is possible to reconstruct what is almost a family tree in reverse for stories. So I found it compelling that there were still common threads from two different family lines: they pointed to a consistent origin, an original story, and therefore also an originating event.

With hindsight, a horse seems an obvious gift for Jimmy Kiss to have given Catherine. He had been born in the Campbelltown district in 1843, the second son of William Kiss and Elizabeth, Thomas Kennedy's daughter. Working out what he did between his birth and his marriage to Catherine Higgs in Cooma in 1861 proved hard, because the Kiss and Higgs families were really on the frontiers. As cattlemen, their lives were spent in the saddle tending their herds in the Southern Highlands and Monaro plains, up into the Snowy Mountains. There was not a great deal of scope to get into newspapers or other people's diaries that way. I only know of Joshua Higgs's great traversing of this territory because he made a point of telling a newspaper editor later on in life.

After their father William's death, Jimmy and his brothers seemed to have carried on the family business, and done so extremely successfully. It was later recalled of Jimmy that 'His brothers, David, Billy and Tom, were the largest cattle dealers in the southern district in the old days. They overlanded thousands of bullocks across the border to Gippsland'. It may have been though this business that they got to know Joshua Higgs and his family.

Ultimately Jimmy seems to have left the cattle business and gone more exclusively into horses. And he was reported to be a natural rider. 'Like his brothers,' it was said, 'he was a splendid horseman.'

Although often out on country alone, the Kiss brothers' riding skills were all on regular-enough public display. They were regular attendees at the Cooma races, and so this is the part of their world which is documented the best. Until he married and set up on his own, Jimmy almost certainly lived with his brothers and worked in the family business, so it is very likely that he attended at least some of the races to watch his oldest brother Billy, who seemed to take the lead for the Kiss boys. And it further helps suggest how Jimmy came to marry the daughter of the sometime jockey Joshua Higgs.

On a clear St Patrick's Day in March 1857 Billy entered the Cooma Maiden Plate, riding Mr Pendergrass's six-year-old horse, Clear the Road. The race was run in two heats of a mile and a half each. An accustomed rider, Billy may have been confident, but his mount was a slow starter. In the first heat, Stranger, ridden by an Aborigine named Charlie, instantly took the lead, maintaining its jump to win by a length and a half, and giving Charlie the win. Billy did better in the second heat. Despite Clear the Road clearing the start last, Billy raced the horse hard and came in second. To do so, however, he had ridden a little dirty and crossed the path of Sir Robert, another competitor. The stewards penalised Billy and he was awarded only third place overall.

In the next race Billy rode Mentor, for Mr Wright. The horse was a bit old and also started a little slow. For most of the race two horses battled side by side, an unnamed Aborigine on Rory and a jockey named Lawler on Crab leading the pack. As the crowd watched the lead horses strain for inches Billy made his move. The old slow starter was given encouragement and raced up the pack, passing one horse after the other. Soon he was level with Rory, then past, then level with Crab. Over the last half mile to the finish line Mentor and Crab raced neck and neck. 'The riding of the jockeys was excellent', spectators commented, and the two horses 'were much punished as the goal was neared', but Crab beat Mentor to the post. The second heat was a repeat of the first, with Crab and Rory leading, and Mentor closing, but ultimately failing to take the lead. It was noted that 'Mentor had evidently seen his best days, but ran beautifully for his age'.

In his third race of the day Billy again rode into second place. He was at least consistently good.

The following day he entered his own horse, William Tell, who performed well in the first heat. The rider was not specified, but Billy was definitely riding again on the third and final day of the races. The first race was the Squatter's Purse, a £75 prize for Monaro-bred horses. Mounting Mr Wright's SpingyJack, Billy easily won the race, leading the whole field to win a length and a half in two heats.

Clearly, season to season, little rivalries between the jockeys developed. In October 1858 Billy won 'the championship for the district of Monaro' on Stranger, beating the Aboriginal jockey Charlie on Pelham. In the first heat Stranger passed Pelham, and despite Charlie furiously whipping his horse, he was unable to retake the lead. In the second heat Stranger won by five lengths. As so often was the case, it was noted that the 'jockeyship of Kiss was excellent, and was much admired'.

The following year, Billy won the second of the St Patrick's Day races, again on Stranger. The victory was achieved by a whopping eight lengths. But on the following day Billy was accused of acting under his employer's instruction to bribe Charlie to lose the race. Disqualified and shamed, it would seem, Billy appears to have relinquished his sideline business as a jockey in the Cooma fields, although he maintained an interest in horse-racing in Bega in subsequent years.

Because they were in public races, Jimmy's older brother's feats of riding were recorded. However, Jimmy is not down in the documentary record as being there at this time. Almost certainly he was on the periphery, quite possibly even standing on the dusty sidelines cheering. But for whatever reason, being a jockey was not for him. Perhaps it was too structured or contrived a setting for horsemanship—or perhaps he was left to tend the herd while Billy went to town to race.

But Jimmy certainly could ride well enough. Someone who knew him said, 'it was a common occurrence to see him throw his hat or stock-whip to the ground, and, galloping past, stoop from his horse and pick up either article'. It is the very image of a confident bush horseman, riding hard and fast, eyes on the target. As he approached, he would lean down, holding the saddle with one hand. Reaching out, he could then snatch the hat from the ground. It is easy to imagine him deftly pulling it onto his head, and tipping the hat to a nearby girl or two, Catherine Higgs perhaps.

Jimmy had other tricks as well. He could 'jump off his horse at full gallop, and throw himself in to the saddle again'.

These were not just party tricks. They were skills that originated from his earliest days in the saddle tending cattle, taking them through the high country and over the mountains to the Victorian side. This was not horseracing. Rather, these were the skills of a horseman of the country, who needed to be able to collect his gear on the run, to stay in the saddle if needed, to move quickly, and to manage his horse deftly across the wild landscape.

And so while Billy won races, it was Jimmy's skills that entered into folklore.

My first introduction to Jimmy's legendary riding skills came at a gob-smacking research moment, the sort of bombshell that makes a person stop and wonder if they have read things correctly.

I was sitting at the computer looking at newspaper articles online through the searchable database Trove. I had only just started to look for information about James Kiss. I did not even yet know that he was routinely nicknamed Jimmy. I searched his name, and was going through the results, not having been very particular about the dates—it was a preliminary search, and I knew that later reminiscences could be very useful starting points. It was only supposed to be a few moments at the end of an hour or so of something else I was searching. There were a few other James Kisses coming up. A boxing match in Western Australia, for example, or the many annoying results from serialised stories where James Kiss*ed* somebody.

One newspaper headline, containing a sizable story about Jimmy, seemingly prompted by family reflections following the death of his daughter, caught my attention, and I read on quickly and rather sceptically. The sub-headline informed me that a 'Riding feat of James Kiss (Father of late Mrs C. Duck) gave "Banjo" Patterson inspiration to write famous poem.' I glanced back up at the headline: 'The Man From Snowy River'.

My initial thought was a straightforward question: do I have the right person? I read on with this and other questions pecking at the front of my mind. His birth year matched. Tick. His wife matched. Another tick. This was definitely my James Kiss, no doubt about it. My second thought was that nobody was going to believe this—everyone will think I'm making it up.

This was the article in *The Picton Post* that first alerted me to the tale that Jimmy had given his wife Catherine a wedding present of a horse named Robin. Patterson's poem, it explained, 'was written following a rare feat of horsemanship by one of the youths of Coolringdon … who, in reality, it is said, was none other than Jimmy Kiss. This 16-year-old lad's feat of rounding-up a renowned brumby inspired Patterson to set his deed to verse'. I wondered whether this was really possible: was I descended from the Man from Snowy River?

Quite a few people have claimed to know who the real man from Snowy River was, so I was naturally cautious. Patterson himself never seems to have identified any particular person and event, but rather pointed to his experience in his own youth as generally informing the poem. That the poem was first published in 1890 gives a lot of the claimants the wrong timeframe. I had noticed there was a weird disjunction about some of the favoured contenders for them to be the real one. They were good horsemen when the poem was written, not when Patterson was a child. They breached the only thing Patterson ever confirmed about the poem's origins. This, at least, was a point in my favour.

According to the Ducks' information, the Kiss brothers were 'cattle dealing on the Monaro on the country around Coolringdon' when Jimmy was sixteen years old, and the Patterson's 'were shepherding on Gegedzerick' not too far away, which was 'then owned by the Brooks'. If Jimmy Kiss did round up a brumby at Coolringdon at sixteen years of age, then it must have been about 1859, with some allowance for the dubious age-recording practices of prior centuries. It was easy enough to place the Brooks family at Gededzerick in the 1860s, and they were definitely involved in horse breeding by 1868. There were even documented worries about that time at that place of horses breeding with wild brumbies.

Not all the details of the story held up to scrutiny, however. It mentioned the horse Carbine being bred at Coolringdon Station, although Carbine was actually a New Zealand born racehorse. But beyond this, which was incidental anyway, the other mistakes were minor. The recollection of who the owners of Coolringdon were in the late 1850s and early 1860s was incorrect. Rather than the Harnetts, it was the Smiths who owned it, but the Harnetts were nearby at Eucumbene, in the same general area. The story had the year of Jimmy's marriage wrong, but only by one year. And old Mrs Duck's grandmother had been mistakenly given as a Miss Ward, but that was actually her grand-aunt. So there were little mistakes of detail, yet they were all close to demonstrable realities and connections. Considering these were events from three-quarters of a century previously, which neither Mrs Duck nor her children had witnessed, there was a pretty good level of detail. More so when I remembered that it was her children's version of her story. The general context fitted.

The only real obstacle to the Ducks' story is the assertion that the ride took place when Jimmy was sixteen. If this were true, Patterson could not have witnessed it, as he was not yet born. But then perhaps that could explain why 'the stockmen tell the story of his ride', and as Patterson himself hinted, it was his childhood generally, not an event specifically, that inspired the poem. There is also no reason to assume that Patterson did not have the opportunity to witness Jimmy's riding at a slightly later period—he was, after all, a well-known rider in the district.

Considering that I found other people from outside of the family who describe Jimmy's feats of horsemanship, I was inclined to believe at least the general idea that the newspaper conveyed, which was that 'Jimmy Kiss was a well-known rider on Monaro and was never known to be unseated by any bucking outlaw'. If he was such a great rider, then was it possible that Patterson's poem was, although fictionalised, at least partly based on the riding feats of a young Jimmy Kiss, either before Patterson's birth, or in the period of his youth? I knew bits of the poem, but had to look at it again.

The salient elements of *The Man From Snowy River* concern 'a stripling on a small and weedy beast', who joins the chase after an escaped colt who fled to the wild brumbies. With a brother who was a jockey, and the use of mountain horses for running their cattle, both these bits could match Jimmy easily. Then, the exciting action of the poem is that through a magnificent display of riding, the man from Snowy River 'alone and unassisted brought them back'. Being Australian-born (unlike some of the other main contenders), living in the area of Patterson's upbringing (again, unlike other contenders), passing through the Snowy River region on regular cattle runs to Gippsland, and being a well-known rider in the region of Patterson's upbringing in the Monaro and Upper Murrumbidgee districts, Jimmy Kiss has at least a reasonable claim on the title. He was a great rider who had stories told about him, and he lived in the right area at the right time.

Certainly Jimmy Kiss's children believed that he chased a horse while riding a 'weedy beast' named Robin and that this event inspired the poem. That is the core message of the two versions different branches of his family recalled. Most of the other details of the two versions did not overlap, but they were not mutually exclusive.

But as I did all of this historical puzzling I thought about how the real beauty of Patterson's poem is that it is about a man who is typical of his type. Clancy of the Overflow tells the other station hands that 'the Snowy River riders' are men who 'on the mountains make their home' and he explains that 'nowhere yet such horsemen have I seen'. That is precisely why he remains nameless: his identity is irrelevant. He could be any rider or none, an amalgam of real individuals, or nothing more than a literary type. Whether Jimmy Kiss was the inspiration for that particular man from Snowy River is a moot point. The key fact is that he could have been.

And so I find myself suitably connectable to a treasured part of Australia's legendary past. But of greater historical interest is the way that Jimmy Kiss's life charts a transition from a mythical to a post-mythical period. His later years are better documented, yet it was his youth that became the stuff of legend. During this period sufficient numbers of colonial Australians became old and settled enough to commence telling, writing, and absorbing stories about their past, facilitated by increases in both population and the means of creating and retaining documentation. This phenomenon creates a bit of a distinction between undocumented and documented periods in Australia's past, be they quite variable in location and geography. The former period is largely captured by oral traditions like Joshua Higgs's autobiography and the stories about Jimmy Kiss's youthful riding, which in some lucky instances were later written down in that secondary period when events were more likely to be documented at or close to the time in which they occurred.

Throughout the later nineteenth century there was a sense of the passing away of the pioneer days. This was generally captured by Banjo Paterson's later poetry, but also by an increasingly self-aware historicism within the colonies. This is well reflected in the way that local newspapers captured the stories and memories of the 'old settlers', and as the years went by arguments and discussions would be had in their pages about who named what, when so-and-so was there first, when the first store was opened, or even the days when bushrangers had robbed various stations. The convict period, conflict with Aborigines, the gold rush, the great wave of first migrants—all became the stuff of recorded history. The Australian colonies, so youthful, so future-focused, suddenly seemed aware they had their own history.

Each person also had *their own* history, and it was the amalgam of these that made for a wider social stereotype. The Duck family patriarch, William, was typical of this. Two of his sons eventually married two of Jimmy Kiss's daughters. Yet while of the same genealogical strata, William Duck and Jimmy Kiss's stories differed vastly.

William's story ended in the same general area as Jimmy's began. Shortly after arriving in Australia in 1855 the Ducks established themselves in the Camden region. William found work, saved his money and was able to buy land, adding adjoining properties as opportunity and finances allowed. I found it amusing to think they were moving into the area about the same time that the Kisses were moving further towards the mountains, because parts of the families' lines would later join up. It was a sort of historical near miss.

I had known for many years that there was some Duck family connection with that district, but only ever had a vague idea of what it was. Although Mum was the Duck, Dad's parents lived at Picton, in the Camden region, so it was a bit confusing when I was younger. I remember being taken to investigate cemeteries looking for Duck headstones. So in a small way the oral tradition persisted for a few generations that 'we were here', even if I was only dimly aware of it.

After the initial expansion of pastoral settlement had taken place, parts of the Camden region were being developed more intensively for other agricultural pursuits than those that had originally seen it named the Cowpastures. The demand for workers was exceeding supply, especially because cheap convict labour stopped being available after the transportation of convicts to New South Wales ceased in 1840. With a combination of pressures having served to bring about the end of the transportation system, after a half century as a penal colony New South Wales was embracing a new identity as a free settlement.

From the British perspective, history was repeating itself slightly. In the thirteen North American Colonies, originally a bit of a convict dumping ground, cheap convict labour facilitated rapid colonial expansion and economic success. When they achieved a certain level of economic and cultural independence, political independence soon followed, and convict transportation had to stop. This was one of the factors that led to New South Wales being a convict colony in the first place. While larger geo-political factors were certainly at play, particularly a British desire to trump the French to claim *Terra Australis* and gain a Pacific port with access to Asian markets, the excess of convicts that filled England's hulks was in one respect America's fault. Fortunately for the British, when New South Wales successfully transited to free colony, it stayed loyal, and Van Diemen's Land was still available as a destination for what was seen as social refuse in need of reform for a little longer, followed by Western Australia.

But settlers still needed labourers, and the New South Welsh colonial government wanted more settlers and agricultural labourers, so they turned not to England's criminal classes, but their rural populace. Government-run immigration schemes, as tried previously, attempted to bring settlers and workers to New South Wales with financial incentives and promises of opportunities in the great southern continent. Such schemes attempted to ensure a steady supply of labour, not only depleted by the end of convictism, but also by the avaricious pull of goldmining on the working classes.

So in part the decision to stop transporting convicts to New South Wales helped created the conditions for a new wave of migration. It took fifteen years for that change to affect two of my Duck ancestors, who lived in the little Somerset village of Kingsbury Episcopi, which quaintly still carried the Latin tag that made it clear this was the bishop's Kingsbury. The year after transportation to New South Wales ceased, the English census puts young William Duck as a six-year-old boy, living with his father, mother, and siblings at an area just outside of Kingsbury Episcopi called Lower Burrow. The family was still there a decade later, although the sixteen-year-old was by then contributing to the family's income as an agricultural labourer like his father.

An ordinance map from the 1880s, although past the period of William's youth, clearly showed what Lower Barrow was all about. There was a farm there, and hand drawn by the surveyor were rows upon rows of trees. This was clearly an orchard. There was a little cluster of houses, obviously filled with the workers who derived their employment from the farm. William and his father Mathew worked as agricultural labourers, working in these orchards and tending the nearby crops, depending on the season. Meanwhile, William's mother Edith stayed at home making gloves, teaching her daughter to do the same.

Over on the edge of the village of Kingsbury Episcopi proper, William's future wife Elizabeth also lived with her family. On 15 March 1855 they married in the old parish church, nestled by a bend of the River Parrett. Bearing a distinctly squared Norman tower jutting up towards the sky, the church has several stages of building that reveal how over the centuries various additions have been made and features added. It was surrounded on two sides by grey slabs, the headstones of the Kingsbury Episcopi faithful.

To read from this seemingly picturesque scene a migration away from an unchanging past would be incorrect, yet some Australian histories have often focused entirely on change in Australia, without always recognising changing situations overseas. Sparse as the details of William and Elizabeth's pre-Australian existence are, they point to a potentially excited and hurried exit. It is hard to know for sure what prompted the decision to leave, but having only married in March, by June they were boarding a ship for Australia in Southampton. Even if they had planned it before their wedding, it was no mean feat, as Southampton was a considerable distance away. Elizabeth was in the early stages of pregnancy and, whether walking or taking a coach, it was a long journey for people who had grown up in a village like Kingsbury Episcopi. I suspect they may have planned their emigration prior to the wedding.

William and Elizabeth's departure marked a real turning point in Kingsbury Episcopi's social structure. The village's population had increased rapidly in the first few decades of the nineteenth century, by several hundred persons in fact, most likely drawn in by work opportunities as much as natural population increase. But between 1851 and 1861 the population started to fall, until by the early twentieth century it was back to its early nineteenth century level. It had boomed, and the Ducks left just as it was about to turn to bust, in fact they may have participated in the busting process.

Possibly aware of the pressures on workers and the increased difficulty in finding employment, their hope at better prospects probably comforted them on their voyage. And they would have needed a strong sense of hope to see them through the voyage and the interpersonal difficulties of being cooped up. The 500 ton *Gilmore* was carrying 280 government-sponsored passengers. The Ducks were one of ninety-two couples, with fifty children between them. There were sixty-one single men, and only forty single women for them to flirt with. It was a little village occupying a floating box.

For two months they travelled in what was later described as 'much bad weather'. Ships that departed England in the summer generally sailed through the Atlantic just ahead of hurricane season, and the likely passage and timing of the *Gilmore*'s voyage could have taken it through several weather systems that in August reached major storm or hurricane status. Having crossed the equator successfully and started the faster run to the east, the immigrants may have slept more soundly knowing the hurricane-rich region was behind them.

Seasickness was a very real problem for passengers, especially those like the Ducks who had grown up inland and were unaccustomed to life at sea. Only gradually does the body adjust and allow the retching passenger some rest from their suffering. Despite the steady rocking of the ship the Ducks were probably sleeping soundly when they were woken suddenly at 3 am on 31 August, over two months into the journey.

An unexpected wave had hit the ship with tremendous force. Coming up from the Southern Ocean it ploughed into the starboard side, broke over the deck at a diagonal angle, and continued its journey across the sea from the port of the damaged vessel.

As the impact of the rogue wave jolted the ship, part of the deck gave way and water gushed into the cabins below. The deluge hit near the bow, where some of the cabins had been set aside as the ship's hospital, and so it was the sick who were immediately cut, bruised, and drenched. As the ship corrected, the water would have run down the length of the lower decks. Passengers like the Ducks, no doubt suddenly and fearfully awake at the bang and shudder of the impact, were faced with the sound of rushing water. There were six degrees of latitude between the ship and the bottom of Africa. There would have been no realistic prospect of imminent rescue.

On deck, the lifeboat and the small cutter had been destroyed, and as the wave washed over the port side of the ship it took the railings and bulwarks with it.

In the darkness the captain and crew scrambled to check everything was alright. The passengers probably prayed and comforted each other. The sea village was awake, and there were almost certainly tears, cries, silent sobs, and surprised stares. If only they had known that in the lower decks of cargo there were dozens of barrels of beer, ale, stout, and cider being shipped to the colony. Although it was probably fizzed up a bit, the rattled passengers could have turned to liquid means of calming themselves.

But the damage was mostly superficial, and so, carried by the cold winter winds of the Southern Ocean, the *Gilmore* safely navigated around Van Diemen's Land, up the coast of New South Wales, and into Sydney harbour. There is no evidence, and it seems most unlikely, that William and Elizabeth Duck ever went to sea again.

Eventually the family did well, and William continued to farm into his old age. He had left England as an agricultural labourer, the son of an agricultural labourer, living in cottages and tending other people's fruit trees. But after a few decades in New South Wales he was able to help his son Charles establish himself as a propertied orchardist in an area that came to be known as Orangeville. Father and son cleared a 'heavily timbered' hill that had 'heaps of boulders on it'. The reporter who recorded this story thought it must have been 'a herculean task sufficient to dismay the stoutest heart'. But through their effort they had an excellent selection of citrus fruits, stone fruits, and apples.

A couple of years later the Ducks were again visited by another reporter, who saw them laying down manure to fertilise a crop of maize. They had maintained a diversified farming economy, successfully protecting themselves against the vagaries of the weather and the market. The journalist struck up a conversation with William about the land, commenting on the apparent richness of it.

'Oh! you think so,' William replied, 'but we must manure on this friable soil.'

They continued with a few more pleasantries about the manure before the reporter noted, 'The country looks beautiful'.

'Yes!' William responded, 'but we have our disadvantages in times of storm, as an instance during a terrific storm we had to cart up 800 cart loads of soil to fill up the washing away.'

With each of his comments rebutted by William, clearly a man of relatively few words, the journalist left the old man and his son tending their farm. It is a good image of the many years of pioneering work, reduced to a brief exchange. As a sort of summation of the experience of leaving the old world behind and replacing it with a new, it captures that sense of hard work undertaken during the great waves of voluntary migration. William Duck acts like a colonial Sisyphus, carrying on a near-perpetual round of manuring and carting to make the land good.

Even Jimmy Kiss, best remembered as a shadowy rider in the mountains, helps chart the way the land and the landscape was becoming more settled. One of the first recorded things he did after his marriage was to sell potatoes. He had two tons of potatoes to sell in Bega in 1866.

In 1867 Jimmy took an advertisement in the *Sydney Morning Herald*. He wanted to buy a 'bay horse', one of the ones with a dark brown coat and black mane, tail, and legs. So although a sometime potato-farmer, he was still engaged with things equestrian. In 1869 he acted as starter for the Nimmitabel races at this little highland village between Cooma and the coast. He was living at Brown Mountain, the highest mountain on the Monaro plain, in August 1869, so it seems that he had a property of some sort up there.

Jimmy was a reader of the *Freeman's Journal*, a Catholic newspaper printed in Sydney, which helps show that the highlands were becoming less of a wild and isolated place. He had closely followed the coverage of the story regarding the Irish State prisoners in 1869. These were the Fenians, political dissidents who were transported to Western Australia, which had been settled from the mid 1820s. Civilian Fenians were freed in 1869, so Jimmy Kiss took charge of a local collection of money to help them pay for a return passage to Ireland which the *Freeman's Journal* was organising. While he certainly loved his new country and showed no inclination to leave, he was the grandson of the Irish political prisoner Thomas Kennedy. If he knew the story of his grandfather's trial and transportation, he might have felt glad that the British government had finally stopped playing this game of exiling people from their homelands. When a shipload of convicts arrived in Fremantle in January 1868, a number of them Fenians, an era came to an end. It was the last convict ship to arrive in Australia.

It may be somewhat funny to think of a man who could well have been the man from Snowy River sitting in a hut reading a newspaper about convicts. But that is what such highland cattlemen must have done, possibly in one of those small wooden country huts that dot the highlands, with a little snow whitening the hills. Perhaps in a similar hut within the little village of Bemboka at the foot of Brown Mountain, Jimmy may have put his feet up and read the latest news. It was a good thing to do, given the often harsh outside conditions. Only the following month there was reportedly a heavy snowfall, and in such weather the family must have had to huddle together in front of a fire.

Jimmy was well informed about the rest of the world, considering his relative isolation from it. Responding to the charitable cause of the released Irishmen in Western Australia, Jimmy wrote forwarding the money of 'the few that are among us'. There were six names from his district, one of which was his younger brother Stephen. It was an Irish-sympathising section of the population no doubt, but it is an indicator of their social circle nonetheless. Yet even the *Freeman's Journal*, heavily focused on Irish and Catholic news, informed him about events in the wider world and would have provided Jimmy and his friends with much to talk of. The wars of Garibaldi in Italy, the American Civil War, and other major happenings of the 1860s were not unknown to them.

This connectedness to global news reflects the gradual settling down of what was once the frontier. People had time to read the newspapers, and there were enough customers to justify their publication. Certainly there were still major economic and cultural border areas, and in some places there would be until the mid twentieth century. But the populous East Coast of Australia, and the metropolises and their hinterlands, were becoming increasingly settled places. And Jimmy Kiss's changing career maps this out.

The days of tending cattle on the plains may have gently come to an end for Jimmy Kiss soon after his marriage. The family seems to have moved around the small highland towns and villages, as Jimmy established himself as quite a successful businessman. But ironically the first move in this direction took him even closer to the mountains. He apparently became a storekeeper at Bobundara, or at least took over ownership of this business. He was also the proprietor of the Bobundara Hotel, and hosted a large dinner to celebrate his arrival in town. This small village was thirty or forty kilometres due east of Mount Kosciuszko, Australia's highest peak, situated in rolling hills running east from the mountains to the Great Dividing Range where, in the area of Brown Mountain, it drops into the Bega Valley.

At Bobundara Jimmy's name crops up in a court case about a colt that bolted. But there is no suggestion of his having chased it; he was just the employer of one of the witnesses. Jimmy had been there since April 1872 when he became proprietor of the store, which had 'an extensive and varied stock of goods'. Mostly, it would have been food, farming and horse equipment, plus the odd luxury.

But all was not necessarily so peaceful in the little village. In 1873 Jimmy was sued. The plaintiff, John Mangan, accused Jimmy of failing to pay him wages, wrongfully dismissing him from employment, and causing other attendant financial harm. Allegedly, Jimmy first employed Mangan as an accountant to do the books for the Bobundara store. He then offered him work as a storekeeper and a position as teacher at the little private Bobundara school. This was an era of proliferating local schools, and Bobundara was no exception. Mangan, who had been the teacher at Brown Mountain and so was already known to Jimmy, apparently took the position and relocated to Bobundara.

Then, attending a wedding out of town for a few days longer than he had said he would, Mangan returned to find himself locked out, and dismissed from employment. Jimmy had also withdrawn his children from the school, reducing the student cohort and thereby the teacher's salary considerably, and Mangan saw this as a personal attack.

In Mangan's absence, Jimmy had another mate go over the books. He claimed this was because he was illiterate, although I suspect this is a newspaper mistake: I reckon they meant innumerate. Jimmy wrote to the newspaper, and was therefore certainly literate, just not sufficiently numerate to do accounts. This was probably why he employed Mangan in the first place, and it explains why he asked a mate to double-check for him.

It turns out that Mangan had a bit of a dubious track record and had been fiddling the books in his favour, racking up debts against Jimmy. There were even pages torn out of the ledger without explanation, although Jimmy only discovered this after a heated exchange between the two men.

Reading the tiny report almost a century and a half after the events, it is hard to know the full context, but Mangan seems to have been a bit of an unreliable and irascible fellow. At least public opinion seems to have been on Jimmy's side. The jury did not even retire before they found in Jimmy's favour and upheld the dismissal as valid.

There was an unusual follow up which strengthens this sense that the community was on Jimmy's side. Mrs Mangan, with her husband, sued Jimmy for defamation of character. It hinged upon a pair of boots which Mrs Mangan had appropriated. Jimmy accused her of stealing them, and the case hinged upon the word 'stealing', even though Jimmy claimed to have immediately withdrawn the word and substituted 'taking' instead. This time, the legal technicalities lost Jimmy the case, and he was fined. But it was only a farthing without costs: a quarter of a penny.

Jimmy's more settled existence as a shop owner did not mean he gave up on horses; in fact, quite the opposite seems to have been the case. By running a store, he may have had more resources to assist in raising racehorses. I am not sure if he started riding them in competition himself, but he was certainly breeding them. In the Nimmitabel races in April 1872 he entered at least two horses: Pegasus and Tom. Each won a race and came second in a race. Two firsts and two seconds were a good effort for two horses. These regular racing meetings provided an excuse for disparate people to come together and socialise, as much as to compete, and, like the proliferation of little stores and schools, they really show how regional communities were developing with strong social bonds.

Soon thereafter the family were documented as residents of Bega. In June 1873 Jimmy applied for a liquor licence and opened the Royal Hotel. A large and typically Australian hotel, it had wide verandahs, and big squared windows. A surviving photograph of the building from the 1880s when the stone gutters were being laid in front by hand shows a line of men posing for the camera. It is the kind of building that was a meeting place and social hub in towns across Australia. Again Jimmy Kiss's life points to a major development in the Australian landscape: the great age of the large hotels had arrived.

These were more than buildings. Hotels were the centre of a thriving social scene, where events and celebrations were held. They also facilitated the catering of external events. When there was a town picnic to nearby Wallagoot Lake, approximately two hundred and fifty people made the journey by horses and buggies along the dusty tracks to the lake's edge. It must have looked like a mini-migration. Jimmy probably went ahead of the crowd, because he built 'a large booth', which was timely, because soon after everyone arrived, it rained heavily. Those fortunate enough to be nearby found shelter under Jimmy's temporary roof, and he must have inwardly thanked the turn in weather as he sold food and drinks to the milling crowd. His business was 'well patronised', a reporter slyly noted. Those less fortunate simply hid under their own carts and buggies, looking longingly at the merry crowd at the booth.

An ulterior motive behind the picnic was for the townsfolk to contemplate whether there was any possibility that the lake could be used as a port. Bega had come a long way since Joshua Higgs first visited only a few decades earlier. This shift to thinking about making a significant investment in landscape modification again reveals a society increasingly settled in the country. Although the port idea was dismissed because of the problems of silting, the townsfolk noted the alternate possibility of an 'iron horse', which pointed to a later thread of much colonial development. But it is also significant that it was considered a viable possibility that the lake could be developed for purely recreational purposes. They were contemplating the economic possibilities of tourism.

The return migration might have dissuaded the people of Bega about the wisdom of holidaying at Wallagoot Lake. Sodden with the rainfall, what was normally an 'ugly bit of road' became a cart trap. One couple was 'capsized', with the woman 'thrown under the cart'. She fractured a finger and suffered bruises, yet was otherwise alright. But as her husband got off and 'endeavoured to extricate his wife', his attempts to manoeuvre the cart off his wife caused its weight to suddenly shift. Immediately 'the heavy cart fell back'. The impact broke three of his ribs and pinned him against a tree stump. He was lucky to be surrounded by carts full of people ready to help. Several other carts overturned also, including Jimmy's, and one child was even 'run over', although apparently not severely harmed. Despite the chaos, the town still looked forward to another picnic for the following year. After all, the roads could only get better.

Injuries were a normal part of colonial life. I often marvel at the way that past ages report tragedies and mishaps relatively laconically. Broken ribs, carts pinning people, and such grievous wounds were normal, hardly worth reporting unless there was something unusual like several crashes at once, terrifically bad injuries, a local 'worthy' hurt, or a really freakish accident, in which case they could go into extraordinary detail.

Luckily for Jimmy one accident he had clearly belonged in the last category. Being an hotelier may not have stopped him riding, but on one occasion a fence did. Apparently, 'whilst in the act of riding at a fence, the horse swerved, and, with his rider, turned a complete somersault'. It was an amazing accident, which incredibly he survived with only a broken shoulder bone. It was a week before he was able to walk about. But Jimmy knew that such things happened with horses, and he apparently continued to ride them, and to maintain a great fondness for them.

Jimmy even combined commercial interests with horses. He advertised that Pitsford, a thoroughbred, was available for stud between October 1873 and January 1874 in 'good paddocks' in the Bega area. At £2 10s per mare, it had the potential to be a profitable little side business. Two of his brothers were also in Bega at this time, and the three of them were deeply involved in the Bega horseracing scene. In the 1874 Flying Handicap there were three Kiss-owned horses racing, one by David, one by Billy, and one by Jimmy, named Venus.

Family tragedy struck, however, when Catherine died. In working through the records of past lives and actions, it is often hard to get a sense of how people really felt about each other. I find it poignant to think that the future Mrs Charles Duck lost her mother when she was two and a half, and yet into her own old age she still recalled the story of the horse 'Robin' being given as a gift. Either she remembered the story being told to her by her mother directly, or Jimmy told the story to his children after their mother's death. Either way, it shows the way the family remembered her, even if the documentary record does not really say anything.

But the documentary record does hint at Jimmy's pain, because Catherine's illness or death seems to have triggered a return to the mountain country. By 1885 Jimmy was running a hotel at Nimmitabel. A few years later he was again advertising a thoroughbred horse for stud, Bard of Avon, this time in the Gundagai area, further west. He was apparently travelling, which might point to Jimmy Kiss having taken to a wandering lifestyle again once his children were making their own ways in the world.

The hurt of loss does not seem to have made him bitter. In 1885 Jimmy (although it was possibly his son James) came across an injured horse. He was bandaging the horse's broken leg when a boy came along with a gun to put it down. His response was 'don't shoot her, she may get right if looked after'. And while a police order eventually required the animal to be put down, the sentiment towards the horse, the recognition that it was not just a utilitarian creature, is rather appealing.

With the progression of time it becomes harder to distinguish Jimmy from his son James. There was a James Kiss mining in Gundagai at about the same time that I know Jimmy was at least briefly living there, but whether this was him, or whether he was simply staying with his son, I may never know. So often documentary records simply name people and it is the oral traditions that link the names together into a coherent narrative of a person. In this case there were stories known and told about James Kiss by people who knew him as Jimmy. Did they picture him when they read *The Man From Snowy River*? Stories are sometimes recognisable, but often they also seem unbelievable, but that does not make them wrong. After all, when I was a little boy I had very light blond hair, which only darkened in early primary school. And despite its absolute truth, many may now think I am making it up when I tell them that as a kid my nickname was Snowy.

Such is the tension between documented people and their storied afterlives. The passing from childhood to adulthood once saw a person's life increasingly recorded, and this is also true for colonies, regions, and nations. The Kiss and Duck families each reveal continuities and changes in the colonial landscape. Whether it be the shift in use of sections of the Cowpastures from its original purpose to become land on which orange groves grew, or the gradual growth of the towns of Bega and Cooma, many transitions occurred, gradually bringing to an end what contemporaries thought of as the pioneer period. Of course this pattern is regionally varied, and other parts of the Australian continent were yet to even become frontier territory. But for many of the settler generation of people and their children, years of toil meant they could steadily settle down in to some domestic security, even if they kept alive memories of youthful adventures and the freedom of the saddle. But as the hearth and kitchen produces little documentation, and epic stories are generally not typical, it is often tragedy that proves a useful historical tool for peering into the daily routines and lives of people doing everyday things in those brief moments before things go wrong.

CHAPTER SEVEN

DOMESTICITY, DEATH, SILENCE, AND REVELATION MARCH 1866

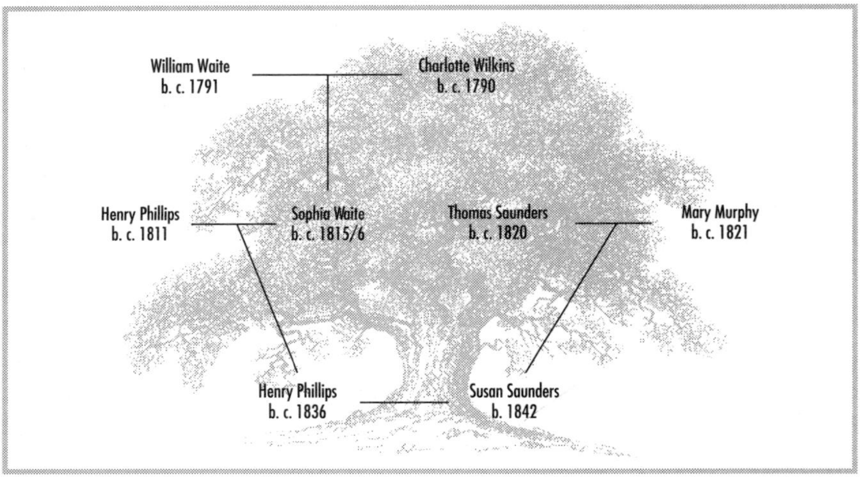

WILLIAM WAITE WAS placed in the ground of the All Saints Anglican cemetery in Sutton Forest, south of Sydney, in March 1866. Many years later, in 1883, the ninety-three-year-old body of Charlotte was buried with him. These events are recorded on the slab that bears their name, in grassy splendour in what is now known as the 'pioneer section'. The printed family notice that said he died aged seventy-five, 'an old and respected inhabitant, many years a resident of Sutton Forrest' records little more than the slab does.

The people of the Australian colonies measured their lives by the profoundly personal moments that officialdom normally reduces to certificates.

Colonial formations, political changes, and even dramatic events of note all frequently took second place to the intensely personal moments of birth, marriage, and death. And perhaps none quite leave their mark like the last. For some, all that remains of these moments of tragic transition are the headstones of the deceased. Moments of grief highlight the transience of human life in the face of narratives of settlement and development. People did not just live in the past; they died in it too. Understanding death helps to uncover the way people of the Australian colonies maintained a sense of family and kinship, and how local communities really worked. By looking at these wrenching breaches from normality, we can get closer to the heart of everyday lives, and what was really significant for the people who lived them.

For example, William's death also triggered the sale of his estate, including the family farm at Mittagong, and that involved a notice in the newspaper, which in turn helps uncover the property for posterity.

Not only did William leave his wife Charlotte behind, but also '5 milking cows, 2 steers, 6 head of horses, 4 working bullocks, dray, yokes, bows and chains, 2 pigs, 1 iron wheeled plough, 2 wooden ploughs, 2 harrows, 1 cart and harness, 1 threshing machine, 4-horse power, with set new wheels, 1 winnowing machine, 3 sieves, block and tackle, 4 bags oats, 1 horse-roller and harness'. He had been more than a hobby farmer, or a poor subsistence farmer scratching the dirt. This was a serious operation. William Waite's move to New South Wales had served him well.

As well as his farm, William left 'a useful family medicine chest, well stocked with a good supply of medicine'. This object conveys a sense that he cared for his family, a minor relic of caring in one of the least well documented family lines I have discovered. It is hard to know what Charlotte thought, looking back over their shared lives of migration and settlement. Perhaps she hated the medicine chest. I suspect she was content to let the farm go, as they had tried to sell out only a few years prior to William's death. And it was from that earlier sale attempt in 1860 that I knew they had 360 acres, 140 of which were cultivated in six fields. The whole thing was fenced with wooden posts and rails. There was a four-room house, with a 'good kitchen and cooking house', a barn, a granary, stables, sheds, and workers' cottages. They also had a 'beautiful orchard'.

While 'for sale' advertisements certainly hype the positive, it seems likely that Charlotte experienced some relative comfort in her adulthood with William. On his death, she probably also looked back on their earlier years together.

Charlotte and William were born and married in Kent, in England, apparently in the port town of Gravesend. But their journey to the colony was prompted by earlier events. In 1803 one of William's older relatives, John, had been convicted of sheep stealing, and the death sentence he received was commuted to transportation for life to New South Wales. John arrived in the colony in 1804 on the *Coromandel* and soon became the assigned servant of Reverend Charles Throsby, colonial surgeon, prominent landowner, and noted explorer.

John was a ruddy fellow, with flaxen hair and hazel eyes, and stood 5 feet 5½ inches tall. His convict placement proved to his advantage, as he earned land and pardon though his good service and prominent patronage. He was one of those relatively rare early convicts that did well by their crime, earning the system a frequently over-exaggerated reputation for being good for those on the receiving end of a sentence of transportation. It helped some, like John, but not all were so lucky.

By the end of 1818 John was settled on land in the Camden Cowpastures area, and had gained an absolute pardon. And, as servant to Throsby, he too turned explorer. One of Throsby's best-known expeditions was to trace a convenient path from the Cowpastures over the Blue Mountains to Sydney's west in 1819, and into the Bathurst plains. They were joined by Dual, one of the first Aborigines to have been transported away from his country, who was recalled from Van Diemen's Land to act as an interpreter on this mission. Another Aboriginal interpreter and a third Aboriginal man acting as 'guide' point out that this was not strictly exploration in the sense of going into the wilderness. It was a foray into rough and foreign-controlled territory, part geographical exploration, part diplomatic mission.

With a successful expedition, John earned the gratitude of Throsby and, with the opening up of the possibility of further westward settlement, that of the government. He was rewarded with a significant land grant. Only a few years later, on 17 May 1825, John petitioned Governor Thomas Brisbane for further land, because he 'has a wife and six children and has upwards of one hundred head of horned Cattle', and wished to purchase additional adjacent land to expand his herd. Unsurprisingly, Charles Throsby endorsed the petition. John had gone from convicted sheep thief to successful cattle baron.

And so, it appears, he invited his relative William Waite to join him, facilitating the immigration of William and his family.

As she looked back, Charlotte would have remembered when they arrived, how, and what the voyage was like. Due to a dearth of records, this dramatic change in their lives remains poorly documented. By 1841 they were on a property at Sutton Forest called Lansdown Park. With family and servants, there were sixteen people at the property, living in a single wooden house. All were members of the Church of England, except one, who was Jewish. In some ways, it might have seemed a full house. But one member of the family was missing.

Sophia Phillips, formerly Sophia Waite, was still in England. When the senior Waites and their children had migrated, Sophia had remained in the port town of Gravesend with her husband and young family. It is a reminder that not all migrants took their children with them, especially when they were adult children who were already establishing independent lives, and gives a different take on that sense that migration could be a wrenching experience. It is one thing for children to leave their parents, but it is a whole other thing for parents to leave their children.

And just as William and Charlotte's migration in the wake of John's transportation suggests that family networks were maintained by correspondence, so too later events suggest Charlotte remained appraised of her daughter's life in the old country. Unfortunately, the correspondence has not survived, but even the terse and unemotional English census records told their own tale and chart the essentials.

In 1841 Sophia and her husband Henry Phillips had three children. Henry was a labourer and there seems to have been a wider Phillips family network. The 1851 census revealed change. Their daughter had left home, as had one of their boys, Henry junior. Moreover, that wider family network had disappeared. Only Henry senior and Sophia were left in Gravesend, with their two youngest boys, William and James. Henry senior was working as a 'Ticket Porter', which may have suggested that labouring work was too difficult. Although only thirty-nine, he died within a few years.

In Sutton Forest in New South Wales, Charlotte must have read about his untimely death back in Kent. Each letter came months after the events described, and each response had half a world to travel. But somehow, the Waites orchestrated a plan. Sophia and her sons immigrated to New South Wales, seemingly with the hope of joining family. Henry junior, her oldest son, returned home to assist with, and join, the emigration of his widowed mother and his two younger brothers.

They sailed on the *Maidstone*, arriving in Sydney in November 1853. Like so many emigrants, their last port of departure from Britain was Plymouth. Sophia could read and write, so it is likely that she knew of her relations' situation in New South Wales, and had an approximate idea of where to find them from their correspondence. When the immigration officials recorded their arrival information, their reasons for coming to the colony were recorded as 'A Grandfather and Grandmother'. These were the Waites, who were 'residing at Mittagong'. Sophia knew where her people were. It was proof of communication of some sort.

Sophia was a 'Needlewoman', so she may have occupied herself with her trade as the ship sailed away from her husband's grave towards her parents' new home. Keeping her mind busy with the distractions of her work may have helped abate the tediousness of the voyage a little. The two youngest boys likely played about the ship, as much as would have been possible. Henry was busier. He was not listed as a passenger as such, but was in fact a 'Sailor', who worked his passage, climbing the rigging, pulling on ropes, and generally doing what he was told to help the ship plough forward.

The ship's records place Sophia in a special section for 'Widows on embarkation'. It highlights that, while it was a bit unusual, her story was not unique. As the waves of emigrants left the British Isles, for some people it was natural to follow their families, whether prompted by opportunity or necessity. The phenomenon is generally known as chain migration. But a better indication of the process comes from an old saying. 'Blood', Mum often told me, 'is thicker than water.' Seeing the Phillips' arrival story put this old phrase into a certain new perspective, a common saying that may have passed down through many families from those times.

But the emotional impact of migration and the stresses of leaving, perhaps through necessity, were shockingly clear for others on this particular sailing. The *Maidstone* was reported free from infectious illness during the voyage. One infant died of 'convulsions', and three were born at sea. The child who died was feared to have been a case of infanticide and was investigated by the Sydney authorities when the ship landed. Single, pregnant, and unwell, Jemima Newton appears to have struggled with her condition and predicament. She had been a servant in a London house, and was 'seduced', in the euphemistic language of the day, before being dispatched to the colonies for the avoidance of any scandal that could injure her 'master'. Although women in the female section noticed that Jemima 'kept her bed improperly', there were no obvious signs of pregnancy until it was too late.

About a month into the voyage, Jemima visited the water closet, and delivered a child. Very shortly thereafter it died, apparently choked by the umbilical cord. Smears of blood alerted other passengers, and the pregnancy was soon discovered. So too was the child. Despite the obvious opportunities presented by a nearby porthole, Jemina could not bring herself to part with its body before she was discovered. For these reasons, she was found not guilty of murder, although she was sentenced to a year in Darlinghurst Gaol for criminal concealment of a birth.

Perhaps with first-hand reports of this grisly story, Sophia and her sons made their way to Sutton Forest, where the Waite family welcomed them. Because they were remittance passengers, having had their voyage paid for them by William, newspaper advertisements directed him to their arrival, and the place and time where he could collect them. So on 15 November 1853, or at least soon thereafter, it seems likely that they were met in Sydney. Sophia was reunited with her parents, practically two decades after they had left her behind in England.

Whole extended families were making the shift to Australia in fits and starts, but, more than that, they were making their way across Australia in fits and starts. John Waite again led the way for his family, moving south to Albury in the early 1850s, at one of the main crossing points of Australia's largest river, the Murray. It was later recalled of these other Waites that the 'journey was made in bullock wagons, and took six months' to get there from Sutton Forest. And young Henry Phillips the sailor, Sophia's eldest son, seems to have decided to follow his cousins. Although his relations seem to have gone for land, Henry was probably drawn by the gold discoveries. He married Susan Saunders on 1 September 1861, at the Presbyterian Manse in Chiltern. He was twenty-five years old and worked as a butcher. She was twenty-one. Their addresses were both recorded as 'Morses Creek, Ovens District', which may explain how they met. This places them in the area of Bright, one of the high country towns in alpine Victoria, part of the wider gold mining districts, which probably indicates that they were participants in the gold rush economy. There were other ways to make money than dig for gold, and it seems that Henry made his by selling meat to hungry miners.

Chiltern was a fair hike from Bright, and may have been chosen for their marriage so that the families could attend the wedding, seeing as it was closer to Albury. One of the witnesses to the ceremony was Mary Saunders, Susan's mother, who crossed 'her mark' to the register. She, at least, had certainly made the trip down from the Albury farm.

In 1865 Henry's mother died. Sophia Phillips's headstone in Berrima records the date of her death, 19 April 1865, mentions that she was fifty-one years old, and records that the headstone itself had been 'erected by her father William Waite'. Henry, so far to the south, probably only learned of Sophia's death well after the funeral. Just eleven months later, his grandfather William also died. His grandmother, Charlotte, grieved her losses without leaving any record. It was the most common yet challenging experience of making Australia home: burying your own people.

AUGUST 1866

Susan Phillips, Henry's wife, lived well into an old age. Soon after their marriage they moved to Albury, where Henry established a butchery and Susan lived out the rest of her life. They had children, and Henry died in his mid seventies in the early twentieth century. Susan long outlived her husband, also dying in a new century and a new nation in 1936. She was then so old that the local newspapers were confused about her real age. She left a large family and was apparently well liked. One newspaper recorded that as 'a little girl Mrs. Phillips accompanied her parents, who had a farm at Eastern Hill, to Albury, and she has lived there ever since'. Another report from 1933 recorded that 'Mrs. Phillips remembers clearly the early days of Albury, where she has lived since she was seven'. Yet neither report captured what was one of the most dramatic events of her young life. After a brief moment of colonial fame in August–September 1866, Susan was probably glad to remain safely out of the papers until her very antiquity made her an object of some local interest. When, in her nineties, the newspapermen asked her about her life, she seems to have chosen to keep quiet about the tragic events of August 1866 that overtook her family.

They caused a sensation that produced a wealth of documentation and coverage, but only concerning the immediate setting and sequence of events. The protagonists were Susan's parents, Thomas and Mary Saunders, and their paths first crossed in Sydney, about the time that the Waites were settling into Sutton Forest.

Twenty-year-old Mary Murphy arrived in Sydney in 1841 on the delightfully named *Glenswilly*. Her immigrant record reveals key details about her life. She was from the little village of Upperchurch in county Tipperary. Her father, Michael, had been a farmer, but was dead. Her mother, Honor, was simply 'his wife there'. Mary was unable to read or write, and her 'calling', as the form put it, was 'House maid'. She was poor, Irish, and Catholic.

Leaving county Tipperary, she made her way to one of Ireland's eastern ports, and was transported by steamboat to meet the *Glenswilly* in Plymouth Sound, one of Britain's busiest ports. From there, she was conveyed across three oceans to New South Wales. Upon arriving in Sydney, Mary Murphy was met with a strong prejudice of the age. Prompted by her arrival, *The Sydney Herald* published an extended diatribe against the scheme to bring in Irish immigrants, 'like so many pigs'. The writer was deeply concerned at the 'proportion of Protestants to Roman Catholics' coming to the colony. There were, he felt, too few of the former, and too many of the latter. It seems that the paper did not realise there was a Catholic priest on board or he too may have elicited comment.

Seemingly making matters worse for the *Herald*'s writer, many of the immigrants 'were from the county of Tipperary, the most infamous county in all Ireland for deeds of violence and blood'. It was perhaps just as well that Mary did not read, but at some point in her new life, her accent and religion would no doubt have been sources of prejudice. Little looks of distrust from shopkeepers, extra surveillance by employers, and such little undocumented encounters of the sort many immigrants experienced may well have encouraged her to cultivate a feisty Irishwoman's tongue.

Yet while she may have been poor, Irish, and Catholic, this was no obstacle to a match, and she was soon married. Mary's husband was Thomas Saunders. He was from Gloustershire and had arrived in Sydney on the *Orestes* in 1839. Many people did not take the English versus Irish thing as seriously as the pundit classes did.

A highlight of Thomas's voyage, no doubt, was the passing of two large icebergs, broken shards from Antarctica straying slowly into warmer waters that gradually melted them away. He was a nineteen-year-old government-sponsored immigrant, and arrived with his first wife, Jane, who was eighteen. They were brought to help provide labour for the developing colonial economy. Thomas was a farm labourer, and Jane, like Mary, was a housemaid.

Quite mysteriously, Jane disappeared from the scene sometime between their arrival and Thomas's second marriage in 1841, but it is not immediately clear how, although an unrecorded or mis-recorded death would be likely explanations. Either way, she was not an impediment to Thomas's second marriage, so whatever had occurred, she did not come back.

The early years of Mary and Thomas's life together is quite obscure. And as was so often the case for them, surviving documentary records were often the product of problems. Unfortunately for Thomas, for example, he saw the inside of Sydney's Darlinghurst gaol. In 1847 he was entered in the gaol register, 5 feet 9 inches tall, with grey eyes. It was a terse account of the man, whose personality was later captured by newspapers and tragedy in much greater detail. The cause of this early incarceration is unclear, but there were later reports that he may have left Mary and failed to provide support. If so, he rethought that decision, because he lived with her after his early release on bail.

Other than this tiny blip in the criminal justice system, the couple basically disappear from easily identifiable records. A year after they married, they had their daughter Susan, who married Henry Phillips, and would later recall that when she was seven years old the family moved to Albury by the Murray River. This would suggest the family headed south from Sydney about 1849. It seems they had been small farmers, and Thomas's legal run-in may have given the family the desire to make a new start somewhere different.

The town of Albury was situated at a place where stockmen and travellers could cross over the Murray River, which is part of the reason John Waite and then Henry Phillips had gravitated towards it. In the early days it was known as the Hume River, after the European explorer Hamilton Hume, although officialdom soon changed its name to the Murray River. Like most of the Riverina, it was already well populated by Wiradjuri people living along its banks, even into the time when my ancestors were arriving there with the first wave of major settlement. Because of this, many of the settlers' children played with the local Wiradjuri children. One settler later recalled meeting a group of Wiradjuri who were fleeing from a spot in the bush in a frightened state. It was of particular interest to this observer, because apparently there was much talk at the time among colonists of the Bunyip, a mythical and monstrous creature supposed by Aborigines to have inhabited swamps and waterholes. He decided to go and investigate. Upon coming into a clearing, his horse saw the beast first, turned suddenly, and threw the rider. He was left facing a stray donkey.

The Saunders arrived as Albury was undergoing rapid growth, transforming from a small village by the river into a town. By late 1850 there was a court house, several hotels, a mill, a school, three stores, 'and a goodly array of slab huts', as one reporter put it. It was said that a house went up every week. It might have been an exaggeration, but not excessively so. People were streaming across the land from the colonial ports, and interior towns were booming. A wooden punt was operated to facilitate crossing the river, steadily tracking back and forth across the flowing water, carrying the inter-colonial traffic. Once Victoria had split from the colony of New South Wales, Albury had become a significant frontier town, as well as a crossing place, and this traffic would increase dramatically with the gold rush. Locals were concerned to ensure a strong police presence so that criminals could not escape punishment by skipping into another jurisdiction across the river.

The great age of paddle steamers had also arrived, but most of the traffic concerned downriver trade, where the Murray connected with South Australia and the Southern Ocean. The colony of South Australia, was 'made' by act of the British Parliament in 1834, and settled in late 1836. It had been one of the corporate planned settlement schemes for British expansion, like New Zealand, that had been topical a generation earlier. In July 1866 a paddle steamer built at Echuca was grounded on its maiden voyage towards Albury, which was still not yet connected to the Riverina network of paddle steamers. Nonetheless, the Murray River was still a highway for carrying produce to the colonial centres and the rest of the world, making this wider region a prominent area of economic growth. The Murray and the rich agricultural valleys formed by its tributaries fed colonial expansion by providing food for cities, income for farmers, and plenty of work. Also capitalising on the rivers were those living on the adjacent pastoral plains, which produced meat, hides, and wool.

I am not entirely sure what took the Saunders to Albury, although I suspect they were hoping to find land and establish a farm in what seemed to be a rapidly developing area. But it proved a good move, for reasons unrelated to farming, but intimately related to the rich alluvial soil.

Like many in his generation, Thomas seems likely to have gotten swept up in the gold fever, which stirred the colonies into such agitation in the 1850s. Already being in Albury seems to have been serendipitous. When the discovery of gold in the Albury district was being reported to the Sydney press in March 1852, it was noted that a 'man named Saunders, a resident in Albury, obtained a nugget half-an-ounce in weight, lying on the surface of the ground'. It must have been an amazing moment for him, caught up in the excitement of possibility, and then to actually strike it so lucky.

Whether he found the gold on his farm, or if it was the means for buying a farm a little out of town, Thomas definitely had one by the mid 1860s. In fact, he was well established enough by 1854 to have worried over one of his animals. On 4 June 1854 Thomas lost his horse in Albury, but he suspected it might have been stolen. Frustrated, he took out an advertisement in the nearest paper, the *Goulburn Herald*, and offered a £5 reward for its return, or a £50 reward for the successful prosecution of the thief. This was another suggestion that maybe he had done well by the gold rush.

But rather than having to unearth their lives from terse advertisements, census records, and the like, as was the case with many of the settler people, the Saunders family's life was put firmly under the public's gaze by the mystery surrounding Mary Saunders's disappearance in August 1866. As a result, I could reconstruct their farm, their socialising, their family relationships, and their words to each other with great clarity.

Thomas and Mary Saunders and their children had clearly settled into the Albury district by the middle of 1866. Susan was living in town with her husband Henry Phillips, and other of the elder Saunders children were making their own ways in the world, but basically within the district. They all had their routines. But they also had their challenges and conflicts.

Thomas and Mary's marriage was not a congenial one. The children later recalled a series of instances of Thomas abusing Mary. He was 'not very kind' to Mary, Susan's sister Elizabeth said, having 'often heard her father threaten her mother'. So often were the disturbances, Elizabeth claimed, that 'she could not remember the threats' except for one time when she heard him 'threaten to throw her mother behind the fire'. That had stuck in her mind.

And sometimes it went beyond threats. Elizabeth spoke of how 'father and mother quarrelled pretty often'. She said that 'he hit her with his hand, but not very often'. Susan also later claimed to have witnessed this behaviour. 'My mother was always much afraid of father', she remembered. 'He is of a hasty temper.'

There was a particular time, perhaps about 1863, when Thomas threatened Mary in a particularly graphic way. 'He then tied her to a beam, and threatened to shoot her.' Three of the children, watching in horror, were reportedly told by their father to each go and get gunpowder, balls, and caps.

Susan's brother John also saw Thomas threatening to shoot Mary, although he placed the event five or six years earlier. He threw the gunpowder into water to ruin it so the threat could not be carried out. He also said that one time Thomas led Mary 'down to a waterhole with a handkerchief round her neck, and said he would make an end of her'. She was apparently choking under the pressure. John claimed to have left home because of this domestic violence, because he feared the repercussions of his attempts to protect her.

His father was 'beating my mother', John said. 'I interfered, and he threatened to chuck me on the fire.'

This notion of throwing people on the fire was clearly one of Thomas's favourite threats. Young Elizabeth 'heard him say so, at frequent times'.

So the children grew up in a world of guns and gunpowder, where domestic violence could escalate dramatically. The family hearth was a potential weapon. But their neighbours seemed unaware.

The children, though, also remembered a period when things seemed to have improved. Elizabeth followed John's example and moved out. She went to live with Susan and Henry Phillips in Albury itself. Their presence in the district may have helped diffuse the tensions somehow. It certainly gave young Elizabeth a residential option that was less combustible. She moved in with her older sister in early 1866. The youngest two, Hester and Mary Ann, continued to live on the farm with their quarrelling parents.

Eventually the fights had diminished. John was gradually able to be on reasonable terms with his father, visiting his parents relatively frequently, although he was often out of the district for work.

The kinship network is on display here, acting as a safety net, with self-reliance and blood ties paramount. It shows a settler family resolving its daily domestic worries 'in house'.

The Saunders' property was next to Schubach's vineyard. One of a group of German pioneers who had headed to the Murray district to establish themselves as vine growers in 1851, Sebastian Schubach soon had his grapes planted. It took a few years before the German immigrants had successful harvests, but by 1865 Sebastian had sent some of his produce to the Rhineland to be entered into competitions, and the names of German and European grapes were familiar to the settlers of this region. Large numbers of Germans gravitated to this part of the colonies, and a thriving German community developed. An Albury newspaper was even printed in German for a considerable time. The proximity of the Schubachs highlighted how multicultural the early colonial countryside could be. But it also reveals that alcohol was readily available.

The Saunders lived in a house on a hill, a little above a barn further down the slope. They had a verandah, from which they could survey most of the property. The harshness of the climate encouraged this architectural feature, so typically Australian, which is noticeably lacking in much of the equivalently aged housing from the cooler Tasmania.

Much of the Saunders' property was fenced. In the winter of 1866 they could see to a waterhole on their side of the boundary with Schubach's vineyard. It was about two feet deep, and had a muddy bottom, and they would sometimes go down there to extract clay. One August day Mary took her son John down to extract some pipe clay. He slipped, and nearly fell in, but she was more sure-footed and stayed on her feet.

This waterhole sat within a cultivation paddock. The field was green with a growing crop, six inches high. Thomas could often be seen busying himself around the property, including carrying bundles of grass. A three-rail wooden fence separated them from Schubach's. On another side, about 50 metres from the house, ran the road. It was the very picture of a perfect smallholding.

And they had the advantage of being fairly close to town. The children often attended functions in Albury, and the parents frequently visited people around the district.

But the memories of many fights and much yelling stayed with the children as they grew to adulthood. And one night during that picture-perfect winter in 1866, when John was working at Cumberoona, a station on the Upper Murray, he had a terrible dream.

After a day at work, on Monday 20 August 1866, John went to bed. He dreamed that his father, Thomas, and his brother, James, 'were murdering his mother and himself'. John woke up, frantic and agitated. In his dream he had been 'trying to get away'. He told one of the other workmen that he had a bad dream, but did not give the details. It bothered him for days, so he planned to return to Albury at the end of the working week.

The day after John had his dream, things were quite normal at Albury. About midday Susan Phillips met her mother Mary, and they may even have had lunch together. The afternoon passed quietly, and the two youngest children went to town to attend a soiree at the Mechanics Institute. These community learning centres put the people of rural Australia in touch with the intellectual trends of the globe. Men and women could attend lectures on topics ranging from the sciences of evolution and phrenology to more literary and cultural pursuits. But sometimes the hall was turned over to the children for music and dancing, as it was on that Tuesday evening.

While her youngest girls were out, Mary went visiting. This time she went to her son-in-law's house, and briefly saw at least two of her daughters. There is no sense of a neat and nuclear generational division between families here. Rather, immediacy and intimacy across generations was clearly maintained with a regular round of visiting and gossiping. But this time Mary was unable to stay for long. She told them that she 'had to go home and set some bread', before then going out again to meet the young girls coming out of the soiree. Mary was planning to escort them home in the dark. Little Mary Ann, momentarily distracted from the fun in the hall, even managed to see her mother going past, presumably on the way home to set the bread.

This image of mother coming home and putting bread on the table in the evening is a recognisable colonial moment. For many farming people 'dinner' was their main meal, and was eaten during the middle of the day. The evening meal, which became colloquially known as 'tea', deriving from the upper classes' between-meal breaks, could be a simpler affair.

The oldest of the children at home, fourteen-year-old James, saw his mother return to the farm 'and set some bread' just as she had planned. He observed Mary and Thomas exchange a few jokes, but they talked little. After the simple meal, Thomas went back out into the paddock where the crop was growing, perhaps for an evening toilet of some sort. At about a quarter to nine, Mary left again for town, and moments later James heard his father's footsteps entering the house. Not long thereafter, father and son went to their respective beds.

At the Mechanics Institute the soiree had come to an end, but Mary Ann and Hester were still waiting there, confused—their mother had not arrived. Mary Ann led the way to one of her older sisters, where she learned that her mother had visited earlier that evening, but was no longer there. When it was suggested that Mary may have been at the Tollards, friends of the family, the children went there, but still they found no mother. Perplexed, perhaps a little worried, the two little girls walked home to the farm in the darkness.

As they entered the house, their father called out to them to light a lamp.

'Where's mother?' he asked them.

Mary Ann told him that she did not know.

'What's the use of talking such nonsense', he asked in apparent agitation, and with telltale signs of drunkenness. 'Tell me where she is at once.'

Mary Ann had no answer. Her mother sometimes spent a night away when visiting, but they usually knew where to find her. This time was different. The little girls went to bed not knowing where their mother was.

With daylight came breakfast. Unsure where Mary was, the conversation was focused on this mystery. James and his father Thomas discussed the situation.

'I wonder why mother did not come home last night', James mused.

'She must be down at Sister's', Thomas replied, before suggesting that 'she might have come home part of the way with the children, and told them not to say anything about where she was going'.

James went searching for her at Hudson's farm nearby and then further afield in the Black Range. This points, perhaps, to the sort of normal socialising range that they expected of their mother. It was not just the town they were connected to. The farming community had its own rural network of connections and friendships.

Thomas said he would go to see Constable Anderson about his missing wife, but apparently the constable was not at home. But through the regular rounds of visits and brief chats, as the people of the Albury district went about their business, word spread that something had happened to Mrs Saunders. She was missing.

Susan Phillips came to the Saunders farm. She knocked at the door, but did not receive any immediate answer and turned to leave. As she headed away her father appeared and asked her if she knew where her mother was. She told him that she did not, but he seemed suspicious.

'Now tell the truth,' he pressed, 'ain't she down there?'—meaning perhaps Albury in general or the Phillips residence particularly.

Susan returned again the following day, obviously increasingly worried, but still her mother was not home.

'Wouldn't it be a lark', Thomas suggested, 'if she was found near at hand, after looking so far away for her.'

The dream-inspired John arrived in Albury from Cumberoona on Saturday 25 August and went to one of his sisters' houses. His wife met him and asked him a question that must have sent shivers up his spine. Had he seen his mother?

'No,' he replied, 'where is she?'

He soon learned his mother was missing, and had been for five days.

The children spent a considerable time looking for their mother. Elizabeth in particular 'felt uneasy', and was searching the family farm on Sunday, even though she had been living at the Phillips' place for the past six months. Elizabeth was the one to find the body.

She saw it from the other side of the fence and screamed as she scrambled through the wooden slats. Mary was in the waterhole, obscured from view of the house by the bank, with two injuries to her skull. Elizabeth called to her brother and brother-in-law, who were both also searching nearby. They hurried over and saw young Elizabeth faint. Someone noticed boot prints in a track that passed the waterhole and warned the others to stay back. Another went for the sergeant. Mary's water-logged corpse gave no signs of life.

She wore the same bonnet and shawl that she had been seen in on the Tuesday night, and a flash of colour from her crinoline contrasted with the grim scene. She lay face down in the water, one hand raised as if protecting her head, her mouth open as though screaming into the water. Her eyes were shut with a sad finality.

The news somehow reached Thomas Saunders and he too came to the waterhole.

'Poor wretch,' he exclaimed on seeing the body, 'this is the expiration of twenty-five years. Oh Lord, Lord, what a sight!'

The local sergeant of police soon arrived and took charge. The scene was studied in detail, the body examined, and the property was searched. A tomahawk and a hammer were both found and thought possible weapons. Thomas was asked to bring his boots down to see if they matched the prints in the mud. It seemed they did. The house was searched and a pair of damp trousers were also discovered. They belonged to Thomas.

Over Monday and Tuesday a preliminary coronial investigation was conducted at the Albury courthouse. The building was crowded. It was the talk of the town. The press was enthralled, and soon so were colonial readers in far-flung centres. The jury in the coronial inquest returned a verdict: 'That the deceased, Mary Saunders, was wilfully murdered by some person or persons unknown, on the night of Tuesday, August 21, and that a strong suspicion attaches to her husband.' Thomas was arrested and taken into police custody.

'Murder', was detailed as the alleged offence on Thomas Saunders's gaol record. An additional notation said that he was 'Remanded for 8 days for safe custody' before being 'sent to the police office' in early September.

His trial attracted widespread publicity. It took place over a number of sessions in early September and early October 1866. Thomas seemed confident about his innocence. He defended himself to begin with, until the judge advised him that a lawyer would be a sensible idea.

It was a moment of familial infamy, recorded through the spotlight of intense press coverage. The multiple trial reports, in addition to the August inquest, built up the details of the scene, the actions of the individual witnesses, the wider family context, and that sense of a series of normal lives thrown into turmoil. But of course there were some discrepancies between the various statements, and even within the records of those statements. There was a delicate line slicing through this wealth of detail, dividing facts, fictions, memories, beliefs, and accusations. Like other over-documented events of Australian history, Mary Saunders's murder provides scope for competing interpretations. And as it does now, so it did then.

A number of the children testified to Thomas's violence and threats, but it was generally thought that the marriage difficulties tended to belong to a distant past, rather than recent years. Even some of the more hostile witnesses agreed to that. And Mary was said to have used bad language against Thomas, so there was thought to be a little give and take, at least in the minds of some of the spectators.

But the trial itself brought out some of the obvious troubled relationships. There were profound moments of familial discord expressed and experienced by the witnesses and defendant. At one point Thomas was questioning a witness giving evidence against him, his own son James, and the exchange between father and son reveals their fraught relationship.

'At any one of the times that I attempted to make away with your mother,' Thomas asked in response to one of James's allegations, 'did you think it was a serious thing?'

'I did', James replied.

'Did you report it?'

'No.'

'Did you', Thomas pressed, 'mention anything of this before you came to this court?'

'No', James responded, 'I don't think I did. I never care about telling anything like that.'

Potentially worse was to come. When the police magistrate asked Elizabeth if she had 'any unfriendly feeling to your father', she simply said, 'Yes'. When asked what the reason was for this, she said nothing. The court report described how Elizabeth 'was silent, and although pressed for an answer both by the Inspector and the Bench, refused to answer'. I could not help but link this information to some of the other details that came out of this case. She was, I knew, the one who had left home to live with her sister a few months previously.

Yet while there was a lot of this character testimony, without a witness to the killing, the case turned on the physical evidence, and here Thomas was at a distinct advantage.

The tomahawk and hammer were first considered the most likely weapon choices, but there were problems with this evidence. Another man, 'named Connors', had been seen on the property carrying the tomahawk only days beforehand. Some suspicion also seemed to attach to him. Moreover, once he had carefully examined Mary's damaged skull, the medical examiner thought neither weapon had inflicted the wounds.

The discovery of wet trousers in a farming house meant little, especially when Thomas had been in the fields on the day of the murder. There was no way of definitively linking them to the waterhole. And the boots were not the perfect evidence they first seemed. James and Mary had visited the waterhole a few days before the murder, and the footprints in the clay could not be proven to belong to Thomas rather than some earlier visit or visitors. The apparent matching of print and boot sizes was also a matter of debate, especially almost a week after the incident.

Against the odds, it seemed, Thomas Saunders was found not guilty.

I found it hard to form an opinion about all of this. At first I too immediately thought Thomas guilty. But as I read more carefully through the trial reports, because of variations in the stories given by different children and problems with the physical evidence, gradually my suspicions shifted towards something resembling 'reasonable doubt'. Though I am not really sure whether he did it or not, the sad fact remains that several members of his family very clearly thought he could have.

Two facts seem to remain pertinent, yet tantalisingly unlinked to this miserable tale.

Firstly, there was Thomas's first wife, who seemed simply to vanish from recorded history. Logically, I know that is what happens with records from that period for people of their class. Sometimes records just did not survive. But then, sometimes, neither did people.

A second thing that may be linked to the murder was the fact that Thomas Saunders himself went missing in 1875. His disappearance was reported in the *Police Gazette*, and his son applied for probate. Apparently, he was not expected back. This police notice provided a physical description which matched the earlier ones I had. He was 5 feet 9½ inches tall, of 'fair complexion', with 'light brown hair worn long and inclined to curl'. From his gaol records I also knew that he had a 'burn mark on right side of stomach', and a 'scar under left shoulder'. These wounds, evidence of a rough existence, were hidden under the 'light tweed suit' he was last seen wearing. As far as I can tell, he was never heard of again.

In the aftermath of tragedy and personal loss, the newspapers lost interest in Mary Saunders's case. Susan Phillips may not necessarily have led a quiet life after her mother's demise, but she certainly left a silence about her life thereafter. Similarly, once Charlotte Waite buried her husband William, her story became even quieter than it had already been, at least in the documentary sense. Australia was a broad place that was increasingly peopled, and many thousands of lives and stories have gradually disappeared. Australia's history is often considered short and perfectly known. Yet it is a place where much remains hidden, some of which will be lost forever. This fact should alert us to how epic our shared story is, composed of so many lost parts. Moments of death and tragedy help cut to the heart of the everyday experiences and emotional bonds of society, but our silences reveal a human tendency to reminisce clashing with an equally human longing to forget.

But some stories have been etched into the landscape, even if they have faded from memory. Australia was dramatically changed by the processes of settlement. The story of how the face of the continent was altered is more complex than a displacement of hunter-gatherer people with farmers, or the displacement of 'wilderness' with pasture, crops, and towns. The modification and maintenance of Australia's landscape by Aboriginal traditional economies took many forms, and the impacts of European encroachment were similarly varied, even if both broad groups often displayed characteristically broad patterns, and some of the ways of using the land that Europeans brought with them had disastrous ecological results. Europeans also brought new ways of constructing society and telling stories, some of which, ironically, drew upon perceptions of Europe's medieval past, whether it be through the built environment, outlaws in the forests, or the bringing of game animals.

CHAPTER EIGHT

BATTLERS, BUSHRANGERS, AND BUNNIES 1871

FANNY MILES WAS born on 15 January 1871 at Gooramadda, just south of the Murray River and to the west of the Victorian town of Wodonga. Her father, William Henry Miles, informed the authorities of the birth in nearby Rutherglen two months later, on 26 March. She was given a family name. Fanny's mother was Susan Frances Atlee, hence Fanny, and had married William Henry Miles in London in 1849. This couple came to the Australian colonies in 1854. And with them, they each brought a brother. Their family backgrounds were decidedly urban. William's father was a grocer, and Susan's father was a builder. But by 1871 the newborn Fanny's parents were farmers. And they were in what later came to be known as 'Kelly country'.

When she was born, Fanny had seven older siblings living. Two others had died. Officialdom sometimes insisted that parents tell them the names of children who predeceased them, as part of a process of verification and identification. As a result, many birth, marriage, and death certificates record dead children. The Miles family were not exceptions to this. The loss of children was a common part of the colonial experience. Even the passenger list respecting their voyage to Sydney on the *Palmyra* hinted at this phenomenon. It was filled out without great attention to detail, and they were simply noted as 'Mr & Mrs Miles & Family'. The number '4' was written next to it, presumably an indication that they already had two children with them.

En route to Sydney from Plymouth the *Palmyra* lost a child to the sea. 'A lad fell overboard, during the voyage, and was drowned', a short account of the voyage noted. This was all that was recorded of the event. The deceased child was not even named. Complementing this tale was another terse record with its own brutal arithmetic. A newspaper reported the Miles family having arrived as 'Mr. and Mrs. Miles and 1 child'. According to another of the ship's records, this child was 'a girl'. They had lost a child on the voyage.

Fanny's birth was one of the events that documented the family having settled onto land. Immediately after their arrival, William had 'spent a few years on the diggings, and at Bathurst' and most likely his family had travelled with him. But by the 1870s, in the wake of the gold rushes, massive immigration, and land tenure reforms, many families were carving out lives for themselves as farmers, or at least attempting to do so. The Miles family was, in this respect, following a similar pattern to the O'Raffertys at nearby Tarramia, the Saunders at Albury, or any number of my other family branches.

But individuals surnamed 'Miles' do not lend themselves to ready electronic searching. This word was a regularly used noun in a colonial setting of rapid expansion and land settlement. Still, those confirmed sightings of this relatively under-documented family, even if complicated by William Henry's eldest son also being named William Henry, reveal a closeness to and distance from iconic events, which can help illustrate a new phase of the settlement of Australia that saw an increase in settlement on the land and a gradual settling down of some of its wilder ways, at least in the broader area between major colonial capitals.

Education and church-building were two features of this period that stand out, with churches and schools usually among the first public buildings in any settler locality. Hotels and general stores were also common early structures, but these had more of a mercantile element and served their communities in different ways. Churches and schools spoke to the aspirations of the communities that erected them. They also reveal, to an extent, the tensions within them, where denominational schooling could be such an issue of religious and political concern.

But a newspaper advertisement in 1871, seeking to fill a position as teacher for Gooramadda's school, highlights several simple features of later colonial society. There was a general consensus that education was good, it was thought the children of rural settlements deserved the opportunity of local education, and literacy was prized.

Complementing this was the increasing development of literary culture, reflected in poems, books, and the high volumes of local newspapers that dotted the land. And with the lecture circuits of public speakers, mechanics institutes, local scientific and religious societies, and other such communal intellectual endeavours, the people of colonial Australia were relatively well informed of wider events and swam in a wider cultural pool than just their nearest village or station run.

Colonial Australians also enjoyed the varied 'fads' of their period. And one long-lasting favourite of the nineteenth century was the neo-gothic. Pointy medieval-like church buildings were extremely popular throughout the colonies, increasingly so as the century progressed. These often replaced simple wooden predecessors, as the settler people built structures to affirm to themselves and each other that they were settled people, with a strong cultural history and modern aspirations of a merry future drawn from a love affair with the medieval world generally, and 'merrie England' particularly. And to adorn these built testaments to good intentions, gothic furnishings were installed, most notably the stained glass that graces many old Australian churches. One of the earliest Anglican churches to be so adorned in Tasmania, at the little village of Buckland, was done so successfully that, well into the twentieth century, many later residents and admirers came to believe, quite falsely, that it contained a genuine medieval window.

Gothic trim and gargoyles adorned public buildings and corporate headquarters—especially in the major cities—and parks and landscapes were adorned with gothic features such as monumental figures and fountains, and gates with pointy curling iron trim. Even the stories that people read, wrote and told often conjured up the medieval European past in the colonial Australian present and future. Louise D'Arcens's *Old Songs in the Timeless Land: Medievalism in Australian Literature*, Stephanie Trigg's *Medievalism and the Gothic in Australian Culture*, and a wide range of other fascinating studies are increasingly revealing the way the neo-gothic impacted on

Australian life. So significant is this medievalism to understanding colonial Australia that it is now a field of historical research in its own right. But the key to understanding the phenomenon is simply to recognise that this colonial affection for the medieval was more than just cultural memory or affectation. Part of an international movement, it reflected a renewed interest in recapturing some sense of what the medieval past could do for the Victorian British Empire and its outposts. Stories, myths, and legends from and of the medieval world all influenced the way that colonial Australians presented and saw themselves. Robin Hood, the Green Man of the forest, Arthur and his Knights of the Round Table, and other such figures were treasured by the many people in Australia who knew them. And perhaps no other group of figures in Australia were so subjected to this cultural lens than some of the later bushrangers.

The first bushrangers were people who ranged in the bush, often a simple story of convicts or soldiers on the run from society, generally sustaining themselves through some criminality. A number, such as the Aboriginal man known as Mosquito, could be all of these. A warrior transported to Norfolk Island and then Van Diemen's Land, he was famously utilised in tracking down vandemonian bushrangers, before himself going on to lead a band of local Aborigines, robbing and killing settlers.

Later versions of bushrangers tended to originate as poor farmers, wage labourers, or other variations on the general theme of an economic lower class. Once bushrangers, they were often considered simply to be brigands, murderers, thieves, or highwaymen, depending on the circumstances of their individual case and personality. It was the tendency to live within the protection of the Australian 'bush' that lent them the collective designation, more than any other particular set of behavioural characteristics. Yet some, through particular successes, personality quirks, or particularly frightening actions often gained notoriety and entered into local folklore traditions.

Typical of this later notorious group was Ben Hall, in some contemporary commentary referred to as the 'Bushranger Chief'. Hall seems to have taken to the bush to escape debt, a criminal past, and what seemed to him like official persecution. He led a gang which audaciously robbed the entire lower half of the colony of New South Wales, at least so it seemed at the time. There were dozens of reported and remembered thefts, but murder was not Hall's thing. Following a traditional format, some of his actions were simple raids on isolated farming properties, or highway stand-ups. His death in 1865, the result of being gunned down by police, was a cause for scandal because the New South Wales government had passed an Act of parliament which allowed the authorities to declare persons 'outlaw', meaning any person could shoot them on sight without warning.

The practical realities of bushranging, the popularity of neo-gothic forms of literature, an active press, and colonial historicism and folklore all combined by the 1870s to foster a certain romantic attitude towards some bushrangers just while the phenomenon was starting to show some signs of waning. While the increasing population and gold rush provided bushrangers with abundant targets for theft, these also provided a greater social cohesion in the face of predation and engendered a greater likelihood of capture. The spreading lines of railways and telegraph wires through the settled districts helped make large-scale bushranging less tenable.

But it was still a threat. During 1871 alone there were several active bushrangers. Writing to the *Benalla Ensign* in January that year, a 'Sharp Shooter' sarcastically suggested the removal of police from the upper Victorian region was a sensible government move to allow the bushranging industry to flourish. And in July the *Bendigo Advertiser*, reporting New South Welsh news, noted how a 'bushranger named Kelly has been committed for trial at Bathurst on a charge of highway robbery'. It was not the infamous Edward (Ned) Kelly, but it was proof there were still rangers in the bush.

Yet even as the phenomenon was less of a direct threat to many districts and communities, at least in the colony's urban centres—it was still a continued danger in its rural fringes—it became a sort of nostalgic focal point. Bushrangers were the perfect literary character for the Victorian epoch. Stories of their exploits were serialised for mass consumption. If the convict era reflected the harsh institutional power of the modern empire, the escape into the bush seemed a sort of physical return to the medieval woods. The criminal's excesses could be brought on by belonging to a 'degenerate class', the horrors of transported servitude, or personal relationships that had gone badly. Whichever way it was framed for readers, it fit within a simple literary frame and a largely tragic format.

Fictionalised bushrangers thus fit the parameters of the romantic neo-gothic genre: they were complex individuals, struggling internally over doing good or evil. They could fight oppression or unfairness, or be ironic oppressors in turn. Even the setting helped the allusions. Bush clearings worked as forest glades as settings for encounters and hut battles conjured up the stereotypes of siege warfare. But perhaps most significantly, bushrangers could indulge in chivalrous behaviour such as showing courtesy to women, giving opponents the option to surrender, and displaying a confident superiority with arms. Indeed, the literature rubbed off on would-be bushrangers, and the courteousness of some real bushrangers fed the literature.

So when in the later 1870s a bushranger robbed banks and distributed money to the poor, donned an armoured suit, and died in a tragic siege intended to liberate (perhaps in a deluded fashion) the people of north-eastern Victoria, his actions were inspired by a wider context, and fit rather too perfectly into a ready-made literary mould. He did seem inspired by Irish resentment of the English occupation, the oppressiveness of the class structures that were in place in a far-from-egalitarian colonial Australia, and a range of other issues. The actual personal impact of the real Ned Kelly on colonial Victoria was relatively minor. It was his public persona, projected through newspapers, gossip, and folklore, which had the widest impact on his country. In popular memory he has become a sort of merry man, gentleman, and knight. But even in this he was and is a walking amalgam of literary tropes: medieval, neo-medieval, and from within the early modern rogue literature that delighted in the sneaky cleverness of some vagabond criminals. By this he became a distinctly Australian symbol, but, ironically, one which highlights the colonial love affair with the very 'merrie England' which invaded Ireland in the first place.

These cultural caveats aside, due to its proximity, bushranging was a real worry for colonial settlers like the Miles family. Kelly tried crossing the Murray River at Gooramadda after murdering three policemen at Stringybark Creek in 1878. And so intense was the police chase that one group of police pursuers actually fired on another group of police in the Gooramadda area. There were no injuries, but there would have been much embarrassment.

This sense of official humiliation probably aided the bushrangers to cultivate a lovable rogue image. Irishmen like John O'Rafferty may have read the accounts of bushrangers with amusement. Rich men impoverished, police officers taunted with powerlessness—it was appealing stuff for people who saw themselves as battlers, not just against the elements, but also against the social structures of their world.

And liked or loathed, there was also an entertainment factor, which bushrangers could and did play to. From Gooramadda, the Miles family moved into New South Wales, and eventually William settled to work in Wagga as a butcher. But before that, they spent some time at Wantabadgery, a farming district to Wagga's east, on the north of the Murrumbidgee River.

When 'Captain Moonlight', a bushranger acutely aware of his public image, approached Wantabadgery Station on 15 November 1879, two of the occupants were a Mr and Mrs McMiles, who worked as station hand and cook respectively. It was not quite my ancestral couple, but their shared locality and similarity of name both highlight my Miles family's proximity to the bushranger phenomenon.

Moonlight and five other armed men opened the rear gate and pointed their guns at the surprised servants. Moonlight ordered them to 'Bail up', and then to hand over all the guns in the house or be shot. Samuel McMiles was forced to smash open the storeroom door with a sledgehammer, and the raiders ate and drank. The bushrangers had a group of hostages, which soon grew in number.

During the afternoon, visitors arrived and workmen returned, as did the station manager, and each little group was taken prisoner. Moonlight was keen to ensure his men were courteous, particularly to women, even while they were raiding the property. And so they all spent a night in captivity, with more arrivals joining them the following day. Moonlight, despite his protestations of concern, showed a darker side when he shot a horse, apparently because it reacted badly to taking the bridle.

In the end, there were some thirty-five captives, and word spread through the district. Police converged on the station from Wagga, Gundagai, and other smaller nearby settlements, concerned that the Moonlight gang may have been composed of elements of the Kelly gang. The bushrangers left the station in a confusing confrontation with the first police to arrive, who had advanced on the station and been encircled by the gang in turn. But seeing themselves in the rear of the police and therefore clear, the gang bolted.

Discovered at a nearby hut soon thereafter, a gun battle ensued, witnessed by a considerable crowd that had come from as far as Junee. While my Mr and Mrs Miles were not inside the Wantabadgery Station, it is quite likely some of the family watched the final confrontation at McGlede's hut. The people of the district were seemingly treating the event like a sort of picnic.

Two bushrangers were killed and Moonlight surrendered, to be eventually hanged for his crimes. The show over, the crowd returned to their normal lives.

Except, that is, for Susan Miles, who likely had to learn of the local excitement from others. In late 1879 she could have been beginning to suffer from the condition that three years and five months later was given as the cause of her death: paralysis. She died on 15 October 1883 and was buried at Wantabadgery. But the larger chronic condition may have been exacerbated by stress associated with an event that potentially concerned her husband or son. On 23 September 1883, two horses were stabbed by someone on Oura Station, which is adjacent to Wantabadgery. The *New South Wales Police Gazette* for October noted that 'One of the horses has since died'. And, for reasons now entirely and permanently unclear, the *Gazette* added that 'Suspicion attached to William Miles'.

While seemingly not going any further than suspicion, fear could easily have turned to desperation, and perhaps rash action. And the seeming inevitability of bushrangers getting caught and punished meant that the biggest bushranger-related fear that many colonial people might have had was not to die at the hand of a bushranger, but that a family member would become one and end their days at the end of a rope.

1874

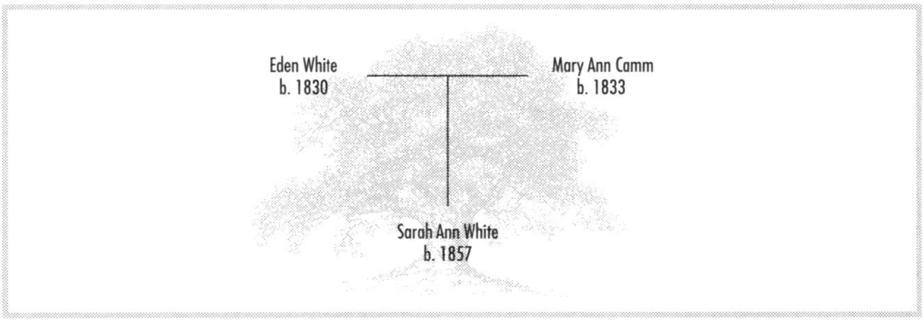

Colonists regularly faced death and injury, without the aid of bushrangers. Many Ann White died on 25 March 1874 of what her death certificate described as 'Accidental Haemorrhage, Preceding Labour'. Having a childbirth go horribly awry was one of the most dangerous of all colonial incidents. Occurring at 'Boho near Violet Town', roughly in the middle of Victoria, this childbirth-related death resulted in her being buried the following day in the Violet Town cemetery. Mary Ann was the daughter of

Joseph and Mary Camm, who, on the outskirts of very early Melbourne, were regularly visited by their neighbours' cows. She had married Eden White, a labourer from Oxfordshire, in Melbourne in 1851. The couple remained hidden from easy historical surveillance for about twenty years. In 1857 when my connection to them was born, Sarah Ann—one of my great-great-great grandmothers—Eden was still a labourer and the couple had three children living and one who had died. They were still in the Boorondara area, perhaps taking charge of the Camm property in the wake of Joseph Camm's death. Then the Whites apparently moved to the Violet Town area in the mid 1860s as part of that wider settling on the land which was a familiar family story, and they were certainly at Boho by 1871.

So it is worth bearing in mind that on a daily basis Moonlight, Ned Kelly, and other bushrangers probably meant relatively little to families struggling with their own concerns, even those like the Whites situated in the middle of 'Kelly country'. Whether they sympathised with the outlaw, resented the brigand, or simply enjoyed tales of derring-do, even those settlers right in the heart of bushranger territory did not necessarily give bushrangers the same attention that historians and folklorists often do. Our land is big and individual bushrangers usually only ever ranged over a fraction of it.

In one sense bushrangers were simply yet another pest to authorities and settlers alike; in some ways they were treated like many Aborigines, particularly those in Tasmania: removed, then romanticised. A far bigger threat was looming over the farming communities of rural colonial Australia. What contemporaries were truly worried about in the later part of the nineteenth century were not men in armour, but little critters in fur.

Introduced into the Australian colonies by the European settlers, rabbits provided gentlemen and gentlewomen of leisure with a suitably traditional source of pleasure: hunting. But, perhaps beyond any reasonable expectation, they thrived, and, like the colonists, spread in waves throughout the land until they eventually reached plague proportions.

During the later 1860s and early 1870s rabbits were a regular focus of interest. Their skins had become an export commodity and their flesh provided food for a great many people, but their increase and spread proved to be a significant problem for agriculturalists and pastoralists. The advance of the problem was not quite explosive, but more like a rapid creeping, rather like two key new technologies of the age, the railway and the telegraph. Looking at town records across Australia, you can often see their newspapers nervously discussing where rabbits have been sighted in neighbouring areas, until eventually they are confirmed in the district.

By 1874, when Mary Ann was buried at Violet Town, both the railway and the telegraph connected it to Melbourne. The man who buried her was typical of this age of closer settlement, when a wave of farmers battled against rabbits and the elements to establish themselves on the land.

Eden was one of several children born to Eden White senior. According to the English census of 1841 this Eden senior was an agricultural labourer. Having grown up in a large family supported by a labourer, it is no wonder that Eden junior and his brother Richard seem to have decided to try their luck in Victoria. They may have seen it as the opportunity to turn around some of the family's recent misfortunes. As I worked back in time through the English records I found that Eden senior had been a farmer. Then, in 1830, he left his farm at Kingston in Oxfordshire for reasons unknown. These reasons, whatever they were, precipitated the decline in the family's wealth and social standing. It had been a large property of 99 acres, containing wheat, barley, beans, oats, peas, and some animal stock. Over a period of weeks the stock was auctioned, and even the still-growing crops were sold. The failure to complete the harvest pointed to real desperation. Things got bad enough that the household furniture was also sold.

So two of the White boys left their parents and travelled to the other side of the world. Like many of the people who immigrated to the Port Phillip District before it was even the colony of Victoria, Eden and Richard arrived as assisted immigrants. They were young men, eighteen and twenty respectively, who arrived at Port Phillip on the *Mahomed Schah* from Plymouth on 5 July 1848. They were described as farm labourers from Kingston in Oxfordshire, and while Richard could read, Eden was unable to either read or write.

I was confronted with Eden's illiteracy when I saw the resister of his marriage to Mary Ann Camm in 1851. The document is filled out by the registrar. But between his first and last name Eden gave an 'x' as his signature. The notary identified this as 'his mark'. Mary Ann also gave 'her mark', another 'x'. By the time he came to bury his wife in Violet Town, Eden may have learned to read, but he was still 'unable to write'. It is one of the major methodological problems of research into the farming communities of colonial Australia: history is written not so much by the victors, as the writing classes.

Wanting to share a sense of the place that Eden experienced, I decided to take the visual approach, and simply look at the district. So I visited Violet Town one year, on what had become an almost annual drive between Melbourne and Junee. Even before taking a specific interest in the place, I had often noticed the name and thought that I should stop and have a look. As I became interested in my family story, and worked out some of their details, I had made a point of visiting the districts with which I knew I had a family association, looking at landscape, buildings, and cemeteries. Violet Town was prominent on the list and convenient, being on my drive home for Christmas. So I decided to see if I could find the White headstones. Violet Town is a tiny place, so I did not think the stop would take too long.

If there was one word to perfectly capture that day in Violet Town, that word is 'hot'. It was far from the best weather or time of day for a cemetery expedition. But, regardless, I duly pulled off the highway about lunchtime. I was greeted by a sign that informed me that Violet Town was the 'Earliest Inland Surveyed Township'. In the mid 1830s a party of convict shepherds were driving sheep through another valley near the Violet Creek when they were attacked by a large group of Aborigines. Several of the convicts were butchered, and the rest fled. This came to be known as the 'Faithful massacre'. The colonial authorities responded with a military expedition that failed to find the attackers, but the incident did encourage a greater degree of militarism in the pastoral frontier, both official and unofficial. Violet Town was planned in 1838 as one of a number of outposts that would provide settlers with a string of protection running the length of a developing inland road between Sydney and the Port Phillip District Settlement.

The squatters who settled the region, many of whom had come up from Van Diemen's Land, then continued to wrest the land from its original inhabitants and fill it with sheep. Bad habits, I suspect, may have been learned during the pastoral settlement of Tasmania. Reporting to London about the Faithful massacre and his plans for a military outpost at Violet Town, Governor Gipps was outraged at a rumour he had also just heard that 'twenty two human beings, including several women and children' may have been killed by settlers in retribution on an entirely different group of Aborigines '500 miles' away. This, it turns out, was to be the Myall Creek massacre. Aborigines who had camped on a settler's station were killed by a group of visiting stockmen. The very public trials and eventual execution of offenders brought some of the frontier violence into a more public light.

Many stockmen had had good working relationships with local Aborigines, and continued to do so. But for others less enamoured or tolerant of the country's original inhabitants the twin massacres may have simply encouraged a greater silence on the poorly documented frontiers.

After the Faithful massacre, however, the 'Earliest Inland Surveyed Township' drifted into obscurity. The surveyed township was not really a success. It had been planned during a drought on what later turned out to be swampland, and the first military outpost was located elsewhere. Even the creek was renamed Honeysuckle Creek. The tiny village struggled to compete with some of its nearby neighbours for the Sydney–Melbourne road trade. Only when gold was discovered in the middle of the nineteenth century did a town really begin to develop, although in less swampy ground that was adjacent to the area first surveyed.

By the time the Whites were entering the district, the Indigenous people had suffered dramatic population decline and economic and cultural disruption. Many had adjusted to the new colonial reality, but the waves of immigrants and the desire for closer settling of the land had prompted the Victorian Parliament to take the colonial initiative in regulating its Aboriginal population with the 1869 *Aboriginal Protection Act*. This built on a growing tradition of colonial race-based administrative and 'protective' legislative models like that of the 1855 *Chinese Immigration Act*, which had attempted to restrict Chinese immigration and better control Chinese immigrants. Other colonies soon had their equivalents for their Aboriginal and Chinese inhabitants.

Race had become of increasing concern for a range of reasons including land hunger, old cultural prejudices, and fears about labour competition and attendant threats to standards of living. But it was the new cutting-edge scientific advances in the understandings of 'race', which helped usher in what can be thought of as Australia's racist century, where legislation affirmed what science seemed to maintain. This popularised offshoot of Darwin's theory of natural selection applied what is often termed 'social Darwinism' to people, focusing on notions of biological differences between peoples and racial competition. And with scientific affirmations of racial difference came strong notions of an objective and absolute racial hierarchy. This prompted increasing concerns about what was termed the 'half-caste' problem, because, ironically, it was thought to represent or threaten the supposed weakening of the higher races by the lower. It was nonsense, and bad science, but populist nonsense, and long-lived science.

So Victoria's *Aboriginal Protection Act*, ostensibly for the good of what was thought of as a 'dying race', ushered in an age of reserves, a new feature of the colonial Australian landscape. It provided for governmental administration of the minutiae of Aboriginal lives such as their place of residence, and allowed for the control of their income and for the 'care custody and education of the children'. But while in large part justified by theories of race, the notion of paternalistic custody and the core concepts, administrative structures, and mechanisms of the new laws and regulations clearly derived from the English Poor Laws, and this was broadly applied to other select segments of the population in not entirely dissimilar ways. The English Poor Laws were also, coincidentally, partly the originating source of the legal parameters of the convict transportation system. And while the transportation of convicts shared similar attributes with the treatment of Elizabethan-era vagabonds, so too many an Aboriginal reserve, when perceived as an administrative structure rather than a place, looks remarkably like an eighteenth- or nineteenth-century English workhouse. In each context persons could be effectively designated as wards, being thus effectively made into legal children, or otherwise placed under some form of custodial authority. Administrators had powers to limit movement, absorb wages, determine diet and daily routines, and make other such arrangements on the behalf of their inmates, convicts, and Aborigines. The settings changed, as did some of the particularities and justifications, but the fundamental concepts underpinning this treatment had been practised long before being deployed over the lives of Indigenous peoples.

Having pulled off the Melbourne to Sydney road, I drove down the main street of Violet Town. I noticed in particular an old wooden house, which was falling into a state of honourable dilapidation. I easily could imagine the old heady days in Violet Town when the gold rush came and settlement expanded. When the Whites first arrived in town, they may have smelled fresh paint and seen some of these houses being built. As part of the wave of selectors who came to settle as farmers on what had previously been large squatter runs, they saw the long-planned town finally grow into life.

The village was even smaller than I had expected. I followed the signs and drove out of town to the cemetery. I parked the car under a tree, got out, and commenced looking. It was forty-two degrees, and there I was in the middle of the day wandering around a tiny little graveyard, with nothing to shade either me or the headstones. No wonder so many of the inscriptions on the graves were badly faded, I thought. Beside the site ran the Hume

Highway. The pre-Christmas traffic zipping north and south provided a distinctly modern humming and swishing soundtrack to my expedition to find a nineteenth-century ancestor. There was a thin strip of scrub shielding the dead from the traffic.

As I walked up and down the rows, there were Whites everywhere, but no Eden or Mary Ann. I amused myself by noting that Violet Town cemetery was very colour-conscious. As well as Whites, there were some Browns, and several of the women were named Violet. There was even a slightly chipped violet-painted park bench. I noticed that it was fairly dusty—clearly no one had sat there recently. Being a curious fellow I could not help but read some of the inscriptions, even after I had determined I was looking at the wrong one. One of these gravestones, a simple cross, was inscribed 'Our Dear Little Violet, Died 29th July 1890, Aged 3 Years. "The Lamb is in the fold."' More than a century later it was touching to see some faded plastic flowers, and a faded blue plastic toy turtle, sitting atop where she lay.

But Eden and Mary Ann were not so fortunate to be remembered at Violet Town. It was quickly apparent that Eden had buried his wife and some of his children here, but if he was in this cemetery, no one had erected a headstone for him in turn. Sometimes people buried all of their children, leaving no family to return the favour. And frequently people could be buried before their children even learned of their death if those children lived at a distance. Eden's was most likely one of the unnamed grave markers, or perhaps even just a patch of otherwise innocuous grass or dirt. The whole experience left me with that sense I sometimes get of just how harsh the Australian landscape can be, and how difficult life must have been for previous generations. Thinking about life in the old days I got in the car, turned the air conditioning up, and continued north and east towards nearby Boho, where the Whites had settled.

Boho is now a locality. Like most of these, it is a name that attaches to an area, generally marked by a church, a schoolhouse, or in the case of Boho, by an intersection. Having failed to find Eden or Mary Ann in the Violet Town cemetery, I decided to have a look at Boho, which is only a few kilometres to the east. I knew that the White's selection was in that area, in its heyday almost a little village community, but now it is just a road running through an area with a name.

So from Violet Town I drove under the grey cement highway underpass and headed east, taking the road that would loop through Boho and back to the highway. I did not expect to see much, but thought the little detour would give me a better sense of the land my ancestors worked. Driving along in air-conditioned comfort I thought about how the change in the Whites' circumstances and lives reflects a major change in the Australian farming landscape: the expansion of small selections into what had previously been a squatter colonial frontier. That smallholder past is still inscribed on the land by little roads, localities, old schools, and isolated churches.

Commencing my drive into Boho, I crested a hill and saw a picture-postcard little agricultural valley, with blue hills in the distance. It is a beautifully picturesque landscape. Although I was visiting in the heat and haze of the middle of a summer day, I could still see how in the softer morning or evening light this could be the perfect setting for a painting by Eugene von Guerard or Nicholas Chevalier. In fact both of these artists travelled in Victoria in the same period as the Whites.

I was surprised at how recognisable it was. It reminded me of the area around Jugiong in New South Wales, another little valley in a rural border-zone between hills and plains, just inside the hilly bit. And as I learned more about the Whites at Boho I saw more connected themes and experiences between the two places. One of my favourite histories of rural Australia is Michael McKernan's *The Valley*, which charts a similarly small settlement with a distinctly Australian history. I could see how the Whites' story charts a kind of rough history of Australian settlement: arrive with little, work hard, settle on land. It could be an American story, or a Canadian one, or Argentinean. They were hardy people of the earth, whose stories I was piecing together with the limited details provided on certificates and the like.

The death of Mary Ann in 1874 must have been devastating for the family, but records of the event leave little trace of their grief. The following year she had a granddaughter named after her. In this tough and lonely landscape life had to go on. Eden even remarried within a few years.

More information becomes available about Eden as he aged, in part because of his particular prominence in one of the most significant struggles of his age: the war against the rabbit. Bushrangers threatened individual farms or small communities, but rabbits nearly spelled the end of many settler farming communities.

'We have been informed by Mr. Eden White of Boho', the *Euroa Advertiser* reported, 'that he trapped 265 rabbits in January last, and this month 200 besides having killed about 400 including young ones.' By February 1885 a plague was upon the gardens of Eden.

Looking over the pages of the *Euroa Advertiser* revealed a massive conflict that would come to engulf most of the continent. There was not a wealth of specific detail, and little newspaper notes reduced day-long battles to a sentence. To trap 265 rabbits must have involved some sort of arithmetic of conflict: x traps times y rabbits per day. On average, Eden White scored 8½ rabbits each day of January. I worked out that 14½ *baby* rabbits were killed on average every day in February, on top of the 200 fully grown ones. However calculated, this conveys a real sense of the problem the farmers faced, because this was just one property. The land that I had thought Guerard and Chevalier should have painted was actually pockmarked with fresh burrows. These holes threatened the skeletal integrity of any horses, people, or stock animals whose legs may have slipped into them.

Pests swarmed the ground, eating down to the dirt. No wonder the farmers hunted them so fiercely and mercilessly.

By January 1886 there was 'a large heap of scalps' in the Violet Town hall that were 'under the stimulating influence of the warm weather'. The smell must have been of an incredible foulness. Among that pile were '44 dozen scalps' from the day before the report, 'most of them being from Mr Eden White's Boho.' That was another 528 dead Boho rabbits. The following year, many of the residents of the Violet Town district enjoyed their Easter holidays shooting 'the Boho rabbits' in little 'parties'. Many of the estimated 1000 rabbits reportedly 'bit the dust' on the White property.

The 'fusillade on the hills' of Easter 1887 did not stop the plague. But they did provide little sideline businesses for some people, and it is possible that Eden White also profited from this. The government paid a bounty on scalps, which was a way of helping reduce the problem for the farmers. It provided a financial incentive for entrepreneurial trappers and shooters. But this conflicted with another business, which was to sell the rabbits on for meat to the Melbourne market. If scalps had to be turned in, the meat would not keep quite so well. Because of the scale of his Boho rabbit problem, Eden was appointed to count the rabbits as a way of placating both interests. Between June and November 1887, a trapping party on his property recorded the taking of 6500 rabbits. Boho, it seems, may have been feeding Melbourne: not sheep and cows, but rabbits.

From 1890 the introduction of wire netting helped to bring the problem under some semblance of control, and Eden's agricultural prosperity improved. He had 'famous potato patches', the harvest of which was eagerly awaited in 1893. In the same year he celebrated ten pounds of wool from the first of his sheep that was shorn, and had a noteworthy 100 per cent success rate with lambing. He even introduced the use of lucerne into the district as a feed for sheep, with excellent results.

The other part of the rabbit solution, however, brought its own problems. Phosphorised pollard baiting involved mixing unstable chemicals and fuel, with resultant fires. Little baits surrounded by poisoned rabbits were combustible timebombs, occasionally going off and setting parts of the country on fire. From a later perspective it is a bit Monty Pythonesque: the rabbits' last revenge.

I am unsure whether it was a rabbit-corpse related one, but the White farm was threatened by a significant bushfire in February 1898. As with rabbits, bushfires became a bigger problem simply because there was a greater population to be affected, and the lack of Aboriginal firing traditions may have been a contributing factor as fuel built up over the years. That summer was a particularly bad one for the Victorian rural community, with fires raging across much of the colony. It was an old fire that had destroyed several paddocks a month earlier, and continued to smoulder away in the forested hills nearby before dramatically flaring up again. A change of wind turned the fire back towards the settled Boho area, and even threatened Violet Town. It was reported that at one point 'Eden White's property was in peril, but 27 workers, by united effort, drove the fire back'. That little sentence, like so many others in this story, hints at a much deeper reality. Thousands of words are spent on bushrangers, but these sixteen words much better capture the essence of some of Australia's gravest colonial battles to defend hard-won homes.

Despite all of his trials, Eden White did seem to enjoy some prosperity. The Whites had lost their farm in Oxford, and Eden arrived in the colony as a labourer, and then once again the Whites were a propertied farming family. A longer generational look at the migration experience gives it that greater level of nuance. What I rather suspect had been his original dream appears to have come true, not just to improve his chances, but to restore some of the family's dignity.

In 1894 a travelling journalist passed through the area and visited Eden, leaving a description of the man and the farm. In a 'hearty fashion', and probably still with his Oxfordshire accent, Eden told the visitor that 'There's nothing to see, it's only a small garden to grow a bit of fruit for my own use'. The visitor noticed two large walnut trees, which apparently earned Eden a little extra income from selling the nuts. Unfortunately, this journalist was most interested in digressing and informing his readers about the various sources and quality of food products, and only gave the barest description of Eden's property. Eden explained to his visitor the many benefits of his new 'Planet Jr. cultivator'. It was a horse-drawn contraption that helped him weed, sow, and plough his potato patch.

But at least it seems that the visitor had some sense of humour. He described the various apples in Eden's garden: Stone Pip, Emperor Alexander, and Lord Nelson. But he did not mention any snakes, so he missed an opportunity there. However, he did provide a reasonable impression of Eden's home. 'There are also', he noted, 'quinces, lemons, and oranges.' A vine apparently climbed one wall of the house, weighed down with grapes. It was a garden that had been lived in for many years, a place where picnics were held and family gatherings took place. Fresh produce was eaten, the fruit of both land and toil. As I drove through the Boho district I noticed a couple of orchards and wondered if it were possible that the cuttings for them had come from the old Oxford-born farmer.

Sadly, within a few years of the journalist's visit the old man who had battled the rabbits and worked the earth was showing signs of serious illness. For three years doctors attended him as he wasted away from stomach cancer. When he died, the funeral 'was very largely attended'. It was a sad end to an early battler's story, but I was glad to know he had been carefully buried in the soil of his new home, even if I had not been able to locate him precisely. Three generations of my family had lived at Violet Town, and until I investigated the Whites I had never known the connection.

A few years after that visit, I also went to the Wantabadgery cemetery to look for Susan Miles's grave. It proved another hot day as I made my way to the tiny country cemetery that nestled on the slope of a hill. And there, once again, it turned out to have been another unmarked burial. But this experience of looking for family in the landscape proved very instructive of wider processes, and highlighted the proximity of the simple farming people to the issues of the day that have attracted considerable historical attention. Understandably, both bushranging and the advent of legislative polices that ultimately led to a policy of 'White Australia' are of interest to folklorists and historians. But what interested the Whites, and the Miles, and the other settler families of colonial Australia were the more immediate issues of housing, income, food security, and family. Everything else was of secondary interest. Yet precisely because of the capacity of industrial developments to impact on those core issues, settlers in this period followed technological advances with particular interest. Whether it was on the basis of something as simple as improved ploughing tools, or because of the arcane complexity of steam-powered engines, few settlers would have doubted that they lived in an age of great technological progress that was getting underway right before their eyes.

CHAPTER NINE

THE INDUSTRIAL EVOLUTION OF QUEENSLAND 1874

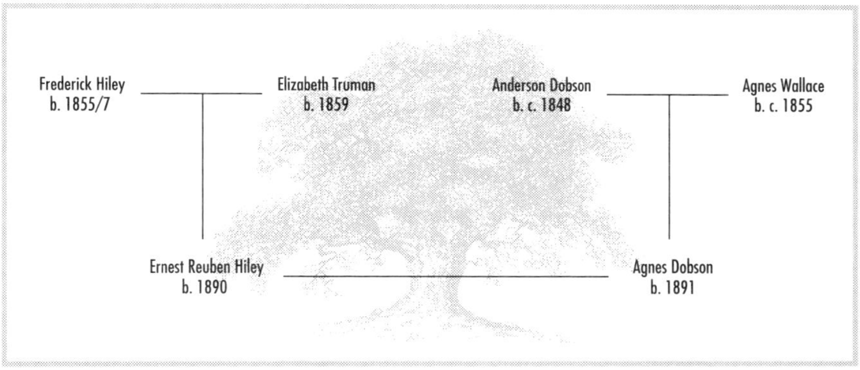

PETTIGREW'S MILL, on the bank of the Brisbane River, would have been a noisy place to work, even for a clerk. Fred Hiley got his first job in the Australian colonies at that business, probably through the assistance of his older brother Percival, who worked there as a mill engineer. At Pettigrew's sawmill the increasing dominance of machinery in the colonial economy was on noisy display. One reporter visiting the site was surprised at the proliferation of 'labor-saving contrivances'. There were large wooden sheds filled with noisy furnaces and big boilers. These powered a complex array of chugging wheels and pistons, which ran circular saws, bandsaws, and a range of other machines. These sheds were the natural colonial extension of the cotton mills of Yorkshire, from whence the Hiley brothers came. Queensland, like other colonies, was industrialising, and the Hileys were helping it to do so.

And one feature of Australia's Industrial Revolution is that it closely complemented the processes of closer settlement. While other industrialising places certainly saw a rebalancing of settlements, previously marginal or unused land being modified, and frontiers of occupation and industry advancing, in Australia this was on a continental scale. The old forests were being cut in the distance and brought to Pettrigrew's Mill as large 'rafts' of logs pushed and pulled into position by two dedicated steam-powered tugs on the Brisbane River. A giant steam-powered crane was on site to do the heavy lifting, and there were localised rail tracks for manoeuvres between the wharf and the mills. The logs were sawn, trimmed, and shipped from this industrial complex, or carted to build the suburbs of the growing town. It even had its own blacksmith on site to maintain the machinery, so the Hileys would have been kept busy.

And although the business had started as a timber mill, the steam engine's power had also been tapped to mill grain and corn, providing a whole other side of the business for Fred's account ledgers to keep track of. As with the wood, the corn and grains grown in the treeless fields could be brought to the same factory, ground, bagged, sold, and shipped. This was the noisy centre of the colonial enterprise.

Fred and his brothers grew to young manhood in Industrial Britain. Daniel, their father, was a loom engineer. Looking into their pre-Australian past, I soon found the family in the English census records. And, as so often happens with this sort of research, I quickly got carried away tracing each generation back in time. Daniel's father, Thomas, was a 'carpet weaver', and Thomas's father, William, was in turn also a 'weaver'. This continuity of occupation struck me as a strong family tradition, surviving for multiple generations. Unfortunately, I lost the Hiley trail, and had little luck with the maiden lines either, until I found that William's wife, Nancy Skelton, was traceable. She was the daughter of John Skelton and Abigail Greenwood, born in Sowerby, Yorkshire in 1727. With relative ease I was able to go back one more generation to discover that Abigail was the daughter of John Greenwood, taking this part of my family back into the seventeenth century. Something about that name, Greenwood, really resonates with me. But this exercise in curiosity, undertaken by following the paths of the family back to the murky Greenwoods, also revealed the story of England in a shorthand way. And it also helped to explain this family's eventual move to Australia.

I do not know what John Greenwood did, but his daughter married a mason. Their daughter, Nancy, married a weaver. They sired a carpet weaver, who in turn produced a man whose job was described as 'mechanic'. My line had come from the woods to the Industrial Revolution in a few short generations—from the potentially medieval to the inescapably modern.

The records of baptisms and marriages place the family at Sowerby and Warley, small villages just outside of Halifax in West Yorkshire, for a few generations. Even Daniel was born in Warley in 1814. Both villages were within walking distance of each other. It all felt so very 'Ye Old England' somehow, even if I was only looking at lists of places, names, and occupations. But then sometime in the early nineteenth century Thomas Hiley moved his family to Northowram, another village on the Bradford side of Halifax, showing the growing urban pull and the rapid pace of industrialisation.

The 'Industrial Revolution' as an historical 'thing' has lost a little favour over recent generations of scholarship. The term implies perhaps too much of a sudden technological shift and does not have a commonly accepted definition: by 'Industrial Revolution' some people mean a period, others processes like factories, and others technological advances such as steam trains. And even as a vague sort of label, the 'Industrial Revolution' tends to downplay the steady developments of processes and technologies over what were often long periods of time. It neglects the subtle interplay between technological and social shifts, and can mask important social, cultural, and technological continuities. It also frequently affirms a sort of lone-genius model of historical advancement. All in all, it struggles to be applicable to a definable time and place, as chronologies and sequences of industrialisation vary regionally across the globe. But after Daniel married in Northowram and took his bride Sarah and growing family to Bradford, they lived in the suburb of Manningham, and there can be little doubt that this was a highly industrialising age. No wonder he was a mechanic.

The family was large, and did well to survive the cholera. Daniel and Sarah had ten children living with them in 1861, split evenly into five sons and five daughters. Having traced the family line back some way, I could see the persistence of family names like Sarah, Thomas, Mary, William, and Nancy. Four stood out as not having an immediately obvious source: nineteen-year-old Henry, and the youngest three, Jane, Fred, and Hannah. Perhaps these were named for other lateral relatives I have failed to track.

But the family's connection with the mill was immediately obvious by their occupations. Three of Daniel's sons were also mechanics, Sarah junior was a 'cotton winder', and the other women were each listed as 'factory worker'. Even the ten-year-old Jane worked in the worsted factory. At that time Fred was a four-year-old 'Scholar' like his older brother Henry, but by 1871 he too was a mechanic. The later census gives slightly more detail. Three of the children had left, but those that remained were all working: 'Drawer Worsted Mill', 'Weaver Worsted', 'Mechanic Fitter', and young Jane had progressed to being a 'Comb Setter'.

The fact that they were working in a machine-powered mill is neatly illustrated by the fact that Daniel, with his son Percival (a delightfully Arthurian name, I cannot help but think) and two 'iron manufacturers', applied for patent protection in 1857 for inventions that improved 'power looms for weaving worsted, cotton, silk, woollen, and other fibrous substances'. These men were not simply experiencing the Industrial Revolution; they were tinkering with the machines, and pushing it onwards.

What precisely prompted a number of Hiley boys to migrate to the Morton Bay settlement is uncertain. But I like to think they may have watched their grandfather Thomas, the carpet weaver, and thought their odds for improving their situations were better in Queensland. Grandfather Hiley's household in 1841 was large, quite diminished in 1861, and by 1871 the seventy-one-year-old widower was living by himself. He was still a 'carpet weaver'. His short census-derived story has a slight echo of George Eliot's *Silas Marner* about it. And perhaps Grandfather Hiley's children, nieces and nephews, and all their descendents, read their futures in England in his lonely and tired old weaver's hands.

Eventually one of them decided to go, perhaps thinking that the colonies provided more mechanical opportunities, and this triggered what amounted to a gradual familial migration for the generation of Daniel's children. First went Percival and his wife Abigail on the *Sultana* in 1862. The engineer must have done well enough to send good reports. William emigrated next, a saloon passenger in the *Royal Dane* in 1871, suggesting that this line of the Bradford Hileys had similarly achieved modest success. Then Fred went, arriving in Brisbane on the *Indus* in October 1873—he was a remittance passenger, so one of his family members in Queensland had already paid for his voyage, which shows once again that there must have been a great deal of corresponding between migrating families. And, in this case, a multi-decade immigration was orchestrated. I like to wonder what the now lost letters said. How would Percival articulate the differences of geography, climate, and culture between Brisbane and Bradford? I wondered how much agency the sixteen-year-old Fred had over his move. I suspect it was a lifeline of sorts, because his migration seems to have been precipitated by the death of his father the year before.

Eventually, others would also follow. Nancy Hiley was another remittance passenger, coming in the *Clara* in 1879. Daniel came by the *Carnatic* in 1881, and Thomas by the *Merkara* in 1883. After generations living in the same part of West Yorkshire, a large chunk of the family made the dramatic shift to Queensland.

So although working on the books and paperwork as befitting the 'scholar' of the family, Fred was following his brothers into the mechanised world of 1870s Queensland, and bringing the experience of Yorkshire to bear on the colony. Percival illustrated this particular family's expertise, when he drove the first 'Road Steamer' through Brisbane on 5 April 1870. Going to see the steamer's various trials was quite an event, one loaded with obvious symbolism. When Percival drove the aptly named *Pioneer* past 'a large number of spectators', then past the Parliament building and the hopefully suitably awed parliamentarians, it was pulling three wagons filled with stone, weighing some 21 tons. Although visibly struggling at times, it managed to pull off most of the manoeuvres impressively. This mechanised beast of burden was a very large and lumbering sign of the times, which Elizabeth Truman may have seen chug slowly by, if she had come in to the town from Kangaroo Point. For old colonists like the Trumans the sight may have been amazing, but for the mechanically minded ex-factory men, such mechanised power was obviously the way of the future, and they helped bring the new technology of the old world to the new.

Percival would have been pleased that the 'steering apparatus appeared to work much more satisfactorily than previously'. But he may also have been frustrated when the *Pioneer* got bogged, although quite appropriately for a symbol of progress, it did so in the parliamentary grounds. Crossing Alice Street, 'the wheels of the waggons sunk considerably into the soft earth, and, in consequence of one of the bolts between the cylinder and boiler giving way, the load had to be abandoned, and the "steamer" returned to the wharf'.

That visible proof of automated progress was, however, in tension with another feature of Queensland's colonial growth. Looking at this early part of Fred's career I found an advertisement in the paper from his brother Percival which references another colonial phenomenon. In the same year that he drove the giant mechanical steam-beast, he was asking for 'Farm Laborers' for 'Mrs. Dawson's Sugar Plantation'. Pettigrew's sawmill was the designated information point, and Percival the contact person.

When Queensland separated from New South Wales and became a colony in its own right in 1859, as if on cue some historical trends of the early 1860s aligned with the colony's new optimistic vision for a prosperous future. To start with there were concerted efforts to rapidly expand the settlement and to develop the whole of Queensland. This was still a frontier society. And one of the major endeavours was the establishment of sugar plantations, a crop deemed suitable in the climate, and desirable as a product to export to the swelling cities and increasingly sweet palates of the colonies and Europe. The supposed interruption to Europe's sugar supply, courtesy of the American Civil War of the early to mid 1860s, provided Pacific Ocean agriculturalists with an opportunity to muscle in on global markets. At that point some settlers had only relatively recently lost the cheap convict labour to which they had become accustomed, however, and so to compete with the cheap slave-sugar of the Americas, and to move into slavery-free sugar markets, they had turned to indentured labour.

An 'indenture' was a fixed term contract with fixed wages, and in some other contexts it has not entirely unfairly been termed 'white slavery'. But in Queensland, concerns about the inability of 'white' labourers to work effectively in the tropics, as well as the proximity of plentiful cheap 'coloured' labour, drove many plantations to seek indentured labour in the Pacific region. Over the next half-century, many thousands of Pacific Islanders would go to work in the farms of Queensland, many voluntarily, but many also 'blackbirded'—kidnapped—and put into waged service. Many Chinese labourers were also brought to Australian colonies at this time for similar reasons, and to work in similar situations, eventually prompting legislative attempts to restrict 'foreign' immigration by the organised ('white') labour movements. In ways that had not been so clear before, race became politicised, with the coincidental blessing of a new scientific consensus.

It was through the physical ornamentation of the building containing the politicians, however, that the Hileys left a particular demonstration of the new industrial age that is still recognisable in the urban landscapes of many

Australian towns and cities: wrought iron decoration. Later in the decade one of the Hiley brothers was part-owner of a company that manufactured architectural ironwork, and a notable output included the iron railing for Queensland's Parliamentary Buildings. It was a contract that perhaps owed something to the displays of the *Pioneer* in the early 1870s.

Another Hiley ironwork product of note was the 'cast iron balustrading' which was used in the completion of Brisbane's Albert Street Wesleyan Church. The Hiley brothers were prominent members of the local Methodist Church, so this was more than just a business opportunity.

The religiosity of the early colonies turned up occasionally in my research for various ancestors. Although not from this line, my Catholicism was certainly passed down in a way that can be fairly easily traced backwards through the family tree, just as other sects can be for other branches of the tree. For the Hileys, Methodism was very important. During my trawling for information, I turned up a recorded interview conducted with Sir Thomas Alfred Hiley in 1974, a Queensland politician and cousin, which spoke particularly of the religion of his father's generation. On first spotting the interview I was intrigued, so I clicked on the link through the National Library of Australia and listened to the voice of a distant relative speak of his childhood in Queensland. He was the son of William Hiley, another of Fred's older brothers, and, in a deep, patriarchal register, he characterised his youth as 'not days of ease and comfort'. He spoke, for example, of their lack of hot meals on Sundays because it was the Sabbath.

The Hileys being Methodists probably explains in part how Fred Hiley met young Elizabeth Truman, because the Trumans were also active Methodists. The Truman family story was relatively little documented after those early years, but it was clear they stayed in the same area. I could find John Truman advertising to let out a house, and also threatening prosecution against anyone who detained his milking cows. On establishing himself as a grocer, he passed from the pages of the newspapers, except for the time when a cottage he owned was burned down, or when his young son was struck by lightning during a particularly fierce storm. To the amazement of many, the boy survived, despite being temporarily zapped unconscious.

And Elizabeth's fleeting comments about the past provided me with some of those little views of lived history. In 1924 the Brisbane Centenary Celebration Committee quizzed her for her recollections. 'It needs no picture theatre', she recalled, 'to give a transformation scene of our progressive town of Brisbane.' She mainly commented on floods and bridges. A passing mention that she was among a group of children to meet the Duke of Edinburgh in 1868 alerted me to the possibility of getting a sense of one particular, if unusual, day in her childhood.

The sound of cannon fire around dawn warned the Trumans to be ready. They knew what it meant, because they had been practising for days, as part of preparations the townsfolk had been making for weeks. The Duke had arrived.

Getting dressed, they hurried to town, as did everyone. The Prince made footfall in Queensland shortly after 10 am on Tuesday 25 February 1868. Among the large crowds gathered in the streets of Brisbane were several of my ancestors. An hour later a procession commenced, and Elizabeth was among a group of 'little smiling faces' strategically placed near the Royal Hotel on Queen Street. She was among a few thousand of them who 'sang the National Anthem in a very pleasing, and indeed affecting manner'—or so the paper said. And reading this reveals the symbolism of empire in a particularly blunt form. Here was my first Queensland-born ancestor, singing 'God Save the Queen', on Queen Street, in Queensland.

Such anomalies aside, it was the regular routines of work and church that structured their lives, and probably helped bring about some of their more important, but undocumented, personal moments, like the meeting of Fred and Elizabeth, and their eventual marriage.

But that is not to say there was no romance. To my amusement, I noticed two passengers on the *Culgoa*, a regular coastal service ship, travelling together from Noosa to Brisbane in October 1876. Named right before 'Mr. F. Hiley' was 'Miss Trueman'. Assuming Miss Truman to be Elizabeth—I hesitate to think it was a sister—it was a flitting pre-marital documentary record that linked them in a tantalising way. Usually, I could only track the meeting of ancestors by the rather imprecise and formal means of their marriage certificate. Although I suspect this pair already knew each other from church circles, I could imagine the exchange of pleasantries if they encountered each other on the boat. And perhaps they were able to gain a better sense of each other than normally occurred in the very public chit-chat of post-churchgoing meetings. Even if it were Elizabeth's sister, it may have created just the right avenue for Fred's introduction.

If it was a secret rendezvous, it involved a two week wait, so it was quite probably simply a pleasant coincidence. This Miss Truman had travelled to Noosa from Brisbane a month earlier, whereas Fred had only travelled there two weeks previously. By then, he had left Pettigrew's sawmill and become a travelling salesman. He had rather had to, in fact.

Being a good Methodist, Fred was probably at church when a fire started on a Sunday in November 1874. A spark from one of the boilers had landed in some corn husks and started to smoulder. It happened regularly, so nobody was particularly worried. Even Mr Pettigrew himself saw it and still went to church. Provided it did not spread it was not a threat, and smouldering detritus was not uncommon. But it did increase in size and intensity, and quickly too. Shortly after midday, one of the workmen noticed that some of the wood had started to smoulder. He grabbed a bucket of water, but failed to prevent the fire spreading. He ran to get help.

In his absence, with 'a good stiff breeze' blowing, burning chips and curls of milled timber floated on the developing convection currents into the air. Drifting upwards and outwards from the growing fire, some of these stray chips encountered various other fuels in the highly combustible environment. Dried timbers, the oils of pine and gum, and the ubiquitous sawdust all contributed to the conflagration. The poor workman 'returned only to find the place hopelessly ignited'. Within fifteen minutes the whole building was a roaring 'sheet of flame', and a tower of fire crackled 'hundreds of feet into the sky'. The churchgoers were unlikely to have missed it as the service finished.

Fire brigades mobilised to save the adjacent buildings and to try and contain the fire as best they could. With a mighty effort, they managed to stop the spread by strategically deploying hoses and water pumps, but they could do nothing for the building. Undoubtedly it drew a crowd of spectators, and Fred may have been watching as the force that powered the mechanical revolution devoured the machinery and the buildings that harnessed it. He probably would have given a thought to the accounts that he kept.

So with his place of work a smouldering ruin, Fred looked for another job. He gained employment as a 'Salesman in the employ of Messrs Butler Bros.' and was to remain a member of that company for the remainder of the nineteenth century, steadily working his way up to the position of general manager. This was a saddler and farm-supply business which serviced the pastoral and agricultural districts, a pointed reminder that the colonial expansion was driven by animals, particularly horses, as much as by humans and machines. The position saw him engaged in a great deal of travel throughout Queensland, of which only a tiny fraction is discernible in the documentary record. It was later said that he 'had travelled all over the State'.

Only when the travel was by boat was there any realistic chance of my being able to find a record. There are references to him on the regular service between Brisbane and Noosa on the *Culgoa* in the mid 1870s, for instance, and he can be tracked to Townsville two decades later. His documented travels map some of his business interests, if not his particular activities. It was this frequent movement that placed Fred and a Miss Truman on a voyage together two years before Fred Hiley and Elizabeth Truman married and settled in Kangaroo Point.

Between Fred's sales travels and Elizabeth's domestic life, they left little record of their activities. In 1884 Fred was a founding member of the Commercial Travellers' Association of Queensland, and in 1890 he was president of the organisation. Fred clearly never forgot his roots. He became a member of the Yorkshire Society, and Elizabeth joined this organisation as well.

Elizabeth played a prominent role in the Methodist Church in Brisbane, undertaking activities like hosting a fundraising bazaar and various tea parties. Although she travelled, and can be found doing so on shipping lists, her life was mostly lived on the immediate country of her birth in the environs of Kangaroo Point.

Fred's respectable position saw him enrolled as a juror in a number of prominent cases in Brisbane in the 1880s and 1890s. In one of these, a man named McNeil was charged with having shot a Pacific Island boy named Taraharpa while on a recruiting mission in mid 1884. The jury found the defendant guilty, and he was sentenced to death. It was yet another indicator of the very close connection that the development of Queensland had with the Pacific region and its people. Whereas the Trumans had witnessed some of the impacts the land frontier had had upon Aboriginal people, the Hileys—whose documented lives related to the period a few decades later—were encountering Australia's Pacific frontier. Almost as if to further drive home the shift, when looking for evidence of the Trumans' first arrival in the 1850s, I found a later copy of the ship's passenger list that was written on a printed form dating from a much later time. This document, before being used to copy an old shipping register from the 1850s, was intended to regulate shipping arrivals according to the 'Pacific Island Labourers Acts of 1880–1892', as the printed title and specialised columns made clear.

It is bizarre to think that some of the first evidence of my family's intersection with some of the sentiments and legislative structures that formed the 'White Australia Policy' was by having their names inscribed on a documentary relic of that regrettable development.

As if to underscore the delicate economic situation for labourers in the later nineteenth century—who were subject to the changes in supply and demand for labour and therefore often particularly interested in questions of 'foreign' labour—I had great difficulty tracking my other Queensland connection, the Dobson family. Labourers and their families tended to be ephemeral in the contemporary documentary record, captured only by major life moments—immigration, criminal trials, births, deaths, marriages, and so on—and without some extraordinary activities, fortuitous record-keeping, or later reminiscences their entire lives can pass by leaving only the barest of historical traces. Grandma's mother, who married Fred and Elizabeth's son Ernest, was Agnes Dobson, the daughter of Anderson and Agnes Dobson, who migrated to Queensland in 1879 on the *Clara*, with their son, also named Anderson. Unfortunately, Grandma was not really able to tell me a lot about her mother's people. Nor, really, did the documentary record offer a great deal more.

The *Clara* came from Glasgow, bringing with it a remarkable quantity of beer. It also brought bricks, clay, and lots of iron products, not to mention some typically Scottish items: herrings and whisky. The material development of Australia was being supplied from the workshops of Industrial Britain as well as the colonial ones, and the taste for a touch of 'home' was being met with ship holds filled with Britain's export goods. The British immigrants who were struggling to adapt to their new colonial reality were also, in so far as money and opportunity allowed, well connected materially and gastronomically to their birthplace.

They also brought their accents with them. Fred Hiley no doubt had a rich Yorkshireman's burr. So too would the Dobsons have brought their aural particularities across the oceans. Agnes was born in Liverpool, her maiden surname Wallace hinting at a Scottish past. Anderson was Irish-born, from County Donegal. His father lived in Letterkenny in 1833, as revealed through the tithe books. The great taxation survey of 1847–1864 gives more information, but a sadder story. An Anderson Dobson was listed as a lessee in Letterkenny, renting a property from Viscount Southwell. Under the heading 'Description of Tenement' is simply written 'Ruins'. All the valuations were dashed as nothing. In 1866 Anderson Dobson senior died, perhaps prompting his son's emigration first to England, and then to Queensland. In Liverpool Anderson worked as a cattle dealer, as indicated on the baptism record for his son. This trade may have explained the couple's decision to try their luck in Queensland.

When the *Clara* arrived in Australia it was unable to unload. There were two children with fevers on board when it anchored in Moreton Bay on the last day of 1878, so, by law, it faced the prospect of quarantine. While the ship awaited instructions from the health officer, one of the children died. The captain was furious, frustrated by a wait of 'four days' for instructions from the government department. The ship was then placed under quarantine. For twenty days the passengers and crew were kept waiting before a government health officer boarded the ship. He was not satisfied, and dithered for a few days over the health of one of the crew.

Enraged, the captain somehow managed to get a letter to the press. Fred and Elizabeth Hiley may have read the public letter, and perhaps discussed the plight of the ship. It must have been a tense time for those on board. After weeks at sea, anticipating landfall, they were stuck, unable to move, in clear sight of land. Fortunately, three days after the letter was published the *Clara* docked, and the Dobsons could walk on their new homeland.

The fear of disease was genuinely held, not only by the government, but also by the community at large. Swelling colonial towns were just as threatened by epidemic disease as were the cities of Britain, and the densely populated urban environments were precariously close to the major arrival ports. Fortunately for Australia, though, its island nature brought possibilities for controlled immigration, and therefore controlled quarantine, that many other governments could only dream of. But for labouring immigrants like the Dobsons, seemingly fleeing difficult circumstances in the search for a better future, the government's measures must have seemed unnecessarily harsh and uncaring. As the crew and passengers watched the burial of a little child at Mud Island in the middle of Moreton Bay, with the safety and prospects of the settlement so close, hope and bitterness may have taunted them. It could easily have seemed like the colony did not want them.

When young Agnes was born in 1891 she was the Dobson's eighth child, and that pretty well marks a large proportion of what can be known about the family. Relatively poor, white, and working class, they drifted inland at some time and settled at Toowoomba, where Agnes was born. What they did and how they lived can only really be guessed at based on the common experiences of people in their class and position. Anderson may have worked in the developing pastoral industry, or as a field labourer in the agricultural sector. Either way he worked beyond the scope of easily discovered documentation. In the early 1900s Anderson, or his son of the same name, worked as a farmhand. In 1906 Agnes senior was a nurse in Toowoomba, a fact only revealed because she was called to give evidence in a trial against a woman accused of killing her own child. According to census records the Dobsons were living apart, quite possibly because of the nature of Anderson's work, but Grandma also intimated to me at one point that Anderson may have been a drinker. The story of this side of the family was one of documentary obscurity, and it makes clear the problems in making sweeping generalisations about past peoples and attitudes based on supposition rather than direct evidence.

The year of young Agnes's birth marked a remarkable yet little-known episode in Australia's history, where, following widespread persecution in Russia, there was some talk in London of a settlement for Jews in the Australian colonies funded by the wealthy philanthropist Baron de Hirsch. Although not terribly advanced, the plans, once public, were excoriated in the Australian press, and the various colonial governments wrote to London to express their disapproval. In all probability the newspaper storm was over before the Dobsons heard of it, but the conditions for labourers in the Australian colonies in the 1890s were not fantastic, so they may have shared in a general sentiment of self-protection and distrust of outsiders. With the colonies gripped by serious depression, unemployment and underemployment were all too-common experiences, and such conditions bred attitudes of hostility, which were played upon by those with political and pecuniary agendas. As the colonies headed towards federation, there was an increasing and ugly focus on racial purity, which had built up as a common motif of public commentary over the previous few decades. Part of this was a product of that new scientific view of the world, with a hierarchy of biologically defined 'races'. But partly it was also simple economic fear. The idea was to ensure the preservation of opportunities for 'white labour' by excluding the competition that came with 'coloured labour'. Whether Anderson shared this opinion I may never know. I certainly would not ascribe to him attitudes common to his period without cause, any more than I would like future historians to believe my views necessarily corresponded with those common to my time.

But the idea that competing labour would be brought in to undermine workers' wages and bargaining potential was not entirely unfounded, even if the reaction to the de Hirsch rumours seem excessive. Early 1891 had been a divisive moment for the colonies generally, Queensland specifically, and organised labour movements even more particularly. Coordinated strikes by unionised wharfies in Queensland, in solidarity with and on the behalf of unionised shearers, highlighted the asymmetrical balance of power between workers and their employers. There were riots and scuffles, marches under the 'Eureka' flag, and heavy-handed responses. But there was also the creation of a more organised electoral block of 'Labour Electoral Leagues'. Anderson Dobson's role in any of this, or thoughts on it, we simply cannot know.

And the same applies to Fred and Elizabeth Hiley. Without a clear written account it is impossible to be certain what view of these issues they held, if any. It is recorded in excessive detail what Agnes Dobson wore on the day she married Ernest Reuben Hiley at the Kangaroo Point Wesley Church, in December 1915: 'a pretty gown of white silk crepe with an overdress of French lace with a design of raised flowers', with a lace bodice, and a train with orange blossoms and such like. The interiority of many past people, however, remains firmly hidden from the historian.

Fortunately Elizabeth Hiley's social position gives a little scope to peer into her attitudes on some issues of wider historical import from a slightly later period. In 1925 Elizabeth presided over a meeting of the Maree branch of the Queensland Women's Electoral League, where the United Party candidate was speaking. The party platform was for a white Australia policy, just as was Labor's position. But the holding of the meeting in itself spoke to a new political awareness of a class of people that had not been evident in Elizabeth's childhood: women.

In looking at Elizabeth's life, she does not really give the impression of being a likely suffragette and probably would not have considered herself in this light. But she was, in her own way, clearly affected by this major social change of the following century. Yet apart from a brief mention that she was there, there was no further information about Elizabeth. Her primary role at this meeting appears to have been mainly to open proceedings and offer a tacit stamp of approval by sitting and listening to the political man give his speech. It is strange to read his talk, because nearly a century later, it has recognisable themes. The speaker lambasted the opposing party for fomenting class antipathy and irresponsibly managing taxes and government spending. It seems to be an early reflection of the Australian political model: ugly dogs barking at each other.

But it helped provide me with a solution to a problem that had been pestering me. I had begun wondering about how Elizabeth Hiley and her daughter-in-law might have got along, if at all, considering that Agnes was clearly from the labouring classes and the Hileys were upper-middle class professionals at least. Politically, they were more likely to have been on opposing sides of any electoral ballot.

The clue to Elizabeth's potential acceptance of her daughter-in-law was in Elizabeth's 1878 marriage, and her favourite author. In one of Elizabeth's reminiscences, she recalled having been given Charles Dickens's work in twenty volumes as a wedding gift, which she continued to treasure over half a century later. 'These are still in perfect order', she wrote, 'and I prize them very much.' She described how 'Dickens's books were a delight to me, and the one I liked best was *David Copperfield*.' It was an interesting insight into her character, her tastes, and the way she may have conceived her own story. Especially because it was a book where a number of the characters escape from their problems in Industrial Britain, and make good in Australia. It was analogous in broad ways to the stories of her parents, her husband and his siblings, and perhaps even her daughter-in-law.

Dickens's tale of workers who made good, often by marrying well, appealed to Elizabeth in theory, so perhaps she delighted in it in actuality. And then maybe she and Agnes also shared a sense of commonality that transcended class and political affiliation, and in many other cases race and gender: they were both born in the same country.

Historians tend to focus on periods and on continuities and changes. But big histories, broad geographies, and the overlapping lives and stories of historical actors often thwart simple divisions and easy conclusions. The Industrial Revolution did not simply happen in Britain and then come to Australia, any more than did the rise of the labour movement, men's and then women's suffrage, or even the rise of the nation state itself as a conceptual basis for larger communal relations. These notions all filtered into the Australian colonies as they were developing, and bits also filtered back out. And while the relative lack of a fully complete and comprehensive set of extant entrenched social structures perhaps gave Australians a slight edge over other places in adapting to such changes, none of it happened entirely without outside input or even output.

But being connected with the outside world was only part of the challenge of modernisation, because ensuring reliable means of transporting people, goods, and information was crucial. And nothing reveals the complementarity of, and competition between, old and new better than the race between the ultimate symbol of industrialisation, the railway, and a Cobb and Co. coachman, who just so happened to provide me with my middle name.

CHAPTER TEN

COACH ROADS AND RAILWAYS 1878

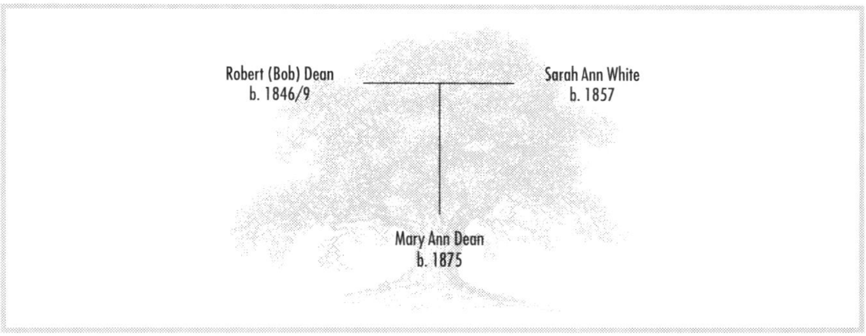

WRITING UNDER THE nom de plume 'Pegasus', after the winged horse of Greek mythology, in 1878 a newspaperman made the long trip from Sydney to Melbourne. He did this for two reasons. Firstly, he wanted to experience and describe the journey, most of which was then possible by rail, and he was interested to see how the inter-railway link was developing. The railways had gradually been extended out across the colonies from the metropolitan centres, and by 1878 the two largest cities of Sydney and Melbourne were almost connected. Only the gap between Wagga and Albury, the flat flood-plains of the Riverina, remained untracked. Pegasus's second reason to travel was to see a horserace, the Melbourne Cup.

The train trip from Sydney to Wagga seemed to provide nothing but a source for complaint. He moaned about stale food and uncomfortable seating and sleeping arrangements. He went so far, in fact, as to characterise the refreshment provisions as 'more like what might emanate from the commissariat providing for Russian prisoners on their way to Siberia'. Clearly Pegasus did not sleep well on the last stretch to Wagga.

The train pulled into Wagga as day dawned, slowly crossing the impressive raised bridge over the Murrumbidgee floodplain, an engineering marvel. Circling to the east of the town, the engine chugged smoke into the sky, and the couplings joining the carriages curved the length of the train westwards as it followed the tracks and slowed to a halt at the Wagga station. Passengers who wished to continue south and catch the Victorian train to Melbourne had to travel on to Albury by coach. The passengers disembarked onto the platform and walked out of the station. There, ready to collect their luggage, was a four-horse carriage already standing by. The muscled man ready to drive them was Robert 'Bob' Dean.

Having whined about the railway food, Pegasus said relatively little about the coach ride, despite it being part of his ostensible purpose in taking the trip. After he and the other passengers boarded the carriage the horses commenced their long pull. Fortunately for the equine team the slightly hilly country immediately around Wagga soon gives way to the broad river floodplains, and they could maintain a steady pace through long stretches of flat country. The coach and passengers encountered 'a little rain and some mud', but, thought Pegasus, they 'didn't get on so badly'. He 'determined to look on the bright side of things' and found that he 'had a very satisfactory journey'. In part this may have been helped by the little 'wash, and a good breakfast' that they had at Billabong fifty miles into their voyage. Pegasus did, after all, seem very fond of eating well.

There were several horse changes along the way, which allowed the coach to continue beyond the endurance of any one set of animals. It was a clever system that many coaching operations used to help travellers cover large distances in the quickest possible way.

One of these horse teams proved a bit difficult, but were successfully managed by 'the perseverance, and', Pegasus thought, 'I might say strength, of the driver'. For a man whose own words were hardly ever recorded, this focus on his physical presences, his strength and his skills proved common to a number of descriptions of Bob. And as if to reward the compliment, despite the length of the journey and the slight delay caused by the problematical team, 'Bob negotiated the last 11 miles, from the change, in 66 minutes', bringing the passengers into Albury 'in good time'. What is now a drive of about an hour and a half had taken over ten hours.

This stretch of country happens to be one I passed through when continuing north from Violet Town and is one I am very familiar with. Because of the regularity of his route and the importance of the mail delivery, one of the most crucial services provided by coaching operations, Bob must have been a well-known figure. It is likely that several other branches of my family may have encountered him. An old Holbrook farmer and former coachman remembered Bob when reminiscing about the great days of the coach runs, but did not know quite what had happened to him. Most likely, Bob left the Wagga–Albury route relatively shortly after Pegasus's description was penned. The railway was inexorably reaching south from Wagga and, seeing this, he may have decided to move before his work became redundant. It seems to have become a great theme of his life, and one that affected most of his contemporaries and colleagues.

The sale of wagons for the Wagga–Albury route in 1878 shows that Bob was at least winding down those operations, but it also reveals that he had been in business on his own. This had served him well for a time, but he then turned once more to working for the major coach companies, as he had in the past.

Bob's career in coaching had started in Violet Town, in the days when it was the end of the Victorian railway line up from Melbourne. In 1872 he had courted and married Eden and Mary Ann White's daughter Sarah Ann, who at the time was working in Violet Town as a 'House-Maid'. She seems to have left home and found employment off the farm, even though she was only sixteen. Robert was born in Cheshire, and was recorded as being twenty-three years old when he married Sarah Ann. I rather suspect he may have cut a dashing figure, at least in the eyes of the teenage girl. He may have still had an accent, and there are hints that he may have had an impish and youthful spirit. In contrast to the tight signature of his bride, Bob signed their marriage document with a quick 'R. Deen', using one of several variant spellings of his surname. The double 'e' and the 'n' flowed in a rapid running script that made each letter bigger than the one before it. I could be mistaken, but I thought I saw confidence in the smooth script.

When precisely Bob walked into Sarah's world I am not sure. His early career likely involved being one of the boys employed on the coach 'stages', where the horses were swapped with fresh ones at regular intervals. Generally, these stages were established at hotels, where passengers could find overnight accommodation if they chose to stay or quick refreshment while the horses were changed if they were continuing onwards. Unusually, the marriage certificate between Sarah Ann and Bob showed that the bride actually married a 'groom', the second such instance in my family line after William Kiss. This task required a multiplicity of skills, involving the ability to manage animals and equipment efficiently. On the other hand, Sarah's duties most likely involved making beds and preparing foods, and a never-ending round of washing and cleaning: pots, pans, sheets, clothes, shelves, bedrooms, fireplaces, chamber pots. If she had seen Bob working through a Violet Town window, his life may have seemed a world away, or at least to offer the opportunity of an existence somewhere away from Violet Town.

Because of his age, Bob was clearly on the cusp of working as a full-time coachman, and may have started to take some of the shorter runs under instruction or on his own. This surely must have increased the appeal for Sarah. Her youthful move into town and employment might hint that she was avoiding her father's farm at Boho. And she might have dreamed of seeing other parts of the country by marrying a coachman. There was also a whiff of danger about the role. This was 'Kelly country', after all, and at the time of their marriage there were bushrangers about. Bushrangers often saw coaches as the equivalent of an ATM.

In mid 1872, shortly before their marriage, winter storms rolled across the Victorian sky and dumped rain throughout the region. Each creek and river now became a potential disaster, and the coaches had to proceed with caution. The Beechworth-bound coach left Violet Town on the last day of June heading north but only got as far as the bridge over Honeysuckle Creek. The bridge was underwater and the coach had to turn back. Trying again on Sunday it got as far as Benalla, but was again stopped by the bad condition of the roads further north. The mail, which had travelled from Britain, bringing tidings from distant relatives and business acquaintances, had to wait a few days more. With a pretty girl in lace and a strong man driving horses, and a constant round of separations, anxious waits, and triumphant returns, the courtship might have played out like a period-piece bonnet drama.

Eventually they rode off to the next major town north of Violet Town and married.

By the 1870s Benalla had grown into a thriving regional centre. Sarah and Bob's wedding there marked the commencement of a very mobile life for the couple. Mapping their children's births shows that the Deans moved around the upper Victoria and lower New South Wales border regions over the next couple of decades: Violet Town, Benalla, Wangaratta, Albury,

Wagga. Their daughter Mary Ann, my great-great grandmother, was born in Violet Town in 1875, however, so the family clearly maintained some links with the Whites. Mary Ann's birth certificate, rather unusually, showed that the mother had aged two years, but the father was still twenty-three rather than twenty-five. While sometimes numbers could be written with sufficient similarity to make reading them difficult, in this instance the integers were unmistakably different. I wondered if the age disparity was deliberate or accidental. Remarkably, the mother was the witness. Such mistakes like this did happen, but I like to think it might have been a little joke. But it was a joke that could be read two ways. On the one had it could be yet another mark of affection for a youthful man at ease with himself, but, equally, it could be the sign of a woman who thought her husband was not growing up.

Bob worked for the firm Robertson, Wagner and Co. as the decade of the 1880s opened. Driven by the need to service un-railed territory, however, 'thrilling experiences' became more common for him from about this time as he worker on ever-marginal routes. As the railway lines north and south linked up, the nearest obvious major employment for coachmen was either in the connections between small towns branching off from the railway towns, or in peripheral country that was not yet connected by arterial railways.

It seems that Bob took employment with Cobb and Co. on the Temora runs very shortly after leaving Wagga. Cobb and Co. was an extremely successful coaching business that had been founded in the 1850s in Victoria and had grown to service much of the Australian countryside. It had even spread its operations overseas, running similar services in New Zealand.

Temora was a minor gold rush town at this time, and Bob was employed on the busy Cobb and Co. routes to and from Temora, Cootamundra, and the important railway town of Junee, my hometown. Bob clearly got a few months or years of employment ferrying people and mail between these towns, but eventually the railway caught up with him there also. With less need for large passenger coaches, the Cobb and Co. route wound down. At Temora there were some final celebrations in recognition of the achievements of the coachmen who had kept the communities connected. One day in October 1881 he made his final run between Temora and Junee. Bob mounted a giant team of twelve horses tied to two coaches and with a slight flick of the reigns he wheeled horses and coaches around the wide main street of Temora in a stately U-turn. Clacking, clicking, and creaking, the coachman headed east.

Regularly driving coaches hundreds of miles each week must have meant that Bob and Sarah's marriage had its share of difficulties, and the winding down of the major routes through competition with rail must have created added burdens of money and separation. One of the few other records of Bob's activities in these years comes from a brief report in 1884 that a Violet Town magistrate had rejected Bob's appeal of a previous case. Sarah had sued Bob for maintenance. It seems that they were separated. Working hard in an industry under pressure may have contributed to the marriage becoming strained to breaking point.

The next time that Bob is clearly discernible in a documentary sense comes from a month after he failed to appeal the court's decision. He was working in the Monaro plains, carrying passengers between Cooma and Queanbeyan in the high country of New South Wales. When he had headed off from Temora it seems that rather than go further west he had continued east into the highlands where there were fewer immediate signs of a potential railway link. The solid and rocky Snowy Mountains were a formidable barrier even to the mighty steam engines, he may have thought. But if so, he was wrong. Splitters were already preparing logs for the tracks.

Living in this territory at this time, and being a horseman of sorts himself, he may have known some of the Kisses. But while old Joshua Higgs could speak of walking between Sydney and Cooma, the advancing railway connections had left some Cooma residents frustrated with the slow pace of the coach connection. In January 1884 the *Monaro Mercury and Cooma and Bombala Advertiser* complained about the slowness of the Tarago and Gunning routes. The paper detailed how over the 103 miles between Tarago, north of Braidwood, and Cooma, the coach travelled 'just a trifle over five miles an hour' and took 'twenty hours'. They advocated accelerating the trip to an average of at least seven miles an hour so that when the mail arrived, there would be more time to respond and get any replies posted on a timelier return run. There were even recommendations of nine miles an hour coming from the postal department. 'Surely', the paper stated, 'we have all had enough of the absurd rate'.

The publicity seems to have been timed to coincide with a new competitor in the Cooma coaching market. Pooley and Malone, Bob's employers, whose advertisements graced the front pages of the newspaper, were faced with a new rival, C. Scott and Co. The new coach company announced its services under the banner 'No more monopoly', immediately below Pooley and Malone's usual advertisement. They covered the same routes, and even used an identical line-drawing image of a two-horse cart. Between new competition and an agitating press, the pressure must have been on to deliver ever faster service.

When at 6 am on Tuesday 26 February 1884 Bob drove the newly built three-horse mail coach, with ten passengers, out of Cooma, he had only recently joined the Cooma–Queanbeyan service. He had excellent references from his previous employment at Cobb and Co., and more than a decade of coaching experience under his belt. He had been in Pooley and Malone's employ for only about a month, possibly having been hired as a way of using more experienced drivers to speed up the service. The journey was expected to take nine and a half hours, arriving in Queanbeyan at half past three. This was not the train-connecting service, so Bob was not under a particular pressure to rush the journey, but the passengers were probably aware of the recent agitation. Wary of each other's potential disapproval, they may have clambered into and onto the coach as quickly as possible.

Two families climbed up into the seats inside the coach. When Mr and Mrs Body and their two children squeezed in, Mrs Body probably boarded first while her husband held the youngest, only several months old. Passing the baby to his wife, and helping his two-year-old boy climb up, Mr Body probably then allowed Mrs Cohen and her little girl Daisy to get in—it would have been impolite not to have held the door for the other lady, before he also boarded, possibly giving her a hand and helping lift young Daisy in.

Mr Betts, the Cooma district surveyor sat on the box, at the front of the carriage with Bob. Mrs Walsh of Nimmitabel also climbed on to the box, probably given a hand by Bob, and seated herself between the two men. She was the wife of the Nimmitabel police constable. She and Mr Betts likely knew each other sufficiently well to exchange pleasantries. Her fifteen-year-old son William climbed onto the back of the coach with Percy Dawson, son of the Cooma police magistrate, who was on his way to university. The young men almost certainly knew each other because of their father's shared occupations, and may have struck up a friendly banter.

With a familiar flick, Bob started the horses. The road followed the valley plain north as the sky grew lighter with the rising sun. As the hours ticked by the summer day grew hotter. Inside the cabin, with the two women probably chatting and the children playing or sleeping, Mr Body may well have been reading the most recent of the Cooma papers. If so, he would have learned of a woman entering the Sydney parliamentary buildings with a whip because a member of parliament had not responded to her letters. The paper also detailed that there was a crisis of some sort in the Sudan, and that some books had recently arrived in Cooma from the Phrenological Society.

At the village of Michelago, about halfway through the journey, another passenger joined the coach. The Honourable Mr Ryrie, Member of Parliament, was on his way to Sydney. He squeezed his way into the cabin with the two families, perhaps smiling and shaking hands with studied expertise. The journey was progressing favourably.

But as the coached neared Queanbeyan a sense of apprehension may have grown within those who had taken the road before. To reach Queanbeyan the coach had to descend a dangerous winding track to make the final approach to town. On one side was sheer rock cliff, on the other, a drop. There was a four hundred foot descent to a small bridge over a culvert. Robert and the passengers were aware of this, and so, as a precaution, the coach was stopped at Guise's flat, where new leather pads were attached to the brake block before the descent was attempted.

When they reached Stringybark, above the final descent, there were still concerns about the brakes. It was a new coach, not yet proven reliable, so they stopped again. The coach stood still in an open landscape in the mid afternoon sun as Bob and Mr Betts rechecked all of the mechanisms and the pads. The horses probably welcomed the unexpected break, and their heart rates slowed. But without the breeze from the momentum it would have been baking hot inside and out of the coach. Ignoring this discomfort, the men took their time. Mr Betts depressed each of the brake pads so that Bob could see up close if they were functioning properly. All appeared to be in working order. But Mrs Betts, poised with a view of the slope, and obviously nervous, suggested that the passengers should consider walking down. The men decided, however, that it would be safe provided they guided the horses slowly, so she remained seated on the box. Not seeing an obvious malfunction, and being a very experienced and reportedly cautious coachman, Bob thought that he could manage everyone down safely.

As they urged the horses forward, Mr Betts and Bob, who were on either side of the box, each kept a foot on a brake. But, despite having their feet depressed hard, it quickly became apparent that the brakes were slipping. The friction on the leather pads against the turning wheels probably caused a burning smell, but only the two young fellows on the back were likely to have smelled it. Mr Betts called over to Bob that his brake was failing. Bob called back that 'It was all right', which was more about reassurance than reality, because Bob immediately also pointed out that his brake, too, was weakening.

As the wheels turned, unrestrained by the leather pads, the carriage gained momentum. The dynamic of the vehicle shifted as the horses ceased pulling and were instead driven to run downhill by the weight of the carriage and its complement of passengers pushing them. With a rocky embankment on one side and a chasm on the other, the only thing that Bob could do was to keep the horses and carriage running straight. A trip would be fatal. Mr Betts suggested intentionally running the carriage into the bank, but Bob simply stated the facts: 'There is nothing for it but to keep them strait, Mr. Betts.' A guaranteed accident was no solution to a probable one. The steepest part of the descent was at the top, and it seems that Bob was striving to hold horses and coach straight in the hope that the brakes could engage properly as the ground levelled off.

The passengers later remarked that Bob kept his cool, even as they approached a turn in the road near the bottom of the hill. But as the coach began to oscillate from the speed of the descent, all semblance of control by man or horse was lost. Gravity and momentum were in control. The coach, mostly filled with women and children, raced down the hill to the tune of their screams.

Approaching the bridge over the gully, one of the horses tripped. The coach was flipped onto a log that was designed to guard the approach. This had the effect of exploding the carriage into shards. The passengers on top, including the driver, were all thrown into the air. Bob landed face down in the gully. Several lost consciousness, including Bob. What remained of the carriage underbody was flung on top of two of the horses, which proved unable to extricate themselves, despite trying frantically.

The inside passengers were now instantly and unexpectedly outside. Betts was unhurt, and his description of events reveals the immediate aftermath. In the gully were the twitching forms of Bob and the two boys who had ridden on the back. Mr and Mrs Body had been thrown clear and landed side by side. Mrs Body screamed for her baby, but amazingly the child was soon found unharmed, having landed on a curtain from the destroyed coach. Their little boy, much to everyone's surprise, also walked out of the body of the wreckage, without any signs of serious harm.

But it was a horrific scene. Among those in the gully and the remaining passengers there were fractured skulls, broken bones, cuts, and bruises. Mr Betts and Mr Body started attending to the wounded. Mrs Walsh was trapped under part of the carriage and needed help being extracted. She had several broken bones and was bleeding from a gaping wound to her head. Part of her skull was exposed. Mrs Cohen also had a severe head wound, with deep cuts to the scalp. Bloodied and dazed, she had been knocked unconscious, but woke as Betts approached. Asking after Daisy, Betts simply reassured her that Daisy was fine, even though he had not yet seen her.

Daisy, it turned out, had survived, but she had fallen into the culvert, right onto the unconscious form of Bob. When Betts noticed her, he returned the dazed but intact child to her mother.

As the horses expired, the men gathered the cushions from the coach to make the wounded women as comfortable as possible. They used the coach's curtains to stem the bleeding as best they could. They then dragged the member of parliament, who was 'prostrated with shock', over to the other survivors, before turning to the three males in the culvert. Percy had landed in an almost seated position with his head against a rock. Trying to give him some whisky to revive him, Betts 'pulled a small piece of quartz out of a wound in his head'.

Bob was face down and slipping from the gully into the culvert under the bridge. Mr Body climbed in and managed to turn Bob over and, seeing him breathing, administered some medicinal whisky.

William Walsh, they thought dead, 'and placed what we thought were his remains in a decent position on top of some of the mail bags'. He was, however, still breathing, but only just.

Betts ran on down the road for help. He found Mr and Mrs Snell, who lived nearby, and the couple sprang into action. Mr Snell ran to Queanbeyan for help, and Mrs Snell took water to the wounded. It was an hour after the accident, in the heat, with the wounded suffering from blood loss and shock, before they even got that water. A sergeant and a doctor, galloping on horses, eventually arrived from Queanbeyan. Seeing the devastation, the former immediately turned back to get a cart while the doctor got to work. Soon buggies and carts arrived to carry the wounded to Queanbeyan. The last to leave conveyed Bob to town, aching from a broken collarbone and fractured shoulder, as well as internal and possible spinal injuries.

The seriously wounded passengers were taken to friends' houses, and Bob was placed in the hospital. New to the region, he did not have the same contacts to call on.

A doctor was called from Braidwood to attend. Operating on Dawson, he repositioned a section of fractured skull, and the operation proved a success. William Walsh, however, succumbed to his injuries. Bob was reported to have been in a 'critical condition' with a 'concussion of the spine'.

But Bob was a tough fellow. He was convalescent for a period, recovered, and continued to drive coaches.

Gradually the railway connected the Monaro towns, and the necessary coach connection to Cooma shrank. In late May 1889 the railway was eventually opened, the final leg from Michelago to Cooma having been completed. I am unsure precisely where Bob worked in the months and years immediately after his injury, but he was clearly getting caught in a terrible pattern. As I watched Bob's story unfold I could not help but feel sorry for him. His working life got harder as he got older. Marginal districts needed coachmen because they were difficult to access with rail. They might not have been off the beaten track, but they were certainly on beaten tracks, and this made the task harder. And then, after a period of service to a community, he was pushed on again by the eventual arrival of the iron horse.

Trawling through the newspapers of regional Australia I eventually picked him up again in 1890. In a funny way it felt like he was following Joshua Higgs, the old cattleman, because he too had gone from the Monaro to Gippsland in Victoria. Bob was driving the mail coach between Bruthen and Omeo for his previous employers Cobb and Co. Rather ironically, the wide publicity of the crash probably helped grow his reputation as a 'careful man' and a competent driver, because there was wide press coverage of his calm reaction during the crisis. Coach malfunctions and crashes did happen often enough, but to have only one fatality from such a catastrophic crash as occurred in 1884 was a miracle.

But still, I wondered how he got back on to a cart after such severe injury and marvelled at how resilient the man must have been. The years of driving, and the accumulation of injuries, must have taken a terrible toll on his body, so I imagine that Bob had similar aches to those that I get in my arm after having broken it when I was fifteen—a dull and persistent pain.

Bob probably had many of these aches, and may too have had mended bones with weather-predicting properties. He would have accumulated them over a lifetime of small bumps, bruises, and fractures.

Driving the cart between Bruthen and Omeo, Bob must have been bumped and rocked constantly by the motion of the coach, each day an aggravation of old wounds. And yet still he drove. I like to think I have done some hard work. I have mended fences in forty-degree weather. I have had ten-hour days of hard digging as an archaeologist. I have been fruit-picking, shelf-stacking, and a range of other tiring tasks. But I am kidding myself if I think I can stack up to Bob Dean's work ethic. Running horses across rough terrain every day of his life, having so few incidents, and surviving, is all really quite remarkable. He must have been an incredibly tough man.

Yet further illustration of this came in June 1890. There had been heavy winter rains in the Victorian alpine regions, and residents at Bruthen, bordering the coastal plains near Lakes Entrance at the bottom corner of Australia's Great Dividing Ranges, reported half a week of continual rain. On the night of Wednesday 25 June, the Bruthen townspeople were alarmed that the Tambo River had risen five feet in the last twelve hours. As it was, the river was twenty-four feet above its summer level. The normally fast-flowing pebbly stream was now a much mightier thing. Spilling over its banks, it inundated houses, flooded barns, and destroyed crops. Many animals unable to get to higher ground were swept away and drowned.

All the while, Bob Dean waited. The coaches were 'unable to get through'.

At Bairnsdale, a catastrophic flood was predicted as the Mitchell River spread over the coastal plain. Houses along its river were underwater. The river had rushed and frothed over the land so quickly that most people had been caught unprepared. Barns full of seed and hay were swept clean like one of the mythical tasks of Hercules. Stockmen were seen rowing around their paddocks, driving surviving cattle and sheep to higher ground by boats. The residents of the town flocked to line the bridges and observe the devastation unfold, and the members of the rowing club scrambled to move their boats to higher ground.

Omeo was isolated and had received no mail for several days, so the coachmen began to contemplate alternatives. With the coaches unable to cross the rivers and with some of the smaller settlements simply underwater, one of the coachmen, either Bob or his colleague Cain, travelled from Omeo down the Tambo River valley as far as the little settlement of Ensay, about halfway to Bruthen. Then, rather than continuing down the main road, he attempted to ride a packhorse over the mountains to get the mail through. Two days later a search party found and rescued him and his horse, both stuck in boggy ground. He had failed.

The frustrations were felt keenly in the community. Despite the unsuccessful attempt to get the mails through, 'a large meeting of the business people of Omeo' gathered in the Omeo Shire Hall on 30 June. They were agitating for a resumption of mail delivery, and passed a resolution 'to call the attention of the Postmaster General to the fact that no mail has been sent or received from the local postoffice for a week'. They proposed another alternate route for a packhorse. Their agitation seems to have been misplaced, however. Seeing that the waters had begun to recede, one of the dedicated mailmen actually successfully traversed the roads from Omeo to Bruthen on horse on the day of the meeting. The waters of the various rivers were rapidly falling, and sections of the plains were now sodden, but no longer underwater. But his report of the condition of the roads was dire. 'Great slips of earth' had left the road in a 'dreadful state', impassable to coaches, and dangerous even for lone riders.

The postal service was aware of the potential danger, and 'issued instructions to the effect that no passengers were to be booked but the mails were to be delivered as usual'. With the business community agitating for regular mail delivery, and the roads gradually improving, the coach service was ordered to resume its runs on the usual roads. So when Bob left Omeo with the mail coach on Saturday 5 July 1890, there were no passengers on board. Bob was driving alone along the muddy tracks, probably wondering if the Tambo River crossing was even possible for a coach.

The river was still in flood at the crossing. The track ran into the water, and even the bridge was still covered. A horseman had presumably already crossed the bridge, so 'Thinking the bridge had stood' and would be structurally safe just beneath the surface of the flowing water, Bob started to drive the team and carriage across.

But the horses stepped into a watery void. Part of the bridge had gone. Immediately caught in the 'raging flood', they started to drag the coach and rider in with them. Bob 'made a plucky attempt to cut his horses loose', but failed, and carriage and driver were pulled in also, to be tossed about in the turbulent waters.

Although starting to break up under the surge, the coach came to a halt on an outcrop of granite. Fighting the pain of three newly broken ribs,

Bob struggled out of the water and clambered on top of the submerged carriage, now sitting precariously mid-stream. Still tied to the coach, the horses drowned in the torrent as Bob clung on and waited.

He spent a wet, cold, sore, and lonely night alone on a broken carriage in the flooded Tambo River.

The next day help arrived. The waters had continued to fall, and when a rider came, he was able to swim his horse across to Bob and effect a rescue. So, as the carriage continued to break apart on the rocks, Bob was taken to safety, and the mail was sent on.

People in the region were surprised because they 'had always thought the crossing fairly safe'. A local subscription was taken up for Bob, and later both Bob and Cain each received 'a purse of sovereigns' from the people of Omeo as an expression of gratitude for trying so hard to keep the mail going without complaint.

That year, 1890, turned out to be a particularly bad year for Bob.

On yet another Monday run, Bob had departed Bruthen for Omeo at 5 am on 13 October with three passengers on board. Aspects of the route were similar to those that had precipitated the Cooma–Queanbeyan disaster of six years before. Bob came to a stage of the journey that took him on a downhill run towards a bridge. On one side was a precipice, on the other, a rock cutting, with a steep decline leading to the bridge, which crossed Monkey Creek just north of Bruthen. At this, one of the most dangerous of possible moments, one of the reigns broke.

This time, because of the 'deep precipice', Bob decided to steer the carriage closer to the bank, but it was so close that the carriage clipped it. The horses, unable to be fully controlled, swerved, causing the carriage to flip. It landed on its roof, which was 'smashed to atoms'. Fortunately, the various injuries that resulted were not fatal. Bob and one of the passengers even managed to continue their journey.

A mate of his later recalled that Bob 'had a hand like a shoulder of mutton'. When I first read this description I instinctively looked down at my own hands. Could mine have firmly grasped the reigns in those moments of crisis, I wondered?

I gradually built up a picture of Bob Dean, searching through slim newspaper reports, but he had been difficult to trace because of spelling variations and name combinations like Dean, Deen, Deane, Robert, Bob, which greatly hindered efficient digital searching. He was also quite ephemeral in the reported news—always there but rarely recorded. His name generally only appeared in the press when he had an accident, or, much later, when people began to reminisce about the old Cobb and Co. coaching days and the best-known coachmen. One of the people who later remembered him mentioned that when Bob did the Deniliquin to Hay route in the 1890s, he travelled '300 miles a week for several years'.

Bob's shift to those western districts, the dry, flat country of New South Wales's western Riverina, came when his employer transferred him off the Omeo service. Once again the railway was creeping closer, and such an experienced driver may have been of greater use in the western agricultural districts. Firstly, he was put running between Hillston and Carrathool, a dry flat expanse beyond Griffith that was part of the Deniliquin to Hay route of the great western internal arterial road, and he seems to have taken on longer duties in that section. Bob drove large coaches, capable of carrying eleven to seventeen passengers, and drawn by teams of between five and eight horses. Remembered as a 'good timekeeper' on the 'plains and sandhills between Hay and Deniliquin', Bob ran these coaches day and night up and down the long, dusty, and bumpy outback roads.

In the mid 1890s Bob once again started his own coaching partnership, basing himself at Deniliquin and running the mail coach to Balranald, almost two hundred kilometres to the north-west. The route proved a success, and he was able to buy out the partnership and go into business on his own.

The year prior to visiting Violet Town and Boho for the first time, I happened to do the Melbourne to Junee Christmas run via the Great Ocean Road, then up the interior. Deniliquin was where, on a forty-five degree day, I stopped for lunch. As I drove into town from the south I was on what is still known as the Cobb Highway. Had I arrived a bit over a century earlier I might have seen Bob's six-room cottage, with its six-stall stable, and coach house, and a garden with fruit trees on an acre of land. I like to think that the fruit trees and multi-roomed property means that Bob and Sarah Ann had resolved their earlier differences, but it is hard to know for sure.

Bob auctioned some 'household furniture and effects' in 1902. '1 Hawker's Waggon and Harness', a 'Dray and Harness', a 'Spring Cart', and '2 Draught Horses and Quantity of Harness' all went, and a few years later the house went as well. But between auctioning some of his equipment and trying to sell the house, he managed one more crash, on the road between Deniliquin and Hay. It seems he was once more employed as a Cobb and Co. coachman. A little outside of Wanganella he was 'taking his team through a boggy patch of the road' when suddenly the lead horses veered unexpectedly. The coach wheels, caught in the mud, locked, and the coach was overturned. Bob and one of his passengers were thrown off. Bob was the only person hurt, receiving 'an injury to his eye and minor abrasions'. Despite being thrown off the coach, and undeterred by the danger, Bob 'pluckily held on to the reins and prevented the horses from bolting'.

While such coaches continued to run, their days were numbered. In 1912, during a drive from Balranald to Deniliquin, a motor car came off the road and crashed into the edge of the Barratta Bridge. As it was travelling at speed, the passengers were all thrown from the vehicle. Fortunately, they all escaped serious injury, but the driver was badly hurt. He was taken to Deniliquin, where he had both his legs amputated, but unfortunately he still died. The age of the motor car had disastrously arrived on Bob's old route. The driver's surname was Dean.

After selling his house in 1906, Bob became very hard to track. I know that Sarah Ann died in 1934 at Corowa, near Yarrawonga, where her daughter Mary Ann had married John O'Rafferty, the son of the miner, in 1893. These twin events place the family in the Riverina border district, albeit not as far west as Deniliquin. But Bob remains elusive. As the various newspapers recorded people's reminiscences of Bob Dean and the great days of coaching, the man himself fades from the scene, as if he drove over the horizon one last time and never came back.

Living beyond the iron-tracked dividing line between the settler past and a more settled future, Bob Dean, with his travels and troubles, illustrated that cobweb-like interconnectivity that was helping to draw the colonial peoples into a more unified whole. Internal borders both political and physical were gradually being overcome, the latter often with great difficulty. And so the question of federation owed its ultimate answer in some considerable part to the railway engines, and to the coaches, horses, and coachmen they often replaced. But even as the Australian colonies looked to their natural geographical unity, parts of the colonial economy were reaching out into wider geographical regions like the Pacific Ocean, where tall ships still sought fortunes, and empires struggled for domination.

CHAPTER ELEVEN

SYDNEY'S OCEANIC FRONTIERS 1880

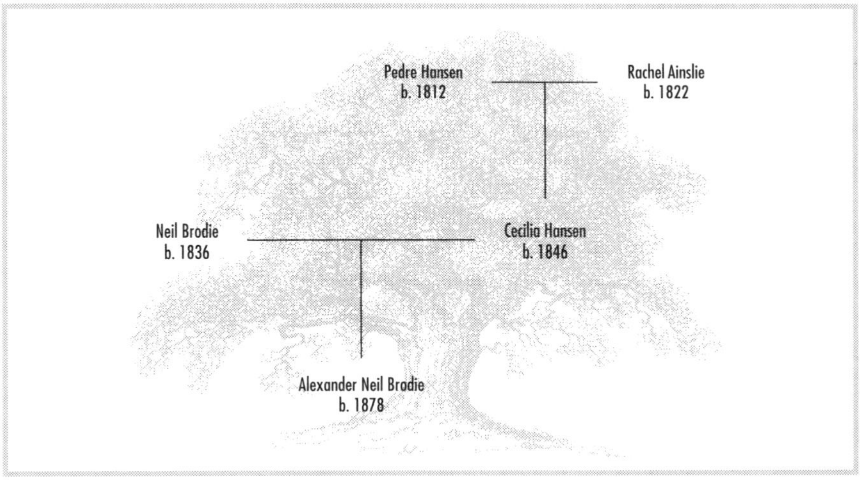

CECILIA BRODIE RUSHED to the wharves with her daughter in tow. Another ship was coming in to Sydney Harbour with news. The two black figures hurried towards the water, cloth and lace flapping from their exertions, with tears welling in their eyes. Despite the late November weather, they were dressed in mourning clothing. Since September of 1880 word had reached Sydney that the *Ariel* had been wrecked among the South Sea Islands. The story was that the ship had hit a reef off some island, before the crew escaped by boat to shore. The exact location of the disaster was unclear, variously given as Bougainville, Guadalcanal, Georgia, or Sunday Islands. No other trader appears to have made contact with the captain, Neil Brodie, or members of his wrecked crew, and attempts to discover their whereabouts proved fruitless. In Sydney, where his wife and family lived, it was believed that the *Ariel*'s crew had landed safely on an island, but were threatened by 'the treachery of the natives'. At last report two of the crew had already been poisoned. This information supposedly came from Islander sources, believable because Neil was a well-known trader in the area of the Solomon Islands to Australia's north-east. The intelligence was slow in getting from the area of action all the way to Sydney, generally through the testimony of other traders.

The sensational story of the *Ariel*'s loss was reprinted throughout the colonies, with papers in diverse regional centres like Adelaide, Wagga, and Bendigo picking up the story. People were interested in the Pacific Ocean, and in the colonial endeavours in the islands to Australia's north and east. Histories of Australia are often focused primarily within a continental or national framework, perhaps with some recognition of the origins of its various peoples. But even very early colonial Australia was more than a place for history to play out within neat geographical confines. New Zealand, for instance, was colonised not by Britain so much as from New South Wales. Indeed, during the earliest phases of New Zealand's colonial settlement, it was governed from Sydney. And this oceanic outlook continued throughout the remainder of the nineteenth century, as the Australian colonies became major trading centres for mercantile engagements across the surrounding oceans. And among those who made their living by trading in Australia's nearby seas was Neil Brodie. Proving the mercantile significance of this focus, when the *Ariel* was reported lost one of the first points that commentators mentioned was the insurance. The ship was covered for £1000, and the cargo for a total of £750. The South Sea Islands were big business.

As word reached the colonies that another trader had been attacked by the Islanders, and there was no news or sight of Neil or his crew, it was increasingly believed they could have become 'victims of the natives'. By early December his family had begun to mourn, assuming the worst.

Cecilia was no longer the little Australian girl of the Mayor's Fancy Ball, but she remained connected to her family and the area of her youth. Her husband was often at sea, so she certainly maintained close links with her parents, the Hansens, who also lived in Peacock's Point in the inner-harbour

Sydney suburb of Balmain. Cecilia lived in Ainslie Cottage, built by her father Pedre, and named for her mother's maiden name.

In October 1871 the cottage had been threatened with fire, a fact revealed by Pedre's grateful letter of thanks in the newspaper. 'I beg to tender my most grateful thanks', he wrote to several people in particular, 'and other neighbours who so kindly assisted in extinguishing the fire which occurred in the cottage at Peacock's Point, Balmain.' Urban fires have always been a particular threat to cities, especially in densely built areas, and Sydney was no exception. Pedre was sure that without help, 'the whole of the place would have been burnt to the ground'. The loss of such a valuable property would have been a concern from a financial standpoint, and there was also likely a nostalgic association with Ainslie Cottage. At the time of the fire, Neil was somewhere in the Pacific Ocean aboard the schooner *Lavinia*, engaged in the South Seas trade.

So the Hansens were an important support network for Cecilia, and while her own activities were domestic and thus unconducive to leaving documentation, her father's story provides some wider familiar and social and economic context. Pedre placed several other advertisements in the *Sydney Morning Herald* over the years, which provide some insights into the man, and into the wider family's situation in Balmain during this period. He had done relatively well in Sydney. The Danish boat builder's personality comes out, in a strange sort of a way, through these newspaper advertisements, not normally an individualistic set of records. There were odd bits of lost property that he tried to reunite with their owners: a spar, a set of oars, a watch, a key, a seal. The advertisements had the same basic formula: I have found this—if you can describe it and will pay for the advertisement, then you can have it back. It is a strange sort of businessman-like honesty. So honest was he, in fact, that he advertised finding two ducks and a drake on his property. A less scrupulous man might have simply discreetly eaten them. He certainly was not a Danish Viking of the marauding and pillaging sort.

In fact the same advertisements suggest that he was regularly attending the Scots Presbyterian church, because that was where some of the items were found. This too was a slightly ironic turn considering the Vikings' fame derives in large parts from their sacking of churches. The influence of his wife seems discernible here, as she was originally the Presbyterian. And, again rather untypically, Pedre's advertisements gave a sense of his feelings for Rachel. They had originally occupied 'Ainslie Cottage' before giving it to the Brodies, so he had named his domestic home for his wife. It had six rooms, a hall, a verandah, a garden, and 'a well of never-failing water'.

His honesty may have in fact caused some problems, with people making promises on his behalf. One of his advertisements was that 'I will not be responsible for any debts contracted in my name, without the written authority of Mrs. Hansen or myself'. But this too revealed at least that he trusted his wife sufficiently to allow her to contract debts on his behalf. And the contracting of debts was not the only problem to come from being scrupulously honest. In 1865 he had been sued for slander by a local politician, D C Dalgleish.

Pedre had written 'that Mr. D. C. Dalgleish had attempted to bribe my vote for him against my own conviction by offering me money'. Considering what else it is possible to garner about Pedre's sense of honesty and fairness, a false accusation would seem rather out of character. But, unable to prove the bribe, he lost the case and was forced to issue a retraction. At the moment of signing the retraction he may have felt quite gutted at being compelled by the law to tell a lie. Alternatively, perhaps he felt true remorse for a sin committed. Of the two options, though, the former seems perhaps the more likely, because he publically recited the original accusation by quoting it within the apology. This, at least, might have made it possible for members of the community at the time to read between the lines while keeping Pedre on the right side of the law. This trick may have worked, and many electors must have agreed that Dalgleish was not to be trusted, because he was not re-elected.

Pedre had a couple of other encounters with the law, but nothing terribly serious. A couple of teenage boys were caught stealing iron from his wharf in 1864, and one year he was fined for allowing a goat to stray around Balmain. This reflects the colonial reality that this was a combined domestic and shipping–industrial district, and the Brodies and Hansens lived very nearby their wharves and ships. Families fed themselves from their gardens as much as possible, and a goat was a natural accompaniment to the self-sufficiency that the colonial economy demanded. So too were milking cows, so it was not surprising to find evidence that Pedre and Rachel had one of these as well.

At the end of the 1860s the Hansens moved to Pyrmont, another nearby inner-harbour suburb. Following his advertisements through the 1870s, more of his personality comes through the tiny printed lines. One concerned a lost dog which he found on 16 May 1873. He advertised having found the 'Black Retriever DOG', and gave his usual statement that the owner could have the dog back by 'paying expenses'. But it seems that no-one came forth. Pedre must have developed a soft spot for that lost dog and adopted him, because a few months later, in October, he was offering a £1 reward for anyone finding a 'Black Retriever DOG'. He even threatened prosecution against anyone detaining him.

But his business also comes through the advertisements in this decade. There are, for instance, several boats advertised for sale in 1870, such as 'Two 12-ton Ballast Boats', 'a Ketch', and the 'Schooner, Hannah', which he noted was 'ready for sea'. This may have been the same ship *Hannah* that was wrecked south of Sydney a few months later. The first sign that the ship had been wrecked was the discovery of a board bearing its name being washed up near Bulli. For such a name board to wash up, the ship must have suffered catastrophic damage and its fate would therefore have been known immediately. So perhaps the only sign that a number of people had lost their lives was a name, possibly only recently touched-up by Pedre.

That he was quite actively repairing boats, often for resale, is clear, and this probably constituted a significant proportion of his work, a reminder of just how busy a port Sydney was. On 8 June 1871, for example, he advertised wanting 'a good boat, about 24 feet long'. He must have got it, because the next day he advertised for 'two good shipwrights this morning' to help him start the work. But as well as repairing and refurbishing he was also clearly building boats, and while these were probably built to order, or sold directly to the major traders, some were clearly built to sell on speculation. During the first half of 1873 he advertised on three occasions for shipwrights, two in January, six in May, and four in June. Clearly the yard was kept busy that year with the cutting and carving of wood, the banging of wooden pegs and rivets, and the caulking of the hull. By late June he was ready to advertise the ship, 'a new cutter, about 45 tons burthen', and was prepared to offer it with or without a copper hull-covering. The copper would protect the hull for longer, and just by offering it Pedre showed how colonial shipbuilding was competing with what Britain itself could offer.

So it is hardly surprising that the busy boat builder Pedre and the island trader Neil moved in the same circles. Neil brought my surname to Australia on the *General Windham* in 1860 when he was a twenty-four-year-old able-bodied seaman. A Bible in my grandfather's possession helps identify the family's immediate origin. In it was written 'James Brodie 1 Oct 1848 Ardrossan School'. This was probably Neil's younger brother, named for their father, and places the family in the Scottish County of Ayr. Various certificates and census records also put the family in Ardrossan, where Neil was born.

Neil's father was not born there, however, and probably came from further into the highlands. The Brodie Clan has good claims on being amongst the oldest in Scotland. Centred in Morayshire, in the far north-east of Britain near Inverness, the family seat is near the little village of Nairn, not far from Culloden, where many of them fought on the losing side of the 1745 battle when Bonnie Prince Charlie made the last attempt by the Stuarts to retake the throne of Britain. By one line of reasoning, the name Brodie is thought likely to be of Pictish derivation, linking the clan to the indigenous people of pre-Roman northern Britain.

Neil eventually made his way to Greenock, the dock suburb of Glasgow, a major port and growing industrial city. Here he almost certainly boarded his first ship, and thereafter spent most of his life on the sea.

Neil's arrival in Sydney on the *General Windham* in May 1860 seems to have been his first visit to the Australian colonies. This was a large immigrant ship, which had departed London just before Christmas 1859, but was delayed in the English Channel by poor weather for a couple of weeks. During the run through the roaring forties it had faced particularly bad weather. Rolling and fighting against heavy gales, the ship battled for several days against heavy easterly and south-easterly gales rather than catching the usual westerly winds. The crew would have been dashing about in the pounding rain, struggling to stay upright and remain on board, fighting against the roaring winds and rolling deck. Meanwhile the passengers prayed, slept, and vomited in the relative safety below.

Eventually, the wind and waves thrashing against the ship's hull took the railing from the port side of the ship and carried it off into the Southern Ocean. Lacking a protective barrier, the work of the seamen became even more dangerous. When the 'topgallant bulwarks were carried away, and the foresail and mission topsail blown out of the bolt ropes', the quick actions of the crew may have saved the *General Windham* from catastrophe. Eventually they arrived safely in Sydney.

Unfortunately able-bodied seamen are not easy to trace in the documentary record. They moved around a lot, and without knowing where they went, it is hard to know where to look. The *General Windham* left Sydney by the end of May for Melbourne, and Neil may have been on board, or he might have opted to stay in Sydney, or he may have boarded another ship—the possibilities are almost endless. The rollicking life of a sailor was full of such uncertainties. Split-second decisions about what work to take could carry a person to the other side of the globe. But it rather looks like he had decided to base himself in Sydney.

When I again spotted Neil re-arriving in Sydney it was aboard the schooner *Native Lass* in March 1862. He would certainly have had some adventures in the tropics. This was a collier, which had carried coal from New South Wales to somewhere in Torres Strait, before continuing to the island of Java in the Dutch East Indies, modern Indonesia, and picking up a return cargo at Batavia. It was a good illustration of the way the colonial economies were regionally interconnected. The *Native Lass* returned to Sydney filled with sugar, coffee, pepper, and rattans.

In November 1862 Neil again crossed the pages of the inbound shipping registers for Sydney. He was an able-bodied seaman on the *Louis & Miriam*, a brig trading between Sydney and New Zealand. This ship was advertised at this time as Sydney's 'favourite trader' and regularly ran between Sydney and other growing colonial outposts in New South Wales, New Zealand, Victoria, and Queensland. It was one of many little ships that were keeping the colonies connected with each other, and particularly with the growing metropolitan centres like Sydney. As with the *Native Lass*, Neil's engagement with the *Louis & Miriam* appears to have been a once-off. Crews were generally very inconsistent. Sailors would sign up for each voyage, which mostly resulted in high crew turnover. The odd cook or crew member might do two voyages, but they would certainly not have served on each of the ship's many trips, and most sailors only seem to have done the one.

In this particular instance the *Louis & Miriam* had left Sydney for Wellington with a cargo of tea, biscuits, and other sundries. Although he was only briefly in Wellington harbour, Neil would have seen a growing settlement. With its big squared warehouses on the waterfront, Wellington was nestled among green hills on the edge of a broad harbour.

Neil visited at a time of relative peace for New Zealand, which was riven by a series of conflicts during the 1860s. The Taranaki War had ended only the year previously. In a striking parallel to the American Civil War that was also raging in the early 1860s, the Taranaki War saw the regular use of trench warfare. Digging themselves in to their fortified pā at Puketakauere, the Te Āti Awa were able to inflict a major defeat on British forces. It was a gross embarrassment to imperial pride. In response there was a concerned British focus of military might upon the islands to Australia's east, bringing defeat, subjugation, and further conflicts in its wake. The Waikato War commenced in the North Island in the year following Neil's short visit. In none of this was there a straightforward British versus Māori dynamic because representatives of each group supported both sides of the conflict, such as Pākehā Māori (Europeans who lived with and as Māori), or the so-called 'friendly' Māori, who could be more closely aligned to the settlers than with the 'hostile' Māori combatants. Nonetheless, the effect of the outbreak of war was that commentators, in many cases, tended to describe the basis of the conflict as being primarily on racial lines, especially in the Australian colonies—in Australia frontier conflict had already primed colonial commentators to speak of ethnic conflicts and race wars. There was also a ready colonial Australian participation in the New Zealand conflicts, with Australian-born men going over to join the various militia regiments.

But Neil missed these conflicts. The *Louis & Miriam* returned to Sydney with 200 hides, 25 tons of potatoes, and 420 bags of sugar. Stepping on to the shore of the Australian landmass, Neil once again disappeared from the easily discernible record for a time.

Although it is possible that Neil Brodie may have crossed paths with Cecilia Hansen in one of his early visits to Sydney, a real courtship is only likely from the time when he had achieved the rank of captain, and therefore had the financial potential to be a good marriage partner. It was extremely appropriate then, that the earliest reference to him holding that title was when he arrived in Sydney on 2 October 1865 as 'Master' of the 51 ton schooner *Princess Alexandra*. Most likely it was a relatively young ship, or had been renamed. In one of the great royal matches of the Victorian period, Alexandra Caroline Marie Charlotte Louise Julia of Denmark, or Princess Alexandra as she was popularly known, was married to Albert Edward, Prince of Wales, in 1863. The ship would have been named in honour of this new Danish member of the British royal family.

But Neil brought the ship into Sydney Harbour with a crew of only four men, including one 'Henry Parkes', although not *the* Henry Parkes of Federation fame. The ship had been at Baffle Creek, a settlement a bit north of where Bundaberg is now, and in the hold were 90 casks of tallow, 400 hides, three tons of bones, and two tons of horns. This was the produce of the far fringes of the pastoral frontier, being brought to the Sydney markets.

From the time of his arrival in Sydney in this ship, Neil appears to have been based at Sydney, and I cannot help but think that the 'Australian girl' played a part in this shift in behaviour from a roving sailor to one with a stable home onshore.

There are records of him travelling as a Sydney-bound passenger on the ship *Rangatira* twice in 1866. In the first he was coming south from Queensland on a voyage from Port Gladstone and Port Denison early in the year, although at which port he boarded is unclear. Then, later in the year, he travelled as a passenger from King George's Sound and Adelaide via Melbourne, although again it is uncertain what port he was actually coming from. One possible explanation for this one-way travel was that he was delivering ships. But the simple fact that he was able to travel this way really highlights the growing interconnectedness of the Australian colonies, a whole generation before federation. Adelaide had grown into a sizable town, demonstrating the success of the concept for the planned-village model of immigration that prominent advocates like Edward Gibbon Wakefield imagined for the colonial world. By the mid 1860s Melbourne, too, was enjoying considerable success, with money drifting through it courtesy of the Victorian goldfields. The presence of several Chinese passengers on both of these voyages indicates once again that a certain colonial ethnic and cultural diversity existed, especially in the port towns, as non-European travellers were not unusual.

Neil was still a relatively junior mariner, however, and had to secure consistent employment where he could. He seems to have found that chance in 1867 aboard the O'Doud and Co.–owned *Captain Cook*. Neil was employed as chief officer on the ship on a voyage from Pioneer River, the settlement later known as the town of Mackay, to Sydney in January 1867. The ship was aptly named, in this instance, because in 1770 Captain Cook had charted that part of the Australian coast; however, it also made the ship difficult to search, because of the ongoing hoo-ha about Cook in the press in the 1860s leading up to the centenary of the British 'discovery' of Australia's east coast.

Even though Cook already knew Australia was there, and was really only engaged in a detailed mapping expedition, the historically minded of the 1860s were busily discussing his exploits and preparing a range of celebrations and memorials. It was a useful historical benchmark from which to measure 'British' Australia, highlighting the sort of pan-continental discourses of colonial history which went on to inform sentiments about federation.

Following that first voyage Neil was employed as captain of the *Captain Cook* for the remainder of the 1860s. On one occasion in 1869 he lost a man overboard—the poor sailor reached for a bucket of water over the side of the ship, lost his balance, and fell. The ship was brought about, a boat lowered, and Neil himself climbed the rigging to direct the rescue efforts. But it was in vain. The man was 'unable to swim' and could only be seen for a few minutes before slipping beneath the surface. Neil had the ship stay 'about the spot for nearly two hours, and had two hands aloft on the look out for any sign of him', but after trying their best they had to admit defeat and continued the voyage.

The ship that bore Cook's name ran a regular service up the length of the East Coast of Australia to Port Denison, Cleveland Bay, and then westwards into the Gulf of Carpentaria, so Neil was well travelled across Australia's east and far north. Only several years after the disastrous Burke and Wills expedition overland from Melbourne to the Gulf of Carpentaria, the Gulf had become a regular sailing destination. Moreover, in 1869 the South Australian government had established a settlement at Port Darwin, at the top of what was then part of that colony. Throughout the 1870s, with British and colonial authorities wary of other imperial powers making claims on the region, and wishing to exploit the nearby resources and trading routes, the north of Australia was finally being settled in some earnest.

The goods that Neil traded to these northern outposts and the eastern settlements in between were a mixture of desirables and necessities. During 1867 and 1868, for instance, Neil's recorded voyages from Sweeis Island and Brisbane to Sydney saw the hold filled with items like wool, 'hogsheads tallow', salt, and tea, the products of colonial outposts or items traded from further afield. The outwards voyages from Sydney were usually filled with the mixed implements, necessities, and luxuries that frontier towns and colonists wanted and needed: tobacco, rice, soap, rope, buckets, and so on. Neil was thus very much on Australia's mercantile naval frontier, which was itself supporting the continually expanding pastoral and increasingly agricultural frontiers and their urban centres.

The delivery of thirty-three bales of wool by the *Captain Cook* in Sydney in June 1868 was typical of the primary produce that was facilitating Neil's perpetual voyaging. Each year Neil made a couple of voyages supplying the frontier towns, and then took their produce back to Sydney. He would be at sea for most of any given year, and this was a pattern that continued throughout his career. Charting his arrivals and departures from Sydney, I could see that he only rarely spent more than a month or so there before once more sailing out between the heads into the Pacific Ocean.

But in his final voyage for 1868, between August and November, he must have spotted a new opportunity, and this changed the direction of his business. In November 1868 Neil sailed back into Sydney with something new in his hold. In addition to nineteen bales of wool, there was 3½ tons of bêche-de-mer.

Bêche-de-mer has several names, such as trepang or sea cucumber. It is a slug-like creature that inhabits shallow tropical waters, feeding on the seabed. And it was a valuable commodity for the Chinese market, where it was used as a delicacy and as medicine, with supposedly virility-adding qualities. Since at least the seventeenth century sailors from Makassar in the Indonesian archipelago had sailed to the northern coast of Australia to harvest bêche-de-mer. In a number of cases they are known to have formed close relationships and fruitful economic partnerships with local Aboriginal peoples. They established seasonal camps, where they would harvest and process the bêche-de-mer, salting and drying it so that it could then be sold on to China. It was Australia's first sizable export market.

So the *Captain Cook*'s trade in this commodity is an early illustration of colonial merchants entering into this valuable trade. Bêche-de-mer would thereafter be one of Neil's main objectives on his trading missions into the equatorial seas of the Pacific Ocean. The traders were actively starting to seek out other tropical products like coconuts and coconut-derived products, tortoiseshell, and anything else they thought they could sell. And it might have been this new economic potential that gave Neil the courage to marry Cecilia, because in late December 1868, only about a month after his re-arrival in Sydney, he married the daughter of the Danish shipwright in a little ceremony at Pedre Hansen's house in Pyrmont.

The newlyweds then occupied the Hansens' former residence at Ainslie Cottage in Balmain, and enjoyed the New Year celebrations in each other's company. On Monday 4 January 1869, loading of the *Captain Cook* commenced. By 13 January Neil was gone, sailing north towards Rockhampton.

Neil was safely back in March, but, as was quite usual, he made a second voyage for the year. In this second trip for 1869 Neil took the

Captain Cook to what were simply noted as the 'South Sea Islands', a broad term that could mean practically all of Melanesia and Polynesia. From this point onwards, with only rare exceptions, he was routinely travelling twice, sometimes three times, a year. When I was first mapping all this out, I was fascinated by the level of detail with which I could theoretically chart his life. Certainly I could really only measure arrivals, departures, and sometimes encounters or events at sea, or at his various destinations. But in terms of the amount of historical visibility, none of my other ancestors had yet come close to being quite so observable as Captain Neil.

But I realised as I was going through some of these accounts that there was another side to this story. Neil had limited time in Sydney, which means that he also had limited time with his family. No wonder, I realised, that Grampy knew so little about his own grandfather. There was little opportunity for the family to get to know him. One of the few bits of oral history that was passed down was that one time he must have gone on a bit of a bender when returning to port, and the children were frightened of the intoxicated man, who likely seemed quite a stranger.

And while I searched as many of the relevant newspapers as I could, I often came back to the *Sydney Morning Herald* to help me build a framework of his voyages. This was his home port, so its papers provided the most information about his comings and goings. As I trawled the pages for references to Neil, I realised that I would not have been the first person to have done this. Cecilia, also, must have followed the shipping news with particular interest.

An important part of most colonial port papers, the shipping news section provided details of recent arrivals and departures, and also recorded imports and exports, and often also which ships were sitting in harbour. It served a function not entirely dissimilar to a stock market report. It was not a foolproof record of ships' activities, but it was pretty good nonetheless. And in addition to these basic commercial facts, the paper recorded little descriptions of the voyages of arriving ships, and, importantly, what ships they encountered while at sea or in foreign ports. So for someone like Cecilia Brodie, apart from verbal reports received from friends and acquaintances, the papers provided the only information about ships at sea that they could get.

From all of this information it is possible to build up relatively detailed understandings of individual voyages. Neil's first voyage on the *Lavinia* is a good illustration. When he had arrived in Sydney aboard the *Captain Cook* in August 1870, it was his last voyage on that ship. He left the employment of O'Doud and Co. and bought himself the schooner *Lavinia.* From then on he ran ships on his own, often with a Sydney-based partner to act as agent. Departing Sydney on 9 September 1870, again after having spent only about a month with his family, he sailed towards the Solomon Islands, for the first time as captain of his own ship.

On 30 September he encountered the *Rose & Thistle*, another Sydney-based trader—one which, as it happens, Neil bought a few years later. Even more startling, on that same day the *Rose & Thistle* also encountered the *Captain Cook*, similarly heading north. This information could not have reached Cecilia until 6 December at the earliest, when the *Rose & Thistle* reached Sydney.

The *Lavinia* was reportedly off Cape Pitt, at the southern end of Nggatokae Island in the Solomon Islands, when the *Captain Cook* passed it on 6 December 1870 while returning to Sydney. It was mid April 1871 before Cecilia could have known this.

At some point he visited the island of New Britain, at the Papuan end of the Solomon group. While he was there, some of the Islanders on Neil's ship informed him that they had either seen or heard of 'a white woman and child' on the island. Neil sent one of these men to find the woman and child, and an eighteen-month-old distinctly white baby boy was found and brought to within sight of the ship. But the Islanders would not permit the child to be taken onboard. Soon thereafter a white woman was spotted through a looking glass among a group of Islander women, but again Neil was prevented from making direct contact. Neil discovered the bowsprit of a wrecked vessel, the apparent explanation for these castaways, and he made sure he reported the discovery upon his return to New South Wales.

Only in April, after at least four months trading with Islanders and gathering and processing tradable commodities in the Solomon Islands, did Neil turn the *Lavinia* for Sydney. He left the island of San Cristobal on 18 April 1871, having lost one of his crew while there, whose death and burial is recorded in the arrival documentation. In little under a month he had sighted the Australian coastline near Moreton Island. He reported that the voyage back to Sydney was subject to 'strong southerly winds' and 'a highly disturbed sea'.

In a strange afterword to his discovery of the castaways at New Britain, the apparent survival of some 'white' castaways on the island was later confirmed by the *Captain Cook*, but gruesome details of murder and enslavement were added. It was widely believed that there were originally four castaways, two men and two women, but that one of the men had been killed, one of the women died, and that the others were 'sold' to Islanders.

This information came to light in another bizarre overlap, where the *Captain Cook* returned to Australia with the passengers and crew of the *Dehli* on board, which had been wrecked at sea. These people were fortunate that, on the second of his 1871 trips, Neil was sailing the *Lavinia* in the immediate region of the tragedy and was able to come to their assistance and take them on board. Contacting the *Captain Cook* through his local agent at Rubiana on the island of New Georgia, Neil was able to arrange for the rescued people to be transferred on to the *Captain Cook* for its return to Australia. Not only did Neil have a local agent, but in some places also small coconut plantations for that other popular tropical commodity.

So while Cecilia was following news stories of ships being wrecked, Islanders attacking people, and scanning for the slightest hints of where Neil might have been and when he might have been returning home, he was busily establishing himself as one of the most prominent of the traders in the Solomon Islands, with a range of European and Islander collaborators. He inhabited a world of clear blue seas, sandy beaches, and tropical foliage. He even had a complement of Islanders on most of his voyages, some of whom also visited Sydney with him. Therefore, when Cecelia feared his loss in 1880 she was familiar with the routines and timings of trading voyages. It must have taken a lot for her to don her mourning clothing.

Cecelia knew that not all was well in the islands. Even the *Sydney Mail*, commenting on the *Ariel*'s disappearance in September 1880, knew that Neil had had past brushes with death. 'On one occasion,' it said, 'when he had charge of the *Lavinia*, schooner, that vessel was taken by natives, and nearly all on board were murdered.'

The South Seas were a complex zone for human interactions. Islanders had a range of economic and religious systems, including various rivalries, which make it hard to generalise about the area. Beyond the broad distinction between Melanesian and Polynesian peoples, there were smaller units based on tribal affiliations, islands, villages, and families. It was also an area witnessing increasing European and colonial activities, further complicating the picture, and Islanders were adapting to the relatively new arrivals, and changing as a result.

Notable during the 1870s was the way that trading in the South Sea Islands, itself a major development of Australian-based economic expansion, competed and intersected with another colonial expansion that had a similar geographical reach but a different economic motive and model. As already seen, demand for labourers in Queensland and northern New South Wales fostered 'blackbirding'. Neil publically criticised this phenomenon as harmful to good relations in the area and disadvantageous to traders. Violent kidnappings fostered some legitimate resentment within Islander communities, but in turn this was often violently expressed against any colonial arrivals in the regions affected. Moreover, the depletion of manpower could destabilise Islander power structures and inter-group relationships, thereby making the violent settling of old enmities more common, and potentially exacerbating existing and traditional tensions and conflicts.

There were, however, also positive and meaningful economic relationships forged between Islanders and plantation owners as part of an extensive and legitimate labour trade. Many Islanders voluntarily travelled to Australia to work for a set number of years as indentured labourers, because they were then capable of earning enough money to return to their villages as rich men and establish themselves as prominent and important members of their communities. Many Islanders were also used to working on trading vessels like Neil's for a season, so it was not a complete break with their experience to extend this to a period of a few years further afield, or for Australian-based plantation work to facilitate their later employment by Europeans in the islands. But although historians may argue over the extent to which colonial activities may have led to increasing conflict and mistrust in the region, Neil, like other contemporary traders, had no doubt that the South Sea Islands were potentially dangerous places.

Neil recorded an outbreak of hostilities with a group of Islanders in May 1872 in his ship's log. He had arrived and anchored at 'a small bight' on the east of the Florida Islands. With the assistance of 'the chief Demo' and a party of Islanders, the crew of the *Lavinia* had a successful ten days of fishing for bêche-de-mer. After this they sailed to another spot more suitable for drying the catch. His men included some Islanders, who, for a couple of months each year, became crew members of the *Lavinia* while it sailed around the various islands of the South Seas. They helped him build little 'houses' for drying and curing the bêche-de-mer, as well as helping harvest and prepare the catch for transport.

Neil and his crew were alert to the danger. 'The natives at that place', he noted in his log, 'indicated treachery.' They were rather unusually committed to carrying their weapons with them as they went about their business. Despite his suspicions, Neil was hesitant about leaving because the drying process was underway. But he clearly expected trouble. Within a few days he was making defensive preparations, telling his men to keep the local Florida Islanders off the *Lavinia*, to retreat to the ship at first sign of trouble, and generally 'to be very cautious' and keep their personal firearms handy. He also readied 'the large guns', bringing the *Lavinia*'s weaponry to bear on the shore.

Over the next few days there were no incidents, but, as his log reveals, he was still nervous. Finally the tension got to him, and at the end of a week of suspicion, he decided to head off in the whaleboat with 'Louis Nixon and five of our natives' to look for another harbour.

As the whaleboat rounded the coast, and the *Lavinia* disappeared from view, the wind picked up. Neil, concerned that the whaleboat would not be able to return to the schooner if they went any further, gave up and returned to the ship.

Approaching the schooner, he spotted the first sign of trouble. An Islander was swimming towards the whaleboat from the shore. He was one of Neil's men, and he seemed to be escaping whatever had happened.

Pulling the man into the boat Neil turned the whaleboat towards the shore to investigate. Rowing safely beyond the breakers Neil saw that the 'Florida natives were yelling and brandishing their spears at us'. His stomach must have sank at the sight, and then he must have looked at the *Lavinia* with dread as he turned the whaleboat towards the suspiciously noiseless ship.

Leading his men on board with weapons ready for action, they found 'not a living soul on board'. It was, he wrote in his log, 'one of the most horrible sights imaginable. James Shearer was lying alongside the windlass with his head split open, and several wounds in his side; Charles Wolf was lying amidships with his head battered in, and his brains scattered over the hatches; George Sellars was lying aft with his head very nearly severed from his body'.

Carefully watching from the bushes, Islanders now rushed into the water and started swimming towards the boat. But they were not attacking; they too were fleeing. This group comprised the remaining survivors of Neil's shore crew. They were desperately trying to get through the surf to the safety of the retaken ship. Neil dispatched the whaleboat to rescue them while directing the readying of the *Lavinia* for departure. Hostile Florida Islanders were continuing to congregate on the beach 'in large numbers yelling'.

When everybody was on board, the *Lavinia* sailed for safety. Five dead were left on shore, as well as the dead on the ship, all of them Neil's men. Once safe, the crew cast the bodies of the slain men from the ship into the sea, and, washing 'the blood off the decks', the *Lavinia* made for friendlier waters.

When the *Lavinia* limped back into Sydney with a reduced crew, Cecilia must have worried even more than usual when, less than a month after safely arriving, Neil again departed for the Solomon Islands. But he returned unscathed a few months later, and this relatively uneventful voyage might have allayed her fears a bit. Perhaps, she may have hoped, he was being more careful.

In March 1873 Neil sailed out of Sydney Harbour as captain of the *Lavinia* one last time. When he returned as a passenger on the *Beagle* that September, he certainly had another story to tell.

The voyage had been typical. Sailing, fishing, and trading around the islands. On 16 July he arrived at Port Praslin at New Ireland, with the local Islanders 'being quite friendly'. Relating the story some time later, he said, 'I have been here several times, trading with the natives, and as everything was going the same as formerly I had no suspicion whatever that they intended any mischief, as they had no arms whatever in the shape of tomahawks or spears'.

A few days later a large group of Islanders boarded the boat to sell tortoiseshell. Only when they refused to leave was there any suspicion of foul play, but Neil and his crew were caught completely unprepared. In a moment, the Islanders rushed the crew. Two men were killed, and others were pushed overboard. Even Neil was grabbed and manhandled overboard. His reaction, as he told it, must have been like something out of *Pirates of the Caribbean*. 'While they were in the act of throwing me overboard I managed to get my right hand adrift: I got hold of my revolver and shot one of them while I was going over the rail.'

Surfacing after the fall, he swam for a nearby canoe. Fending off a tomahawk blow from one of the two Islanders already in the canoe, Neil fired at them and they fled into the water. He waved the men in the whale-boat over, climbed in, and smashed the canoe.

Meanwhile, they had drifted close to the shore, and the Islanders there began to throw rocks at the *Lavinia*'s survivors. Retreating, Neil and his men fired a few times to dissuade the rock-throwers, but kept their ammunition in reserve in case a concerted attempt was made to attack the whaleboat by canoes.

Closing with the *Lavinia*, with himself and his crew firing on their own ship, Neil was surprised to see little flashes. The Islanders who had taken the ship were returning gunfire with gunfire. More worrying, however, was the sight of some hostile Islanders bringing the burning wood of the kitchen stove up to throw at the whaleboat.

Having nervously watched the proceedings unfold from the yardarm, Billy, one of Neil's Islander crew, quickly descended, dodged the hostile attackers, and dived into the water. He was soon picked up by the whaleboat. Neil and the remainder of his crew stood off from the *Lavinia* for about an hour and a half, but it was obvious to all that there was no hope of retaking the ship. With no other option, he turned the whaleboat towards Duke of York Island.

It was a forty mile journey, and took them all night. They had no food or water, and there must have been moments of great despair as they rowed beneath the stars.

But they did survive, and 'were received very friendly by Johnny, the chief of Port Hunter', Neil recalled. For two months they lived with 'Johnny' and his people, until the HMS *Beagle* was spotted and it rescued Neil and his crew.

The *Beagle* was one of Australia's first warships, built in Sydney in 1872 to patrol the Northern coast. It was commissioned in part to deter European blackbirders. As the representative of British naval might it returned with Neil to the site of the attack to investigate. Landing and looking around the deserted village, they could discover none of Neil's stolen goods, but the Islanders once again commenced to attack. Blank cannon shots failed to deter them, and only the use of 'rockets' seemed to have any effect. There was no sight of the *Lavinia*.

Later in the year HMS *Sandfly*, another of the Australian Station schooners, tried to further investigate the *Lavinia* event. It turns out that the ship was destroyed the day after it was taken. Traders like Neil often faced this sort of hostility. Blackbirders tarnished the reputation of legitimate traders and recruiters, and Neil expressed annoyance at their actions in making the region more dangerous. But there were also inter-tribal conflicts into which the Europeans could unwittingly step. Often enough, Neil's Islanders may have been the primary target of hostilities.

After the *Beagle* returned Neil and his crew to Sydney he was able to cash in the *Lavinia*'s insurance and acquire the *Rose & Thistle* to continue trading. But this ship did not last long. In March 1874 it was towed back into Sydney Harbour, having only just survived a hurricane while among the islands. It had lost part of its cargo, and the mast had to be cut away to maintain stability when the risk of capsizing was imminent. Reportedly 'she was whirled about by every change of the storm perfectly helpless, but fortunately escaped any damage'.

In October 1874 Neil captained the *Ariel* to Fiji, which may have been his first voyage on that ship. This set of islands, another locus of British colonisation and plantation-economics, was the other main outpost of British mercantile interests, and helps map out the scale of the area these merchant traders covered. Ships heading that way carried mail for the United States, which was then conveyed from Fiji to Hawaii and on to California. The next year Neil took the *Ariel* to Townsville, illustrating again how Neil's voyages reveal a complex web of economic and therefore social ties. From Java to Wellington, Rubiana to Suva, Neil literally charted the extent of empire. And while it was nominally part of a larger British one, its centre was Sydney. This was the oceanic empire of New South Wales.

Although Neil ran the *Martha Ellen* to the South Sea Islands in 1876, it was the *Ariel* that became his major trading ship for the remainder of that decade. And while he escaped major harm himself, in 1877 he reported seeing 'a quantity of wreckage, consisting of a deckhouse and vessel spars' which had drifted ashore on some of the islands, giving grim evidence of another ship's poor fortune. In early 1879 he was the bearer of the grim news that another trader and three of his local crew had been killed, further evidence of the violent reality that many traders faced.

So when he sailed out of Sydney Harbour on 25 March 1880, he was acquainted with the dangers of hostile Islanders and hurricanes, and was as experienced as any sailor in facing these threats. But when word trickled back of disaster, and then a two-month silence followed, Cecelia and her children donned their black clothing.

And then, against all odds, the *Ariel* sailed back into Sydney Harbour on 29 November 1880. Cecilia and her daughter were told the news, and still in black, they raced and met him at the wharf and 'proceeded on board'. It was reported of the reunion that 'the captain's relatives were in deep mourning apparel for their supposed loss, and their joy may be imagined when they heard the schooner was in the harbour, bringing her entire crew back without the slightest mishap'. For the reporters who scooped the story, the husband and family's reunion was 'as joyous as it was affecting'.

Neil had apparently learned of the rumours while still in the islands, and considered cutting his voyage early to return and reassure his family, but decided that the business should go on. Yet the voyage, although not disastrous, attracted attention, and so Neil's log and additional comments leave a reasonable account of the trip.

Having left Sydney in March, he was in the Solomon Islands by April, recruiting some Islanders for his trading cruise. He picked up '11 boys as labourers'. One of these, Neil soon realised, was 'Jimmie Fiji', who had been 'one of the ringleaders of the *Lavinia*'s massacre'. As it turned out, this proved no real obstacle to the voyage. Neil continued on to one of the islands, and left two of his crew, James Martin and Thomas Evans 'to procure island produce'. He provided them with provisions and items to trade, telling them 'I would not be back under five months'.

In late May the *Ariel* arrived at Simbo, where the local Islanders also 'recognised Jimmy Fiji as the ringleader of the *Lavinia* affair' and wanted Neil 'to put him on shore, which I would not do'. It seemed another indication that internecine conflict was a part of the violent outbursts against European traders. The internal dynamics of inter-tribal and inter-island relations were often overlooked by colonial commentators, and some subsequent historians, who were largely focused on what Europeans did and what was done to Europeans.

Neil, having refused to hand Jimmy Fiji over, said that 'to pacify them I told them I would give him to the first man-o-war I came across'. This assertion of British justice seemed to leave them 'quite satisfied', and helps explain how through gunboats and diplomacy the British were gaining political traction within parts of the region. By playing arbitrator, they could gain authority and exercise power.

But Jimmy Fiji never had his encounter with British naval justice. 'During the night of the 29th May,' Neil noted, 'being at sea or in the morning of the 30th, he was missing. We searched everywhere for him, but could not find him; whether he fell overboard or committed suicide we cannot tell; but we all supposed the latter.' If someone pushed him into the sea, no one told the captain, and Jimmy Fiji's fate officially remained a mystery.

In September the *Ariel* arrived at Ronogo, one of the Solomon Islands, and Neil was somewhat taken aback to find the local chief was surprised to see him. Apparently word had gone around that the *Ariel* had been wrecked. 'Every place we arrived at,' Neil said, 'the natives were astonished at seeing the ship and crew all right after the yarns they had been told.'

A possible source of the rumour was discovered when Neil went to retrieve James Martin and Thomas Evans, but found them missing. Nearby Islanders informed Neil that another trader, Captain Schwartze, had arrived, told Evans and Martin the *Ariel* was lost, and then 'succeeded in getting' Neil's copra (dried coconut) and other island produce. Neil chased down one of Schwartze's ships, and 'caught him on the Guadalcanar coast'. 'I boarded her', he said, 'and found Martin and Evans on board', whom he took aboard the *Ariel*. When he returned to Sydney, he had 83 tons of copra in the hold, as well as other Pacific products.

Gradually, through such voyages, the South Sea Islands were becoming better known, and reports could be more specific about Neil's various destinations like Solomon Islands, Noumea, and New Caledonia. But the fact and reportage of violent confrontations in the late 1870s and early 1880s spurred colonial and imperial authorities to take notice of various 'offenses', 'murders', and 'massacres'. They gradually resolved to come to the aid of legitimate traders, and to punish cruel merchants and treacherous Islanders alike. In hindsight the process has more than an echo of the Australian land frontier about it. There was nothing quite like a little conflict to help justify extending the *Pax Britannica*.

In 1881 Neil reported 'numerous attacks' on his ship. His return to Sydney in November 1881 again attracted media attention for the particular hostility Islanders exhibited in the Admiralty Group. An extended precis of Neil's log set the scene: 'They arrived at Nares Harbour on the morning of May 3, and at daylight an immense fleet of canoes, more than the usual number, came from Wild Island, and surrounded the vessel, under the pretence of offering bêche-de-mer and pearlshell for sale. The captain and crew, however, were not without some experience of the treachery and deceit of these tribes, and consequently were prepared for any emergency. Presently, as all eyes were fixed on their chief, he gave a sign, which was responded to with a shower of spears being sent from a hundred tawny arms, and directed towards the captain, mate, and crew, and a portion of the crew who were in an open boat towing the ship. The latter were got on board at once, and each being armed with his gun, sent a few bullets among the natives, which had the effect of making them retreat to land as quickly as possible, where they kept up a beating of tom-toms, accompanied by war cries and yells for many hours.' Only one of the crew had been slightly wounded, an Islander from Rodango.

A week and a half later, the *Ariel* was visited by two different groups of Islanders, coming from further afield, which each wanted to trade. One group had bêche-de-mer and pearlshell; the other group, potatoes. Neil traded with each, but as they left to return to their own villages, one of the groups was set upon by the Nares Islanders who had previously attacked the ship and crew. The Nares Islanders 'made an onslaught upon one of the two lesser ones [groups], that were quietly making their way to shore, and binding them hand and foot, they plundered the local canoe of everything tangible'. Then Neil and the *Ariel* crew watched what followed with horror, having been informed by 'a high authority', presumably British or colonial government or military official, not to interfere in domestic conflicts in the islands. 'The unfortunate bushmen were mercilessly tomahawked by their savage captors,' it was reported, 'their cries being heartrending to those on board the *Ariel* whilst the death blows were being administered.' The *Ariel*'s mate later spoke of it to a reporter: 'They let into them with their tomahawks', he said, 'and it was pitiful to hear the cries of those poor savages. We hardly knew whether we were doing right in not firing on the murderous lot.'

Soon the *Ariel* was again targeted by the Nares Islanders, who were seen off with more gunfire, but the ship was eventually driven to depart. But, encountering another trading vessel soon thereafter, Neil arranged for the two ships to return to the harbour and continue fishing in tandem. By relying on their combined strength, it was hoped to better exploit the area with less danger. Nonetheless the two ships were threatened, and it was thought best to leave the area and avoid it in future, even at the expense of leaving before the fishing was complete.

The reporter who conveyed all this to public notice drew attention to the hypocrisy of claims for being 'the pioneers of civilization', when well-armed representatives of a 'civilised' power could 'not be permitted to stop such murderous attacks by one body of savages against another'. While clearly many Islanders rejected European and colonial visitors to the region, particularly perhaps where it involved the exploitation of their coasts, others welcomed them, and these, it was increasingly felt, deserved protection. Moreover, the 'colonial' fishing was mostly conducted by Islanders, who benefited materially from this by access to marketable goods and commodities brought by the trading ships en route to the islands, notably including guns for hunting and warfare, so this was no simple European interloper situation, and the trading routes were not simple one-way plundering exploitations. And then there were traditional and newly developing intertribal and inter-island discords and conflicts, which regularly spilled over into bloody feuds and local warfare. So it was more than just the attacks of Islanders on traders and missionaries that inspired greater British involvement in the region, there was some recognition that it was a troubled area.

As well as local wars, Neil also witnessed wider dramatic shifts in the region. He continued to sail from Sydney to the South Seas throughout the 1880s and into the 1890s in the *Ariel*, *Martha Ellen*, *John S Lane*, *Thistle*, and eventually the *Renard*, formerly HMS *Renard*, which was a sister-ship of the *Beagle* and the *Sandfly*. Decommissioned from the Australian Station, the ex-naval ship was converted to trading before Neil acquired it. He continued to employ Islanders, and mostly traded peacefully with Islanders for the rest of his career. Yet he was still witness to the changing dynamics of the region. And one of these shifts, prominent moments of which he actually witnessed, were of global significance.

In 1893, he encountered the British warship HMS *Curacoa*, which was steaming around the islands and planting the British flag on all of the islands in the Solomon group not already claimed by the relatively new German Empire. Neil even witnessed the negotiations and ceremony at Simbo. The arrival of German expansionism into this region was the main cause of this sudden British interest in making claims, but, as Neil observed, the long familiarity of the Islanders and the British with each other's languages and customs meant that the exchanges were not naively entered into. And so the island trader was again the bearer of significant news. Neil's account of Britain's successful annexation of the islands had international ramifications, and received widespread publicity. As did his reports of poor treatment in the new German protectorates. German authorities were now flexing their power in the region, restricting British shipping and trading, and prompting Neil to remonstrate with the German Consul in Sydney upon his return.

As I researched and read such varied accounts of Neil's adventures I was amazed that this was the first I was learning of practically any of it. How, I wondered, could these not have passed into family lore? This was Grampy's grandfather, after all. And these were exciting stories of the R L Stevenson sort that I used to read as a boy, yet here they were in my own family!

But perhaps the answer lay in the only really strong piece of oral tradition I had about him. The one certain fact that I always knew was that he was lost at sea.

Farewelling Cecilia, Neil sailed out of Sydney Harbour on the *Renard* in August 1893 and never returned.

In mid September the Sydney-bound *Thistle* passed the *Renard*, which was still heading north. It safely arrived in the Solomon Islands, conducted its usual trade, and with full holds turned for Sydney. It was spotted passing the Marau Islands on 20 January 1894, still in the Solomon Islands.

Almost certainly unknown to Neil, there were two cyclonic weather systems between the *Renard* and Sydney. But it was said that 'in point of experience in hurricanes, he probably had no superior in the Pacific', so maybe he did know but decided to risk it. Maybe he only found out too late.

By late February it was obvious that the *Renard* was 'overdue'. Inquiries were 'made as to her whereabouts'. Every sail to enter the harbour must have given Cecilia and her children a mixed pang of fear and hope.

News that a derelict hull had been sighted must have caused the family a great sense of dread. Unable to get near enough for a 'close inspection' because of bad weather, the *Thistle*, once again on a return voyage to the Solomons, seems to have sighted what 'was part of the hull of a vessel of about 100 tons. The few timbers sticking out of the water here and there were about the size of a small trading craft'. The captain of the *Thistle*, although not entirely sure, thought it was probably the *Renard*.

When it reached Sydney, this news caused even more questions to be asked of every trader. The *Renard* was, as one writer put it, 'away quite long enough to cause a little anxiety'. No-one knew what had happened.

'Word of the whereabouts of the Sydney-owned schooner *Renard*, which left Sydney for the Solomon Islands, is still awaited with concern', the *Sydney Morning Herald* noted on 25 April 1894. The next day the steamship *Aldinga* arrived in Sydney with bad news that added to the *Thistle*'s account. It was the *Aldinga* that brought reports of Neil's position on 20 January, which placed him in a bad position in relation to the cyclone that he would have passed through. It all pointed to 'the loss of the vessel and probable loss of all hands, although', the reports noted, 'it is too soon to abandon all hope'. It was possible that some of the crew had either reached an island, or been picked up by a passing vessel.

Eventually Cecilia donned her mourning clothing again, filed for probate, and after a year Neil's death was officially pronounced.

But his name lived on; not only through his descendents, but in another way. Personal loss, economic gains, conflicts and the politics of empire aside, Neil also helped advance scientific understanding of the wider region, both ethnographically and biologically. The *Illustrated Sydney News* of 26 January 1878 carried a large image of scenes from 'The Solomon Islands', including a village and 'King Tom'. This drew in part on Neil's adventures with the *Lavinia* of that year, and the study of Islander traditions has been facilitated by the sorts of encounters Neil had, and the records he left, as well as those of missionaries and various military or exploratory navigators. Coincidentally, the newspaper also happened to carry an image of Sydney's Lane Cove, where Neil built a home for the Brodies. What Neil's encounters with the peoples of the Pacific most helped to achieve, however, was to provide firm evidence of the complexity of the situation, and the diversity as well as similarity of island peoples. He was attacked on a number of times, but he spent more time working closely with Islanders than he really did with his immediate family. He was the embodied link between Lane Cove and the Solomon Islands, proof of how colonial Australians looked outwards to sea, as much as they looked inwards to the outback.

And that seaward gaze had a particularly nineteenth-century touch, revealed because Neil donated a number of items to the Australian Museum in Sydney, like a cuscus (a marsupial), a 'collection of fishes from the Solomon Islands', and various tropical seashells. His interest in the Pacific was, therefore, not simply economic. And as early as 1871 John W Brazier honoured Neil by naming a species after him, *Helix (Geotrochus) Brodici*, for having 'brought this and other species from the Solomons'. In one of his voyages in the *Ariel* in 1879 Neil had provided 'transport, and facilities', for James Cockerill, a noted naturalist and collector. So, in the same way that Pedre Hansen's advertisements, or Cecilia Brodie's reactions to her husband's losses and returns, reveal something about them, tiny snippets of information seem to relate something of Neil's personality. He liked science, it seems. And in that, in the later nineteenth century, he was hardly unique. But, even while German ships advanced through the Pacific Ocean north of the Australian colonies, the real war looming seemed to be a civil one. There were growing divisions within the colonies.

CHAPTER TWELVE

THE SCOURGE OF SECTARIANISM 1887

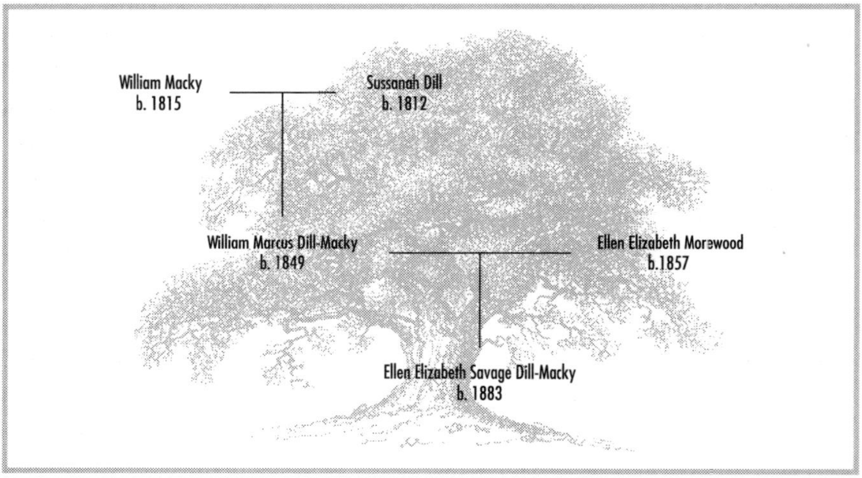

ONE OF THE prophets of sectarianism, the Reverend William Marcus Dill-Macky—son of the Irish republican would-be goldminer William Macky—was installed as minister of Scots Church in Sydney in 1887. The colonies had seen some outbursts of sectarian discord previously, primarily concerning a sizable Catholic minority. Prejudice and mistrust were certainly present within some communities and between families, where various sects had occasionally eyed each other suspiciously, but things had not really reached major proportions until the later nineteenth century. Just as the colonies were seriously beginning to contemplate joining together in a federation, several factors were aligning to make sectarian conflict an increasingly prominent part of the social and cultural landscape of late colonial Australia.

Mass Irish immigration in the middle of the nineteenth century was one element, boosted in its effect by the horrors of the great hunger of the potato famine. The Irish brought their grief and grievances with them to Australia, especially when they felt they had been pushed or taken from their homelands. Complementing this focus on historical injustices were persistent and increasing calls for a modern remedy, and so the agitation for Irish independence from English rule became an issue which colonials of Irish extraction and descent followed closely. Adding to the mix was the way that the Catholic episcopal hierarchy of Ireland was a significant institutional voice for change, and the Catholic Church in colonial Australia had become increasingly Irish as the nineteenth century progressed. Even many Catholics of English descent could point to the centuries of legal oppression, and longstanding traditions of anti-'Papist' doctrines and diatribes that proved a uniting concept and rallying point for several forms of British Protestantism. In some ways the restoration of the Catholic Church in England and Scotland in the early nineteenth century actually fostered some prejudice within Britain as large industrial cities saw the building of new Catholic churches to serve large immigrant Irish populations. In the minds of many people in Britain and its colonies, the Irish Catholics were an insidious 'other', whose primary allegiance was to a foreign power. The Australian colonies therefore seemed ripe for considerable trouble, and a landmass utilised by the British to address some of its 'Irish problems' was poised to become the setting for sectarian conflicts.

Aided by these factors, and a great many others, the Irish question about Home Rule for Ireland was a political issue of great interest to people in colonial Australia. Opponents of Home Rule thus often saw it as the herald of 'Rome Rule', an argument that Dill-Macky himself put forward frequently. In advance of Australian federation, public debate was often framed around issues of religion, race, loyalty, liberty, culture, and democracy in strikingly recognisable ways. And into this mix stepped a very effective speaker, whose oftentimes puerile arguments were welcomed with great fanfare by large and noisy segments of the population.

Dill-Macky had left his ministry in Draperstown in the north of Ireland to come to New South Wales, and that particular background context informed his attitudes and subsequent behaviour. His notions of Ireland, the Catholic Irish people, and Catholics generally, were all broadly formed by the sectarian context of the Ireland of his youth. As a child he played on the cannon named 'Roaring Meg' that sat on the walls of Derry, and he would imagine himself fighting against the army of James II & VII which besieged the city nearly two centuries beforehand in 1688. He also became a member of the local 'Apprentice Boys', essentially a Protestant gang for youths, and participated actively in annual celebrations of the city's siege by shutting the city gates and burning effigies. It seems that in his childhood he inhabited a Protestant versus Catholic worldview which quite literally belonged to the seventeenth century.

Later in life, Dill-Macky provided an account of his youth and background in the *Watchman*, a Protestant paper which he himself started. This was probably the closest thing to an official autobiography, so 'The Life Story of the Rev. W. M. Dill Macky D.D.' probably reflects his own chosen understandings of his childhood. He clearly remembered it as having been a deeply divided world. On the one side were the Protestants, who were good, intelligent, loyal, and part of the wider British family and tradition. On the other side were the Catholics: superstitious, unthinking, disloyal, ungrateful, and blinded by the hegemony of Roman religion and the sinister plotting for global domination of the Pope.

Graduating from youthful gangs, he went on to study religion and was eventually appointed as a Presbyterian minister in Draperstown. Having descended from the colonists that had settled in Ireland three centuries or so earlier as part of the English invasion and occupation, Dill-Macky's views were not uncommon for his class and background, and his career choice was likely to have exaggerated these. As an active and very vocal opponent of Catholicism itself and of any suggestion of Home Rule for Ireland, which was still at the time ruled by Westminster, he soon made himself unpopular with the Catholics of the town.

Dill-Macky made himself a target of resentment by belligerently voicing his attitudes about the native Irish and their capacity to govern themselves. He was undoubtedly a rousing speaker, capable of whipping crowds into some fervour, which probably only made the situation worse. But the effective language of division also had its uses, and local politicians asked him to speak on their behalf, giving him a wider audience than he may otherwise have had.

Dill-Macky's mother, Susannah Dill, was the daughter of a Presbyterian minister. The Dills were a quite prominent clerical family, and certain 'father issues' aside, this probably in part explains the hyphenated surnames of two of William and Susannah's children who went on to be ministers. It was quite likely that he gained his strong sense of militant Protestantism from the Dills, perhaps fuelled by an old family tradition suggesting that the Dills came to Ireland in the seventeenth century from Europe with the invading army of William of Orange, and therefore may have been part of the forces that 'liberated' Derry. William was a Dutch prince whose English wife Princess Anne gave him a tenuous, but ultimately successful claim on the English throne. This wider sequence of events was effectively the last victorious invasion of both England and Ireland and, although partly just an extended palace coup, it was so successful a coup that it is better known by the propagandistic post-conquest label for the event: The Glorious Revolution.

Dill-Macky's own recollection of his family's story recorded hints of bitter divisions that lasted down the centuries. One of his reverend uncles apparently preached in the very Catholic south-west of Ireland, and was known there rather unflatteringly as 'The Cock of the North' by the locals who did not take to him. The title implies a sort of preening nature, but it was also the name of a military bagpipe tune famously used by the Gordon Highlanders. It could therefore be taken to allude to a certain Scottish 'church militant', perhaps implying he was full of wind.

Even Dill-Macky's marriage in 1880 to Ellen Elizabeth Morewood reveals Dill-Macky's colonial and establishment connections. She was the daughter of a government medical officer. Ellen's mother was from the Savage family, whose ancestry supposedly goes back to the Norman Conquest of England. The general milieu of Dill-Macky's family life was thus very British imperial. They were descended from English colonists of Ireland, proud of that fact, and did not trust the natives.

But largely absent from Dill-Macky's discussion of his family was the story of his father, William Macky. The semi-official version ran that William Macky was 'a well-to-do farmer' who had gone to the goldfields, hoped the family would later join him, and then disappeared. Unsurprisingly, but very tellingly, none of William Macky's American exploits or republican attitudes were so much as hinted at. It appears that Dill-Macky had simplified and sanitised his father's life for later retelling. He may well have held feelings of abandonment, and perhaps embarrassment and resentment, which exacerbated certain prejudices of his place and period. He was forever after a proudly loyal British subject, and fiercely Protestant, the opposite of his republican father.

The immediate explanation for Dill-Macky's relocation from Ireland to New South Wales seems to have been his brother. Dr James Macky had established himself in the colony as a colonial medical practitioner, and wanted to bring his family over. So in 1886 Dill-Macky resigned from his Draperstown ministry, and he and his young family, with Mrs James Macky and her children, all boarded the *Austral* and headed to Sydney.

One of the colonial newspapers that commented on the arrival of the *Austral* was the *Freeman's Journal*, the Catholic paper Jimmy Kiss subscribed to. The article headline was 'More Priests for Australia' and the text that followed gave the details of the return to Australia of two priests who had been abroad in the United States of America and Europe collecting money for the rebuilding of St Mary's Cathedral in Hobart. I suspect the Reverend Dill-Macky may not have been so pleased to find himself on a ship with these two Catholic priests, plus four more, and at least one soon-to-be postulant nun.

Family and individual specifics aside, Dill-Macky and the six Catholic priests and a future nun were all on the *Austral* for much the same wider reasons. With expanding populations, there was growing demand for religious leaders in the colonies, and many saw it as their duty to leave their homes and go and minister where the need was. The Australian colonies were very religious places and sections of the population were remarkably religiously literate. The idea of an increasing secularism, in the sense of a society where religion was relegated to personal and private thoughts, is a simplistic and anachronistic reinterpretation of the past. Most socialists, for instance, considered themselves to be Christian socialists. And the wide spectrum of social reformers, whether against slavery, racism, class prejudice, and the death penalty, or advocating for issues like workers' rights and welfare reform, frequently did so with reference to the Bible. Even sometimes seemingly anti-religious publications like the republican-oriented and white workingman–focused (and often blatantly racist) *The Bulletin* were predicated on the knowledge required to get the various jokes.

And the nineteenth century was a heady time for Christian religion generally. Wide social, cultural, economic, and industrial changes encouraged the major churches to continue to develop their theologies, liturgies, and structures, particularly aided by the advancements in the social science disciplines of history and archaeology. Complementing this, geology and palaeontology were developing new scientific understandings of the world, and these were being advanced and challenged both within and without the major churches, especially regarding the origins of humankind. Many of these issues would not be fully resolved until the middle of the twentieth century or beyond, if at all. More specifically, within the British world the Anglican Church was both inspired and torn by the Oxford Movement of the 1830s and 1840s, which broadly advocated a liturgical and spiritual return to its Catholic roots, slightly turning away from the Calvinistic model of prior centuries. Methodism and other forms of 'low-church' Protestantism spread throughout the empire with colonists, bringing a renewed Biblical literacy throughout the empire. And Catholics, particularly the Irish, re-established themselves prominently in Britain and planted themselves firmly in the soil of Britain's colonial outposts.

In Rome, Catholicism faced the loss of Papal temporal power as the Papal States crumbled during the nineteenth century, in some ways causing an outdated and clunky renaissance court in Europe to sometimes rail against modernity, ultimately perhaps one of its greatest public-relations disasters. From 1870 onwards the Pope lacked any sovereign territory at all until the late 1920s. Yet the church also faced down some of the core ideological frictions facing the modern world, and Pope Leo XIII's 1891 encyclical *Rerum Novarum* on the 'Rights and Duties of Capital and Labour' provided a means for workers, employers, states, and the poor to navigate their responsibilities towards each other. It proved a foundational framework for the development of the field of human rights and, with its particular focus on human dignity, the United Nation's *The Universal Declaration of Human Rights* of 1948.

And Catholicism also continued its spread throughout the globe. With mass success in South America, the Philippines, Asia, and Africa, it seemed to some observers to be encircling the Australian landmass. There were even 'foreign' religious orders filled with the likes of Germans and Spaniards and other nationalities attending to Catholics in Australia, including to Aborigines, as well as the massive investment of Irish priests and religious men and women tending to the Irish settlers. For the boy who had played at defending Derry, this situation seemed a new siege, with conspirators already within the city.

Furthering the impact of religious and nationalist movements in a British imperial framework were some basic structural developments. When the *Austral* 'made the second fastest passage on record from London' up to that time, the combination of faster shipping, international telegraphic cables, and persistent cross-oceanic loyalties and interests all meant that the Australian colonies were well informed and concerned about European and other international events. Arguments for and against Irish Home Rule were closely followed within Australia, just as many other international events were, although perhaps not always with the same levels of vested interest as the Irish question. Family and cultural ties still bound many people in the Australian colonies to Ireland. When Thomas Kennedy was transported for treason in the 1790s, his opportunities for political agitation were practically at an end. But almost a century later, when Dill-Macky emigrated, the situation was quite different. The mass migration of Irish people, particularly in the wake of the mid century famine, provided the conditions for sectarian conflicts to spill over into the colonies to a much greater extent than had previously been the case.

Giving no hint of the discord he would bring, Dill-Macky commenced his ministry innocuously enough. The Scots Church community commenced a programme of church repair, refurnishing the simple building in Church Hill near Sydney's modern-day Wynyard Station. Dill-Macky and his family lived in a two-storey tenement attached to the church, serving what was quite an inner-city suburb, with a number of other denominations nearby. He was soon advertising his sermons in the newspapers, and the subjects he spoke on were fairly standard fare. Every week there were two sermons, a morning and an evening service, each with a different topic. 'Character better than wealth', for example, was the subject at 11 am on Sunday 26 June 1887, and 'Fidelity' was at 7 pm.

But the advertisement pages also revealed that he had got himself invited as a guest speaker at the '12th July Celebration' of the Goulburn Orangemen. The Orangemen movement originated in Ireland, and nominally demonstrated loyalty to Britain via reference to William of Orange. They saw themselves as defenders of religious liberty against foreign powers and Catholic absolutism, typified by their seventeenth-century bogeyman, the French King Louis XIV, and the very idea of the papacy. The ideological roots of this lay in the mid seventeenth century, which had seen much political turmoil in Britain and Ireland. The essentials of this were a civil war, followed by the deposition and decapitation of King Charles I, an ascendancy of Puritanism under Oliver Cromwell, followed by yet another invasion of Ireland, rebellions, monarchical restoration, wars and alliances with both the Dutch and French, sectarian conflict at home and abroad, and the looming figure of King Louis in France. But while ideologically drawing on this longer heritage, as an organisation the Orange Order strictly originated in the later eighteenth century, one of the many sectarian organisations of the period, opponents of and contemporary with Catholic groups like the Irish Defenders.

Dill-Macky's own particularly retrospective brand of Presbyterianism had primed him for this audience. A precis of Dill-Macky's speech was printed in the *Goulburn Herald*, the first of many of his speeches to be so recorded. He lamented not yet being an Orangeman, but expressed his desire to join. He made the listeners laugh at his trouble adapting to the antipodes, especially mosquitoes at night. And he was already convinced 'that Australia was destined to become a great and mighty nation'. But despite these opening comments, his fixation was on Ireland, the Irish, the Catholic Church, and especially the Catholic Church in Ireland.

'Irishmen are exceedingly gullible', he said, before suggesting that 'if the people were told what England had done for her during the past fifty years they would be led to love England'. This last fifty years was, of course, a period of time which covered the famine, when English policy in favour of the free market allowed market forces to redirect needed food away from hungry mouths, and where 'English' law facilitated the eviction of indebted tenant farmers. Rather pointedly, Dill-Macky's argument bears cultural comparison with jingoistic nationalism, which became increasingly common at this time, and also with fascism, the heyday of which was not too far around the centennial corner. He created a caricature of a whole people and a system of belief, neither of which he really seemed to understand, and ignored the wider context, and then posed an alternative yet positive caricature of his idealised group. He was arguing from prejudice, rather than depth of knowledge, and speaking to a very receptive audience.

Dill-Macky's speech continued in this vein, arguing that 'home rule' would mean 'Roman rule for Ireland', including a potted racial analysis. 'There were two nationalities in Ireland,' he said, 'the Saxon and the Celtic. The north of Ireland was Saxon, and was Protestant and loyal to the backbone.' The audience applauded this bit. 'The south and west of Ireland', Dill-Macky continued, 'were Roman Catholic and disloyal.' He was clearly excited, and must have presented a frantic figure on stage, raising his voice and feeding off the excitement of the crowd as he concluded loudly by calling out, 'God save England, God save Scotland, God save Ireland, and God save the Queen'. He failed to mention Australia, but the crowd applauded loudly anyway.

Two months later, in September, he was again out of Sydney, this time opening the Picton Presbyterian Church. But his travels, and pointed hostility to Catholicism and Irish Home Rule, began to bring him some unpleasant attention. Back in Sydney he advertised that the regular Scots Church evening sermon on 18 September was 'A Review of the Sermon preached by the Rev. John Ryan, at the Consecration Ceremony in St. Mary's, on Sabbath, the 28th ultimo'. He was deliberately and directly picking a fight. To be fair, he was responding to a sermon about the apostolic succession, Papal primacy, and assertions of the pre-eminence of the Catholic Church, which was hardly terribly sensitive either. While Dill-Macky was certainly on the more extreme end of sectarianism, it was not a thing ever only owned by one side, and each of the churches had their hotheads and cooler minds.

The following week Dill-Macky's sermon was on 'Papal Infallibility and the sacrifice of the Mass', ramping up his attack. His service was disrupted by the crashing sound of broken glass. A large rock had been thrown through the church window. His reaction is unrecorded, but it would not have been out of character to have pointed to it and gesticulated wildly as if it was a God-sent message that the Catholics were bad. Whoever threw the rock, as such things are wont to do, it most likely only encouraged Dill-Macky. The next year he was a fully fledged Orangeman.

Dill-Macky had only been in New South Wales for a little over a year when the colony celebrated a century of European colonisation. He chose 'Religious Patriotism' as his evening sermon theme, a suitable topic sure to draw a crowd. But it was not Australian patriotism he was on about, but rather his favoured British Protestant patriotism, which he again reflected on in February when he gave a public lecture about the siege of Derry. He 'gave a graphic description of the sufferings of the people besieged' and 'of the patriotic conduct of their leaders'. Having partly grown up in Derry while his father went in search of gold, he would have been able to offer good descriptions of the setting, perhaps drawing on his close affinity with the cannon 'Roaring Meg'. After he finished talking, he and his hundred-strong audience sang the national anthem: 'God Save the Queen'.

When Britain's Australian colonies had first been established, Britain was but one of a number of European empires, each striving for some global prominence. But by the later nineteenth century Britain's older main rivals had fallen a bit behind, and the newer rivals were yet to seem particularly threatening—at least many British people were convinced that this was the case—some, like Neil Brodie in the Pacific Ocean, knew differently. But in the suburbs it was a period of quite bellicose British self-satisfaction, when Britain really did seem to rule the waves, and enjoy perpetual sunshine. And it was one of the great ironies of empire that its strongest adherents really believed that it was the *Pax Britannica* that enabled them to live in peace and liberty, ignoring the fact that having an empire generally involved removing other peoples of their liberties. Later that year Dill-Macky would tell listeners in a speech at Wollongong 'that the granting of Home Rule to Ireland meant the surrender of the freedom and religious liberty that had been purchased at such severe cost by our forefathers'. Where he saw settlement, others saw invasion and repression, and each side struggled to see the other's point of view after generations of hostility.

Being a rousing speaker, he was regularly invited further afield to give talks. In 1888 alone he could be heard giving talks in Goulburn, Wollongong, Gundaroo, Nowra, Queanbeyan, and even a little-known locality called Canberra. Good railway connections allowed him to trip inland for a day or two at a time, and up and down the coast, all throughout a network of settlement leading out of the colonial metropolis. Probably no other of my ancestors was seen and heard in person by as many people as the Reverend Dill-Macky. No wonder some later commentators referred to him as a 'demagogue'.

Dill-Macky certainly had a certain 'culture warrior' status. But beyond his rousing speeches, his other interests and activities, although less well documented, help reveal wider concerns and developments of the period, and help soften the image he projected of himself.

For instance, a boating tragedy reveals that he enjoyed fishing. In this case, however, the day of recreation turned into a day of sombre duties. A nearby boat capsized, and Dill-Macky was soon part of the rescue, attempting, unsuccessfully, to resuscitate a child. He spent the remainder of that day comforting the shocked survivors and travelling to inform two mothers that they had each lost a child and one a husband. This was a side of his life the papers rarely reported, excepting only in exceptional circumstances like these.

And through charitable activities he showed his concern for Aboriginal peoples. By the late nineteenth century the Aborigines had not faded away as many commentators expected. Many Aborigines were fully integrated into the colonial economies. Many lived in fringe camps and reserves segregated by means official and unofficial. In very remote areas, others still lived in very traditional ways on traditional lands, although as pastoral expansion continued on the fringes of the settled districts such liberties were nearing their end within a generation or so.

With his brother Richard, who also came out to Sydney as a Presbyterian minister, Dill-Macky was one of a number of attendees in St Stephen's Church in Sydney in August 1890, where the idea of establishing 'a mission to the aborigines of Northern Queensland' was proposed. In fact it was Dill-Macky who proposed the motion that 'this meeting expresses its hearty approval of the proposed mission'.

Dill-Macky was also a member of the Aborigines Protection Association and attended a number of its meetings in the 1890s. Founded in 1881, this organisation administered and assisted a number of mission stations. Aboriginal peoples' experience of the missions is really quite varied, and although missions have come to have a very poor reputation, this generally reflects the troubles of later years and greater government interventions. In many initial instances, the missions' attempts to educate children, their provision of work opportunities, and their role in providing rations all facilitated the continued survival of Aborigines in areas where their traditional hunting and gathering opportunities were gravely restricted. The Aborigines were, it was believed, being protected from the worst elements of European culture.

And this focus on Aborigines was part of a wider set of concerns also directed at colonials generally, and this was shared by all the major Christian denominations. Although never a teetotaller, Dill-Macky was involved in a number of temperance initiatives aimed at reducing the effects of hard-drinking and gambling, particularly on the family economies of poorer women and children.

As an organisation that relied on charitable donations, the Aborigines Protection Association was limited in what it could do. The meeting reports reveal significant numbers of Aborigines voluntarily attending services and schools at the various missions like Cumeroogunga, Brewarrina, and Warangeada. The numbers of Aborigines present at the missions were recorded by officials as daily averages, because Aborigines would come and go, largely as they pleased. The fact that hundreds of Aborigines were fed and housed was a great achievement, and there were efforts to make the missions productive farms, which in theory would allow Aborigines a means of getting experience and training that would help them participate in the colonial economy. Yet when Dill-Macky gave a speech in 1894 in response to one of the reports detailed at a meeting, he stated that he 'regretted one thing about the report, namely, that the total income from donations and subscriptions only amounted to £310 12s 7d, and the Church ought to awake to its duty in the matter'. The biggest problems with these early missions, Dill-Macky thought, were the lack of public support and interest.

And following this line of his activities I found a sentence that helped me to see past some of his silly thoughts about Catholics and Irishmen. In an age where Darwinism had led to a proliferation of theories about the biological distinctiveness of races, where the primitiveness of darker-skinned people was taken as a given, and where there was a general scientific consensus that Aborigines were a lesser form of person, William Marcus Dill-Macky told this well-intentioned meeting quite simply that 'aborigines were as intelligent as whites'.

On a number of occasions Aborigines from the missions even attended these meetings, and sometimes children performed songs. The Association certainly reflected paternalistic ideas of civilisation and progress common to the period, yet, however culturally insensitive the missions could sometimes be, and though badly managed at times, generally their hearts were in the right place. But unfortunately the Aborigines Protection Association lost out to its notorious government-sponsored rival, the Aborigines Protection Board, which took over its responsibilities in 1897. With legislative backing and official powers, the Board ushered in a more active and increasingly harsh period of governmental intervention in Aboriginal affairs. It marked a wider shift in focus away from smaller initiatives aimed at encouraging Aborigines to learn the Gospels, to a larger insistence that they reject the Dreaming.

Yet, through the Presbyterian missions, Dill-Macky continued to know and assist Aborigines, and on at least one instance in the middle of 1900, Scots Church Sydney was filled with Aboriginal voices singing hymns, perhaps the first Aboriginal religious gathering on that spot for over a century.

Meanwhile, the colonies were moving towards federation. Dill-Macky was a supporter of the Commonwealth project, and in fact went even further. In 1899 he told a Presbyterian tea meeting that 'loyal though he was and conservative though he was, he did not hesitate to express his belief that Australia would one day become a republic'. It was a position he had held throughout that decade. In 1891 he gave a talk called 'The Genius of the Three Nations—England, Scotland, and Ireland', which he regularly repeated throughout the Australian colonies during his life. In it he expressed that he 'hoped that those living at the present time would see a federated Australia, and later an Australian republic, when the people would be united and would work along in harmony under the three great emblems—the rose, thistle, and shamrock'. By the time he was speaking at the 1899 Presbyterian tea meeting, he had perfected his phrasing and introduced another flower. He fully expected Australia had 'a great and glorious future' where 'the fragrance of the waratah would mingle with that of the rose, the shamrock and the thistle'.

This lecture on the English, Scottish, and Irish was clearly extremely popular. He gave it regularly throughout his whole speaking career, across large swathes of the country. Fortunately, a number of the local papers published lengthy accounts of his talk, so it is possible to get a sense of just what he said and how it was received. And while there was quite a bit of poking fun at entire peoples based on racial and cultural characteristics, especially the supposedly disloyal southern Irish, it was mostly delivered and received in quite a jovial spirit. It was, I tend to think, something like a Billy Connolly routine for Presbyterians. Perhaps with fewer swear words but more racism.

The late nineteenth century was a period when people in the Australian colonies, especially in the cities, seemed to be craving entertainment. Dill-Macky's lecture series was one response, but his involvement in other items also highlights what else was available. Clearly Orange Lodge marches and sing-a-longs could rouse a fighting spirit, but there was also the curious new Sydney experience which he visited: the Cyclorama.

This was in essence a large circular painting, contained in a specially built round brick building. Visitors would enter through a tunnel and emerge via a staircase into the centre of the room. They would then find themselves surrounded, as it were, by the illusion of being in the centre of a foreign scene. When it opened in 1889 it contained the experience of being in the middle of the Battle of Gettysburg in the United States of America's Civil War. Dill-Macky was listed in an advertisement as one who viewed it favourably, saying, 'My second visit. Simply marvellous. No one should miss it'. I did wonder if he would approve, however, of the advertisement offering half-price tickets on Sundays.

In some ways the Battle of Gettysburg suited the mood of the period, which had a certain militaristic flavour about it. Curiously, Dill-Macky was a prominent anti-war campaigner but also a military chaplain. In April 1889 he attended the weekend military camp 'at National Park' outside of Sydney, where large numbers of people flocked to watch the volunteer forces manoeuvre. Artillery, infantry, cavalry, and mounted riflemen, all paraded, marched, tramped, and drilled to the admiring gazes of their friends, family, and sweethearts. There was even a mock invasion, with defensive pits, guns, and an obliging naval force that did the attacking. Australians had played at storming beaches long before they really did it.

But as well as being a period seeking entertainment, it was a time of acute economic distress, and rising tensions between labour and capital. For Dill-Macky this was experienced mostly through a staggering array of charitable connections and activities. He was involved with the Sydney City Mission, where he shared board membership with prominent figures like the Australian-Chinese businessman Quong Tart. This organisation ran soup kitchens and provided emergency housing. Thousands of meals were given to desperate people each week, and the government was pressured to provide blankets and shelter for the many city homeless. Similarly, Dill-Macky was involved in what was euphemistically called 'rescue' work, helping women escape destitution-induced prostitution. Orphan homes were established and funded to help abandoned or lost children. And the spiritual wants of people were mixed with some of these initiatives through various missions: the Bethel Union—which provided services for seafarers—the Bush Missionary Society, and the unusual but apparently successful mission to the theatres later in the 1890s.

In one prominent speech in 1896 in Sydney's Town Hall, Dill-Macky pointed to the distress in his own neighbourhood, where he 'could name half a dozen families around about his church who were depending upon their husbands to get a few scraps of work'. He also 'could personally testify to the inability of large numbers of men to find employment' and went on to propose a fund to 'at least supply them with bread', because 'it was the duty of every man, no matter to what section of the Church he belonged, to follow the example of their Master and try to provide bread for those who were starving'.

And this destitution probably in part explains why twice during this broad period Dill-Macky's own house was robbed. In both cases the thieves were caught trying to resell the items at the local pawnshop. Once it was a silver plate, but the other time it was just a garden hose. On another occasion a sailor asked for food at Dill-Macky's own house, and having been fed, tried to sneak back in. Spotted by one of Dill-Macky's daughters from a window, he too was soon arrested.

So while it was a period of intense cultural development, it was also one of wealth disparity, class and cultural conflicts, and even a growing sense of the divide between the bush and the cities. Perhaps nothing exemplified this so well as the poetry battles between Henry Lawson and A B 'Banjo' Patterson in the pages of *The Bulletin*, where what I tend to think of as Australia's first great rap battle was played out. The two wrote a series of opposing poems, variously painting the bush and workingman's life as a place of gloomy hardship and misery versus one of manful pride and liberty. Ultimately, these disparate views are best remembered in the tension between the capable man from Snowy River and the mournful and desperate suicide of a swagman in Waltzing Matilda.

Even the Presbyterians were not free of discord. On 6 March 1894 many members of the New South Wales Presbyteries gathered in St Stephen's Church in Sydney. Dill-Macky was there, along with many other ministers, to participate in the General Assembly and to hear the new moderator. The Scottish-born George MacInnes, a well-educated minister, had been elected to the leadership position. The attendees also looked forward to an entertainment tea meeting afterwards, which was run by the Women's Missionary Association at the Young Men's Christian Association rooms. But as the ministers assembled, there can have been little warning of the theological tempest about to be unleashed in the normally quiet church.

Prayers were said, and the outgoing moderator gave a sermon. Then the General Assembly was formally commenced with a roll call. The new moderator, MacInnes, was introduced, and started his first address. His topic was 'The Bible, a sufficient witness to the self-evidencing Christ', but the lecture title belied its argument. He referred to shifting theological understandings within Protestantism, away from seeing the Bible as a 'verbally inspired and inerrant code of rules', to one that recognised the social and historical conditions of its compilation, and he sought to read it with this critical awareness in mind. In short, he was suggesting that the Bible, as read by the average Presbyterian, was not literally the unvarnished, complete, perfectly translated, and perfectly transmitted Word of God.

It was a dangerous thing to say. To Dill-Macky's ears it sounded suspiciously Catholic. And so, as soon as the speech ended, he spoke up.

'I desire', he called out, 'to publicly record my dissent from the address which we have just heard from the chair.'

Several voices were heard to agree with 'Hear, hear' and 'So do I', but the Moderator ignored them, and directed the Assembly move on to other business.

But Dill-Macky would not let it go. He probably started sharing his thoughts over tea and biscuits in a state of some agitation immediately after the moderator's address. Then, using the technique he had first used against the Catholic priests of St Mary's Cathedral, he delivered a sermon in Scots Church the next Sunday, rounding on the new moderator's position and explicitly responding to the address. He probably spent days furiously thinking, writing, and marshalling his arguments, all to dissuade his listeners from doubting the absolute reliability of their Bibles.

On Sunday he stood up to an expectant crowd. Dill-Macky's sermon was called 'The Verbal Inspiration of the Bible'. This was an explicit statement in itself. He opened by quoting a bit of the prophet Isaiah, and moved on to address more fully what he saw as the new moderator's misguided position, framing a deep schism within the Christian world. 'In our times', Dill-Macky said, 'we have two Gospels, each calling itself Christian, and each asserting its superior excellence. The one is satisfied to rest on the testimony of God, to stand by the old landmarks', which he went on to characterise as 'the old evangelical religion'. This, his flock were left in no doubt, was his side.

'The other Christian religion', he continued, 'states that Christianity, like any other system of knowledge, has evolved and developed.' It was a slightly simplistic view, but his whole approach was one of straightforward and opposing binaries, so the lack of nuance is not surprising. 'Is the Bible', he asked his congregation, 'an infallible record, or is it not?' He concluded by asserting his views that 'the address of the Moderator has given a handle to infidelity and to scepticism which they had never received from the Church in this colony before, and secondly it has bolstered up the argument and the practice of the Church of Rome'.

And indeed, the Catholics were greatly amused by this argument, as no doubt were many fellow Protestants and other theologically minded observers. The Catholic *Freeman's Journal* responded to Dill-Macky's tirade by pointing to the inherent ridiculousness of a position that held every bit of the Bible to be literally true: 'To take the Bible in a strictly literal sense, as it is translated—word for word, accent for accent, is of course absurd. For example, in the book of Job we find reference made to "the four corners of the earth"; but where is the sane man who would argue from that line (as Parson Dill-Macky and his clique must do) that the world is flat?'

The wound caused by the questioning of Presbyterianism's approaches to the biblical texts remained open for several months, and the fissure received widespread publicity, until in June a settlement was formally reached. Each side admitted of minor misunderstandings, and the divine inspiration for the original texts, conveniently lost many ages ago, was freely admitted by all. It was a weak backdown from the brink of serious schism.

Dill-Macky won his next major battle, part of a wider burst of inter-colonial political activity in 1897 concerning the proposed Federal Constitution. He was one of a number of commentators that advocated the inclusion of some recognition of God in the document and went so far as to 'credit' a Catholic who proposed an amendment to this effect. The debate even saw Dill-Macky characterising Edmund Barton, soon to be Australia's first prime minister, as 'a very poor theologian'. And then in the same speech, given at an Orange Lodge celebration, he thundered to the crowd: 'Let the Legislature remember that behind it was the people who created it, and who could unmake it.' This point was apparently loudly applauded. It was in some ways a profoundly ironic moment, I noticed, and wondered whether he had ever read Rousseau's *The Social Contract*, which argued that the basis of legitimate government was derived from agreement between the people and their rulers rather than divine appointment.

Yet, with the will of the people, it was so. There was overwhelming popular support for the idea, with Jewish leaders, as well as various Christian denominations, all advocating some recognition of a higher authority than the state itself. When the Australian Constitution was passed it included a reference to God, albeit in a fairly muted form: 'Whereas the people of New South Wales, Victoria, South Australia, Queensland, and Tasmania, humbly relying on the blessing of Almighty God, have agreed to unite in one indissoluble Federal Commonwealth', it said, in the opening to the document. Western Australia, dithering over federation, missed out on being in the document's opening lines, pointing to the very close-run nature of the federal movement. New Zealand, originally also part of the discussion, was given special mention to join at a later time.

But another key word in that opening sentence of the Australian Constitution is the word 'indissoluble'. Many of the people that voted to create the new Commonwealth of Australia, which was formally born on 1 January 1901, had lived through the years of the events reflected on the Cyclorama of the Battle of Gettysburg. They had seen that the greatest threat to national unity did not necessarily come from without, but could come from within. Even recent Presbyterian history could vouch for that. Civil strife was the greatest threat to national unity.

And Dill-Macky was on the right side, at least to my mind, of another major unifying issue. He 'spoke strongly in favour of extending the suffrage to women' in 1899. By 1902, however, his Catholic prejudice was causing him to have some limited reservations about this. He thought it possible that nuns would be restrained from exercising their free will by their superiors.

His prominence, his skill as a speaker, and his known pastoral work all led to Dill-Macky gaining a variety of leadership positions as the centuries changed. In 1899 he was Moderator of the Presbyterian Assembly of New South Wales and his portrait was taken and published in the *Australian Town and Country Journal*. This sort of public standing only increased the reach of his views. He notably took up the question of church precedence at official functions, rounding on the Anglican Diocesan Synod of Sydney for not insisting that their archbishop should take precedence over the Catholic cardinal at official functions at Government House. He also criticised the Governor for attending an opening service at St Mary's Cathedral. It caused some embarrassment when he turned out to be misinformed about what had been said in the homily, and that parts of the written version that could have affronted the Governor had not been delivered.

Further embarrassment came as Dill-Macky retired from the moderator's position. He had, it was reported, suggested that the bubonic plague, which struck the city in early 1900, could have been a form of punishment for the sins of the city. The outbreak of this disease, the same as the medieval Black Death, resulted in some social panic, more than a hundred deaths, and the quarantining of parts of the city. Dill-Macky's supposed theory may have been a misreported view, especially as he was concerned to ensure people in quarantine were ministered to, but it was probably not entirely unbelievable to parts of the reading public. Some of his views seemed, even by the standards of the final months of colonial Australia, rather outdated.

But in other ways he was surprisingly modern. He took to riding a bicycle, a fact revealed only because he had a serious crash in 1897. Apparently he came off near his church on a Saturday, and within a few days some internal injuries left him bedridden for at least three months, causing his doctors quite some concern.

Even light newspaper jokes at his expense revealed how the colonial world had changed. In an 1898 *Sunday Times* section called 'Our Telephone', he was the target of a joke about 'The Reverend Dill-Macky, Exchange'. It was a mock telephone conversation and spoke to his moralising about Sydney's vices. Late colonial Australia may have seemed like an almost anachronistic world, where people could have both the plague and telephones.

But from Dill-Macky's perspective the greatest threat his world faced was not plague, but Catholicism. As the new century started, he continued to beat the same war drum more loudly.

Sectarian discord burst from the bedroom to the courtroom in one of Australia's strangest celebrity trials. In early 1901 a new trial was being heard on Arthur Coningham's suit to divorce his wife for adultery. It was a media sensation because of the allegation that Alice Coningham had committed adultery with Father O'Haran, the priest who was administrator of St Mary's Cathedral in Sydney. Allegedly this had taken place in 1898 and 1899, in either the cathedral itself or the adjacent buildings.

Arthur Coningham's suspicions might have been raised by his mixed marriage. Alice was a Catholic, and regularly attended services at the cathedral. But the couple had a stormy relationship in general. During a fight with her husband, Alice allegedly told Arthur of the affair, and Arthur told his concerns to Dill-Macky. Because of his close association with the case, Dill-Macky was labelled by some parts of the press as 'Coningham's Chaplain'. The first trial fell through because the jury could not agree on the evidence. Coningham's first lawyer was even charged with encouraging witnesses to perjure themselves. There were suggestions that a second lawyer abandoned his case after learning Coningham stayed with his wife during the divorce application period. It was all a bit of a farce.

In the lead up to a retrial Dill-Macky tried to inflame public opinion against Catholic witnesses with the rather bizarre assertion that, because of the sacrament of confession, they could lie in open court. Dill-Macky seemed to suggest that because Catholics believed confession had absolved them of sin, sinful events were, to their minds, somehow undone. The newspapers loved it; the public laughed at it; the Catholic Church rejected it. Eventually, the jury did not buy it either. It was a rare case of a civil jury being asked to consider matters of church teaching as a matter of law, or at least an odd Dill-Macky-esque version of another church's teaching.

As the new trial approached, Arthur Coningham discussed the case with Dill-Macky and a clerk named James Exton. The three were discussing the new jury and had a list of the potential jurors. Dill-Macky was keen to ensure 'no publicans were on it'. They, he thought, were all either Catholic or sympathetic to the Catholic cause. The document turned up in court during the trial and the striking of jurors it highlighted proved to be a major sticking point for Coningham's cause.

There was another problem for Arthur Coningham. While being examined as a witness, James Exton revealed that 'Coningham carried a loaded revolver'.

Both amusing and alarming for the judge and jury, Coningham responded to this by saying, 'Yes, I have it here.' He then took a revolver out of his pocket.

The judge made the plaintiff give the gun to a constable. Coningham did so, but then, almost as if not reading the situation properly, he asked the constable to check how many chambers it had.

Then the cross-examination started, and Dill-Macky's close involvement began to further unravel.

Exton said of the weapon that Coningham 'told me it belonged to Dill-Macky'.

The lawyer questioned him further. Dill-Macky had apparently handed the gun to Coningham on the night of their meeting to discuss the jury.

‘What did he do with it?’ the lawyer asked Exton.

‘He’, Exton said of Coningham, ‘went out of the door and escorted me down the Glenmore road to within 100 yards of where Mrs Coningham lives.

According to Exton, Coningham then said, ‘If anyone molests you, shoot him.’

The trial went on for fourteen days, but the evidence was too thin. Ominously, a new range of dates for the alleged adultery were given, later revealed to have been given by a mole named ‘Zero’, a rival Catholic priest with some grudge to bear against the administrator of the Cathedral. But even these failed to stick. This only added to suggestions of conspiracy by the plaintiff which were hard to shake, and Dill-Macky was very embarrassed by involvement in the whole thing. He eventually broke an unusual and awkward silence with a public letter claiming that ‘I felt him to be an injured husband’ and stating that ‘I was compelled to do all in my power to right what seemed to me a wrong done to him’.

To many people it seemed like he had been rewarded for poor behaviour when Dill-Macky gained an honorary doctorate soon after the trial. But this was for his wide-ranging mission work, with connections stemming throughout Australia, China, India, and the Pacific, and also for his pastoral leadership. It was perhaps also related to his teaching work. In 1899 he had been appointed a lecturer in Systematic and Biblical Theology at St Andrew’s College at the University of Sydney, and the doctorate would certainly have been a welcome addition in that role.

I found his doctorate, much to my surprise, when I visited Sydney’s Mitchell Library, in the State Library of New South Wales. I had caught a train to Wynyard Station on a bright spring Sydney morning and had gone to have a look in the Scots Church. The building is not the one in which Dill-Macky ministered, but rather a larger replacement, which is now topped with elegant high-rise apartments. But the neo-gothic facade at the ground level still gives the building a churchy look and feel, and there is still a chapel inside. As I left, I noticed pamphlets trying to persuade me that people and dinosaurs lived together.

I walked east to the State Library and waited for the delivery of a family album of Dill-Macky’s stuff to the reading room. When it arrived, I could see pictures of him as a boy and a young man, his thin wife, his old mother, and various other family members. There were matriculation certificates from his school, Lodge membership materials, and, among other trinkets, his doctorate. It was strange to see these archival relics of a man I felt I had come to know relatively well. A complex man's life, it seemed, was almost reduced to a collection of letters, certificates, and photos.

The collection was mainly geared towards his ministerial and combative side, which really did not surprise me. As he got older he kept up his speaking tours, even visiting Wagga in 1901. In part this was a response to a new sectarian initiative, the Protestant Defence Association, which he helped establish in mid 1901. There was a great push over subsequent months to establish branches throughout the country, and Dill-Macky even travelled to New Zealand to help establish a NZ Defence Association.

To Dill-Macky's mind, and that of many of his followers, 'a great conflict was drawing nigh in connection with the educational movement'. The Protestant Defence Association expressed deep concerns about the new nation's identify, views which were vastly different from those of people like Dill-Macky's unfortunate father. In a speech in September 1901 Dill-Macky thundered from the podium that 'It was our pride and out boast that we were members of the great British Empire. It was our prayer that the Union Jack might long be our flag, and that our connection with the old land might remain a permanent one'.

The crowd cheered.

By the twentieth century, Dill-Macky was used to roaring crowds. He travelled the country, visiting local halls, and giving rousing speeches to crowds that seemed slightly fearful that their ascendancy was somehow under threat.

In March 1903 he travelled to Wyalong, a district in the South West Slopes of New South Wales, still a relatively young goldmining town. Mining persisted after the gold rush as a serious venture, and it is possible to see a mining frontier move through the continent in a somewhat similar manner to the pastoral frontier. For Dill-Macky, travelling from Sydney, this must have felt like the real back of beyond. Flat and dry, it was populated by strong men whose clothes and faces were dirty and dusty, and whose accents were very frequently Irish. It was the wrong place to give an anti-Catholic or anti–Home Rule talk.

The Wyalong Anglican and Presbyterian ministers both reportedly spoke out against Dill-Macky coming. This highlights how the Protestant Defence Association reflected cultural worries of a section of the Protestant communities, but did not necessarily encompass a unified or coherent Protestant theology shared by all Protestants. It is also a reminder that things done in the name of a religion do not always really originate from or properly reflect the tenets of that religion. Wyalong's Protestant ministers' relationships with local Catholics were fine, and they did not wish to see sectarian strife brought to their community.

But at 8 pm on Thursday 26 March 1903 the meeting started, and it was well attended. It was held in the Excelsior Hall, and entrance was by admission. Beyond that it is hard to be precise. The details get fuzzy because of what followed, and there are multiple, competing accounts of what happened.

As Dill-Macky began to speak, trouble was brewing outside the hall. A large crowd had gathered, apparently to protest against Dill-Macky's meeting and his agenda in stirring up sectarian strife. Soon rocks were flying, hitting the iron roof and breaking some windows. Men inside the hall reportedly broke chair legs off to use as weapons and rushed to the doors with these simple clubbing instruments. The women and children were ushered away from the doors and windows. There were some reports of gunshots being fired outside.

Responding to the disturbance, the local police magistrate read the Riot Act and demanded the crowd disperse. Many voices continued to yell and shout throughout the town. Some men from within and without the hall came to blows in the street. Those inside the hall apparently sang 'Rule Britannia' as this was all happening. Wyalong became a montage of chase scenes, bloodied fists, faces contorted as they yelled, children crying, and figures in the dark—all to the resounding chords of a very familiar triumphal song of battle.

The idea of 'Rule Britannia' being the soundtrack to a sectarian riot in far inland Wyalong strikes me as a moment that well expresses the tensions and ironies of this whole period. The whole logic of the Protestant Defence Association was that its members felt they were defending themselves against aggressive forces, yet their meetings naturally solicited this sort of reaction from frustrated people. One of the quickest ways to make a person mad, I have learned, is to start by intimating that they are already mad. Most people can only say 'I'm not angry' so many times before it becomes untrue.

Yet while correspondents and newspaper editors saw the Wyalong Riot as a tremendous story, the reality seems a little less dramatic. Certainly a man badly hurt his eye socket, either tripping while fleeing or being beaten, depending on accounts. There was considerable damage to the hall and also to the property of a sympathising shopkeeper. But this, when coupled with suggestions from locals that it was mostly young and bored youths doing the damage, might suggest there was some opportunistic violence for the fun of it going on as well. Not much happened in Wyalong normally, and anybody looking for a fight could easily enough adopt a convenient banner for the duration of the conflict.

And the police magistrate did quell the disturbance, which could easily have slipped out of his control, and this points to the participants generally acquiescing with the rule of law. The people were happy to have a brawl, but for the most part it did not go too far, all things considered. Apparently Dill-Macky was able to continue the meeting, which wrapped up about 10:30 pm. It certainly was not a night in which the social order entirely broke down, as some of the papers made it out to be.

But the widespread reports of the riot actually encouraged further trouble when Dill-Macky next went to Temora, another nearby goldmining town. There, prompted by news of the Wyalong precedent perhaps, almost the same sequence played out. Speaking in the Salvation Army Hall, Dill-Macky was interrupted by broken windows and yelling from a hostile crowd outside. One report said, 'it was the most disgraceful fracas that Temora has ever witnessed. Crowds paraded the streets looking for Dill-Macky till late in the night'. Apparently they tried to block him from accessing his own hotel and, by his own account, Dill-Macky had to be escorted from the hall by the police. He had no doubt that the experience of Temora was actually worse than Wyalong, and I wonder to what extent he may have pondered his own role in this, or whether the riotous behaviour simply confirmed his lifetime of suspicions.

In July that year he travelled to Wollongong to give a good old-fashioned anti-Catholic speech at the annual Orange Lodge celebrations. As the meeting started, a letter was found, warning the organisers that there was a bomb secreted in the town hall. A device was found hidden under the podium where Dill-Macky was due to speak, and it was discreetly removed. The audience had no idea, and Dill-Macky spoke anyway. It was suspected to be a hoax plot with a fake bomb, largely because of the warning note, but it must have made many people nervous. The Commonwealth of Australia was only a few years old and seemed to be on the cusp of major sectarian violence.

And inflaming the situation, Dill-Macky continued to travel ever more widely, giving his views a hearing in far-flung parts of the country. Soon after the Wollongong episode, he was in Melbourne, then Adelaide, before travelling inland to Broken Hill. He attracted huge crowds at each place, perhaps as many as 12,000 people in Melbourne, for instance, in what one headline called, perhaps with a wry editorial observation, 'Monster Demonstrations'.

Two years later, in 1906, Dill-Macky visited Tasmania. It was a rough voyage down, and one writer offered as proof of this the fact that 'two circus horses on board were washed down the hatchway'. A circus was a good analogy in some ways because the Orangemen phenomenon and the Protestant Defence Association gatherings, while ideological, also had a huge entertainment aspect to them that helped to pull in crowds. Dill-Macky was notorious, and people wanted to see and hear him because of that, not always because they shared his views.

Trouble was anticipated as Dill-Macky travelled throughout the island state giving talks at many towns, but generally the trip proved uneventful, at least in the sense of causing no major public disturbances. In some ways, it seems to me, the mood of the country had stepped back from that line.

In following his peregrinations I saw the same hostile language coming from Dill-Macky, but little reaction to it. I did some rudimentary testing of a theory, searching on reports of Orange marches as a guide. I noticed that there was a bit of a bell curve effect. Orangeism attracted considerable attention from about the 1870s but had practically diminished by the 1930s. The peak of Orange marching activity in Australia was really about the year 1900 and a decade either side. The pattern was not an accident, as it generally matched the period when Home Rule for Ireland was being seriously discussed and waned considerably as other ideological movements like communism and fascism began to attract greater attention, and bigger concerns like world wars eclipsed it. It seemed almost like those who liked to fight in the name of things simply found new names, and new conflicts, and the twentieth century would provide plenty of scope for that.

Dill-Macky returned to visit his beloved British Isles, but when he came back to Australia, he seems to have been almost disappointed in the land of his birth and the Isles he had so publically defended as the centre of a peace-loving empire of human liberty. And it was not just about politics: the British religious scene had changed. The success of the Oxford Movement in the Church of England particularly depressed him. The Anglicans in England were almost Catholics, he thought. Even the Scottish Presbyterians sometimes skirted with idolatry by embroidering their communion tablecloths.

In many ways it must have seemed that the world had moved on, and Dill-Macky had loudly and publically tried to hold it back, and failed. In an interview with him conducted in Adelaide in 1909, the interviewer revealed that Dill-Macky 'had been sent abroad by the Protestants of the Commonwealth to refresh and recuperate'. But this sounds a bit like positive spin. It is hardly an accident that he was encouraged to leave Australia in the wake of sectarian strife. He even seems to have fallen out with his students at the university. In his addresses to them he was still sticking to his earlier ideas about verbal authority and the Bible. He seemed to have been fundamentally stubborn, and his students got up a petition against him.

The 1909 Adelaide interview focused on Dill-Macky's various impressions of the United Kingdom. He thought that 'the suffragettes have injured their own cause by their peculiar methods and extreme forwardness'. He contrasted this with the situation in New South Wales where 'women's vote has been helpful to the best interests of the State' and was perplexed that the English were, he thought, too conservative to listen to him on this issue. He was a natural conservative, but it was good to see that some of Australia's progressive thinking had rubbed off on him.

He also thought that the British 'Government has been so anxious to please everybody that it has succeeded in pleasing nobody'. This was a sentiment I immediately recognised, briefly bringing on my own sense of disappointment in the poll-driven politics of my own historical epoch.

When the interviewer asked Dill-Macky a question on the 'Condition of Ireland' his response was harsh. 'I have never seen it', he said, 'in a worse state than at present. The landlord class have been practically banished, and a peasant proprietary established.' His father would have been happy for Ireland, I thought, even if the son was displeased.

And this may have prompted Dill-Macky to think carefully about the nature of the Australian political scene. In July 1910 he gave his annual Orange Lodge address with a fiery attack on the three-headed dangers of the Labor Party, the Catholic Church, and socialism, his new Cerberus. He encouraged his listeners to vote Liberal in the forthcoming state election. A few weeks later he was at it again. 'Never forget,' he called to the crowd, 'that Rome is determined to dominate Australia.' But in October 1910, no doubt to Dill-Macky's despair, Labor won the election. 'Fighting Mac', as he had come to be known, had failed to win over enough of the people.

Dill-Macky's address that July in 1910 to his Orange Lodge listeners provides a good insight into why Dill-Macky's influence was waning. He suggested there was an international plot to invade England and place a Catholic on the throne. Directing his listeners to the likely invader, he settled on Germany, apparently oblivious of the religious makeup of that country, which was almost evenly divided between Protestants and Catholics, and where Protestants actually tended to be over-represented in the army because of Prussian military traditions. It was yet another of those beautifully ironic moments I had discovered. He was right, of course, in seeing war between England and Germany looming, but he was seeing it entirely through the lens of a seventeenth-century sectarian worldview, rather than a late nineteenth century and early twentieth century imperial one. His was the perspective of a Northern Irish British Protestant settler family in 1688. He failed to see that the dangers of the coming century were not derived from Christian sectarianism, but rather from nationalism, empire, capital, and class.

After Dill-Macky died a memorial tablet in Scots Church said of him that he was 'A champion for righteousness and freedom and one of whom it can be said he never feared the face of man'. He certainly had a great concern for all kinds and classes of people, which was expressed with real charitable action. I admire him for this, and I greatly respect his sense of faith and his dedication to the Gospels, even while I do not share his millennial version. But I cannot help but see the profound impacts of his fostering of division. He helped push Australia to the brink of serious civil conflict, ostensibly in the name of unity, empire, reason, and liberty. But he did this with quick recourse to accusations of disloyalty and a simplistic failure to understand the people he accused of unreason. It is a terrifyingly familiar image. Even more worrying than Dill-Macky having held such views is the fact that he had such an enthusiastic audience. Rather than the egalitarian and easy-going people of national mythology, peacefully coming together at the dawn of the twentieth century, many Australians had proved themselves capable of vehemently turning on some of their own.

And further damning the myth of a peace-filled federal Eden was a great and popular yearning to be part of the British imperial project. Federation was a great achievement for democracy, certainly, and provided a model of secure and stable governance of which Australians could and should be proud. But not all was perfection. Aborigines were relegated to a secondary position in the new nation, the language and policies of a 'White

Australia' denigrated large ethnic minorities, and sectarianism bayed angrily. And while all this played out, many men and women left their homes, their families, and their communities to participate in Australia's last colonial war and its first federal bloodying.

CHAPTER THIRTEEN

THE EMPIRE'S MOUNTED RIFLEMEN 1901

GOOD DENTAL HYGIENE among children was, the *Sydney Morning Herald* reported in February 1901, 'a matter of both military and national importance'. This short line about teeth captures two major features of that year. Firstly, there was a new nation, less than two months old. After many years of agitation, the *Commonwealth of Australia Constitution Act*, a statute of the British Parliament passed in 1900, came into force in 1901 as a new nation's founding document. And secondly it hinted at the fact that as it formally came into being the Commonwealth of Australia was at war.

The *Herald*'s concern with children's teeth also highlights a third feature of 1901. The process of colonies becoming states joined together in a federal commonwealth was relatively seamless. The new *Dentists Act* illustrates New South Wales blithely continuing to regulate its domestic matters. The law was passed in the colony in late 1900, but some of its provisions were due to come into force in the state '[f]rom and after the first day of January, one thousand nine hundred and one'. The legislation shows how the period that straddled the moment of federation was one of both continuities and changes. Rather than violently wrestling independence from a tyrannous autocracy and making a clean slate, as many nations like to remember their births, Australia's foundation was more like autonomous governance granted by royal charter to large medieval towns, and a little like the *Dentists Act*—it was the administrative result of governmental decree.

And in that memorable but innocuous year of 1901 one dentist, Alexander Neil Brodie, made a decision that took him away from dentistry for a while. This saw him traverse issues relating to national identity, still being formed and articulated amidst the apparent paradox that Australia was peacefully founded while embroiled in foreign conflict. He experienced Australia's relationship with a mighty empire first-hand, and assisted that empire to assert its continued dominance over subject peoples and neighbours alike. And this choice to temporarily abandon his profession was perhaps encouraged, at least in some part, by tiresome bureaucratic changes to the local regulation of dentistry. At least, so the timing might suggest.

Prior to 1901 it was a mix of overseas professionals and local amateurs who had worked on the teeth of the New South Wales colonials. Alexander's career was really just getting started, so, because of governmental dictate, he was possibly anxious about his future in the beginning of what Manning Clark, one of Australia's most popularly influential historians, characterised as 'The Age of the Optimists'. Fortunately Alexander seems to have undertaken some form of apprenticeship, possibly with his brother James, also a dentist, with whom he worked for a while. Therefore, Alexander would have been eligible for professional registration under the *Dentists Act*. He had worked in the Strand Arcade in Sydney, part of Sydney's beautiful downtown wrought iron shopping district, so he may even have welcomed the opportunity to present himself as a certified medical professional. But then, perhaps he felt it was another instance of the law interfering in his life.

This all came on the back of a difficult period in Alexander's youth. His father's disappearance in 1894 had left Cecelia having to apply for probate of Captain Neil Brodie's will. She had several children to support, and while there was equity in property, this could not be immediately accessed. Neil had, in effect, to be declared legally dead. Strangely the insurers were more understanding than the law. In July 1894, the insurers had paid out the loss of the *Renard*, but the courts prevaricated over whether Neil might not still be sitting on an island somewhere. And, although Neil had told Cecilia in August the previous year that he would be back by December 'or the beginning of February at the very latest', and a hurricane and several months had intervened, the court wanted to give it another month to make a round year.

So for the young man, perhaps the new nation's military engagements overseas provided a dramatic alternative to dealing with the nuisances of official dental registration. Early in 1901, coincidentally the moment the *Dentists Act* came into force, Alexander applied for overseas military service. Oral history has it that Alexander offered to be a military dentist with the forces being readied for the Boer War, but was told that they 'already had one'. Apparently, good dental hygiene was not what was needed on that distant front, irrespective of the *Sydney Morning Herald*'s focus on the future military importance of strong teeth. Still, enthused perhaps by a mix of patriotism, curiosity, and adventure, he enlisted as a mounted rifleman in the 3rd NSW Mounted Rifles.

At the time, and seemingly ever since, Australians have been rather attached to the notion that the continent produces natural warriors. But the military authorities did not share this opinion, and as a result of their cynicism about natural national martial abilities, all potential mounted riflemen had to undergo a shooting test and then a riding trial. Far from being the archetype of an Australian knight, Alexander had never even ridden a horse before. It was not long before he came off, hitting the ground hard and breaking one of his fingers. But, undeterred, and apparently unnoticed by the instructors, Alexander got back on the horse. Fearful of being barred from service, he kept his injury hidden from official observation and somehow managed to pass his tests, only revealing the story to his family. Over the weeks that follow his broken finger set, thereafter always locked at a slightly odd angle.

On 21 March he steamed from Sydney with C Squadron on the *British Princess*, bound for Durban. He was now Sergeant Brodie. Before departure, the whole of this contingent was photographed, squadron by squadron, at Sydney's Randwick Racecourse. The photographs were published in one of the newspapers. And so, when I was looking for what I expected to be fleeting references to Alexander's activities, I was surprised to find him, arms crossed, in uniform, staring towards me, wearing the famous slouched hat.

The Commonwealth of Australia was only several weeks old when Alexander had this picture taken. It is probably that sense of a nation being engaged in a complex and quite murky colonial war at the moment of its founding which has long encouraged in me a particular fascination with Australia's Boer War in South Africa. This conflict seems to sit awkwardly across neat historical periods, and complicates and challenges many aspects of our later national mythologising.

But it is a difficult conflict to follow. The origins of the war go back a considerable way, and it requires a great deal of context to make much sense of why it happened. The fact that in Australia it is known as *the* Boer War rather misses the nuance of what actually played out in South Africa over several decades. Really, the conflict that started in 1899 is the final dreadful failure of politics and diplomacy to forge a solution to a range of problems concerning notions of race, land, autonomy, identity, capital, and empire, among other things. The ins and outs of some of the causal politics can easily do a person's head in.

It probably was not all that well understood by many people in the Australian colonies. But when war was finally declared between Britain and the Dutch Republics (Orange Free State and Transvaal) in October 1899, the Australian colonies, New Zealand, and Canada all enthusiastically offered to help. At least their political classes did, matched with much hearty cheering and flag-waving on the part of the wider citizenry.

This enthusiasm seemed driven more by a sense of contributing to the honour of the British Empire, than by any military need regarding the defence of a particular small part of it. But the early stages of the conflict only exacerbated this sense that honour was at stake. The Boers, as the enemy was collectively termed, inflicted a series of humiliating defeats on the British forces stationed in South Africa. Largely farmers with guns, the Boer commandos, as their units were generally called, proved incredibly capable as mounted infantry. Practised riders and shooters, they were good fighters if not traditional soldiers. Many were well equipped with modern German-manufactured weaponry. Supported by artillery, the Boers went on the offensive and soon drove back the limited British forces, and surrounded key towns.

News from the war generally reached Australia fairly quickly. One of the interesting things about the war, borrowing from reporting traditions of earlier conflicts, is the way that it was covered by newspaper correspondents. Winston Churchill was one, as was A B 'Banjo' Patterson. Because of the undersea telegraph cables connecting the globe, and the regularity of ocean travel, it was possible for reporters to keep readers at home well-informed of the progress of the conflict. Travelling to the warzone and embedding themselves with regiments, these men provided readers with accounts of the movements, battles, and experiences. Reports were telegraphed from South Africa to London, and then down through Asia to Australia, and longer descriptions were posted, and shipped from Cape Town to Australia's capital cities.

A number of these correspondents published accounts of the war, often written and published while the conflict was still in progress. These books give a particularly great sense of how the conflict was playing out, how it was experienced by the writers, and how it may have been understood by the readers of the time. The immediacy of these books, written during the conflict, indeed published before it ended, helps provide a sense of the 'vibe' of empire. Some of the details might be off, the analysis can be misplaced, several predictions get proved wrong, but the feelings seem very true to the historical moment. They have a general sense of racial superiority, which extends to denigrating the 'Germanic' Dutch Boers, expressions of annoyance at a little country attacking their mighty empire, a genuine shame in British surrenders and defeats, pride in British victories, fear and hope for friends, and a strong sense of the inevitability of Britain's coming victory. This was the type of material which my ancestors may well have read. In fact, they would have been hard pressed to find many alternative views.

Australia even had its own correspondent-authored war history: *How We kept the Flag flying: the Siege of Ladysmith through Australian Eyes*, by Donald Macdonald, published in 1900. On the front cover of my copy is a big picture of the Union Jack. Macdonald opened his account with a description of leaving Albany on the West Australian coast. He was heading to South Africa before fighting had even started, anticipating a war. The ship travelled, as he put it, 'across the Indian Ocean, which is so rapidly becoming a great English lake'. He self-consciously made a point of describing how unused to war he was, simply for being 'an Australian novice, whose experiences of fighting had hitherto been confined to such a small bush affair as the destruction of the Kelly gang of bushrangers, or a second-hand recital of the revolt of the Ballarat miners at Eureka'.

I think that G W Steevens's *From Capetown to Ladysmith*, also published in 1900, gives a good sense of the almost jaunty attitude to war current at the time. He was in Ladysmith, besieged by the Boers and cut off from the world. This little town was the focus and objective of the British world, which admired the plucky resistance of 'their' men. Catapulted into world fame by the siege, the whole Ladysmith affair played out though Steevens's words like a mix between a game of cricket and a medieval siege. A steady pounding of artillery was the daily routine, although this was often broken for lunch and during the night, and always on Sundays. The cannons were named and known, like the way that a medieval sword of legend might be. 'Long Tom' did not have quite the ring of 'Excalibur' about it, but it almost seems to belong to the same tradition. Unfortunately for him, Steevens's account of a bored, almost lethargic duel was brought to a sudden end when he succumbed to the enteric fever, which killed more people in that war than bullets did.

Winston Churchill's description in *London to Ladysmith* of travelling to the conflict, witnessing it, and even participating in it, is more action driven. It starts with his passing a ship of Australians on his way south. He too sets up Ladysmith as a modern castle, the object of a rescue mission. But it is an anti-castle, situated on the low ground, and surrounded by gun-clad hills. And, whether consciously or not, Churchill also seemed to indulge in a neo-gothic version of the war. Soldiers with regimental names like Hussars and Dragoons recall the great age of continental war against Napoleon, even the use of navy guns and gunners seems to suggest the military traditions of Francis Drake. But realising this I remain perplexed that Churchill did not make the obvious connection with another Dutch Republican battle against a great empire: the Dutch had fought off the Hapsburgs, the senders of the Spanish Armada, the empire that once threatened England. I do not think he saw the irony, or, if he did, he kept it to himself.

But Churchill, racing to the conflict, encountered and described images that resonate with the modern world. There were bicycle-based troops in this war. There were armoured trains bristling with cannon, iron armour, and gun holes. Churchill naturally saw this as the iron horse, the knight of the day, even though its armour failed to protect him from capture. A train in which he was a passenger was ambushed, so Churchill was caught and interred in a prisoner of war camp, although he did eventually escape. Following his flight from captivity, Churchill joined with the British Army on its march to rescue Ladysmith. He shared with other observers the same obsession with the pluck and skill of the British soldiery, and a sense of the honour and destiny of the empire. Knowing his later prominence, it is hard not to read Churchill's descriptions with a particular sense of future dread. He described battles where the sides bombarded each other's entrenched positions and sniped away at exposed heads. In one passage he describes a 'lad of nineteen' whose 'right trouser leg was soaked with blood'. Churchill asked the boy if he was wounded, but was told, 'No, sir; it's only blood from an officer's head'. It struck me as particularly poignant because stamped across this old yellowed page in fading blue ink is the labelling of a past owner of my copy of the book: 'Australian Comforts Fund Southern Division'. It was a book provided for the Australian soldiers of a later war, possibly read while recuperating from injury. I struggled to see how such descriptions would comfort them and pondered the possibilities behind some of the dark stains on the book's other pages.

But, sure enough, despite some initial setbacks and embarrassments, the empire managed to roll back the Boer forces and relieve the besieged towns of Kimberley, Ladysmith, and Mafeking. The British captured the enemy capital cities Bloemfontein and Pretoria, and by the middle of 1900 it seemed like honour was restored and the war was nearing its completion. The British formally annexed the Dutch Republics. A number of the journalists posted a last report and then went home to finish their manuscripts.

Unsurprisingly, many of the Boers rejected this settlement, and a guerrilla war developed. Relying on local support, they could disperse and strike at British infrastructure or isolated military elements. The British really only controlled the territory directly under the boots of their concentrated forces. They needed more men.

As Alexander Brodie's ship left Australia, another of my relatives was just about to complete his voyage to Africa. James Edwin White was the son of Eden White of Boho. In 1899, rather than follow his father into farming, James joined the Victorian Railways. He worked as 'a porter at the Violet Town station', carrying bags and attending to the travellers. He was thought to be a 'bright' fellow and was known for having a 'genial and obliging nature'. Well respected for his courtesy and professional conduct, James was known to many people and was well liked in the little town.

His opportunity to leave Violet Town came with a transfer to Spencer Street Station in Melbourne. He got to work in the signal box and for a time watched over the coming and going trains steaming in and out from the busy lines. It was soon the scene of a major public display.

On the last Sunday of January 1901, 'the heavy gates of the Spencer-street railway station swung open'. Then company after company of uniformed men marched out, with their legs and arms swinging in unison. A large crowd had gathered for the spectacle, aided in their arrival by special trains and tramcars converging on the station during the previous two hours. The streets of Melbourne were 'filled with dense moving masses of human beings', the very opposite of Sunday's normal emptiness. But the crowds, principally dressed in black, were relatively restrained. And the sombre line of marchers, some 'three-quarters of a mile long', processed towards the Exhibition Building, where the memorial service was to be held. The State of Victoria was mourning its namesake. Queen Victoria was dead. An era had ended.

But again the war challenged easy partitioning of time. *The Australasian*'s coverage of the procession was followed by the headline 'Troops for South Africa'. The paper detailed the 6th Victorian Contingent's imminent finalisation, preparations for 'the federal contingent', and then particular military preparations by each of Western Australia, New Zealand, South Australia, and Queensland, before moving on to describe some of the 'Indian troops' recently arrived in Melbourne.

Amid such heady imperialism James joined the 5th Victorian Mounted Rifles. Formally enrolled in February 1901, before the month was out he was en route to South Africa.

Even before Alexander Brodie's arrival in South Africa, the broad nature and direction of the conflict was changing from large sieges and set battles to a guerrilla war, as James was to experience.

Sometime on 4 May 1901, James sat down to write a letter to his parents. He told them that he was 'in the best of health and thoroughly enjoying active service'. One of the unusual features of Australia's participation in the Boer War is that relatively little official documentation has survived with which to track the actions of individual units and soldiers. But unlike some later wars, where censorship tried to restrict such frank accounts, Australians could and did write detailed descriptions of their activities to family and friends back home. Many of these were published in local newspapers, preserving a record of the documentation, even where the original letters have not survived.

About the time that James wrote this letter in early May 1901, some of the letters written by the Victorians back in March were being received in Australia. Troopers wrote of travelling towards the area of operations in a cattle train. To the tune of the click and clack of the rail, perhaps wondering if the Boers had sabotaged part of the line, as they were prone to do, the company 'travelled up day and night through the most barren and stony place'. There was apparently 'nothing to be seen on either side of the line except bare and stony kopjes', as the rocky hills were known. Eventually they arrived in the former Orange Free State, which was greener, with notable grasslands.

The fresh arrivals were keen for some action and were surprised to hear that a number of the Australians who had already been there a while were sick of it, and keen to go home. The new Victorians' major two complaints seemed to be that the military had ordered the nearest pub not to serve them, and bottled beer was grossly overpriced. But otherwise war seemed okay so far. James was probably still enjoying the novelty of foreign travel, and the austerity of military life may have had some appeal, reminiscent of camping holidays or rabbit-hunting excursions at Boho. The former railway porter was now wearing a khaki uniform, rode his own horse and carried a rifle and bayonet.

He was soon in action. The 5th Victorian Mounted Rifles were attached to General Beeston's column, a combined force driving the Boers from the Rhenosterkop area. In all likelihood James had not yet had his first taste of battle when he wrote home. When it came, other men in his contingent recorded the details in their letters, and the surviving correspondence, although each a particular experience, can be used to build a picture of the whole action.

James was in the 4th Division of G Company, and both he and trooper Bunting each wrote to their respective parents of their exploits. The middle of May was a particularly active time for the 5th Victorian Mounted Rifles. Bunting noted that the company 'had been in a skirmish or fight every day from 19th to 28th May'.

From the middle of April the company had been regularly deployed as part of General Beeston's column, sweeping across the land and rounding up the Boers. Many of the Australians seemed distressed when writing of these duties. As well as general scouting and combat roles, they were employed in rounding up women and children, who were often living in tents and were discovered hiding in isolated valleys from the invading armies. After capture, the newly imprisoned families were placed in concentration camps for the duration of hostilities.

In addition to this unpleasant duty, the Australians often had to kill captured animals, burn crops, and destroy houses. For the young trooper from Violet Town, whose own family were isolated farmers, the exercise must have been particularly distressing. The Australians found themselves at the pointy end of Lord Kitchener's scorched earth campaign.

And because of regular and long riding, the Australians' own horses were being overworked. Tired men and horses scoured the grasslands, constantly on the watch for Boer ambushes and the telltale dust clouds of mounted Boer commandos, but mostly finding themselves being directed against civilian properties.

One of the troopers from the 5th Victorian Contingent wrote home that it 'would take too long to explain everything, so I will just give a list of captures, &c., of the column up to April 25: - Destroyed two steam flour mills, took charge of 368 women and children, 68 prisoners of war, 12 surrendered, 33 Cape carts, 2032 head mixed cattle, 583 trek oxen, 3000 sheep and goats, 35 mules, 14 donkeys, 54 horses, 116 rifles, 245000 rounds of ammunition, 95 wagons, and 1 engine and thrasher'. The trooper was writing on what later became a resonant date: 25 April, ANZAC day.

The first military engagements that Australians undertook on their nation's behalf were, to say the least, messy. With such letters being written by hundreds of Australians and then read in households, towns, and newspapers across the new nation, it is easy to understand how profoundly many Australians went on to feel a need to wipe clean Australia's military record. When a later conflict gave them the chance, many Australians adopted the flawed notion that the nation enjoyed its first bloodying and 'birth' on a beach in Turkey on 25 April 1915—at least, those who believed the propaganda did. But that national mythological package needs to be understood not just as wartime propaganda or a grief-stricken re-imagining of events. It makes sense only by contemplating what had gone before. Almost any take on the 1915 landing on ANZAC Cove provides a much more reassuring image of Australia's role than the image of Australia's bloodied afterbirth, where women and children were violently wrenched from their homes and put in camps, many of them to suffer and die of starvation and disease. Australians' enthusiasm for the Boer conflict gradually waned in the face of such reports.

And this attitudinal shift was not despite the soldiery; rather it was, in part, precisely because of their first-hand accounts. Participation in this war did not necessarily mean agreement with its conduct or its conductors. Of General Beeston, one trooper wrote home simply, 'He is not too well liked'.

Yet, despite the overwhelming forces ranged against them and the savagery of the British plan to subdue the countryside and all on it, the Boers valiantly and stubbornly resisted the British advance.

The letters from members of the officer class often had more actual military detail, and suggest a slightly different attitude. Lieutenant Hennessy in James's company described the actions of a few days in late May to his family. On 26 May the company had its first major battle with a Boer commando of about 1500 men. Two divisions of the company attacked, one led by Lieutenant Murphy, which meant James probably participated. To the sound of nearby artillery fire, a cat and mouse game played out. Horsemen would rush to take seemingly undefended ground, only to find Boer marksmen hiding in the grass—at first they were mistaken for ostriches. The soldiers exchanged shots until darkness ended the battle and each side retired to rest before again fighting the following day. During this clash, James was probably on the other flank with Lieutenant Murphy 'bundling the inhabitants of the farm house out into waggons'.

The following day there was 'some sniping again', but nothing Lieutenant Hennessy thought worth reporting home. The Boers 'again made a stand' on the third day of this drive, but as their numbers thinned and the artillery was brought into action against their positions, it seemed like the resistance was beginning to wane. It was a very typical engagement of the sort Australians fought in this stage of the war: small-scale fights, with horseman racing into contact with each other, dismounting and engaging in a ranged shooting match, using the terrain for cover as opportunity provided.

Concerted skirmishing continued between the two groups for a fourth day, 29 May, which, interestingly, was a day covered by three of the various letters sent to home audiences. Lieutenants Hennessy and Anderson each wrote descriptions of the action, and James's friend Private Bunting also gave an account. It is notable that even in the rather confused and repetitive actions of General Beeston's drive the letters mostly corroborated each other, differing only in minor details.

The men of G Company got up early, breakfasted, and readied their horses and equipment. It was another cold winter morning in the hilly and tussocky grasslands of southern Africa. At 7:30 am they left camp, which was a little town of tents in the wilderness. The dawn lightened as the sixty-man company was diverted at an angle from the main column, which continued its inexorable march to tramp the Boer country into submission to monarch and empire. The men of G Company were told that they were being 'sent 8 miles to a place where some notorious train wreckers named Frickhardt lived at Driefontein'.

For three hours they rode without any incident or sight of the enemy. By about 10:30–11 am they were '5 miles from main column'. The further they went, they must have realised, the more likely an encounter became. The Boers would probably avoid the main column after the action of the past few days. In unfamiliar territory, the fifteen men of 4th Division were sent ahead. Lieutenant Murphy was in charge of the scouting party, and troopers White and Bunting were among the fourteen mounted riflemen under his command.

The scouting party rode on for another three miles before they spotted the enemy. They could see 'about 50 Boers on the skyline of a kopje ahead'. Lieutenant Murphy ordered a charge, and the men raced forward 'at full gallop'. But it was in vain. By the time they reached the top of the hill, the enemy had disappeared. The scouting party had discovered and lost the enemy within a matter of minutes.

The hill they were on overlooked a farm. There was a small ring of kopjes, and in the centre of them were a farmhouse and a round animal yard, known locally as a kraal. The scouts assessed their position. The rest of their company was half a mile back, in support, with another scouting group several hundred metres off to their right. There was no sign of the enemy. They decided to advance on the farm.

The Victorians reached the next kopje. And then 'the Boers, who had been in hiding, sprang their trap'. Well hidden in grass, behind rocks, in the kraal, and over kopjes, the Boers had lured the scouting party into an ambush. The only warning was the sound of rifle fire, which was too late for some. Shots came from both flanks and the rear, and the Victorians were caught in a devastating and deadly crossfire. 'The Boers rushed from all quarters,' one man recalled, 'and on the advance Private White was shot dead, poor fellow.'

The war had abruptly ended for the likable railway porter from Violet Town. The widely reported death of Lieutenant Murphy in the same engagement provides further details on what happened. 'They waited for the Victorians, and shot them like rabbits', one of the letters said. Fortunately

James's father did not have to suffer the knowledge of a lost child, as he died while James was away. The same was not true for his mother, however, who soon afterwards received the terrible news, delivered either by train or telegraph via the Violet Town railway station.

Trooper Bunting, who survived the assault, was captured and disarmed by the enemy. But he escaped to tell his story of the engagement. In a five word sentence that carried a dreadful echo, he conveyed his sense of loss: 'My mate was shot dead.'

But while James's war was over, the campaign against the Boers continued. 'We buried our dead the next day with military honors', Bunting wrote, and the company again mounted up and moved on.

In the meantime, Alexander Brodie and the 3rd New South Wales Mounted Rifles were part of Colonel Remington's column, operating in the Transvaal. The regiment arrived in South Africa in the middle of April, so it was only in early May that they commenced serious operations. Once again their movements and activities can be tracked through published letters in Australia, generally printed a month or so after the events described. And in one of the more bizarre yet fortunate such records, the captain of C Squadron, in which Alexander was a sergeant, even had a large extract of his diary published in the Sydney *Evening News*, leaving a day-by-day account of the actions.

The diary commenced on 13 May 1901 and reveals how movement itself was the main occupation of the Mounted Rifles. That day they 'moved from Vlaklaagte to Kaffrespuit'. Apparently an officer took ill, the third from the squadron. On the following day they simply 'Went to Leeuspruit'. The day after, they 'marched northwards, and had a 10-mile gallop after 200 Boers. No casualties. We captured 200 sheep'. As these tiny references reveal, Alexander and the New South Welshmen were engaged in very similar activities to James White and the Victorians.

C Squadron had a few skirmishes that month. On 16 May they were in the rearguard of the column when they were attacked on their right flank. With the aid of a cannon detached from the advancing column to provide support, the Boers were driven away and Alexander's group 'had no casualties'. The next day they followed up their minor success. 'Chased Boers that had been following the rearguard for ten miles in the direction of Bethel,' the diary said, 'and burnt the house where Botha and Smuts had slept the previous night.' When I learned that I had an ancestor in the war, I had never entertained the idea that he would be so close to key figures, even if only in the form of watching flames destroy a farmhouse where the enemy's leaders had slept. Having destroyed the property, they took the animals. 'We captured 500 head of cattle and sheep', the captain noted.

Heading towards the town of Bethel, C Squadron had a 'sharp engagement'. The captain was no more specific, other than noting that they 'had four horses shot'.

The diary does not convey the stress and exhaustion the men must have felt, but sometimes it is possible to uncover more of a sense of things from a close reading of the terse notes. They left camp the next day at 5 am, information that was not usually diarised, which suggests it may have been an early start. And this was followed by 'a running fight all day', where the first human casualties were recorded in the diary. From this point onwards records of human deaths became more common, those killed mentioned briefly, buried quickly, and left in the rear as the column moved always onwards. 'C Squadron has done everything that has been required of it', the captain noted in a rare reflective moment, before noting that it 'is bitterly cold of nights here'.

A few days later C Squadron was ordered 'to charge a kopje', where they 'captured four prisoners, two horses and saddles', before chasing after a Boer convoy they had spotted in the distance. 'Shelled it, and returned to camp' was what the captain said of the attack, mentioning only one additional detail: the capture of 'a few Boer families'. The next day was spent guarding the main column from a hill, before 'blowing up three farm houses' and bringing 'the women into camp'. Kitchener's plan was clearly being put into terrible effect by the New South Welshmen. Regiments from New Zealand and Queensland were engaged in similar activities, some of which C Squadron encountered in its advance. The combined British forces were enacting a massive operation to clear the land of all opposition.

For C Squadron, a small part of the greater British strategic sweep, the war continued like this over the remainder of the month, with minor skirmishes and the regular capture of prisoners and animals.

The captain was mightily pleased by C Squadron's performance. Writing on 6 June, he gave an account of the past few days. 'We had hard fighting for the last four days, and C Squadron has won great praise from the General. The day before yesterday, while in command of the advance guard, and after a five-mile gallop, we came right on to General Botha, Schalk

Burger, Smuts, and a number of the Transvaal officials. At 800yds we poured volleys into them, and unhorsed eight, wounding many, one of them supposed to be Botha himself.' Too few to 'effect captures' and too far from supporting forces to be entirely safe from being cut off, C Squadron returned to the safety of the column, where the general toasted their engagement.

'We have had', the captain mused, 'some miraculous escapes, bullets falling like hail all around us, and not a man of C Squadron has been hit yet, although two have had their horses shot. We have lost in the regiment three killed and eight wounded, and two died of disease'. As he wrote in his diary after a supper of 'broth, boiled fowl, potatoes, cabbage, bread and butter', he reflected on how it was all very 'excitable and enjoyable'.

This was an officer's view, and the ordinary soldiers and non-commissioned officers like Alexander may have looked on the adventure differently. Although not a member of C Squadron, Trooper Issac Bewley from E Squadron wrote home about this time with another perspective. 'Life in South Africa is not what it is cracked up to be', he noted. 'Three biscuits and 1lb of meat a day is the regulation allowance', which was easily lost to flies and other fellows if not watched carefully. 'We have been in the field now over five weeks, fighting almost every day', Bewley complained, 'it is cold over here. Frost an inch thick every night, and we have to sleep out in that weather. Yes, war is all right, but it's not the game (for us) that it's cracked up to be.'

But clearly the C Squadron captain felt it was a bit of a game. 'He was stalked like a kangaroo', he detailed, writing of one encounter with the enemy where they killed a man. Yet even his jauntiness wanes as the diary extract reaches its conclusion. 'Flour and raw mutton ration', he noted, because there was 'no wood to cook it; men hungry'. Soon there was 'a night march' and another day where they simply 'went on and on'.

In July a medical officer attached to the regiment was worried. 'We have had a fairly rough time of it', he wrote, 'in fact, I think the General is working the men a bit too hard, but the New South Welshmen have stood it pretty well.'

As well as writing to friends and family, as the war continued many of the men wrote home to comrades who had been wounded and returned to Australia. After action, news of casualties gradually filtered through the military administrative machine and then via telegraph to London, and eventually word reached Australia. And so the Sydney *Evening News* of 12 August 1901 reported what my family dreaded to hear: 'near Heilbron

14th July: No. 1120, Sergeant A. N. Brodie, 3rd Regiment N.S.W. Mounted Rifles, slightly wounded'. Often tales of injuries got home through formal and informal mechanisms, so they likely knew of it without the aid of the paper, but if they had not, they may have taken solace in the adjective: 'slightly'.

I endeavoured to find an account of the action that wounded Alexander, but could not find one. The official record was terse, but fortunately family tradition helped to fill out the detail. Apparently he was shot while using a small shrub for cover with another trooper. Presumably they were engaged in one of those ranged shooting matches that seemed a common part of this war. Having used their horses to track the enemy and get in range, or perhaps having been ambushed, the Mounted Rifles spent their time fighting with their feet or bellies firmly on the ground. In fact, when he was shot, Alexander was 'facing the enemy with another fellow', and lying prone to give himself as low a profile as possible.

When lying down, soldiers did their best to keep their heads down when not actually aiming and firing. This results in the highest and therefore most exposed part of a hiding body being, ironically, the bottom. And this was where Alexander was shot, specifically, 'in the right buttock'.

'The wound was a through and through of soft tissue', fortunately for Alexander. A fleshy wound in the bottom is better than many of the alternatives. And it brought him home from a war that he was never afterwards very keen to talk about. Yet before he left, he had one more ordeal. He was taken to the field hospital for treatment. While there 'a severe storm came up, blowing the tent down'. The wind, howling through the flapping canvas, caused the centre pole to topple. It fell on one of Alexander's fellow patients, killing the man, who was still in his bed.

In November 1901 Alexander arrived back in Sydney, having trained, been sent to war, fought, been shot, and returned, all in less than a year. During the time he had fought in an overseas campaign, the university had not yet fully established its Dental School, despite having been planning it since the start of the year.

By then, public interest in the war was fading. The big battles and honourable rescues had passed into memory, and the ugly guerrilla war continued. At the start of that month even Alexander's jolly captain started a letter with a telling sentence: 'The end of the war seems as far off as ever.'

Eventually, in 1902, the war did end. The formal termination of hostilities was a final official blip in a story that had already faded away in the minds of many. Between the war's start and end Australia had federated and Queen Victoria had died. Despite the continuities it did seem a time of change, and of moving on, and a distant and dirty conflict was of limited interest in people's daily lives.

But for some the war continued to be raw and real.

Mrs White received James's letter on Monday 10 June 1901, informing her that he was well and happy. By then he was already dead. News of his demise reached the town on 15 June, the following Saturday morning.

Trooper White was the second of Violet Town's young men to be killed and buried in South Africa. Private Charles Edwin Williams had been killed in battle in February 1900, one of the first of the Victorian contingent soldiers to fall, and soon thereafter the town had begun to prepare a memorial. News that James White had also been killed reached the town before it was completed, so his name was also added. The monument was unveiled on 3 July 1901, only a little over a month after James was shot dead and buried. At about 2 pm, a party of mounted riflemen marched into the town. But the train was late, so they dispersed, and only reformed when the train arrived with more soldiers and spectators. Many probably thought of the young railway porter whose name was covered with cloth. Several dignitaries took up seated positions, and apologies were recorded from those unable to attend. A member of the Legislative Assembly gave a speech, suggesting that the monument did credit to the townsfolk and 'was absolutely the first of its kind which had been erected in the Commonwealth'. He stressed how it 'showed that those who remained at home fully recognised the sacrifice made by the men who went to aid the empire's cause'. 'Australia might congratulate herself on the broad and free lines of the constitution under which she flourishes' he went on, before finally the cloth was removed.

Carved in red granite with gold lettering on one of Australia's first memorials to the Australian dead of a foreign war are the simple words: 'In Memory of Private James Edwin White, 5th Contingent V. M. R., Killed in Action at Middle Kraal, South Africa, 29th May 1901. Pro Deo Et Patria.' For God and Country, the last bit means. In the Commonwealth of Australia's first year, it marked the beginning of a new phase of Australia's town and city architecture.

Trooper White is remembered on two other memorials. He is on the Roll of Honour at the Australian War Memorial in Canberra. This large structure that sits at the foot of Mount Ainslie was prominently placed in relation to Parliament House so that Australia's leaders would be reminded of the potential results of their decisions on the lives of ordinary Australians.

But at the time of James's death the sites of both Parliament and the memorial were still sheep paddocks.

In 1904 another monument with James White's name on it was unveiled, this time in Melbourne. It was described in a Victorian paper as a 'splendid column erected by the members of the Fifth Victorian Contingent to the memory of their comrades who fell in South Africa'. This paper also commented on the way the regiment of Australians were poorly served by being 'placed under the command of Imperial officers who were quite inexperienced', and that the British were arrogant in their dismissal of the Australian soldiery. It is hard not to detect a whiff of myth-making here that would carry down the ages. Alexander Brodie's captain, who compared hunting Boers to hunting kangaroo, was certainly Australian, after all. And this captain's great pleasure at being noticed and applauded by his general points to a distinctly Australian urge to impress the empire, which sits awkwardly with that other urge to blame it when things went awry.

Learning of this monument, I decided to visit it. Staying in downtown Melbourne where streets were once filled with the massed supporters of empire, I walked one clear morning down Swanston Street, past the magnificent Flinders Street Station, across the Yarra, and towards the Victorian War Memorial. Removed from its original position, the Fifth Victorian Contingent Memorial was immediately recognisable, tucked slightly to the side in a patch of greenery. I walked up to it and searched for James's name. It is a three-sided thing, with inscriptions of the places of battles, and I soon saw 'Rhenoster Kop' carved around a pillar. This was the place of his death. At the top of this side was inscribed the line 'King And Empire'.

Around the corner, beneath 'Honor The Brave', was the plaque which bore his name. His was the last listed: 'Private J. E. White'. And then I continued around to the final side, which faces the Victorian War Memorial to the Great War. And there was inscribed a final three-word phrase from Boer War veterans who wished to remember their comrades: 'Lest We Forget'.

This line was most likely taken from Rudyard Kipling's 1897 *Recessional*, a poem that was soon turned into a popular hymn, widely printed and known in Australia before and at the time of the Boer War. Written in connection with Queen Victoria's jubilee, its refrain, 'lest we forget', pointed out that God should be remembered as the arbiter of empires, and pleaded that Christ's sacrifice on behalf of humanity be always kept in mind. It became a popular sort of 'battle song', but carried a message that warned against self-seeking glory and unqualified belief in the exercise of human power. When inscribed on this memorial, one of the first to carry it, this phrase had meanings often subsequently misconstrued. More than simply attempting to remember the dead, it pointed to a hope that they were with God, linking sacrifice and salvation. And it served as a very public reminder that even empires were not above judgement, rebuking the hubris of political powers by listing the names of the dead, and thus acting as a warning to future ages against making unnecessary sacrifices.

Whatever prompted Alexander to fight in South Africa, when he returned to Australia he renewed his interest in dentistry. And this took a peculiar turn, remembered only relatively vaguely in family tradition. He went to Philadelphia in America to get his doctorate in dentistry, working his way there on a cattle ship. I managed to find evidence of this story in the American immigration records for the cattle ship *Merion*. He had already made his way to England before boarding this ship, which left Liverpool in the United Kingdom on 30 August 1905 and arrived in Philadelphia on the other side of the Atlantic Ocean a bit over a week later on 10 September. Crossing columns 8 and 9 of the US Immigration form, which were 'Nationality' and 'Race or People', the word 'England' was handwritten next to the twenty-seven-year-old Alexander Brodie's name. Deep in my gut I want to correct the form: it should be Australian.

A series of lines were also ruled across the form encompassing all the men listed, and a single sentence was written to cover the various columns like occupation, destination, and such like. It said they were all 'Cattlemen holding Certificates of Admission into USA'. This Boer War veteran was, albeit very briefly, an American cowboy.

He said of his experience of Philadelphia that it was 'freezing cold'. Apparently he boarded with a fellow Australian, and to the dismay and irritation of their landlady, they would heat 'a brick over a gas ring to keep warm'. He had arrived in the northern hemisphere's autumn, so the onset of a Philadelphia winter would have been a rude shock after Sydney.

Once he was qualified, Alexander returned to Australia, stopping briefly at Fremantle in October 1906 on his way to Sydney. As when he arrived in America, an immigration form recorded his arrival, this time denoting his 'race' as Scottish. Even his own country, officially preoccupied with race, denied him the label of being Australian.

Nonetheless, although Alexander was still a long way away from the eastern states that he was more familiar with, Western Australia is undoubtedly and unmistakably Australian, so I suspect that the man that left as a cowboy and returned as 'Dr A. N. Brodie' felt a profound sense of homecoming when he stepped once again onto the land of his birth. And despite some intimation of misgivings about his war experience, he seems to have been in the Australian Garrison Artillery in 1909, suggesting he was still prepared to fight for his country if needed.

But apart from this hint, his focus had firmly shifted to civilian life. Alexander re-established himself as a dentist in Sydney, where he married Ellen Dill-Macky, daughter of the minister of Scots Church. Her father performed the ceremony, with the assistance of her uncle Richard, who had come down from his church duties at Byron Bay. Alexander took up the leisurely sport of bowls, entering occasional competitions between the dentists and the doctors. Through dentistry, he did well enough to invest in some rural property, including owning a sheep station named Yootha at Tooraweenah. Poor health compelled him to take early retirement, during which he developed a love of painting. Grampy retained a number of Alexander's efforts, some of which are copies, I have been told, which helped him to develop his techniques. As a lover of painting who is not a talented painter, nor an expert, they quite appeal to me. But perhaps that is as much the subject as the skill, because what this veteran who rarely spoke of his foreign war chose to paint again and again, until he died while Australia was in the grip of a second world war, were peaceful scenes of the Australian bush.

In some ways the Boer War joined a list of conflicts Australians would rather have forgotten. Both the various frontier wars against Aborigines and the conflicts in New Zealand were part of our military history, yet were often relegated to the status of police actions against rebellious and ungrateful enemies of the civilising power of the British Empire itself. To an extent the Boer War joined this club, later remembered as another dirty colonial war, its unsavoury concluding actions in contrast with the narratives of British martial supremacy and colonial military excellence that lauded its coming and early stages.

But lecture circuits, books, associations, friendships, memorials, and pictures on mantelpieces kept the war in many people's minds. Whether as the purest form of jingoism, the embarrassment of an enthusiasm misplaced, or the grim burden of injury, memory, and grief, the war lived on as a scar on the generation that lived through it, proudly born by some, resented by others. This generation notably included the young boys who saw the uniformed marchers, and many of these boys later grew up to march themselves.

Even after its conclusion, the Boer War continued to inform Australia's engagement with the empire. It proved an historical touchstone for commentary, revealed in the way that during the early twentieth century the Boer War remained a subject of discourse in Australian newspapers. Steadily increasing in frequency of use, mention of the war declined through the 1900s as the decade closed, before creeping upwards again as another war loomed, peaking, not without accident, in 1915. It put into sharp contrast the first 'world war', where in a single action more shells could be dropped than in the entire 'Boer War'. By making reference to this earlier known war, commentators were able to convey the horror of a scale of destruction that had previously been unknown.

Before that challenge, however, the Boer War helped conclude a subtle shift in many Australians' sense of a shared identity. It would not be unfair to say that in 1788 Britain saw itself as having an empire, but by 1901 it saw itself as the Empire, and Australians bought into this shift. Australia's colonial story had commenced in the midst of a British struggle to maintain, extend, and redefine its empire in the wake of a changing global power structure. American Independence, Irish intransigence, French Revolution and global war, the rise of the Russian and German empires, and many other conflicts and threats had taken their toll, yet also seemingly extended British hegemony. Yet Australian histories have so often wallowed in Australian exceptionalism, the idea of particularly local causes and effects of exclusively Australian phenomena, that they have often missed this much bigger picture of which the Boer War was a prominent part and illustration. More than anything the Boer War violently proves that Australia was and wanted to be a partisan part of a global world order. But in the face of such an aggressively outward-looking national perspective is the everyday reality of the post-Federation moment and the fact that much of everyday life in Australia went on rather as before.

CHAPTER FOURTEEN

BLUE MOUNTAINS AND BROWN PLAINS 1912

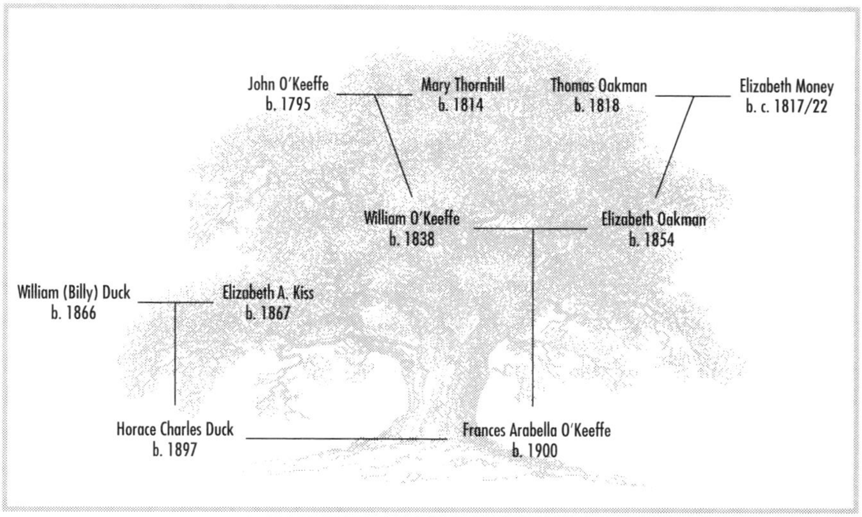

DURING THE WINTER of 1912 a young girl sat down to write a letter. She was in Umbango, a small farming district in the lower western slopes of the Great Dividing Range, which extends up much of eastern Australia, just below the Snowy Mountains. The Umbango Creek runs through a fertile little valley, carved out by the cold snowmelt and gathering precipitation, ever flowing down into the great rivers that run to the west and south.

The young girl was Frances Arabella O'Keeffe, born in the year 1900, the last colonially born of my ancestors. 'Dear Uncle Jeff,' she started. 'There has been a nice fall of rain here lately. All the farmers have their crops in now. There is going to be a football match between Tarcutta and Humula. I like to watch a good game of football. I go to the Humula school. There are about 60 children going to the school; I like going.—Your fond niece, Frances O'Keeffe (11 years 11 months).' She posted the letter to the *Albury Banner* newspaper, and it was published.

In the newspaper, children throughout the region communicated with 'Uncle Jeff', and through him, with each other and a much wider community than their own little valleys or communities huddling on the western plains. He was their 'uncle' by literary convention. And these children's letters, providing specific news of some historical interest, collectively demonstrate the means by which widely dispersed people developed and maintained a common sense of identity. This was the shared childhood of a young nation.

Jeff briefly appended a response to each letter. For Frances, he offered a wish: 'I sincerely hope the farmers will have a good crop this year.' Although Frances's letter was understandably childlike, it followed a pattern quite familiar to other of Uncle Jeff's correspondents and to the wider correspondence of adults during that time. Frances came from agricultural folk very concerned with the weather, as only subsistence people can really understand. Moreover, she reveals that there was a sense of community, local and regional, expressed by sporting and social events. And with other writers, and in the very act of writing itself, she shares a common focus on education, which was slightly egalitarian in its objectives and progressive in its aspirations. This was the ideal of Australia in the early twentieth century: anchored in place and community, looking to the future.

A photograph of Frances taken some years after she wrote this letter shows her aged about sixteen years old, standing beside a horse and what Pa, my grandfather, once told me was a nephew. She is dressed in black, an outstretched arm keeping the toddler in place. He is in white, matching the painted wooden house peeping over an unpainted wooden fence. He also almost blends with the ground, which could be dirt, or probably snow. Frances's shoes are also either muddy or covered in snow. She is dressed for the cold.

Wire netting at the base of the fence highlights that they had problems with rabbits and possibly foxes. This photograph could have been taken in almost any ex-frontier agricultural setting: the Wairarapa Valley in New Zealand's North Island; the Shenandoah Valley in Virginia; or in Argentina or Chile, parts of North America, Eastern Europe, Western Asia, South Africa, or many more. At the start of the twentieth century many people's domestic lives and work routines would have been fairly recognisable to their ancestors from a century or so previously, as well as being recognisable in broad terms to their contemporaries on many parts of the planet.

But even at the time Frances was writing to Uncle Jeff, her secure agricultural world had already begun to crumble. For many Australians, Miles Franklin's 1901 novel *My Brilliant Career*, with its story of feminine frustration at economic hardship, rural isolation, and insecurities about country 'bumpkin' ways, captures the tensions of life and culture in this period with a distinctly Australian flavour. But Frances's early life proved harder than Franklin's literary version. By the time that photo was taken, even before she had written that letter to Uncle Jeff, both of her parents were dead.

The O'Keeffe branch of my family tree spreads upwards into a huge Irish clan from County Cork, whose arrival and dispersal in Australia echoes a familiar colonial pattern. Frances's father, William, was born in Ireland and came out to Sydney in the *Portland* in 1841 with his father, John, mother, Mary, and a few siblings. The young family settled for a time in the Bankstown district, before moving south in that great wave of migration towards Albury and the Riverina, where they established themselves as farmers. Along the way they stopped at Gundagai long enough to have a child, and if they were still there a few years longer they may have seen the Murrumbidgee flood that town in 1852, one of the worst natural disasters in Australia's recorded history. But more than simply reflecting the past, in the early federal period some of this was relatively recent family history.

In settling in Albury, Frances's grandfather John O'Keeffe had successfully moved from labourer to landholder like so many others at that time. According to the immigration records, his wife, Mary, was a nurse. John and Mary had defied sectarian differences, and a fair age discrepancy, to leave a troubled Ireland behind. Love conquers all, apparently, and if it does not, then lovers can skip town. After many years of farming, John died in 1879, leaving a large family with intergenerational ties to his 'new' land. Mary lived to see the colony absorbed into the new Commonwealth of Australia. She was a grandmother to the young of an officially youthful nation, capable of remembering the voyage out on sailing ships in the convict days. As did thousands like her, she provided a cultural, memorial, and embodied continuity between that first arrival and the federal infancy.

Frances O'Keeffe's mother's people similarly marked her world, even by their absence. She possessed a photograph of her Oakman grandparents which she kept and passed on to her son. It had been taken sometime in the later nineteenth century, but was an important object in Frances's life in 1912, one of a few objects that would have connected her to her colonial roots. Frances's mother was Elizabeth Oakman, born in the colony not long after her parents' arrival. The senior Oakmans, Thomas and Elizabeth, came from Cambridgeshire in England, and sailed to Sydney in the *Blundell*, arriving in 1853. They too settled in the Bankstown district, so it is not implausible that young William O'Keeffe knew the baby Elizabeth Oakman. He was sixteen when she was born.

Frances's maternal grandfather, Thomas Oakman, was a farm labourer who had managed to pay £3 10s to put his family on a ship to Australia. His parents were all living in Thetford, in Cambridgeshire, and his wife Elizabeth's were in Ely. He could read and write, Elizabeth could read. The three young children could not, although in Richard's case it could hardly be otherwise, given he was only an infant. Thomas's older brother and family were also on the ship, so it was another case of familial, generational migration, and that pattern continued, eventually bringing the combined families into the hills at the headwaters of the Riverina. But this had all taken place before Frances was born; she had never known any other place or region.

For about two decades the Oakmans worked the small farms and gardens in the Bankstown area that fed the growing and hungry city of Sydney. Like many recent immigrants, and paralleling the O'Keeffes, they probably had a mind to save up and establish themselves further afield on a larger selection. By 1867 Thomas's brother William was a farmer at Tumbarumba, and about this time Thomas and his own family moved south as well, although not as far as Albury. The Oakmans settled in that little locality of Umbango, near Tarcutta, relatively near Thomas's brother. In 1871, when Elizabeth was seventeen, she and William O'Keeffe married in Wagga and went to live at Humula, slightly further up the hills towards Tumbarumba.

By the early twentieth century historians and chroniclers had and were recounting how a sequence of colonies formed, grew, and joined in democratic wonder for the exclusive use of that bizarre literary abstraction: a widely travelled and apparently ubiquitous fellow, 'the white man'. This political narrative, albeit existing in numerous variations, has survived relatively intact into modern times. But the real lived story of Australia, people knew, had been the story of different peoples coming together, often defying the prejudices of the commentating classes. The *Portland*'s Irish and Catholic cargo had attracted the opprobrium of press commentators, for instance, and the Oakmans, despite their gloriously archaic name recalling a heritage as people of the English Woods, were just ordinary labouring people. Their determination to get land to provide for their children and thereby leave wage-bondage behind was the motor of their life's narrative, and Australians like Frances were raised intuitively knowing that the real colonial past was an accumulation of such stories. And so Frances's epic colonial past was framed not by empires and political parties, but by the journeys, struggles, and adventures which ultimately led an English clan to be joined to its Irish equivalent by a wedding in Wagga and land in a place with the unlikely name of Humula.

After being born to William and Elizabeth in 1900, Frances O'Keeffe grew up in a thriving little community, captured in a letter she wrote in 1912 when she was old enough to convey a sense of her surroundings. Her wider family had been, and continued to be, prominent advocates of local development in the adjacent localities of Humula and Umbango. As early as 1880, for instance, a Mr J O'Keeffe seconded a motion at a meeting of local selectors that some political pressure be undertaken to alleviate the burdens brought about by their repayments to the government. Farmers who had obtained their land through conditional purchases acquired it with a deposit, with a requirement that they make improvements to the property, but they often struggled to meet the remaining balance of payments. These smaller farmers wanted the government to recognise how they battled against weather, land, and economy, and to cut them a bit of slack.

A printed application to register a company in 1886, to which some of my relatives subscribed, further illustrates the networks of family. It suggests that those farmers had a bit of capital to put into investments and were willing to try their luck with the company-driven gold schemes of the later nineteenth century. The scheme, rather delightfully, was called the 'Grand United Gold-Mining Company, Tarcutta, Limited'. The shareholders were listed, indicating their various locations, such as Thomas and John Oakman, who were both living in or near Humula. At Umbango were Jeremiah and William O'Keeffe. And there was a Patrick O'Keeffe of Gumly Gumly as well. It pointed to the tendency for families to spread out a little, but also the persistence of family connections within the same general area.

Joint-stock ventures aside, however, the primary concerns of this community were with another form of stock. The yearly animal stock returns of the wider district provide a small view of the properties of these farmers with some of the perspective that most mattered to them. William O'Keeffe's farm, for instance, varied in its agricultural and pastoral activities. In the half decade from 1889 to 1894, William's acreage oscillated by up to a hundred acres. At any given time he maintained between fourteen and sixteen horses, twelve and twenty-four cattle, and nil to twelve pigs. The family farm was not a timeless unchanging thing, but rather a constant work-in-progress, being adjusted to the conditions of weather, workforce, and the markets.

And it could easily be threatened. In 1893 there had been tremendous fires in the area, burning the forested hills and threatening the town of Humula itself. Among those affected, the property of 'Mr. T. Oakman' was reported to have 'suffered by the late fires'. Burnt crops, perhaps smouldering corpses of stock animals, and damaged property all took their heavy toll on the family before passing out of full memory into historical quietude.

Mutual protection from bushfires prompted inter-community organisations, but there was also an active social scene unrelated to disasters. People gathered within their towns regularly and confidently travelled throughout the wider district to participate in major events. In 1890, for instance, some of the Humula Oakmans travelled down to Kyamba for the Bachelors' Ball. And sport, particularly rugby clubs, encouraged towns to interact, while fostering rivalries that cemented local and regional identities. Even after Tarcutta thrashed Humula 36 to 0 in August 1898, Frances could still grow up enjoying a game and the fun that went with it.

Helping such socialising was another of Frances's uncles, Thomas Oakman, who carried his father's name. He bought and enlarged Humula's Hotel as well as running the town's general store. It was not all eating and drinking, though. Humula formed its own School of Arts in 1899. Literary, scientific, and artistic pursuits across the countryside of Australia reveal a people who aspired to a variety of ways of expressing themselves. Australia was never simply a land of sport-mad farmers.

In February 1907, Frances may even have attended the Humula School of Arts' hosting of a 'magic lantern entertainment', where coloured pictures were projected for the delight of the attendees, and some phonograph records were played. Explanations about the images were given for the education of the audience, although it was noted that 'several men on the back seats' had been 'making a lot of noise', thereby distracting the children. If Frances had managed to focus, she would have seen pictures of the Russo–Japanese war of 1904–05, in which the rising Asian power defeated one of

Britain's imperial rivals and stalled Russia's eastwards expansion. Although images of Queen Victoria, Edward VII, and Britain's Royal Navy illustrated an imperial preoccupation, the almost ethnographic focus on Japan, with images of 'a Japanese banquet in a tea house' and similar scenes, reveals a great interest in the wider world, and Asia in particular.

So the settler people worked the land and built settled communities, and this was all still part of an ongoing way of life as the centuries, and generations, clicked over. It was a pattern that was familiar to many parts of Australia as the nineteenth century drew to its close and a new century started. From the original stock runs, through the period of the gold rushes, to the period of more intensive settlement and occupation, the landscape had dramatically changed, and was still changing. Traditional life was disrupted for the original inhabitants as hunting grounds became fenced, stocked, and cultivated. Treated as relics of a passing way of life, old Aboriginal men often became local identities, whose travels through their country was only remembered in print as they approached death or died. Charlie Parr was one later recalled to have been an old man when the Umbango district was settled, his age becoming a defining feature, and one which echoed a wider recognition that Aboriginal people had lived in the land over a very long time.

But the change for Aborigines was not all destructive. Charlie's people had dispersed into the new communities as stockmen, labourers, domestic servants, husbands, and wives. Admittedly such working opportunities could be limited or constrained by prejudice, and domestic service was generally a less positive experience than stock work, which was often remembered fondly. Nonetheless, the fact remains that Aborigines were present in many urban and rural communities, generally as part of the wider working classes. Although often labelled in reports as 'Aboriginal', highlighting their apparent otherness, many Aborigines were able to participate in regional sporting events, helping to illustrate that social barriers were not always unbreakable.

Even the chasing of two Aborigines, Jack and Willie, accused of murdering a lone Russian-Polish farmer at Dora Dora, highlights the racial and cultural complexity of the later nineteenth century and the early twentieth century. A telegram sent by the Albury police to surrounding towns asserted that 'It is quite likely that the murderers may make for the Bland or Humula, where the traces of them were last seen'. They were supposedly former police trackers who had turned criminal and escaped. And the chase after them, which converged on the hills, was partly guided by other unnamed Aboriginal trackers. The pursuers found the tracks in a valley between Humula and Kyamba, but lost them, before heading north in the direction that Jack and Willie were travelling.

They were thought to have sought refuge at the Brungle Aboriginal camp near Gundagai, but to have then split up sometime after their brush with this region, although each was ultimately captured. Both were tried for the murder, found guilty and sentenced to death. A large public petition was presented to the Victorian government, successfully gaining a commutation of their punishments to imprisonment, fifteen years for Willie, and life for Jack. Their story reveals a small part of the way that Aborigines were occupying increasingly ambiguous positions in the new nation. There was no one unqualifiable attitude towards them, official or otherwise. In some instances Aborigines were the object of almost obsessive levels of 'care'; at other times they were ignored or neglected. They could be variously studied, lauded, mythologised, patronised, employed, categorised, and much more, all of which happened individually, collectively, regionally, and nationally, in fact and fiction, in policy and practice.

But undoubtedly many Aborigines found themselves in fringe camps, particularly by the larger river towns like Wagga or Gundagai, which were frequently designated as reserves during the later nineteenth century. It is one of Australia's stupidest myths that prior to European colonisation Aborigines were aimlessly wandering nomads. Rather, subsistence patterns, seasonal movements, and so on were all quite varied across the continent. Climate and cultural practices helped determine social densities and patterns of movement, and in the Riverina this meant a relatively sedentary riverside or tributary creek–side existence for much of any given year. So when the Brungle School for Aboriginal children near Gundagai was established in the late 1880s, this reflected an extant concentration of Aborigines that was relatively traditional in concept, even if European settlement had further concentrated the Aboriginal habitation to and of a specific location.

And unsurprisingly enough, Aborigines gardened and farmed at the Brungle Camp, and tried to find work where possible, while also hunting and fishing to supplement their diets. The government, taking an interest in the site, helped provide rations, further drawing in camp inhabitants for longer periods of time, but also facilitating, some residents of Brungle noted, a dependence relationship that proved inadequate in the face of wider restrictions on movement and a lack of employment options in the district. When two residents of the Brungle Camp were charged with stealing mutton in 1890, their lawyer pointed out that they 'did not get enough to eat and the pangs of hunger caused them to steal'. While government rations were subject to scrutiny and some cynicism, the Aborigines Protection Board also contributed to the improvement of the camp, increasingly called the Brungle Station after the nearby squatter homestead. In 1893 the Board helped pay for a hayshed, illustrating the type of economy towards which the camp was being transformed. Many locals provided work, and even charitable gifts of food and blankets, showing that in some ways the camp was well integrated into its immediate region, with local pressure for the provision of reasonable shelter and food being the main factors prompting official oversight. So much was it a part of the wider community that when in 1906 a spark ignited a neighbour's paddock, many of the so-called 'Brungle Aborigines' came to assist putting it out.

But it was also a place of some tensions, no doubt facilitated by a concentration of pressures internal and external to the community within the wider region. In the summer of 1892–93 a fire had destroyed the crops at the Brungle Camp, and some local residents, fearful of their own farms, suspected that the fire was 'wilfully caused by dissentions in the camp'. This could be true, but it is also worth bearing in mind that a resident of Brungle had spent part of 1890 busying himself 'in obtaining signatures to a petition to have the Aboriginal camp, at Brungle, removed'. As already seen, the colonies and nation was often split over the question of treatment of Aborigines. That Brungle was thought to be a potential safe haven for the fugitive ex-trackers Jack and Willie furthered some vocal local resentment against it.

In part, the problem in characterising the racial attitudes and experiences of the period is one of basic historical methodology. It is generally only when identified clearly as 'Aboriginal' in documentation that people can be written about in this way. Designations such as 'half-caste' represented official control and a scientific obsession with racialism, but people nominally capable of being so labelled often passed into the mainstream of society without mention, as they had since the commencement of European settlement, unless they were seen as firmly belonging to the 'Aboriginal' camp. Many Aborigines lived within the wider nominally 'white' world, just as their Chinese, Middle Eastern, and Mediterranean counterparts did. A 'White Australia' was a sort of official ideology, not a demographic reality.

So regular contact with diverse people is perhaps the originating context for that tendency some people had to see individuals as 'not like the others' of a particular racial group. Those 'others' generally belonged to a distant group, only known in the abstraction, supposedly relegated to the camps, suburbs, shanty towns, or reserves of Chinese, Aboriginal, or Pacific Islander peoples.

Even in isolated areas like Umbango, Europeans and Aborigines were not the only major ethnic groups. This is revealed by little daily interactions, like when Frances's real uncle, Jeremiah O'Keeffe, was charged by the Wagga magistrate's court in 1885 for selling liquor at Umbango without a licence. It was alleged that he had sold 'pale brandy' to two Chinese men. His defence against the allegation was that he had in fact 'refused them when they asked for it'. Specifics of the case aside, it indicates that there was a significant Chinese presence in the wider area. And, if some of them were coming to the hotel for a drink, they were not wholly isolated from the wider communities in which they lived. Moreover, contrary to popular misconceptions, the Chinese presence in these valleys was not all related to goldmining. In addition to the usual crops of oats, barley, potatoes, and the like, Umbango was a significant producer of tobacco, and this was an industry known to have attracted some Chinese enterprise nearby at Tumut.

When the 'Chinese camp' at Tumut caught fire in early 1890, the Chinese occupants were celebrating their New Year. Hundreds of the residents of Tumut apparently turned out onto the racecourse to watch helplessly as the flames consumed the camp, prompting renewed thoughts of 'organising a local fire brigade'. Yet another illustration of Australia's ethnically diverse past, it was also another proof of the sorts of local initiatives that occupied the minds of many of the farmers and town dwellers of late colonial and early federal Australia.

In another instance of this mindset, a journalistic visitor to Umbango explained for his readers the problems the district faced in exporting its produce to market in 1889. He noted how the creeks all produced wonderful crops of everything and that they could be made more productive. The limiting factor was the poor boggy roads, he was told, which stymied transportation. This visitor was surprised to learn 'that one-half of last year's tobacco crop was lying on the hands of the growers, because there was no means of getting it away'. Several thousand pounds worth, he noted, was lying in the Umbango creek. 'I also saw at Mr. O'Keefe's shed,' he reported, 'beside tobacco, 18 bags of oats and 16 bags of barley both of excellent sample, showing the capability of the soil.' This all pointed to what the Umbango people felt they most needed: the railway.

The railway had not arrived by the time Frances O'Keeffe was born in 1900, nor before she wrote to Uncle Jeff in 1912. Since the late 1880s residents of the valleys agitated and hoped for a branch line from the main Sydney–Melbourne line to Tumbarumba, but only in 1911 was serious attention being given to various routes from either Wagga or Junee. In April 1912 a politician symbolically turned the first sod of the line at Wagga, but, as 'a matter of fact, the first sod had been dug out by a plough or scoop some week ago', a commentator snidely noted. As further demonstration of the gradual and slightly inept management of the project, in 1917 the line had finally reached Humula and was running some limited services, but even then it had not been 'officially' opened.

Although Junee was the more important railway centre, Wagga was the bigger commercial one. And so, without any railway to facilitate their trip, it was to Wagga that Frances's maternal grandparents went when they wanted to have their photograph taken late in the nineteenth century. A copy of one such occasion survives in a studio portrait from E Henningham in Wagga. The couple look kindly and appear to be in their Sunday best. Elizabeth's bonnet has a delightfully period look, and bits of lace trim provide a bit of Victorian 'bling'. The existence of this photo tells a little story all of its own, saying a lot about one of the most common relics of the late colonial and early federal past, many of which still have prominent places in households across Australia.

To produce the image, the Oakmans had to have visited Wagga sometime after 1888, when the studio opened. It was situated near the lagoon bridge and had a special anteroom where women could rearrange their clothing discreetly after the disruptions of the journey into town. For the Oakmans, the trip meant hours of travel and probably necessitated at least one overnight stay. Once they had arrived, and with clothing readied, the subjects would have gone into a studio where various props were available to help compose the photograph, similarly to the way a painting would be. The photographer looked to balance the picture, and in the Oakmans' case a tall plant and a small pot plant were used to offset the figures and the bench

Thomas sat upon. The photographer would instruct them how to stand and where to look. They were, like thousands of country folk like them, doing their best to make themselves presentable for eternity.

Sometime after that, a copy of their picture was given to their granddaughter Frances. It was to be the only way she would know her grandfather. Thomas Oakman died in 1899 and Elizabeth soon followed him in 1904. This proved to be a hard period for the family. Frances's father died of the 'deadly influenza scourge' in 1900, the year she was born. There was apparently a significant epidemic in the Tarcutta region, so the baby girl was lucky to survive herself. Illness wracked the population and local papers reveal how fever, like fire, was one of their greatest concerns. It had the capacity to destroy entire communities and wreck livelihoods. And during these hard years other O'Keeffe and Oakman burials also dotted the Humula and Umbango valleys.

In the face of a world where sickness could take lives suddenly, people clung to memories of their connections to people and places. So much so that through her constant presence in photographic form in Pa's kitchen, Frances was a notable part of my growing up in the late twentieth century. Pa really loved his mum, so much so that we jokingly refer to her sometimes as 'Saint Frances'. His sister, my great aunty Joyce, told me that 'everybody loved mum', and that she came from 'a really lovely family'. The O'Keeffe's, she felt, were really good and kind-hearted people. The strongest evidence of this strong sense of responsibility to their own kin came in 1904, when Frances's mother died, and Frances was taken to live within the protection of her extended family network among the hill folk.

Although it was an adult Frances whose photographed image I saw several times a week growing up, there are three pictures of Frances as a girl, all dating from this period when she lived with her wider kin. One is the picture with the horse and the apparent nephew already mentioned. In another, on a property somewhere, Frances and her sister look seriously at the camera. Frances is a pretty girl, reminiscent of my own mother and sister and half a dozen cousins. Behind them is a small and simple farmhouse. Beyond that is bush. The third photograph, taken in much the same spot, is of six children, including Frances and her sister. One of the boys has his hat folded into a slouch hat.

Somebody organised these photographs, paid for them and kept these copies. Carefully posed, they were preserved down the generations. The one of the larger group of kids was torn, possibly because it has been repeatedly handled. In a way these photographs mark the limits of family memory just as they became talking points of familial remembrance. There are thousands of such photographs throughout the antique stores of Australia bearing the images of people that nobody remembers.

Raised within an extended family network, Frances eventually left her home to make a new one, just as so many of her ancestors had done previously. As a young woman she moved to Junee, where she found work at the Junee Cottage Hospital, and met Horace Duck, whom she married in 1918.

Originally Junee was just one of a number of pastoral stations. Taken up in the 1840s, the original Junee run covered a wide area, including the present town. Within the Junee run a little village grew by an organic pastoral process, but did so a few miles west of present-day Junee. This is now known as Old Junee and sits on Houlaghans Creek.

The original squatter, a gentleman with the aristocratic name of Leopold Fane de Salis, was a well-connected fellow. Drawing on his brother's business connections in Hong Kong and political connections in Britain, de Salis was one of the earliest known pastoralists to use Chinese shepherds to tend his flocks. He had brought four of them over to New South Wales from Hong Kong to work on his runs as indentured servants in the 1840s. This was an experiment that was quickly followed with interest and practice elsewhere in the colony. At Junee, Oura, and Darbalara these Chinese men, and others who soon joined them in de Salis's employment, again point to Australia's complex and multicultural past.

The village of Junee that developed to serve Junee Station and its region throughout the middle of the nineteenth century grew steadily in tandem with the pastoral, agricultural, and economic prospects, and demographic trends, of the Riverina and South West Slopes. It became a familiar if relatively unimportant place for shearers and shepherds, bullock drivers and cattlemen, and all the other figures of the nineteenth century interior. But the coming of the railway changed both Junee's fortune and its location.

In the late 1870s the railway line south from Sydney was extending toward its joining point with Albury, and therefore Melbourne. Because the line had to follow the flattest, straightest, and cheapest routes possible, a new railway station and workers' camp a few miles to the east of the old village grew rapidly into a prominent regional town, thus eclipsing the old Junee settlement. Cuddled around the railway tracks that gave it economic succour, Junee had the advantage of being about halfway between Sydney and Melbourne, meaning it was a good place to service engines, to stop and change drivers and other staff on long-haul trips, and to refresh passengers, coal trucks, and engine boilers. Moreover, it was near the Bethungra Hills, which could require multiple engines to climb, and was the site of a major branch line to the western Riverina, hence Junee was also often known as Junee Junction. Official attempts to gazette the town as 'Loftus', in honour of the colonial governor Lord Augustus Frederick Spencer Loftus, fell flat, as people refused to conform their nomenclature to governmental dictate. So Junee it remained.

Combined, these factors meant that Junee became an important place relatively suddenly. And the economic pulling power that eventually brought Frances O'Keeffe down from the hills had also brought the Duck family, albeit a bit earlier.

It was Frances's eventual father-in-law, Billy Duck, who had followed the railway line south to Junee. Born to his fruit-growing parents William and Elizabeth in Camden in 1866, he learned his trade as a butcher working in that town. There is an apocryphal story about him that says he left home at about thirteen years of age with no money and lived in the bush eating berries and snakes while he meandered his way to Penrith. Upon seeing an advertisement for a butcher's boy, he applied, got the job and worked hard at learning his trade. It is a delightful story of the sort that an elderly person might tell his gullible grandchildren in jest, but regardless of its accuracy it highlights his apparent familiarity with the bush from childhood. A more probable and reliable account suggests that in 1888, the year that New South Wales marked a centenary of European settlement, Billy was working for Griffiths' Butchery in Camden.

Billy became a patriarch of the large Duck clan in the Junee district, about whom many stories have been told, in print and in word through family histories and oral traditions. So it can be hard to picture Billy Duck as a young man. Before he entered father-figure territory, however, he was a well-regarded sportsman. He regularly entered footraces and apparently 'boxing was his favourite sport, at which he excelled'. There are also a few family tales and court records that suggest Billy sometimes resorted to his fists to settle arguments, even when he was an alderman.

He was also a rider, often enough entering horseraces. This proved a lifetime interest, common to the period, which was mostly focused on trotting. This sporting association with horses may explain how he managed to meet and marry Elizabeth Kiss, daughter of the famed rider Jimmy.

She too had clearly come down from the hills, albeit even further up in the high country, at some point.

Billy and Elizabeth married in Cootamundra in 1891. There are some discrepancies between various family stories about whether Billy was there in Cootamundra working as a butcher or had arrived in Junee a bit earlier. Pa seemed convinced that Billy had temporarily had a butchery at Old Junee before setting up in new Junee about the time he married. Either way, his stay must have been relatively short, because by April 1892 the couple had their first child, in Junee itself. Billy soon established himself as a prominent businessman in the busy railway town and his progeny would remain there down multiple generations. Rarely over the following century and a bit would there be no Duck's butchery in Junee.

I often visited my uncle's butchery in my teens, in practically the same spot as his great grandfather had established the original one. I would stop in and say hello on the way to school soccer. By then refrigeration was the norm, so the butchery was a good place to stop to cool down a little after the walk. But in Billy's time and that of his son (Horace), and even the early time of his grandson (Pa), hanging sheds were used. Billy had his own slaughterhouse, which was brick with cement cladding. Pa's paddock had its own slaughterhouse as well, a structure with curious grooves, chains, hooks, and other mechanical elements that engaged my curiosity as a boy. It also had an attached hanging shed, the gauze windows tattered and rusted, but once swarming with flies, desperately trying to get to the flesh inside.

During the course of his working life, Billy moved shops a few times, but he was generally never far from the railway. The precise location mattered little, because meat was delivered to customers' houses by a 'cutting cart', which delivered pre-ordered meat. He also carried larger carcass sections on his delivery rounds, so that pieces could be cut on site to requirements. As a result, the butcher's life had a little of the sociability of the postman about it. Doing his rounds of the town, Billy would get to know the people and their stories. He would know who worked on the railway, at the mill, or the foundry. He got to know what schools and churches the families were associated with. He also delivered to the hotels, which fed the town's many visitors. He may even have supplied the impressive railway station dining rooms, where travellers would break their trips north, south, or west, while the engines were replenished with coal and water.

This regular contact with townspeople probably helps explain how Billy soon came to be an alderman, a post which he held occasionally in the

1890s and 1900s. He was a man of paddock and town, who could bargain with farmers, chat in a friendly way with housewives, box with the men and, like everybody else, discuss the weather. This last was seemingly the topic of greatest interest, at least if the town newspapers can be trusted, of which the busy and thriving country town of Junee sometimes had two.

And behind his shop, day and night, the steaming, puffing, grunting engines that brought Junee its prosperity rolled back and forth. An old photograph of one of his shops captures part of the railway station in the background, diagonally across the crossing road and rails, and the signal tower directly behind the shop. Junee, like much of Australia, lived with familiar rhythms as the nineteenth century drew to its close and the twentieth century commenced. Its inhabitants read papers, they played sports, they sent and received letters and telegrams and, soon enough, started listening to voices broadcast over the airwave in their big chunky wireless radios.

Surprisingly, even a place with multiple newspapers can sometimes be historically obscure, and getting an idea of what was really happening in a town, the place's true social history, can be a difficult exercise. Certainly anomalous events are easily enough discovered, like when an unfortunate fellow was 'deemed to be insane' at the Junee Police Court in 1912. He had been found insensible at Wantiool, a bit out of town, with his feet nearly in a fire. The chap had apparently 'complained he had a wireless telegraph working in his head'. It was a sign of the difficulties and fears associated with the new technologies increasingly affecting everyday life in bigger towns throughout regional Australia, which tempers perspectives of ceaseless and beneficent progress. But it also highlights the kinds of things a person may have to do to get into the papers.

Sometimes there is simply too much information to make research manageable. In 1912 alone it is possible to see Billy Duck in considerable detail. In May he successfully tendered for a lease of 'the Junee park at £16' for a year. In September a 'fire destroyed a cottage at Old Junee' that he owned. In the same month he entered the horse 'Dreadnought' in several races. In a mile and a half trot this horse with its ominously modern name came second only to Red Tape, although it did manage some wins. And on Christmas Eve Billy 'and several members of his family, went to Wagga and hired a motor car, and proceeded to Tumut'. On the return journey the car rolled over an embankment, ejected the passengers and left Billy with an injured arm.

ABOVE (LEFT TO RIGHT): William and Elizabeth O'Keeffe (née Oakman). (Private collection)

BELOW: Frances Arabella O'Keeffe with a nephew. (Private collection)

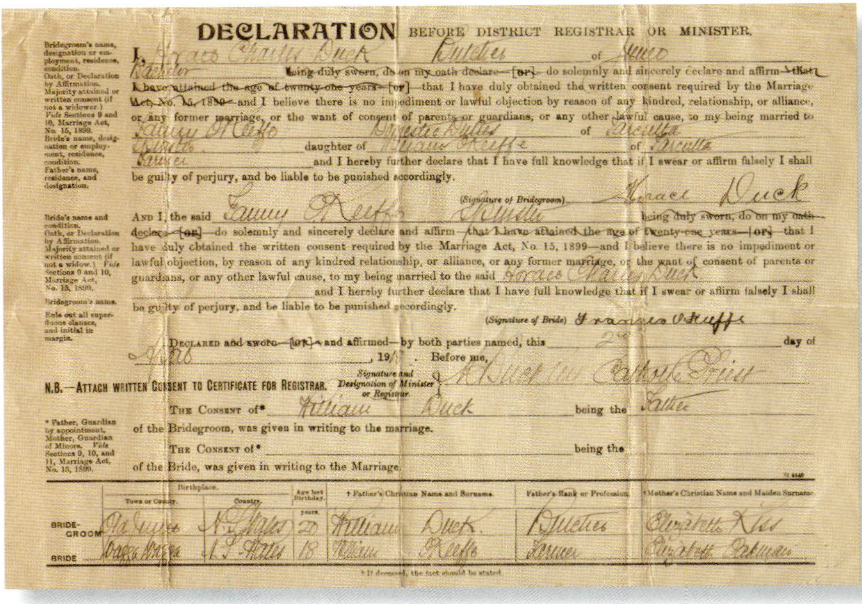

DECLARATION BEFORE DISTRICT REGISTRAR OR MINISTER.

Bridegroom's name, designation or employment, residence, condition. Oath, or Declaration by Affirmation. Majority attained or written consent (if not a widower.) *Vide* Sections 9 and 10, Marriage Act, No. 15, 1899. Bride's name, designation or employment, residence, condition. Father's name, residence, and designation.

I, Horace Charles Duck Butcher of Junee Bachelor being duly sworn, do on my oath declare—[or]—do solemnly and sincerely declare and affirm—that I have attained the age of twenty-one years—[or]—that I have duly obtained the written consent required by the Marriage Act, No. 15, 1899—and I believe there is no impediment or lawful objection by reason of any kindred, relationship, or alliance, or any former marriage, or the want of consent of parents or guardians, or any other lawful cause, to my being married to Fanny O'Keeffe Domestic Duties of Parcells Spinster daughter of William O'Keeffe of Parcells Farmer and I hereby further declare that I have full knowledge that if I swear or affirm falsely I shall be guilty of perjury, and be liable to be punished accordingly.

(Signature of Bridegroom) Horace Duck

Bride's name and condition. Oath, or Declaration by Affirmation. Majority attained or written consent (if not a widow.) *Vide* Sections 9 and 10, Marriage Act, No. 15, 1899. Bridegroom's name. Rule out all superfluous clauses, and initial in margin.

AND I, the said Fanny O'Keeffe Spinster being duly sworn, do on my oath declare—[or]—do solemnly and sincerely declare and affirm—that I have attained the age of twenty-one years—[or]—that I have duly obtained the written consent required by the Marriage Act, No. 15, 1899—and I believe there is no impediment or lawful objection, by reason of any kindred relationship, or alliance, or any former marriage, or the want of consent of parents or guardians, or any other lawful cause, to my being married to the said Horace Charles Duck and I hereby further declare that I have full knowledge that if I swear or affirm falsely I shall be guilty of perjury, and be liable to be punished accordingly.

(Signature of Bride) Frances O'Keeffe

DECLARED and sworn—[or]—and affirmed—by both parties named, this 2nd day of April, 1918. Before me,

N.B.—ATTACH WRITTEN CONSENT TO CERTIFICATE FOR REGISTRAR. Signature and Designation of Minister or Registrar. A. Buckley Catholic Priest

* Father, Guardian by appointment, Mother, Guardian of Minors. *Vide* Sections 9, 10, and 11, Marriage Act, No. 15, 1899.

THE CONSENT of* William Duck being the Father of the Bridegroom, was given in writing to the marriage.

THE CONSENT of* being the of the Bride, was given in writing to the Marriage.

	Birthplace: Town or County.	Birthplace: Country.	Age last Birthday.	† Father's Christian Name and Surname.	Father's Rank or Profession.	† Mother's Christian Name and Maiden Surname.
BRIDEGROOM	Old Junee	N.S.Wales	20 years	William Duck	Butcher	Elizabeth Kiss
BRIDE	Wagga Wagga	N.S.Wales	18	William O'Keeffe	Farmer	Elizabeth Bateman

† If deceased, the fact should be stated.

ABOVE: Horace Duck and Frances O'Keeffe's wedding certificate. (Private collection)

RIGHT: Horace and Frances Duck (née O'Keeffe). (Private collection)

ABOVE: A dust storm in Junee, January 1915. (Private collection)

BELOW: Part of John Thomas O'Rafferty's First World War service record. (National Archives of Australia, NAA: B884, N77547)

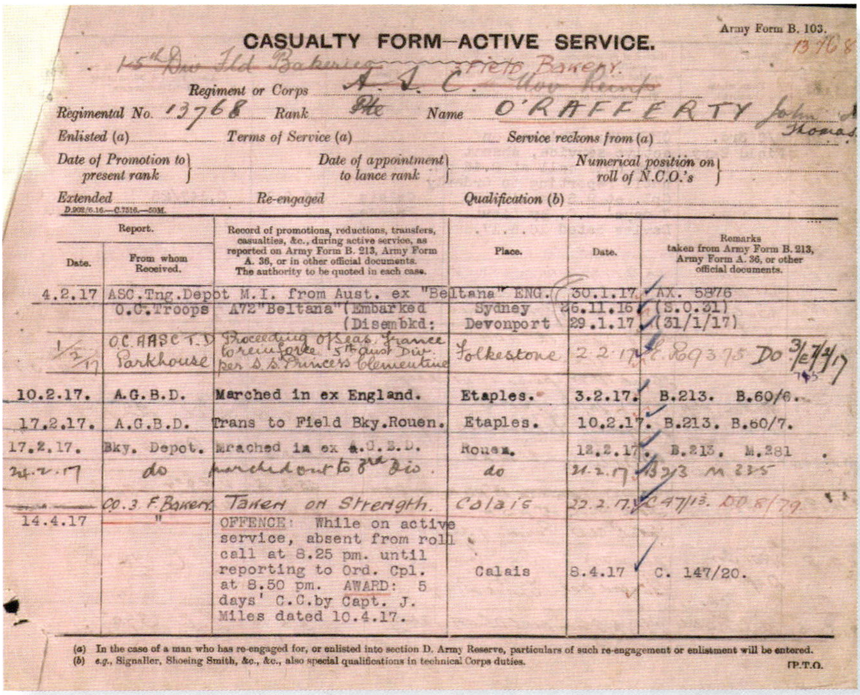

Army Form B. 103.

13768

CASUALTY FORM—ACTIVE SERVICE.

~~15th Div Fld Bakeries~~ Field Bakery.

Regiment or Corps ~~A. S. C. Mov Reinfs~~

Regimental No. 13768 *Rank* Pte *Name* O'RAFFERTY John Thomas

Enlisted (a) *Terms of Service (a)* *Service reckons from (a)*

Date of Promotion to present rank *Date of appointment to lance rank* *Numerical position on roll of N.C.O.'s*

Extended *Re-engaged* *Qualification (b)*

D.902/6.16.—C.7516.—50M.

Report. Date.	Report. From whom Received.	Record of promotions, reductions, transfers, casualties, &c., during active service, as reported on Army Form B. 213, Army Form A. 36, or in other official documents. The authority to be quoted in each case.	Place.	Date.	Remarks taken from Army Form B. 213, Army Form A. 36, or other official documents.
4.2.17	ASC.Tng.Depot	M.I. from Aust. ex "Beltana"	ENG.	30.1.17	AX. 5876
	O.C.Troops	A72 "Beltana" (Embarked	Sydney	26.11.16	(S.O.31)
		(Disembkd:	Devonport	29.1.17	(31/1/17)
1/2/17	O.C. AASC T.D. Parkhouse	Proceeding Overseas France to reinforce 5th Aust Div. per S.S. Princess Clementine	Folkestone	2.2.17	[illegible] Do 3/E 7/4/17
10.2.17.	A.G.B.D.	Marched in ex England.	Etaples.	3.2.17.	B.213. B.60/6.
17.2.17.	A.G.B.D.	Trans to Field Bky.Rouen.	Etaples.	10.2.17.	B.213. B.60/7.
17.2.17.	Bky. Depot.	Mrached in ex A.G.B.D.	Rouen.	12.2.17.	B.213. M.281
24.2.17	do	Marched out to 3rd Div.	do	21.2.17	B213 M 235
	Co. 3 F. Bakery	Taken on Strength.	Calais	22.2.17	C47/13. DO 8/79
14.4.17	"	OFFENCE: While on active service, absent from roll call at 8.25 pm. until reporting to Ord. Cpl. at 8.50 pm. AWARD: 5 days' C.C. by Capt. J. Miles dated 10.4.17.	Calais	8.4.17	C. 147/20.

(a) In the case of a man who has re-engaged for, or enlisted into section D. Army Reserve, particulars of such re-engagement or enlistment will be entered.
(b) e.g., Signaller, Shoeing Smith, &c., &c., also special qualifications in technical Corps duties.

P.T.O.

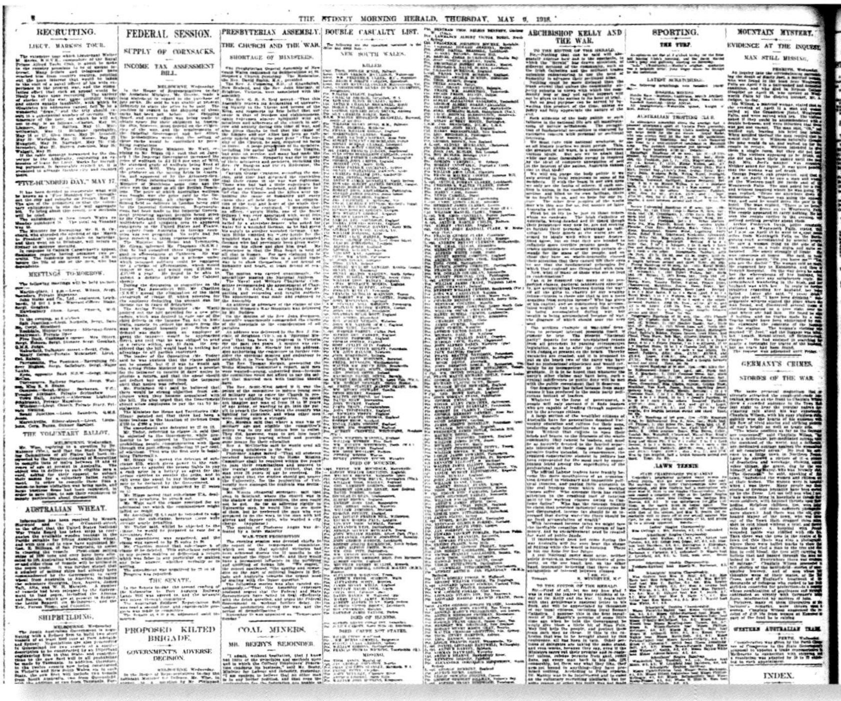
THE SYDNEY MORNING HERALD, THURSDAY, MAY 9, 1918.

RECRUITING. | FEDERAL SESSION. | PRESBYTERIAN ASSEMBLY. | DOUBLE CASUALTY LIST. | ARCHBISHOP KELLY AND THE WAR. | SPORTING. | MOUNTAIN MYSTERY.

ABOVE: Casualties, including William (Bill) James Duck, fill the two middle columns of this page from the *Sydney Morning Herald*, 9 May 1918. (Courtesy of Trove, National Library of Australia)

BELOW: Several generations of my family at the Hiley residence in Kangaroo Point in 1926, including Fred and Elizabeth, and their granddaughter Daphne, Grandma to me, sitting in the front. (*The Sunday Mail*, 21 November 1926, courtesy of Trove, National Library of Australia)

SPECIAL MONTHLY HOME NUMBER

The Sunday Mail

No. 181 BRISBANE, NOVEMBER 21, 1926 THIRTY PAGES. PRICE, THREEPENCE.

DIAMOND JUBILEE OF WESLEY CHURCH, KANGAROO POINT

The jubilee was celebrated in the beautiful garden of Mrs. Fred Hiley's residence in Thorne-street, and portion of the large gathering may be seen in the photograph.

EXTRAORDINARY DISASTER | WILL HE RESIGN? | BLAZING OIL | BOAT CREW'S ORDEAL

ABOVE: A cheque signed by Horace Duck. Business was tough for the butchers in Junee during the Depression. (Private collection)

BELOW: Part of Gordon Brodie's album depicting Australia in the 1930s. (Private collection)

ABOVE: Anti-Aircraft guns firing in defence of Australia in 1942 at Darwin, photographed by Gordon Brodie. (Private collection)

BELOW: In the aftermath of the first Japanese raid on Darwin, Gordon Brodie documented some of the damage. (Private collection)

ABOVE: Gordon and Daphne Brodie (née Hiley), Grampy and Grandma to me. (Private collection)

BELOW: Eileen (née O'Rafferty) and Gregory Duck, Nanny and Pa to me. (Private collection)

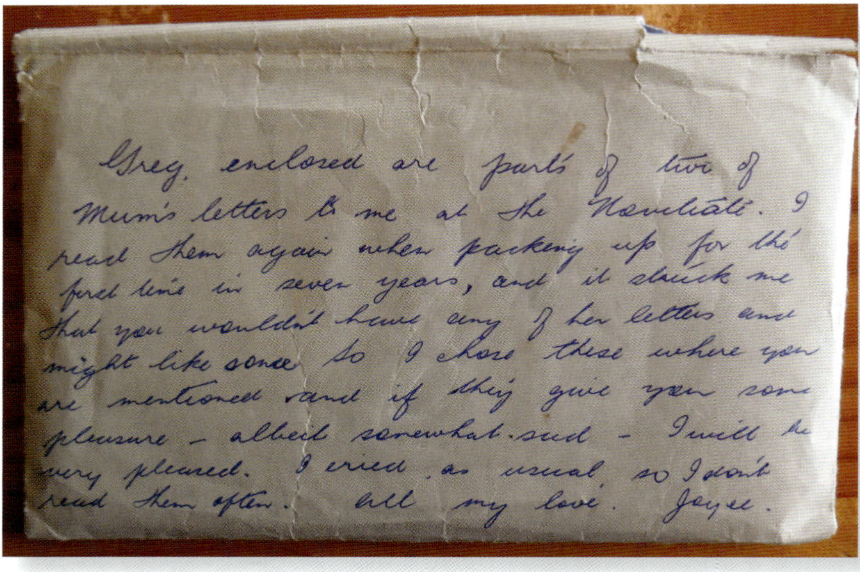

Greg. enclosed are parts of two of Mum's letters to me at the Novitiate. I read them again when packing up for the first time in seven years, and it struck me that you wouldn't have any of her letters and might like some. So I chose these where you are mentioned and if they give you some pleasure – albeit somewhat sad – I will be very pleased. I cried as usual so I don't read them often. All my love. Joyce.

ABOVE: Envelope containing letters written by Frances Duck to her daughter, which Joyce later shared with her brother Gregory. Such highly personal documents provided insights into everyday life in the late 1940s. (Private collection)

BELOW: Pa and Nanny at Manly-Queenscliff beach. This everyday image highlights my many connections with places and people through time, where however distant and different, the past often seems familiar. (Private collection)

But in contrast, with their regular focus on national and international news, business and farming interests, and issues of local government, the local papers can actually fail to give much of an insight into the life of a place. Their readers already knew the local stories; they wanted the wider news. As a way of getting around this, it is useful to look at series of letters about a place printed in other papers. Through these, I have discovered, it is possible to get a sense of the essentials, that is, what locals thought newsworthy for people in other places, with whom they often corresponded with great regularity. One such series of letters is interesting for the prominence the letters give Billy Duck. Writing under the non de plume 'Wombat', a correspondent kept the people of Albury up to date with happenings in Junee through the little column 'Junee Jottings'.

Wombat gives little snapshots of the town of Junee for his readers of the *Albury Banner*, the same paper with the 'Uncle Jeff' that Frances O'Keeffe wrote to. It could thus have been through Wombat that she learned about Junee, reading about it in an Albury paper up in the hills at Humula and Umbango.

In May 1900 Wombat reveals that Junee had an active masonic lodge, a concert for the Catholic Convent School, and the midnight ringing of bells and blowing of whistles in celebration of the relief of Mafeking in South Africa. The country was green and crops were growing well after a period of drought. The next month was 'miserably wet', making for a slippery rugby match between Wagga and Junee, and there was a minor scandal over the Cottage Hospital showing some inequity in its treatment of patients. There was a visit from the railway commissioners and a town deputation to have the gasworks removed so the centre of town no longer had to suffer 'all kinds of noxious smells'. There was a local bazaar and dance to raise funds for extending the Catholic Church on the hill overlooking town.

Wombat's jottings give a steady sense of Junee's balls, dances, parades, parties, and bonfires. It was clearly a place of some activity and had a strong series of networks for socialising. Wombat also captured prominent visitors, like when in late October 1901, 'at the Alhambra Hall, Dr. Dill-Macky, the well-known divine, delivered his popular lecture, "The Rose, Shamrock, and Thistle," to a fairly good attendance'. Apparently Dill-Macky 'kept his audience in good humour throughout with quaint anecdotes and sketches of the characters of his subjects'. There was no riot.

Narrowing in on Wombat's references to the Duck family, Billy's horseracing crops up frequently, highlighting the wider regionalism of this sporting confraternity and the general enthusiasm for competition. Billy raced horses in Temora in October 1902, taking his own horses in the reverse direction of one of Bob Dean's many last rides. It was two decades since Bob had wheeled the big carriage there and headed towards Junee one final time, a marker of how much things had changed and were still changing, at least for those connected to the railway and the telegraph. In February the following year Billy was elected alderman, and he also entered his horse in Coolamon races that September.

Whoever Wombat was, they had a distinctive turn of phrase. Writing of the elections in 1903 Wombat suggested that 'Never has New South Wales sent forth such a poor lot to represent her in the Australian Parliament, and the poorer was generally successful. Junee ladies rolled up in full force, pleased no doubt by the novelty of recording their votes for the first time'. Again, the voting of women highlights a significant change, even while the domestic situations of many people remained similar to that of earlier decades.

That jotting was in the Christmas Day edition of the Albury paper, but Wombat's following news was bad. 'It is with feelings of deepest regret I have to announce the death of Mrs W. Duck, of this town, which sad event took place on Tuesday morning. The deceased was in excellent health until about 10 days before her demise, when she contracted blood-poisoning. All that medical service could suggest was tried, but with no avail. Mrs Duck leaves seven young children, two being infants. The funeral was the largest ever witnessed here, the interment taking place in the R. C. portion of the local cemetery.'

I have often visited this grave over the years, as we have long tended our family's resting places with a regular round of visits. The Junee cemetery is just out of town on the eastern side, on the Gundagai road. That famous song about 'The Road to Gundagai' has some different connotations and inflections in Junee. Its lines about 'mother and daddy are waitin' for me/ And the pals of my childhood once more I will see' conjure up meanings of return to a heavenly home, rather than just being a simple rustic ditty conveying nostalgia for childhood and countryside.

Reading of the death of a family member is a little poignant, even at more than a century's remove. But I had a closer look at the circumstances of her death, which revealed the immediate cause. One of those seven children Elizabeth left behind was named Mary Duck, who had just been born on 2 December 1903, thirteen days before Elizabeth died. It seems there had been complications with the birth. Baby Mary died six days after her mother. And then, to complete the tragedy, Mary's twin, Agnes, joined her sister and mother early the following year.

Mourning his wife, Billy advertised for a Catholic girl to help take care of his children. What little documentary record that Elizabeth Kiss had left generally showed her busy on organising committees associated with Junee's Catholic Church, suggesting some devotion, and it may have been a last wish that this would continue to be cultivated in her children. Billy duly appointed a nanny. Then, three days shy of a year after Elizabeth's death, Billy married Katie McNamara, the successful applicant, and his family continued to grow.

Among the remaining children of Billy's first marriage was Horace Duck, who continued to live in the family home on Junction Street, a few blocks down from the shop, right across from the Western Riverina branch line. It was a small, wooden, old and rickety looking thing, which would shake with the passing freight. After forming a new relationship, it was not long before Billy and Katie moved further out of town, leaving the first children in town to the care of another nanny. There are some disagreements among family members about whether this affected relations between the next generation of half-siblings, which perhaps reflects personal temperaments more than historical actualities. Pa seemed convinced there was no particular bad blood, but it is hard to escape the impression that this made life difficult for a very young Horace. Born in Junee in July 1897, he was only a toddler when his mother died, just like Frances O'Keeffe was.

1915, JANUARY

Among the *Sydney Morning Herald*'s many advertisements for positions vacant in January 1915 were a 'plain cook' and a 'housemaid-laundress' at the Junee Cottage Hospital. By then Australia was at war, and while certainly a preoccupation of sorts, the conflict still seemed a far-off thing. That same issue of the *Herald* opened with a three-part summary of news that conveys this odd mix of urgency, obsession, and detachment perfectly: 'A Zeppelin and three aeroplanes flew over Calais on Saturday night in the direction of Dover. Sixteen aeroplanes were seen over the Channel on Sunday, travelling towards England, but the weather compelled them to return. On the western front the Allies' artillery is gradually assuming superiority over that of the Germans.' And on it went with little snippets of distant actions, before noting that 'In consequence of the war, the Bisley rifle shooting meeting is likely to be abandoned'.

Further in the issue, along with more detailed treatment and commentary, the *Herald* mentioned that 'Volunteering continues healthy in New South Wales'. It also noted that enlistment was being expedited with medical officers on site so that 'the whole business can be got through in one day'. But in little Junee, urban improvement continued untroubled by the distant conflict. In the Cottage Hospital some new linoleum was put down and 'the operating room repainted' in early April. For Frances O'Keeffe, possibly working at the Cottage Hospital by then, doing 'domestic duties', as her wedding certificate later put her occupation, this was a period when the Australian government's advocating of a total war mentality had yet to bite. Life was still going on in a similar way to that of peacetime.

For Horace Duck the main change concerned a name. What had formerly been known as 'German sausage' had by the end of 1914 come to be referred to in some areas as the more bluntly patriotic 'Devon'.

But while the changing of a meat product's name, and even the war that prompted it, reflected a wider political and imperial context, there was a more noticeable phenomenon in the Junee of 1915 of considerable interest to locals. Despite the sometime harshness of the Australian landscape, it was really the pull of ready money and a push for agricultural and pastoral expansion that created conditions for a phenomenon more commonly associated with the United States of America. And evidence for this was among Pa's collection of photographs, with one image clearly given to him by his father Horace. This image was unusual for not being focused on people, a business, or a racing horse. It is of a big black cloud, looming ominously over the townscape. It dwarfed some telegraph lines in the foreground, as well as a hotel, and a few houses. It is labelled 'Dust Storm Junee Jan 19 1915', and a century later the effect is still impressive.

Dust storms are a normal feature of the landscape and tend to come with bad weather and dry years. They vary quite a lot. Some come up quickly as a sort of brown haze, while others grow gradually into a swelling mass before striking. In seconds the impacting dust reduces everything to a rolling, blowing, and biting dark brown. As kids we knew the drill, race around and shut every window, get the clothes off the line.

This early 1915 storm was just one of several that struck Junee and the region at this time and reveals a bigger story. The photograph of the dust storm that hit Junee on 19 January 1915 was probably the one described in a short report in the Wagga *Daily Advertiser*. 'We have received from Mr. Turvin Studds, of Junee', the paper noted, 'a photo of Tuesday's extraordinary dust storm. The snapshot was secured when the huge clouds of dust were within half a mile of Junee, and within another minute the whole place was enveloped in a pall darker than night. The photo gives a very fair idea of the density of the dust.'

This storm was truly enormous and blasted across much of the state. It was a violent and dramatic crescendo to a heat wave the interior had been experiencing. News of its coming travelled in little blips of electricity along the telegraph lines from the towns further west. Urana, sixty miles west of Wagga, gave warning at 3 pm, and by 4:45 it struck Wagga. 'For twenty minutes the darkness was intense, and as the clouds were lifting it was seen that the color of the sky was a fiery red.' In Temora, west of Junee, trees were uprooted, and sheets of iron were thrown about.

The day after, one report said, 'the whole of the State was ... enveloped in a fog of almost impalpable dust'. Even Sydney experienced a haze.

But it was not over. After a day of respite, word came from Narrandera on Thursday morning that another storm was on its way. This time, knowing what the impact would be, residents had time to prepare. Various Duck children probably run around securing windows and bringing in the washing. At 11:30 am it hit, darkening the sky so much that electric lights were again required in order to see. Then heavy rain seems to have washed the dust away.

Throughout the seasons of the storms, Horace was probably working. They kept an eye on the horizon as they did their rounds, ready to secure the cart in the event of oncoming wind and dust. Following his father, Horace had learned the essentials of the butchering business: kill, cut, and chat. He eventually took it over while Billy retired to farming just over the hill where the Junee Correctional Facility now discreetly hides from the town's view. Butchery kept Horace busy on the home front during the First World War. But it probably helped him perfect the confidence and social skills he needed, when opportunity presented itself, to talk smoothly and successfully to the beautiful Frances O'Keeffe. Like many local conversations it probably started with comments on the weather, and the dust would have certainly given them something to talk about.

Dust storms are a natural phenomenon, of course, but they can be exacerbated or even facilitated by human activity. Too many hoofed animals can break up grasslands. Too much mono-culture, especially crops like wheat, can leave fields exposed to excessive erosion. In either case, the top soil becomes loosely bound and more liable to be blown away. This is what created the American dust bowl, for similar reasons, at a similar time, furthered by high prices for wheat on the international markets because of the predictions of imminent war followed by actual global conflict. In a very real way one of the first Australian casualties of the First World War was the Australian landscape itself.

As in America, there was much anticipation that a long war would be good for wheat prices. While agricultural expansion and a European war may not have necessarily caused the Junee dust storms of 1915, they almost certainly contributed. But the photograph of the January dust storm revealed more than a story of simple cause and effect. Australia's historical newspapers contain thousands of references to dust storms, but also disclose a wider pattern. The references increased from the middle of the nineteenth century, and then they suddenly peaked around the 1900s and 1910s, gradually tailing off again to the middle of the twentieth century. In some respects this could reflect the trends in local newspapers, which certainly increased and then gradually decreased. But, broadly speaking, it also matches the very obvious trends of European settlement and its attendant agricultural and pastoral expansion. It is a salutary reminder of the continuities and changes wrought by, with, on, and through land and people at levels variously local, regional, national, and international. If ever an event were to perfectly capture the spirit of Australia in 1915 it was that storm, which served as a portend to humankind of imminent devastation in a great tempest of immeasurable complexity that had no possible excuse of a natural cause.

CHAPTER FIFTEEN

WHEN LEGENDS WERE CRAFTED AND WAR RAGED MARCH 1915

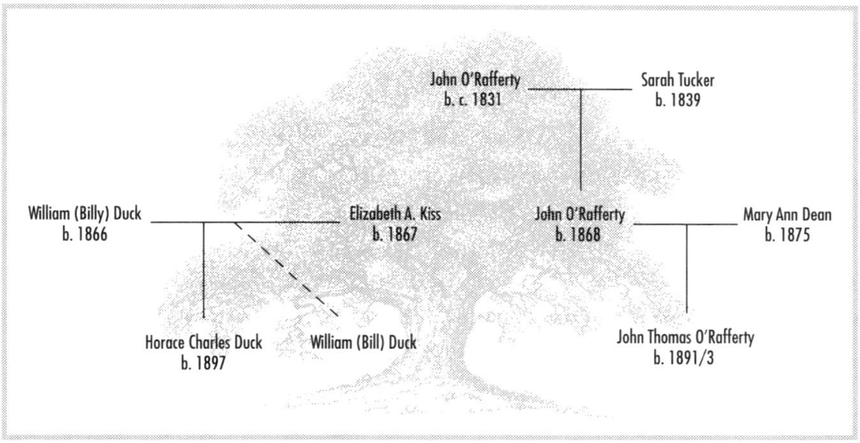

WILLIAM JAMES DUCK, known as Bill after his father Billy Duck, enlisted in the Australian Imperial Force on the Ides of March 1915 in the Sydney suburb of Liverpool. Minor actions aside, Australia's first major component of soldiery in the Australian Imperial Force were now already overseas in Egypt. No doubt Bill had a sense of what he might expect. As had been the case with prior wars, many wrote home detailing their experiences; in March 1915 alone, dozens of letters were printed in local papers throughout Australia, giving the reading public an insight into the campaign in the Middle East and the experience of being overseas.

Press correspondents detailed some of the troops' activities, and in doing so gave rise to an ongoing debate about the behaviour of the

Australians in Egypt: either well-behaved and honourable representatives of their nation, or larrikins indulging in the physical delights of the streets and brothels of a foreign city. The fact is, of course, that they were both, and more, as personal temperament, peer pressure, and moral judgement would determine. Engaging with the debate is to buy into the mythical notion of a singular Australian soldier-type.

Those soldiers who wrote home projected a different and wider series of concerns than the way in which their Egyptian sojourn would be remembered. There were, for example, insights derived from their travels which they felt would serve continued Australian development. 'After seeing Egypt,' one writer stated, 'I would urge everybody along the river to go for irrigation.' Others simply marvelled at the amazing sights like the pyramids and other remains of ancient Egypt. This phenomenon is well known, but perhaps less recognised is how many also explored the markers and culture of modern Egypt, like the mosques of Cairo. Writing home about one such mosque, one Australian soldier described how it was 'beautiful in the subdued light', mentioning that he had taken his boots off to avoid 'sacrilege'. It was an extremely sensitive act for a member of a force that has been dogged forever afterwards with the blight of having generally acted with much racial and cultural insensitivity.

There were, however, many less-than-positive attitudes towards the people encountered in Egypt, like that of one soldier who stated simply that 'Egyptians are a peculiar race, who almost worship the Australians'. The same writer followed up with the observation that a 'feature about the lower class I dislike is that they are dirty'. Another part of his letter reveals that he remained under the impression that the forces were still being readied to be sent against Germany.

But the Australians in Egypt were soon to be directed against the Dardanelles in Turkey, as part of the Mediterranean Expeditionary Force, a cohort of Allied military might drawing on France and parts of the British Empire, notably Canada and India, as well as the Australians and New Zealanders, for whom the campaign has come to take on the significance of a sort of secular book of Genesis. At this time the bureaucratic military acronym ANZAC, which came to stand for a section of a larger combined expeditionary force, then a place and the soldiers at that place, then a century later seemingly as a synonym for all Australian and New Zealand military forces, had yet to gain any real prominence. While nationalism certainly prompted a strong desire for conflict in many Australians, some military regionalism was still evident, which reflects some lack of a yet fully coherent 'Australian' narrative of the war in early 1915. One soldier wrote about how 'we had a sham-fight, N.S.W. Light Horse versus Queensland Light Horse; had some pretty hard riding, but took them nicely'. It was still all a bit of a game.

Having signed up before Australians had commenced serious fighting, Bill Duck might also have seen the war as a bit of fun and adventure. But there was possibly a sense of duty involved as well. With his brother Horace remaining behind to take care of the family business, Bill, like many such men to enlist, was perhaps the family's nominal representative in the global war. Each country, each state, each region, each town, each family of the British Empire was encouraged to do its bit, and in Bill's case, he was it for the Junee Ducks.

On his attestation papers he said he was twenty-one years and two months old. Recording the months of a person's age is something normally only done for children, but the records of would-be soldiers are replete with them, a measure of their collective youth. He was just short of 5 feet 7 inches. His complexion was fair, his hair was black, and his eyes were 'good green', meaning they were good and green—he could see well enough to shoot. Three days after applying to join, he signed his papers and the unmarried butcher boy from Junee was off to war.

Like the soldier writing from Egypt, Bill probably thought he would be sent against Germany, Britain's main rival in the war. Most of the major powers of Europe had been pulled into a series of extended fronts, which were grinding into an increasing stasis by the start of 1915. Nominally, Britain's war had been triggered by German territorial aggression with the invasion of Belgium and the threatening of France. This German activity was part of a series of wider diplomatic and military responses to the assassination of an Austrian Archduke (itself an expression of Yugoslavian nationalism) and a complex network of alliances, which led major powers to variously declare war against each other in late July and early August 1914. In some ways, Britain and the Allied powers were thought to be defending liberalism, but in other ways the war also looks decidedly like a territorial and imperial power struggle of the sort that Europe had often seen before.

Amid this complex situation Britain's scheme to distract the Ottoman forces from the Dardanelles Strait, which was part of a wider Allied strategy regarding the war, slowly and inexorably led the newly uniformed youth towards the famous beaches and hills of Gallipoli.

After enlisting, Bill was assigned to A Company, 20th Battalion, 5th Brigade, AIEF. This much was recorded on his enlistment form. Some of the recruits in this battalion had already served in the First World War in a military capacity as members of the Australian forces which took German Papua in 1914. Although little remembered, it really was the first significant Australian role in the war and was the end-point of the German expansion in the Pacific that Captain Neil Brodie had witnessed about two decades previously.

Finding out about the battalion's history was easy, because Australia is well served by this part of its military past in one particular way: it has a lot of records. The service records of the men and units, individual and official diaries, and the accounts of witnesses, particularly the official war historian Charles Bean, provide historians with plenty of scope to unpack the campaigns and battles.

But, at the level of the individual solder, the story becomes harder to tell. Without diaries, oral histories, or prominent roles leading to their being mentioned in other sources, unpicking the story of an average soldier like Bill Duck can become an exercise in contextualisation. The war diary for the 20th Battalion survives in the Australian War Memorial in Canberra, so it is possible to piece together a rough outline of Bill's experiences. In ruled columns labelled 'Date', 'Place and Time', '20th Battalion AIF', the details roll off the page in snippets of laconic military exactitude: '1915, July, Suez, 0400, Arrived per HMAS Berrima en route from Sydney Australia.'; 'July, [Suez], 0800 to 1500, Disembarked 20th Battn & other unit on ship. Proceeded by 3 troop trains to Palais-de-Kubba near Zeitoun, and marched to Aerodrome Camp Heliopolis.'

Many observers were acutely aware of ancient associations of place and heroism that dotted the landscape of the Mediterranean and Middle East into which the Australian and New Zealander soldiers were sent. That the Australians fought near the site of Troy did not escape notice, and the 'bronzed' soldier image that developed is as much an historical and epic allusion to the bronze-clad warriors of legend as any reference to the tanned skin of the soldiers. And, just reading over this faded unit diary, I too found myself musing on the historical parallels. The terse descriptions had echoes of ancient stone inscriptions depicting the exploits of the army of Ramses the Great, the books that recorded the wanderings of the Israelites, or the chronicles and biographies of Alexander the Great's vast sweeping invasion. Long marches received only flitting epithets, like: '15th Aug 1915, Heliopolis, Battalion entrained in 2 troop trains to Alexandria.'

I was mildly disturbed on Bill's behalf that his time in the desert included training in what was described as 'Musketry'. The war to end all wars was being fought with machine guns, artillery, and aeroplanes, and poor young Bill was being readied for that conflict with skills described by a quaintly antiquated term like 'Musketry'.

Eventually, after a wait in Lemnos harbour on a 'dirty' troopship rather than on shore, with the upper echelons of the officer class 'indifferent' to such conditions, the moment came: '22 August, Anzac, 0200, Arrived Anzac & disembarked in barges'. Bill climbed into the landing craft with other fellows, rolling about as they carefully headed towards the Gallipoli shore and gradually lost sight of other boats. Clambering out with his kit onto a foreign shore, he probably spent a few moments wondering where his mates were—the landing was a mess. With a fraction less than a thousand men going ashore in the darkness, it was almost inevitable that the units became muddled up.

That evening, the battalion moved into position on Bauchop Hill, and some casualties were named the following day. Then, a few days later, the unit was again moved, this time to 'Russells Top' at the very frontline of the Allied positions at Gallipoli. As the days drift by in pencilled notes recording the dirty and dreadful business, the battles unfold in a detached sort of way, with the mentions of the wounded slowly turning from names to numbers. And, at the same time, there was a steady trickle of 'sick' being sent to hospital.

The battalion had arrived in Gallipoli as the last concerted assault petered out, so their contribution to that endeavour was relatively minor. In *Anzac to Amiens* Charles Bean wrote of the Gallipoli campaign that 'Anzac stood, and still stands, for reckless valour in a good cause, for enterprise, resourcefulness, fidelity, comradeship, and endurance that will never own defeat.' This may have a ring of truth to it, but it is also true that Anzac stood for inaction, horror, pain, suffering, and mental anguish. Bill's main duties were defensive, a fact captured in the details of his unit's diary. Day by day through August, September, and October, they were 'In occupation of Trenches'. And alongside this constantly repeated phrase, running down the right-hand column, the numbers of killed, wounded, sick, and returned from hospital were recorded with dismal regularity. It is a strangely patterned relic of the meat grinder of the Gallipoli trenches at the height of a horrifying stalemate, preserved in neat pencilled script on little cards. This is our Gallipoli: a bureaucracy of death.

Bill's service record indicates that he was not among the numbers of those killed, wounded, and sick. For over three months he lived that reality of snipers and shelling, the crack and boom of weaponry aimed at him and his mates, and endured the bitter living conditions that came with occupying those manmade lines which scarred this part of the earth.

On 8 November 1915 they were, as always, 'In occupation of Trench' at Russells Top. It was their last full day there, however, and it was the day that Bill was first injured. According to his medical report, he 'Strained his leg at Gallipoli walking up a hill with a pack on a forced march on 8th November 1915'. Russells Top was a notoriously rough piece of steep and rocky land. But he was not invalidated out of action, and may, somehow and somewhere, have participated in the action of the following day. At midday 9 November, the 20th Battalion handed over the occupation duties for Russells Top to another unit, blew 'H1 Tunnel' and then 'broke into [the] Turkish Gallery from H3 Tunnel'. The frantic running, shooting, and stabbing of that action, the cries and adrenalin, the wounds, the blood, and the gore are reduced to seven pencilled words. The next day's report said simply that the unit 'Took up quarters in Fatigue Gully'.

It was frightfully cold at Gallipoli about this time. For Bill, this seems to have exacerbated a condition apparently brought on by his injured leg. 'After a fortnights walking about the legs began to swell and [he was] sent to 5th field ambulance on 20th Nov', his medical record related. On 27 November he was transferred to the Gallipoli hospital. His unit diary did not capture his personal misfortune. It simply noted that 'snow fell' and '6 Sick evacuated'.

A little more than a week later Bill was back in Alexandria, having been transported by the hospital ship *Dongala*. His unit withdrew from Gallipoli on 20 December, so he missed what was probably the best-managed part of the whole campaign—the retreat.

1915–16

Bill's service record, like that of many soldiers of the First World War, was not a litany of battle successes and glorious actions, but is instead a personal revelation of the administrative machine of which he was but a tiny part. And what that machine was most interested in recording was his battle readiness. So after his being hidden for months in the bloody tempest of actual frontline action, his injury makes it possible to chart him in absurd detail. He was transferred from the 'Greek Hospital' in Alexandria to Cairo. His 'pains' were recorded, but only as a means of assessing his readiness to be returned to battle or to Australia. Bounced from unit to unit, hospital to hospital, his service record noted his conditions: 'Odema', Oedimatic Leg', 'Dysentery', 'Sprained Back', 'To Duty'.

A little slip of paper recorded that a urine test in December 1915 was 'Negative'. He enjoyed a hospital diet of fish, chicken, white bread, jelly, and more. A clinical chart mapped his temperature, heart rate, breathing, and 'Motions', all in order to assess him as still 'Impaired'. Eventually the machine declared him fixed. After a year temporarily attached to a sanitary unit he was transferred to the 45th Battalion in November 1916. Promoted to A/Cpl at Étaples, he was in France, and ready to meet his new comrades in the 45th Battalion.

During the interim, Bill's old unit, the 20th, had been busy. After pulling out of Turkey, the unit undertook further training in Egypt while it was brought back up to strength, before being sent to the Western Front in Europe. In April 1916, while Bill Duck was still recuperating in the Middle East, the unit was preparing to again enter frontline duties. The month opened with a review of the battalion by Lord Kitchener at Steenbecque in northern France. Having previously brought so much distress to Australian soldiers as the author and prosecutor of the scorched earth policy of the later phases of the Boer War, during the First World War Kitchener was made memorable for his pointing finger on recruitment posters.

The next five days were spent in training, and then the move towards the trenches of the Somme sector commenced. On 10 April they 'took up Reserve position' near Bois Grenier. Over the next few days the officers went forward 'to be familiar' with the Allied operations in this area, before finally moving into the 'front line trenches' four days later. Their sector was regularly reported to be 'quiet', although barely a day passed without one or two casualties. After four days on duty they were relieved, and another battalion swapped into the hard duty of frontline defensive work.

On 22 April the 20th Battalion again returned to the forward position. 'Condition in trenches very bad', the unit diarist noted. They had a 'Quiet night', but the next day 'aeroplanes were active' in the skies above. The routine continued on 24 April. 'In Front Trenches. Improvement of defences continued. Normal condition.', the unit diarist noted, with one soldier sent to hospital. The next day was like the one before. Anzac Day 1916, which the 20th Battalion experienced on the Western Front, was reduced to 'ditto. ditto. Aerial activity'. Three were wounded.

The next day their headquarters were shelled, and the following day they heard the dreaded 'Gas Alarm Signals'. And on it went: repairing trenches, swapping in and out of frontline duties and billeting in the rear, facing the threat of artillery, aerial assault, ground assault, gas, and disease. Some days only a few were killed or wounded, on others dozens.

Through June this routine continued, but the battalion was ordered out on the last of the month. They were shifted in early July and spent the first two weeks moving, training, and taking on strength. They were likely being readied to support the anticipated gains of the massive Somme offensive of that month. One soldier, writing home to his family, described seeing 'flashes of light over the sky like sheet lightening, but which we knew to be the reflection of the flashes of the big guns in the bombardment miles distant, too far away to be audible in fact'. It was just like a distant country storm.

The Somme offensive proved a dreadful disaster for the Allied forces. British troops, caught by German machine guns, were devastated. The British lost some 20,000 killed on the first day alone, and roughly twice that were wounded. But the British kept pushing over the following weeks and months as the war's massive scale continued to astound the world.

Having occupied the 'British old front line' in late July, in the area known as 'Sausage Valley', the 20th was soon thereafter ordered to attack an area near Pozieres. A series of difficulties and an inability to reconnoitre the ground delayed the assault. When it started in the early hours on the day after first intended, the Australians were 'badly cut up by rifle and m gun fire and held up by uncut enemy wire'.

Eventually, some Australians gained the enemy trenches and managed to hold them for an hour, but lack of munitions forced them 'to retire back to our own front line'. The unit diarist had to estimate the casualties, but arrived at the figure of two officers and 200 other ranks 'killed wounded and missing'. 'Lewis guns lost', he added.

It would be months before soldiers who lived through this and other engagements got descriptions of their action back to worried family in

Australia. Family members with servicemen overseas would dread knocks at their doors as official word was given of a dead, wounded, or missing loved one. And as had occurred with Mrs White in Boho in the Boer War, letters could and did arrive from those already dead. The grief this triggered was on a scale unexperienced before, and individual responses were varied. But one notable shift was the way that Victorian traditions of mourning, such as wearing large black lace outfits, were in some quarters giving way to simpler habits like wearing black armbands. Some commentators were actively encouraging Australians to bear their grief quietly and keep their public mourning to a minimum. It was bad for recruitment, after all. But an additional factor was that some materials were running short because of the war economy.

But the shortages at home did not prevent support of those away from home yet living. Australians took to supporting their fighting men through various 'comfort funds', which were often organised to support the men of individual battalions. Fundraising committees around the country united in their efforts to support Australians overseas, perhaps coming closer to illustrating any sense of national unity than the fighting actions themselves, which were clearly just small parts of larger Allied military strategies. So money, clothing, various foods, reading material, and blankets were all sent overseas to help the men endure what was now known to be a dreadful war. Women were particularly prominent in this, because, as Michael McKernan in *Australians at Home* has noted, the First World War 'was not the watershed for Australian women as it was for women in other societies'. They did not fill the workplaces of Australia to the same extent as other major combatant nations like England and Russia.

So the comfort funds reveal a tension between ostensible national unity and persistent divisions, gender being a case in point. And other old constructions of a racially and ethnically homogenous nationalism began to resurface and intensify during the war. Although some foreign nationals were interned when war broke out, especially sailors, the outbreak of war did not immediately bring about significant tensions against local 'enemy' ethnicities. Initially many Australians were not really worried by domestic 'aliens' of foreign birth or extraction, especially those settlers who had been farming neighbours for years, perhaps generations, like the German wine-producers of the Murray River that had lived by the Saunders family. But, as the war intensified and was prolonged, official attitudes changed, both prompted by and prompting more populist and public attitudinal shifts.

Calls for more foreigners to be interned were met with action, and domestic 'enemies' increasingly came in for suspicion and incarceration.

Moreover, the Easter Rising in Dublin in April 1916 had reignited fears of Irish nationalism and briefly stoked again the fires of sectarianism. Irish republicans had seized what they thought was the chance at independence while the British military was distracted in France. Armed militia occupied key parts of Dublin and declared Ireland an independent republic. In the face of overwhelming British force it was quickly subdued, ending the largest rebellion since the 1798 riots that had led to Mary Durham being transported to New South Wales.

The sectarian and sectionalist fears did not stop Australians of Irish extraction or Roman Catholic persuasion from fighting for the British Empire, though. In September 1916 John Thomas O'Rafferty—both of these things—enlisted in the AIF. The twenty-six-year-old was assigned to the 3rd Field Bakery. He had previously tried to enlist and been rejected on 'dental' grounds, but his persistence paid off, or perhaps his oral hygiene had genuinely improved. His enlistment, like many others, was published for all to see that he was doing his bit. While domestic referenda to introduce conscription twice failed to pass the Australian voting majority, there was a strong culture of lauding those who went, and in some darker instances shaming those who did not. The Sydney *Evening News*, under the heading 'Answer the Call', listed John O'Rafferty as one of the 'Men who have offered'. The life-giving language of sacrifice and salvation has long roots in the traditions of military service for empire, and reading this list with the knowledge of what many men experienced, it evokes the lists of the dead and wounded that soon followed, and reflected an earlier such trend during the Boer War.

But there was also a powerful new recruitment tool in Australia. The Gallipoli campaign had, undoubtedly, been utilised for propaganda effect. For instance, Charles Bean's *The Anzac Book*, an edited collection of writings from soldiers on the front, helped foster and project an image of the easygoing digger fighting well and bearing up with good humour. It was published in early 1916, and was advertised as 'A National Souvenir'. Others similarly capitalised on the moment, like the artist Percy Leason, whose picture of the 'Landing of the Australians at Anzac' was advertised in the Melbourne *Argus* as giving 'a true representation of the glorious achievements of the First Expeditionary Force', and would serve homes well as a 'reminder of the brave deeds of our Gallipoli Heroes'. There were standard or deluxe versions available for purchase and postage was free.

And so in a bizarre complement to the official propagandising use of the soldiers who fought and died at Gallipoli, the term 'Anzac' became almost a brand. It was used to sell products like an 'Anzac tonic'; raise business profiles, like 'The Anzac Motor Works'; or attract gamblers' attention, like the 'Anzac Handicap'. In fact, in 1916 alone, there are more than 6500 uses of the term 'Anzac' in the advertising sections of Australia's newspapers. And that is only the digitised ones. Many of these were, to be fair, selling poems and stories of the Gallipoli actions, but even that fact illustrates its commercial resonance.

While Australians were in trenches fighting in Europe on 25 April 1916, the first anniversary of the first Gallipoli landing was being remembered around the globe. New Zealand, with the benefit of immediate proximity to the International Date Line, was the first to host a celebration. Other services followed the sun from east to west, although they were held variously throughout the day, because the famous dawn service had not yet been developed. From Australia, over Asia and the Middle East, Europe, and the British Isles, the earth turned towards the sun and Anzac Day was a day of significance and remembrance. As Joan Beaumont characterised it in *Broken Nation: Australians in the Great War*, the first Anzac Day in Australia was 'an occasion on which government mobilisation and private grief converged in powerful public acts of remembrance'. With that first Anzac remembrance day coming only two days after Easter, as Beaumont and others have noted, this coincidence 'invested its rituals with a semi-sacred quality that it retains to this day'.

But the word 'Anzac' also adopted very classical literary references. Allusions to the gloriousness of sacrificing oneself for the honour of one's empire and nation mimicked traditions from ancient Rome and Greece with which writers of the 1910s were often familiar. And this seemed to gradually mesh with notions of the rewards of death in battle, which Pedre Hansen's Viking ancestors would have recognised as the prize of dining in the halls of Valhalla. But in 1916 'Anzac' was not just about past sacrifices. Military authorities were, as Peter Stanley noted in the *Lost Boys of Anzac*, even for the very first soldiers to have landed at Gallipoli, still overwhelmed by the administrative details of notifying next-of-kin of casualties. Yet even while the business of informing family of their losses continued, often months after a death had occurred, in Australia an opportunity was being readied for exploitation.

In preparing for the first Anzac Day, the Victorian *Wangaratta Chronicle* opined that 'We rejoice to see that Anzac Day—April 25—the day made glorious by the Gallipoli landing—is not to be a mere laudatory shout. It will be made a new starting point for enlistment for men for the front'. It then went on to detail the extensive recruitment plans throughout the country planned to coincide with that day. And so it was. On 25 April 1916, the first Anzac Day, Charles Alexander O'Rafferty, John's brother, applied to enlist at Wangaratta and was accepted the following day. Admittedly, he had previously tried to do so in Liverpool in November 1914, but had been rejected. In the new post-Gallipoli enthusiasm for recruitment, the enlistment officer did not seem to mind.

Charles and John both had to take an oath, signing their agreement to it on an official enlistment form, as had former soldiers like Bill Duck. They, and other new recruits, put their signatures to the solemn promise, affirming that they swear to 'well and truly serve our Sovereign Lord the King in the Australian Imperial Force'. They agreed to 'resist His Majesty's enemies and cause His Majesty's peace to be kept and maintained'.

While Charles was sent overseas in September 1916, John's profession and the slightly later timing of his enlistment probably saved him from the frontline. John's declared profession upon enlistment was baker, a simpler version than the same occupation described on his marriage certificate: 'pastry cook'. He joined the 3rd Field Bakery while the unit was being established in Sydney, possibly intentionally. The unit history records that it was poorly equipped, so much so that the newly enlisted men wore a variety of uniform patterns. Although formed in New South Wales, the unit drew on enlistments from Victoria and Tasmania in order to be brought up to strength. A daily routine was enforced, which introduced the men to a regular military round of 'Physical Training', 'drill', 'Rest', and 'drill'. All this was performed 'on a large flat park', perhaps providing an interesting spectacle for passersby.

He probably spent his few days of leave at the conclusion of training in his Willoughby home in the Northern Suburbs of Sydney. Although Thomas and his wife Emma came from Albury, where their respective parents lived, the couple had opted for the big city after their marriage. They had been together for only four years when John enlisted. But while his leaving undoubtedly caused some anxiety, John's enlistment brought the family some income to compensate. A weekly allotment of four shillings was granted to Emma from 11 September 1916 when he commenced duty.

Leaving his wife, the blue-eyed, brown-haired, 5 foot 6½ inch private embarked on the *Beltana* on 25 November 1916 and arrived in Devonport, England on 29 January 1917, the first direct ancestor on this family line that I know to have returned to the British Isles after generations away.

1917

John O'Rafferty was in Britain for only a few days before he was sent to France. His war service record basically shows him baking his way around the French cities of Rouen and Calais. John served much of his war in a uniform of white coat and white trousers. It at first might seem a ridiculous contrast to the experiences and conditions so well known to have taken place in the trenches, but nonetheless this was vital war work and also very dangerous. Thousands of men were kept alive by an overworked supply machine, of which John was a contributing part.

In a letter home detailing some of his experiences, a member of one of the Australian field bakeries described how the 'work is very heavy', often starting at 4:30 am. The long shift would then generally extend beyond 1 pm. Writing in January 1917, a month before John joined the Australian baking operations in France, this writer experienced difficulty adjusting to the climate and conditions of a northern hemisphere winter. 'The weather is very cold,' he wrote, 'and raining every day, and it is starting to snow a bit now. They say next month is the worst month here.'

Likely stationed at either of the French medieval cities of Rouen or Calais, this writer captured the size differential with a distinctly Australian comparison: 'Where the bakery is placed is a much bigger town than Bendigo.' And while he recognised the advantages he had over the fighting soldiery in the trenches, he still expressed a wish to be 'back in England again. It will do me', he emphasised. He had already been wounded and carried a 'piece of shrapnel in my chest', which was 'very sore now and then'. 'I can barely touch the place where it is, as it is so sore', he noted, prompting him to immediately think of how the campaign for conscription in Australia had been unpopular with the soldiers. 'I voted no,' he said, 'and would do so again before I would see conscription in such a place as Australia.' He concluded by adding a wry comment on the prime minister that had advocated conscription and would later strongly advocate for punitive reparations against a defeated Germany: 'I think Billy Hughes's boots were too big for him that time.'

John O'Rafferty was only attached to the Rouen bakery briefly, before being sent to Calais. The Calais bakery was a converted paper factory. It was 'a high brick building' of three storeys where the bread was made by a descending process. On the top two floors dough was made, which was dropped to the bottom through 'schutes'. On the ground floor there were fourteen ovens. An adjacent building held the fresh bread until 'the bread train' was loaded. The men spent their days busily kneading, tending their ovens and stacking the loaves. There must have been a white haze throughout the whole building from the many thousands of flour particles floating in the air. Trains brought in raw supplies, and took away the finished products. The chugging engines and clinking rails added to the constant banging of dough being pounded. The men had to bring in the flour in large sacks at the end of their 'very long' shifts, resulting in many casualties from the literally back-breaking work.

As demand increased, more ovens were added. These were located outside the main building, which was thought a wise precaution against air attack, so that the baking could continue in the event of a successful bombing. The author of the unit diary clearly felt that the military priorities on this matter were insensitive. 'It should be here mentioned', he noted, 'that at this time no protection was afforded against hostile aircraft.' He highlighted how the bakers constructed their own protection 'during their spare time'. This was particularly worrying for the bakers, as there were 'incessant air raids' which were 'very intense'. The raids would take place for hours at a time as the British military supply system was deliberately targeted. While duelling air battles played out above, down below the bakers continued to knead their dough and stoke their ovens to an outside soundtrack of buzzing planes, thudding bombs, and chattering anti-aircraft fire. The unit diarist marvelled that there were no casualties from the anti-aircraft shrapnel, which, after being fired into the sky, then fell clattering on the ground below.

One of the privates in the 3rd Field Bakery wrote home of his experiences when 'we had a visit from Fritz with his aeroplanes'. The Australians endured 'six hours of it, and the damage to innocent civilians and to property was terrible'. Even German prisoners nearby suffered from the attack, and the private indicated there were about '50 funerals'. The toll of the constant harrying from the air began to tell, he suggested. 'We were rather nervous—I couldn't say frightened—but it rather gets hold of you when you don't know where the next one is coming, and the guns are firing in the air at a noise that can be heard somewhere, and shrapnel is falling all about, and there is nothing between you and it but a bit of canvas.'

The private concluded his letter by commenting on the scale of the baking operations. He had heard that women might be soon employed—'lady bakers' was the term he used. And he noted that the Australian military bakers 'were now working three eight hour shifts, and they are putting some splendid machinery in the bakery. One would think it was going to last another twenty years to see the preparations', he thought, before predicting that 'Fritz won't go into another winter campaign'.

The labour demands of this environment were so intense that the British authorities eventually brought in Chinese labourers to assist. An Australian bakery officer noted with distaste the abandonment of a reliance on exclusively 'white labor', something that seems somewhat ironic in the context of a global war where Japan was one of the Allied powers. When the 3rd Field Bakery moved to Rouen this issue of race and food supply raised its ugly head in an ugly war, with it being noted that 'The system of consignment was the same as at Calais, but the loading was done by A.I.F. Personnel instead of chinese personnel, it being thought that no chinese or other element should enter into contact with an organisation which was purely Australian'.

Fortunately, while the administrative officers had time to focus on such things, John was almost certainly too busy baking. Like most that actually did the work, he would probably have been grateful for any bit of help, and if the racists went hungry then more fool them. An average of 40,000 pounds of bread a day were produced, the loaves of bread being bagged twenty-five or fifty to a bag, and sent to feed the many bellies that made up the frontline of the Allied powers.

And among the bags was Australian flour, a major part of Britain's contribution to the war. One such bag, which had been packed in the Euroa flour mill in Victoria in the middle of 1916, was opened by a Belgian soldier working in 'a military bakery' in April 1917. He was surprised to find tucked inside it a letter from an Australian girl addressed to 'A Belgian soldier and sailor fighting for King and Country'. She asked after the recipient and requested a reply. The soldier graciously took up his pen, pleased with the chance to show off his English, which he had gained during a few years spent in England. He was married, thirty-two years old and had a boy and a girl.

'My wife and family', the soldier wrote, 'are always in invaded part of my poor country, which I hope relieved of German rather soon, for at our front some very good and great battles are having place for present. While our army was on the retreat of Antwerp, I had the occasion to see some Australian cavalry. I found them beautiful soldier and horsemen'. He had a friend write an additional note in French, confirming the discovery of the original note, which he appended to the reply. He dated his response 25 April 1917.

April 1917 was a significant month for the Allied war effort. Germany had widened its submarine warfare against Atlantic shipping to include neutral merchant vessels earlier in the year, so after several of its ships were sunk in March, the United States of America shifted significantly in favour of war. In early April America joined the Allies against Germany and by the end of the year also against the Austro-Hungarian Empire.

But offsetting this seeming blow to Germany was political turmoil in Russia. The Tsar had been effectively forced to abdicate in March, prompted by massive workers' strikes, some of which derived from political agitation around International Women's Day in February. The trouble was exacerbated by chronic food shortages. Intended heavy-handed military responses failed, fomenting mutinies instead. For several months Russia endured a terribly delicate and unstable domestic situation, before the Communist Revolution in early November resulted in Russia withdrawing from the First World War in early 1918 and plunging into civil war.

And agitation and resentment against the war and its conditions was not restricted to the Eastern Front. Approximately midway between the two bakeries of Calais and Rouen was the fishing town of Étaples. Here Bill Duck spent four months after having been shipped across the Mediterranean Sea from Alexandria to Marseilles, and may have eaten John's bread there. His whole journey from Alexandria to Marseilles to Étaples was like a history lesson. Alexandria was a Greek settlement in Egypt, and Marseilles was originally a Greek settlement in France. Both cities later became Roman possessions. Étaples, near the border with Belgium, was not far from the old frontline of the *Pax Romana*, the Roman peace that extended, theoretically, throughout the empire from Egypt to the border with Germania.

It was the general area from which the Romans had departed to invade Britain, and Vikings had raided along this coast. It suffered greatly in the Hundred Years War between France and England and gave its name to the *Treaty of Étaples* between the French King Charles VIII and the English King Henry VII in 1492. Napoleon's army had also loitered along this coast waiting for the opportunity to invade England, which never came. And the British camp, quite frankly, lived up to this long reputation of violence, tension, and distrust. In an historical parallel, Étaples was used as a staging ground for British military endeavours on the Western Front to bring on 'His Majesty's peace'. But it was also the site of a significant internal disturbance of that peace, conducted by Australian and New Zealand soldiers. In September 1917, frustrated by poor living conditions, various stresses of the war, and the officious attitudes of the training officers, thousands of men mutinied.

A New Zealander, sneaking out of camp to enjoy a visit to the town as a break from the camp, was arrested. This proved the trigger for mass protesting at the horrific camp conditions. The military police were at first unable to stop the surge of angry men from leaving their camp and entering the town. But, with reinforcements and the threat of machine guns, one of the lesser known battles of the First World War ended. The Étaples Mutiny faded away and several ringleaders were punished, including the execution of one by firing squad. But Bill Duck was not there to protest the camp conditions, he had been sent to the front several months earlier. Nor was Charles O'Rafferty, who by then was already bouncing around the military hospital network in England, soon to be sent back to Australia.

Charles, fighting with the 58th Battalion, had been wounded on two separate occasions. The first occurred on 12 May 1917 while the 58th was, its pencilled war diary recorded, at Bullecourt on the Hindenburg Line and he was sent into action against the German lines. There were many 'golden flares all along our front', there was a 'light shrapnel barrage falling on our right', and 'Enemy heavies shelling area in rear of our lines'. And, to make things worse, it was the middle of the night when the officers decided to strike.

At 3:40 am, 'zero hour', the Allied artillery commenced a barrage on the enemy lines in front of Charles's position, to which the Germans responded with a similar barrage, and 'numerous red rockets with an occasional green flare'. The attack was even supported by aircraft, aided in their bombing runs by ground flares ignited by the soldiers. The whole effect would have been incandescent.

The officer writing the diary recorded incoming reports of initial success: 'everything was going well and men had gone towards their objectives; showing splendid dash when jumping off. Our barrage fire was effective and well placed. Enemy shelled the whole sector heavily'. Soon afterwards, more detailed reports came in from the lines. By 4:35 am one of the companies had been beaten back and was having another push. Seventeen minutes later another report came through that the Australians were in the enemy trench and there was 'fierce hand to hand fighting with rifle and bombs'. By 5:21 am the gain was being maintained. 'We are holding them', it was said, 'and bombing them along trench.' Six minutes later the attack was wrapping up: 'Huns appear to have suffered heavily and are freely surrendering. We have captured strong post and reached objectives.' The other company had similar success, noting that only seven minutes after first encountering the enemy it had 'reached objective' and 'am digging in'.

The main attack had taken a little under two hours. Among the wounded of this day was Charles, hit in the left arm and shot in the left buttock. As the morning dawned, the fighting reduced, and the casualties and prisoners were removed throughout the day, although this was difficult. While the fighting had diminished, the front was still active and 'there were numerous complaints from Company Commanders during the day that our artillery was shooting into our own trenches'.

After extraction from the front, Charles was gradually transported to Calais and then to Brighton in England. He spent a few months in various military hospitals in England, but his buttock wound did not heal sufficiently to return him to active service, so he was returned to Australia by the end of the year and discharged as medically unfit in early 1918. His family in Albury received word of his wound in late May 1917 and of his early return by December of that same year. In the end he spent only one Anzac Day overseas.

Being transported, or marching between positions, and waiting and recuperating ready for action were among the most common experiences of the war for Australians. Like most Australian soldiers of the First World War, Bill Duck's service record is replete with the arcane mysteries of military abbreviation. For those capable of deciphering this almost runic language, these record his official war. Mostly dominated by seemingly constant changes between various units, and cursorily described movements associated with those changes, it is not an immediately intelligible document. His journey across the ex–Roman Empire was recorded by little phrases like 'Attached to 3rd Aust Sanitary Section', 'Taken on Strength', 'Transferred to 4th Bdge', 'Temp attached to 13th Btn', before finally on 20 May 1916 being 'Transferred to 45 Btn'. Interspersed amongst this more straightforward detailing of his major movements were less obvious notations, often minor administrative matters captured in shorthand. His epic travels were a far cry from the *Odyssey* or the *Aeneid*.

The 45th Battalion was composed of many Gallipoli veterans like Bill, and the British strategists were utilising their experience of modern warfare and military discipline. They were planning a sledgehammer strike against the German lines at Messines in June 1917. The assault involved Australian, New Zealand, and British troops, lots of artillery, and military engineers. A now-famous group of diggers dug under the German positions near Messines, and blew heavy explosives below the enemy lines. This proved to be one of the more successful actions of the war, although perhaps not quite as successful as it was initially hoped to have been or was later said to be. In a striking echo of the siege tactics of old, the tunnels were blown, the enemy lines were bombarded, and the waiting troops flooded into the weakened positions. Reportedly some 10,000 Germans died. Bill may have felt the rumble through the ground of the subterranean mines exploding at 3:10 am on 7 June, and possibly seen the flash of dirt into the air signalling the deaths of thousands of men. The artillery, a constant companion of the war, was thumping regularly with one of its barrages, dropping shells directly onto the general area into which Bill was heading.

In the early afternoon of 7 June 1917 Bill and his mates waited on Messines Ridge for the third wave of the assault to commence at 3:10 pm, exactly twelve hours after the attack had commenced. The Germans had certainly lost ground, but their lines were far from collapsing. They had even been attacking the Australian positions held by the 45th for an hour before this third Allied infantry push. The 'hostile Artillery and Machine Gun fire was very fierce, and our losses were heavy', it was formally reported later.

When the Allied attack commenced, the 45th met with 'heavy opposition' from an 'enemy concrete Strong Point' which was well armed and 'heavily garrisoned'. Eventually securing the positions, and 120 prisoners, the Australians held their gains against yet another German counter-attack later in the evening. However, in pulling the lines back to what the commanding officer of the 45th frustratingly described as 'the RED DOTTED LINE', two of their companies had to endure an Allied artillery barrage near that line. For a time they were cut off, beyond friendly lines, enduring 'friendly' shelling. This was described as being 'most unfortunate as it inflicted a number of casualties on our own men'.

Over the next few days the Australians sought to make the best of the dilapidated trenches they now occupied and fend off repeated German assaults. Eventually they were relieved of frontline duties on the night of 10–11 June, and the officers could write their reports and count the losses. Eight officers were dead and eight more wounded. Of the other ranks, ninety-two were killed, fifty were still missing, and 344 were wounded. One of the wounded was Bill Duck, who had received a 'G.S.W. Buttock. R', a gunshot wound in the bottom, on the first day of the action.

This wound triggered another flurry of notation on his service record sheets. 'Wounded in action in the field', a purple stamp recorded. After recuperating for so long, Bill was injured again in the first day of the Battle of Messines, a coincidence in a way, as this was the first time since Gallipoli that Australian and New Zealand units had fought together. Whether he had been advancing on his belly, lying prone on the ground shooting at the enemy positions, or was hit from the side as he charged, he was soon out of the action. Surrounded by death and mud and cries and groans, the soldier somehow made it back to the safety of his lines.

Unlike his Gallipoli injury, Bill's wound at Messines was treated with more immediate seriousness. On 10 June, three days after being shot, and as the remainder of his unit was preparing to hand over frontline duties, Bill was admitted to Reading Military Hospital in England. He had been extracted from the front and transported to safety. And like the dozens who wrote home expressing a 'longing to get back to Australia', as a soldier in Charles O'Rafferty's 58th Battalion put it, or at least safely away from the warzone, Bill was probably relieved.

After a short stay in hospital Bill was sent for continued recuperation to Perham Downs, the site of the Australian training camp on Salisbury Plains. His file is relatively quiet for this period, with only a single 'offence' recorded, an absence of a few hours, for which he was 'admonished' and docked '8 days pay'.

Such absences occur on many military service files, slotted between the transfers and wounds as just part of the war experience. The day after Bill Duck was shot, for instance, John O'Rafferty was 'absent from roll call' in the evening at Calais. Perhaps he was celebrating news of the successful Allied assault. Perhaps it was simply coincidence. Yet it was the first of two such offences recorded for John's time at Calais, with a similar evening absence on 15 May 1917.

1918

At the start of 1918 John O'Rafferty went 'on leave to [the] U.K.'. But he was soon 'sick to Hosp. whilst on leave'. The reasons are terribly, embarrassingly clear, recorded for posterity with the same military precision with which the state of Bill's bottom had been treated. John had a 'Total V.D. period' of forty-one days, then twenty more, then another nine days. His holiday had turned into an extended health crisis.

Venereal disease proved a major problem for all combatant armies in the war, and for the civilian populations to which they returned. Raden Dunbar has dealt with some of this sensitive issue in *The Secrets of the Anzacs*, where he illustrated the prominence of the phenomenon by noting that the numbers of Australian soldiers treated for VD during the war was more than 60,000 men. John was manifestly not alone. The afflicted men elicited a range of complex responses from friends, family, institutions, and country. And, with the diseases often transmitted to wives, and thus on to children, the phenomenon contributed to an international health crisis. Undoubtedly the biggest winners of the First World War were the pathogens. And to make matters worse, in 1918 the trenches of Europe experienced the first blossoming of the strain of influenza that came to be called the Spanish Lady. Once it was present, troop movements and concentrations facilitated its deadly spread.

John seemed to overcome his spate of problems by May 1918 and he was temporarily posted to the Training Brigade in England, rather than being immediately returned to France. Here his military skills, both fighting and baking-related, could be drilled for further improvement, and this brigade also served as a sort of administrative holding area before redeployment to the active theatre. But he was not free of trouble. Throughout the coming months he was returned to hospital with some regularity as 'sick', and with 'stomach' problems of some sort. On one occasion he was admitted with 'Contusions and Abrasions' to his face. Whether he had had a baking accident, or it was some sort of garrison scuffle, it was probably still better than being in France. Although plagued with chronic bad health, John was fortunate enough to spend the remainder of 1918 safely in England.

Much of this time was spent in the camp at Fovant, a little town in Wiltshire in the undulating chalk downs. This area is famous for pre-historic ground carvings of horses, which prompted some of the Commonwealth troops stationed at the Fovant camp to carve unit badges into the hillside nearby. Among those which remain near Fovant to this day is the emblem of the Rising Sun of the Australian Imperial Forces.

Bill Duck started 1918 back in France, having rejoined his battalion two days before the new year. His recovery from the gunshot wound took less than three months. Bill was 'absent' for several days while supposed to be en route from the Reading hospital to the military camp at Perham Downs. He may have taken a scenic way, but he may also have had trouble, as the railways system was overwhelmed with military traffic. He was admonished and docked pay, but not otherwise punished. He did face up to his duty, after all.

And so he was shipped back to the front, his file recording the locations like a series of train stations with an ominously vague final stop: Perham Downs, Southampton, Havre, Field.

It is a familiar pattern for the official record of a soldier's service to have bursts of notation following action on the front. Bill's war record is silent about January, February, and March 1918. Only in April does a new round of writing mark a change in his military status. And once again it was because he became a casualty.

The 45th spent the first two-thirds of March training at Meteren. 'Musketry Instruction' and 'Gas Training' were prominent. The Australians enjoyed a series of inter-battalion football matches, with the unit diarist laconically recording the results: 'Played 46th Battalion Rugby Football. Won by 45th Battalion'; 'Played 48th Battalion Football Brigade Competition Aust. Rules. Lost'; 'Played 12th Field Amb. Rugby Football. Won by 45th Battalion'; 'Played the 48th Battalion Rugby Football Won by 45th Battalion 45 to Nil.' Clearly, they were better at rugby than Australian Rules. They won a soccer match, and lost another Australian Rules game. And then they had to move.

On 23 March the unit diary again became busy recording movement as the Allied war machine seemingly responded to German activities. By then there were Germans through the Allied lines in the area around the Somme. The Western Front had been breached.

They called it the *Kaiserschlacht*, the Kaiser's Offensive, better known to the Allied forces as the German Spring Offensive. It was to be the last major push by the Germans to break the Allied lines, using masses of troops freed up by the termination of Germany's Eastern Front with Russia's withdrawal from the war. Launched in late March, it initially met with considerable success and came close to achieving conditions for a major German breakthrough in the Western Front that would split the Allied lines and facilitate a German victory. But as the Allies raced to defend the city of Amiens and the German soldiers began to outrun their supply lines and artillery support, the attack slowed.

It was this offensive which triggered movement for Bill's battalion. Eventually, on 28 March, at 12:10 am, the 45th was manoeuvred into frontline positions. One company 'dug a line of trenches' near Millencourt, expecting an attack, while another company supported the 47th Battalion at Dernancourt. On 1 April the Germans telegraphed their intention with 'a heavy barrage'. But, despite some infantry raids nearby, a major attack did not arrive. The following day the battalion was relieved. But when the battalion was advancing back to the front on 5 April the Germans, 'put down a sudden and very heavy barrage'.

Digging in, the Australians made it to relative safety in 'Pioneer Trench', and the 45th took up right flank positions near the Dernancourt Road, ready for its attack. Late in the afternoon the order was given, and 'in excellent spirits and anxious for the work before them, the men advanced in fine formation. Heavy casualties were inflicted upon our men by M.G. Fire, but notwithstanding this they advanced steadily in good order, taking their objective'. Such, anyway, was the official record.

Sometime that day Bill suffered a severe gunshot wound to his foot. He was evacuated to England, missing a toe. He spent Anzac Day in the 1st Eastern General Hospital in Cambridge. In Europe the intense German efforts of April were continuing, but gradually they stalled. The war would continue for several months, but Germany's last great chance had failed. And Bill would not fight again. Like John O'Rafferty, he spent the remainder of 1918 in England.

In May, the month following his injury, Bill's family may have seen his name listed in the *Sydney Morning Herald*'s 'Double Casualty List': 'Pte William James Duck, Junee'. The lengthy casualty lists polarised the country, as people's losses were mingled with accusations of cowardice, war-mongering, and hypocrisy. Class divisions, in particular, seemed exacerbated by this. Financial incentives for and against enlisting already troubled the working classes acutely. Economic necessity encouraged some men to enlist because of the economic downturn caused by the war, while others needed to maintain their families by working and could not seriously contemplate going to war without leaving their families in economic distress. And this was sometimes made worse by being badgered about serving nation and empire. Casualties, too, impacted more directly on spouses and children of workers' families who were already struggling with limited income and an absent breadwinner. And this in turn put strain on wider family and community support networks. Nonetheless, the high casualty rates did not dampen all enthusiasm for the war.

On one level continued support was expressed through public demonstrations. Perhaps none quite captures the essence of militant imperial enthusiasm like a mock tank display held in Brisbane. This symbol of mechanised warfare was used to raise money when 'a facsimile of "His Majesty's Land Ships" began a successful offensive to raise money for sixth war loan'. A band, uniformed men, and banners complemented the parade of the 'contraption' along Queen Street. Among the subscribers to the fund was Fred Hiley, who gave £1000.

Such public demonstration of military fervour by the moneyed classes was sometimes resented by those of the working classes, although the jingoism of some public figures often caught the attention of the most vulnerable in society. In July 1918, young Daniel Frank Kiss of Junee applied to enlist. He was a 'Bill Poster at Picture Show', his mother was dead, and his father lived at Sydney. His file shows the application proceeding until it abruptly ends with a handwritten note: 'STOP. Real name Stanley Frank

Shaw. B/C Provided by father'. He had, it turns out, 'Been in camp before [and] gave false name & age'. He was not one of Bill's relatives after all, just a young man who was so desperate to join the great event of his time that he had somehow latched on to the Kiss family of Junee as an opportunity to do so.

Australians were becoming increasingly familiar with returned soldiers, whose often broken bodies and troubled minds were clear arguments against war. When an ex-soldier from the 3rd Field Bakery was found dead of self-inflicted gunshot wounds in Whittingham in New South Wales, it was a surprise to his family and friends alike. He had seemed happy and cheerful, and gave no indication of his intent or explanation for his actions. The coronial inquest could only point to his mental health. Dozens of other soldiers seemed similarly to struggle with a return to civilian life. Of another suicidal soldier, who killed himself in January, the newspaper could only discreetly comment that the deceased 'sustained shell shock, and was afterwards strange in his behaviour'.

The return of thousands of serving men, and the failure to return of thousands more, was probably one of the greatest social adjustments Australia ever had to make. Going to war had been relatively easy, enthusiastic even. But, despite the continued fervour of some for the conflict, war weariness had gripped the country, and any belief that Australians remained united in their support of the war is pure delusion. Two failed conscription referenda, strikes, marches, and so on all decidedly demonstrate things to be otherwise. Many in Australia came to hate the First World War and were very glad when it ended.

Of those who welcomed peace, the families were prominent. I do not know how Emma O'Rafferty dealt with John's absence. They had been married for only three years and two months when he left Sydney for France. Emma was left caring for the children, including Nanny. But even the war's end did not mean immediate reunion. After the Armistice of 11 November 1918, it took some time before all the soldiers returned.

Bill was shipped back to Australia in December. He would later pass on stories about jabbing corpses with bayonets to give their edges an infectious element so as to kill wounded enemy by sickness if they survived the initial thrust of steel. This sickly tale is my one piece of oral history from the First World War, passed on from Bill to Pa to me.

John remained on active duty and was appointed as a driver in January 1919. It was several months before he would get home.

Demobilisation and repatriation took time and brought many problems with it as the nation embraced peace and adjusted to the many memories and effects of war. In a very real way a whole generation was damaged. Two of John's in-laws had also served, for instance. Arthur Bowen Phillips, a clerk, had been a gunner in France, raining death upon the muddy fields. His brother William Henry Phillips, a blacksmith and farrier, had done field artillery service prior to the war, so was part of the pre-war enthusiasm for militaria. He was discharged from his real war service as 'Medically unfit—disability due to Military service'. Perhaps nothing can quite capture the change in mood from well-dressed and rehearsed parade-ground marching and show-shooting to the post-war quietude of broken bodies and the many cenotaphs recording absent bodies which grew like cold stone trees around the county. Australia was made a place of pain. These men and others like them, with the women who had served as nurses or held families together through years of battle, and the thousands of grieving parents, partners, siblings, and children all struggled in their individual ways to navigate the awkward return to civil society. This was the truly epic struggle of the age.

CHAPTER SIXTEEN

RECOGNITION
1919

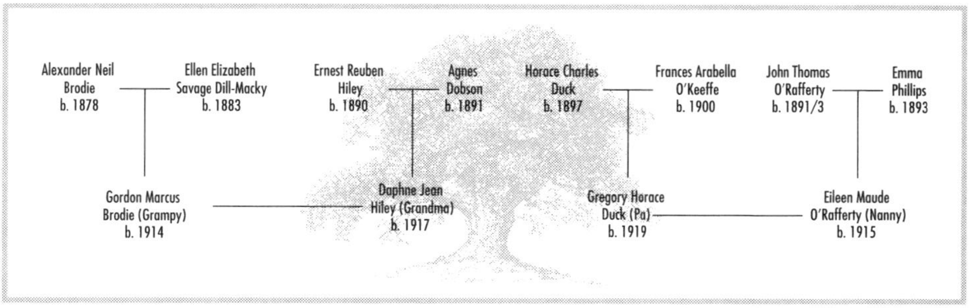

IN JUNEE A SPECIAL Influenza Committee was established by February 1919. The great influenza pandemic had made its way from the trenches of Europe to the shores of Australia. Although some Junee folk likened it to a regional outbreak from a generation earlier, the fact was that this virus was killing people around the world at a rate greater than any experienced in living memory. More people would die of influenza than were killed in the war. In terms of global epidemiological catastrophes, it was a modern equivalent of the Black Death.

To those who lived through it, the First World War had seemed like a long conflict, but in reality its duration was on a par with the Boer War. It was the catastrophic scale of the thing that was different, and the coming of the so-called 'Spanish Flu' extended the suffering of the generation that had already suffered so much. Fortunately for the Duck family in Junee, not too much had really happened in the interim between the war's start and end. Old Billy Duck was fined a couple of times, once for slaughtering more sheep than he had said he would, and another time for supposedly keeping dirty premises. His father, the Camden orchardist, had died. Horace Duck was working in the family business and was not far from completely taking over from his father. Bill Duck had gone to war and came back, albeit one toe short and carrying shocking memories of warfare and lost mates. Other families had endured worse. The names of the fallen were eventually inscribed on the town's cenotaph, which was erected in 1926, but in 1919 the site of the memorial was still occupied by a cannon forged in Junee during the Boer War to celebrate British victories.

As one of the most important railway towns in the country, placed at the centre of modern mass transportation, Junee was unlucky in that the conditions that allowed economic prosperity also facilitated the ready arrival of disease. Expecting the possibilities of sick train passengers becoming patients, a large tent was erected behind the town's district hospital. The annual railway picnic was cancelled, as were various trotting meetings, no doubt to Billy's annoyance. Commercial travellers were told not to visit the town or its businesses, especially places like the Junee railway refreshment rooms where large numbers of people congregated. Butchers like Horace might have been nervous doing their normal rounds with carts of meat, worried that they would either catch the flu or, perhaps, that their business would be retarded by quarantine measures. The atmosphere was tense, and their precautions may have seemed increasingly inadequate. Even the hospital tent was blown down in the first windstorm after it had been put up.

Australians read in horror of the way the rest of the world was suffering from the disease. One Junee resident received a letter from his brother in Wellington in New Zealand, for example, in which the author described being near death for five days with the sickness. The correspondent noted a death count in Wellington of more than a thousand people in three weeks. Such personal testament only added to the fear which public news reports gave the reading public on a daily basis. Mortality and morbidity counts and the frontiers of infection within Australia probably gave a sense that the country was being invaded by a new and terrible enemy. National, regional, and local borders were watched obsessively. While there had been waves of the flu before, of course, this one had the potential to be particularly dire. The world was experiencing another great plague, and so Australia's real battle at home was actually just beginning.

Returning soldiers were considered a particular threat, and towns were torn between welcoming back their own and being wary of all new arrivals.

In Junee, one soldier returned in January 1919 influenza-free, was given a public welcome and then travelled to Victoria with his mother to visit relatives. On coming back to Junee again, officialdom's surveillance machine and various frightened members of the public spotted them. A report was telephoned to Wagga that a man 'in khaki' in company with his mother had 'evaded guards' and boarded the northbound mail train. They were intercepted by the police at Wagga station, who got on the train, placed masks on the pair and ushered them to isolation in the hospital. Meanwhile, the carriage they had travelled in was emptied of passengers and quarantined. The train rattled on to Junee with one empty carriage among the rest, and the offending empty space was fumigated when it arrived. The soldier explained the situation to the police in Wagga, and turned out to be fine. But any other passengers on the train alert to what had happened did not yet know the soldier was clear of infection and may well have feared for their own safety, especially having witnessed the dramatic police intervention.

Travellers on the chugging steam train may have had a sense of being at the centre of the official response to the disease as the engine slowed to a halt, whistling and hissing, at Junee station. It was mandatory to wear masks on the platform and in the railway station, and reports of some people being charged for failure to do so illustrate that most people probably did wear them. Furthermore, an inoculation depot was installed there, which was an effective means of giving a large number of travellers access to the vaccine. By the middle of February more than 1100 people had reportedly been inoculated at Junee station, with the record for a single day clocking in at 224 people. During the course of the outbreak, thousands would be inoculated nationally. While it helped control the disease, whether this helped to calm the public or increased people's panic was a matter for individual temperaments.

Inevitably, before February had even ended, Junee had its first suspected influenza patient. The sick man, a railway worker, was placed in isolation in the kindergarten section of the public school. Classes were cancelled. In late March, six new cases were reported, one of whom died. By then, it seems the idea of using the school had been abandoned and the hospital was dealing with the patients. The Junee Influenza Committee had either been very effective or a touch paranoid. There was another reported case that March. So far it did not seem to be the great wave of infection that wider reports suggested the town should expect.

But the numbers, ominously, continued to rise.

They were using the school again by April, designated as the Junee Influenza Isolation Compound. In addition to this, some infected persons like David Kiss, a cousin of the Ducks, were isolated in their own homes. In May he was placed in confinement in his home in Ducker Street, only a few blocks from the primary school. Complementing these initiatives, the local authorities decided that when business operators became ill, their businesses should be shut for the duration as a precaution. For the first time in memory, some of the hotels began to remain closed to the drinking public.

The Isolation Compound had twenty-five patients in early June and continued to receive high numbers through the winter and early spring. Life still mostly went on, but it did so rather nervously. In August the local returned soldiers were given a function, at which Bill Duck received a pendant as a sign of appreciation for his overseas service. There had been a number of these gatherings, so the town's social life had not broken down, but the atmosphere must have been tense. Every sneeze or sniffle would have attracted worried gazes.

But the situation was clearly improving. By early December the compound had closed and the beds, pans, sheets, and other goods were being sold. In accounting for the expenses of running the facility, it was discovered that a significant amount of money had been consumed by patients in the form of liquor. Auditors calculated that Junee patients had drunk five times the equivalent per patient than the next-highest amount in the state of New South Wales. Patient merriment aside, the compound could be closed because the district hospital had a new isolation ward and sufficient beds to deal with the fewer cases in the latter part of the year. Like a dust storm the pandemic had swept through Junee, done its damage and was mostly gone again. A heavily pregnant Frances Duck must have been relieved to have survived the tense months, and on Boxing Day she gave birth to Gregory Horace Duck, Pa. She later told him that he was a very lucky baby boy to have survived that year.

For my wider family, 1919 proved to be an important year, marking this period as a time of changing generations. The full complement of my grandparental generation had now been born: Gordon Marcus Brodie, Daphne Jean Hiley, Eileen Maude O'Rafferty, and Gregory Horace Duck, the last to arrive. This marked the dawn of a period better covered by oral history and living memory.

And coupled with this was my family's continued movement away from the pioneer world. In early September 1919 Stephen Truman died in Gympie, in Queensland. His death, captured in one article under the heading 'Passing of the Pioneers', recalled his parents' voyage to Moreton Bay in 1852 on the *Maria Somes* and their settlement at Kangaroo Point, and it mentioned his sister's continued residence in that suburb. And although Elizabeth Hiley may have continued to live in the same area, her activities in later 1919 highlight how different the world had rapidly become from that of their parents. In September she was in charge of the 'useful garments' stall for the Central Women's Branch of the Queensland Protestant League's fete, seemingly a typically feminine role. But she was also a prominent member of the Queensland Women's Electoral League and sat with the Mayoress of Brisbane on the platform of the Empire Theatre in November, when the women gathered to hear the Prime Minister address them. Women had at least come to be seen as a voting bloc. When her mother had arrived in Australia, not even all men had the vote. Although she and Fred would continue to provide a link to the colonial world, as would other elderly Australians, the colonial world was increasingly distant for much of the population.

The same phenomenon occurred in Albury, made even starker about the time John O'Rafferty returned from Europe. He spent a large part of 1919 serving as a driver in England, perhaps following the peace negotiations with some interest. By being a signatory to the treaty of Versailles and an active participant in the negotiations, Australia gained some recognition as an independent nation. In this sense the war did propel Australia's international standing. But, by pushing hard for tough reparations against Germany, Billy Hughes also unwittingly helped to set the scene for another conflict.

Yet John's main focus was surely his family back in Australia. His daughter Eileen had been born in 1915 and had therefore spent the first few years of her life without a father present. And when John finally did return, he was racing against his father's illness. John only just made it back in time to see his father in Albury before he died of 'a lingering illness', pulmonary tuberculosis. For two years John O'Rafferty senior had battled against the complaint, surviving long enough to see his two sons safely back on Australian soil. And they stepped into the support of the wider family.

Although Charles had a few run-ins with the constabulary for noisily playing cards in late 1918, he shared his pension with his siblings and mother. And after the war John seems to have decided to return to live in Albury with Emma and the children, having given up their Willoughby home. The people of Australia had faced great troubles, but as the war and the flu moved into the past, each in their own way tried to get on with their lives.

1928

Young Eileen O'Rafferty gained her sixth class school certificate at the Henty Convent School in January 1928. John had stayed in Albury for a while during the early 1920s, before moving into the little country town between Albury and Wagga, in the flat Riverina plains. While still in Albury he had re-established himself as a civil baker, and in 1922 he was fined for not placing his name on the Commonwealth Electoral Roll. He was involved in organising a 1924 football match between the bakers and the butchers of Albury. These tiny snippets of information suggest, at least on the surface, a return to normality, before the move to Henty.

Henty is a regional centre for a wide area of agricultural land and was the ideal place for a bakery. Like many of the towns along the railway, Henty's silo stored grain drawn from the surrounding farmland, ready for transport by train. In the 1927 harvest, for instance, the Henty silo held an enormous 84,000 bushels of wheat. There was certainly plenty for John to work with. And it seemed to be on the increase. In January 1928 the Henty silo was holding 111,100 bushels. It was not quite Old Junee's 228,300 bushels, but it was still a substantial holding.

After the years of drought in the 1910s, and the passing of the war and the flu, the 1920s might have seemed an optimistic time, especially in the country. With a comfortable family life, a successful country business, and children in school, life must have seemed good for the O'Raffertys. At the end of 1928 'Mr and Mrs J O'Rafferty and family motored to Melbourne to spend the Christmas season'. They must have been doing alright if they were participating in that popular new family activity, the road trip.

Holidaying by car was just one of the signs of technological change influencing the behaviours of the people of Australia. Both moving picture shows and wireless radios had changed the entertainment landscape and helped keep Australians current with national and international cultural trends and events. American movies in particular came to be popular with Australian audiences, with 'Ben Hur' screening widely in early 1928. So too did American music become increasingly popular, both the traditional folk and country music, but also the modern jazz and brass band music, which helped introduce Australians to a new type of Australian woman, the 'flapper', as they came to be called. This, like the art deco architectural style that had originated in France and was increasingly common in new Australian buildings, both homes and offices, reflected a new cultural epoch profoundly different from that of the previous century. Not all of it was developed after the war, but by the 1920s these changes had collectively reached a certain critical mass.

But the technology could also be put to more sombre uses, reflecting the raw emotional underpinnings of this age of cultural flourishing. In Junee a 'Movie Ball' was held in the Lyceum Hall in 1928, which served to help raise funds for the debt on the town's war memorial, only relatively recently installed. While the 1920s are often remembered as a happier time, the memories of the Great War continued to haunt the nation and its people. It was in part the misery that came before which marked out the optimism of the period. And the internationalism of the new media, aided by the experience of war, helped to foster political aspirations which looked forward to increasingly better times. Bill Duck ran as a Labor member in the Junee council elections during 1928, for instance, an illustration of the sense that people had that they should get involved to make Australia in the image they wanted it to be.

Yet while some members of my wider family were demonstrably political on occasion, variously on differing sides of the political spectrum, their daily lives were often unconnected with the big political tussles between progressives and conservatives or left and right that tend to dominate histories of this wider period. Instead, their political concerns tended to be local, and their recorded activities often social. The most common documented references to Horace and Frances Duck in Junee place them regularly playing tennis from the mid 1920s and very involved in the local tennis tournaments. Frances also entered the local 'Junee Queen' contest, placing well, but not winning.

Far to the north, in Queensland, Fred and Elizabeth Hiley regularly attended or hosted a round of anniversary dinners during this period, celebrating how far they and their organisations had come. These events speak to their social standing and the relatively self-satisfied situation in which they and people of their class found themselves. These moments and rituals of remembering proved particularly useful for my research as I explored the stories of the Queensland branch of my family tree, and they served the purpose of grounding the family firmly in their Australian situation.

In 1926 the Kangaroo Point Wesleyan Church celebrated its diamond jubilee, and the event was held in what the paper described as 'the beautiful garden of Mrs. Fred Hiley's residence'. That particular phrasing is a good illustrator of complex historical contexts and nuance. There was something almost ironic about the way that Elizabeth was by convention relegated to the status of 'Mrs. Fred Hiley', but there could be little doubt that this was her garden. And the party and the garden took pride of place in a big black and white photograph which dominated the front page of Brisbane's *Sunday Mail* for 21 November 1926.

The tropical foliage is clear in the background, even in the grainy newspaper image, with its palm trees above, grass below, and a huddle of dozens of people in the middle. Heads poke through in the background, which provides a slight glimpse of the house in one corner of the photograph. Two tables, decked with dangling lace, hold bouquets of flowers. The men wear jackets and ties, with a range of older and newer hats, and the ladies have their own uniform of dresses, hats, and ribbons. The very prominent spots on one dress hint at the extensive use of colour that the black and white image masks. The children in the front have smaller versions of these patterns, and for the most part their expressions display their lack of interest. One of those children is Daphne Hiley, Grandma. This is one of those facts that break down time and distance. Elizabeth Hiley, pictured there, is Grandma's grandmother. Someone I know knew someone born in 1859.

But the picture in the garden is compelling for a range of other reasons. I also remember Grandma showing me a copy of that picture hanging in her hallway and saying she did not really know any of the people in it. They were likely relatives and once-close family friends, but remained unnamed and unknown. A few pages into the same newspaper that published the photograph, it is possible to see the attendees' names. Yet the list was too short to mention the children. Grandma was not listed, although her father was.

Elizabeth Hiley had attended her party wearing 'a frock of lettuce-green and mauve striped marocain', and 'a small black hat'. There was an orchestra, tea, and stalls with sweets, cakes, and ice-cream. Flowers on the tea tables were apparently 'shasta daisies and sunflowers'. The event had been organised by the Ladies Church Help Society, with Elizabeth in charge. The newspapers could be very descriptive sources, yet also filled with utter vacuousness, conjuring a sense of a Queensland with some similarities to the world of *The Great Gatsby*. It was all about who was there, what they wore, and what they ate. As a memorial of sixty years of church history, it was rather focused on the present.

A brief report from the social pages of December 1927 reveals that 'Mr. and Mrs. Fred Hiley and their granddaughter, Daphne, are spending a holiday in Warwick'. They too were indulging in the trend for holidaying, which enabled an increasing number of Australians to become more familiar with more of their country as a place to enjoy. Tourism certainly was not new, as the planned developments near Bega in the previous century have revealed, but new forms of independent motorised transport helped widen the possibilities for Australians.

Yet the period also reveals a focus on the persistence of place for some families and their sense of long association. Elizabeth and Fred Hiley appear regularly in lists of attendees at social gatherings, often enough as hosts. In one of the more prominent of these events, in 1928 the senior Hileys celebrated their golden wedding anniversary at Webster's Café Majestic on Queen Street, Brisbane. Apparently, at least according to its own advertisement, it was 'the best dining place in Brisbane'. During the 1910s its increasing numbers of patrons had included many 'discerning men and women', or so the marketing suggested. Good food and orchestral music were also offered, in addition to the chance to rub with the best of society. In 1928 there was an upstairs dining hall, which benefited from 'natural light and big windows'. The food was apparently 'priced at a figure which business men will appreciate'.

But while detailing the event, the reports also linked it to the past it commemorated. In a single printed hit, their lives were rendered in short detail: 'Mrs. Hiley, born at Shafston-avenue, on May 31, 1859, was the second-daughter of the late Mr and Mrs. John Truman, Bristol, Somersetshire, and has resided on Kangaroo Point the whole of her life. Mr. Hiley, youngest son of Daniel and Sarah Hiley, was born at Bradford, Yorkshire, England, on March 10, 1857, and arrived in Brisbane by the sailing vessel *Indus* on

October 8, 1873.' Arrival, the message ran, was followed by persistence and longevity. They had been living at the same address at Kangaroo Point for fifty years, since their marriage in 1878, and were pleased with it.

The event itself was a sumptuous 'banquet'. There was a 'three-tier wedding cake' and dozens of guests attended. A member of the Legislative Assembly presided, the Mayor of Brisbane brought a gift, and dozens of other people were named as attending or contributing to the event in ways clearly meaningful to contemporary readers of the paper, though rather opaque now. 'The tables were decorated with bowls of golden-coloured dahlias, and red roses.' It reads like the kind of colonial tropical setting that conjures up images of Raffles Hotel in Singapore and the long afternoon of the British Empire.

And working in the central business district of Sydney, where he fixed people's teeth, Alexander Brodie saw the towering heights to which the post-war economy and global financial order was driving Australia.

Alexander had become an avid bowler and was an active member of the Cheltenham Club in 1928. The decades before this had not been easy for the family. Unlike the senior Hileys, the young Brodies moved around a fair amount. Alexander lived in Mosman immediately after marrying Ellen Dill-Macky. Then in 1914 they had moved to Killara, where Gordon Marcus Brodie, Grampy, was born. In 1916 they were in Drummoyne, Gordon recalled. 'This house was on the waterfront', he said, 'and we had a small open boat with an inboard Chapman Pup engine.' By 1921 the family was in Cheltenham in a newly built house, with four boys. Rather unusually, each of the boys was sent to a different high school, and it was only from this time that they seem to have firmly settled into a particular part of Sydney's suburbia.

Sydney in the 1920s was a buzzing place in many ways, with a rich architectural heritage to show for it. In the city's centre, St James and Museum underground railway stations were opened in 1926 at different corners of Hyde Park, with those wonderful art deco–inspired designs. Alexander may well have left Museum and gazed up at the magnificent eight-storey T&G Building across the street each morning before he crossed over to work. Later on he will have done the same with its replacement, one of Sydney's earliest skyscrapers, where he apparently worked in a high-rise suite.

As with the other families, the period saw the passing of the last of the settler generation. Alexander's mother Cecelia died in 1927. On one of my visits to Sydney I made a point of travelling out to visit her grave at Woronora Cemetery in Sutherland. It took me about half an hour's train ride from Central Station, and I got out at Sutherland on a windy spring day. The cemetery is not far from the station, so within a few minutes I had found my way there on foot. A crow was hopping about looking for grubs, and the wind was howling in my ears and blasting my face. It took a bit of searching to find the Presbyterian section, but soon enough I had my bearings and found Cecilia. It was a very little plot, I thought. And although I knew the graves were the same size, I could not help but think she must have been a little person.

I read the headstone, with its metallic letters on a marble block: 'In Loving Memory Of Our Mother Cecilia Brodie, Died 18th Dec 1927, Aged 82 Years. Also In Memory of Our Father, Capt Neil Brodie, Lost At Sea, 1894.' I had the chilling thought that the sound of wind in my ears may also have been the last thing Neil ever heard. And then I pondered what a long time it was for Cecilia to have lived without her husband, and for her boys to have lived without their father. I stayed a few minutes, then walked back to the train and left Cecilia to her rest.

Even Cecilia's grave, however, reveals something about how rapidly Sydney was changing in those years. Her parents had been buried in Balmain, but that was no longer an option. The old suburban cemeteries were full, and many were being turned into parks.

Yet, being so busy, the city's population growth probably helped the family survive after Neil's disappearance. There are several properties around Balmain bearing the names of various ships he owned, or family names, which he or his father-in-law had built. They are mostly tenement cottages with verandahs sporting wonderful Victorian-era wrought iron trim, a typically late nineteenth century look, and they dot a landscape filled with similar buildings. Only names like Ainslie, Cecilia, or Lavinia really mark them as particularly different and tie them to my family story. Some of these passed to Cecelia and the rents provided her with income until her death.

The passing of these buildings from Cecelia's ownership, and the appearance of skyscrapers, paralleled other ways in which the built landscape of Australia was shifting. In Wyalong the old Excelsior Hall burnt down in January 1928. The locals regretted its loss, noting that it had 'historic significance from the fact that about 24 years ago the late Dr. Dill-Macky held a meeting there, where a serious disturbance was caused'. And in May the winner of a competition was announced for the design of a new building on 'the site of the Rev. Dill-Macky's old Scots Church on Church Hill, Sydney'. The winner happened to be from Wagga. Changes to the streetscape had been prompted by work on Sydney's Harbour Bridge, and the congregation took the opportunity to build a new combined church and office building, which still stands. Ironically, in some ways, it is a magnificent neo-gothic structure of the sort Dill-Macky would possibly have disapproved of.

Dill-Macky's memory lived on, however, not merely as a byword for sectarianism, but also in the Dill-Macky Memorial Home, an orphanage. It had struggled for financial support during the war, but had survived, and it continued to serve the community. By late 1928 the society that managed the orphanage could boast that the two homes it ran were 'in good condition, and that the financial position of the society generally was very satisfactory'. It was just as well, because the charitable organisations of Australia were soon to face a period of great crisis.

In Junee the built environment was overseen by a council still focused on urban improvement and closer municipal surveillance. A little after Bill's return from Europe, he and Horace took over their father's butchery. This may have fostered Bill's desire to run for office in 1928, even though he proved unsuccessful. They called the rebranded business 'Duck Brothers'. They did well, even though documentary records of their activities tend to point to run-ins with local council. In 1920, for instance, they were fined because 'their shop was not kept free from foul odour'. This was a fairly new shop in Regent Street, built in a growing residential district, which means a local might have complained. The butchery naturally had the capacity to produce great aromas, and smells are rarely obedient to neighbourly boundaries.

In 1925 the state of the slaughter yards was of concern to the council, not so much because of the smell, but simply the location. The councillors did not want a slaughterhouse in that part of town, which was right on the western edge. They might have felt it would discourage residential growth in that direction.

This infuriated Horace, who had recently made a number of improvements to the yards at the insistence of a health inspector from Sydney.

He claimed to have rebuilt part of the yard houses for hanging the meat, on the same place that had been used for fifteen years. Yet his licence was being threatened on the basis that he had supposedly not done so, and the council was leaning toward making him move. It was a typically asymmetrical power relationship. But he fought nonetheless. He wrote to the council and made it clear that 'all improvements were carried out'. He asked them 'whether we have to do all these improvements and then be kicked out, or whether we will be granted a conditional license for, say, six to twelve months until we have a chance to shift the yards'. It seemed to be the arbitrariness of it which particularly annoyed him. Fortunately, he won a temporary reprieve, it seems.

The next year Horace was again in dispute with the council. He apparently had an agreement to feed some slaughter stock on a park area and some of the cattle had strayed through an open gate. Horace once more wrote to the council, denying that the stock was his, which was possibly technically true. He also rejected the idea that he be held responsible for a gate left open, unless he had been the one to leave it so. He turned it round on the council and asked them to repair the gate, suggesting he could take responsibility for impounding the cattle if the council offered him further grazing rights on the park areas. It was a bit cheeky and seems not to have won over the councillors. They were more concerned with what they saw as urban improvement, which generally meant a cow-free town. Other concerns of theirs at the time included the provision of sewage to Junee and the installation of depth markers in the town's dam, in which the populace swam during the warmer months.

And then, like an annual ritual, Horace and the council had another spat in the spring of 1927. Horace still had some grazing rights on the oval park, where sports were played, and some people expressed concerns that sheep grazing there could infect the soil with the disease tetanus. But Horace pointed out that many sheep were regularly bitten by dogs on the field, and showed no signs of the disease, even though it would be easy for such open wounds to get dirty. He also seemed to wonder why the inspectors felt that sheep were the problem, when, if the disease was in the soil, surely the danger to humans came from playing the dangerous game of football on the oval? Although he had not definitively settled the question, once again his logic was pretty sharp. The councillors passed the buck to the health department.

Horace's rather irascible wit was matched by a physically demanding and dangerous job. One of the few other documented instances from this time that involve him was reported in a newspaper from March 1922. It simply said that 'Mr. Horace Duck, while engaged in yarding some cattle last Wednesday, had a narrow escape from serious accident. He was on horseback and a cow charged him, tearing the leg of his trousers with her horn and grazing the flesh of his leg'. He was working on the saddle, something his Kiss ancestors had done since at least the 1820s.

The business of rearing cattle for the domestic market in which Horace was involved was an ancestral tradition that he could have traced back to the earliest days of the colony of New South Wales. Servicing domestic needs had always been a significant part of colonial growth, with regional boom and bust cycles affecting the local and wider economies of the continent and the globe. Some parts of the colonial economies of the past were very international, with large exports of primary products like wheat, wool, leather, timber, mutton, and beef being subject to international prices and the fluctuations in world markets. This was as true of export cattle, as it was of gold or bêche-de-mer.

In mid 1928 Junee even established its own regular 'Junee Stock Market', although this sold animals, rather than shares. Yet telegraph and wireless technologies facilitated regular and long-distance transactions of practically anything, thus enabling the Wall Street stock market in the United States of America to see an inflation of value of a different sort of stock. When, in late 1929 there was a sudden correction in the price of some shares, a cascading global monetary crisis reached all the way around the world into many of the households of Australia.

1933

For young Greg Duck, growing up in the 1920s and 1930s meant a number of things. There was rabbit shooting and camping with mates. There were nights sleeping outside during the summer when it was too hot to sleep inside. There were picture shows, of which cowboy movies were particular favourites. There was also an extended family network. He knew his uncle Bill, who told him stories about the war. He may have heard of his aunt dying in 1933, whose death prompted some members of the family to talk about how one of their Kiss ancestors was probably the man from Snowy River. And his parents continued to play tennis. In 1933 they were each defeated in the doubles finals for men and women respectively in the railway tennis club.

But there were also studies at St Joseph's Convent School. Fortunately, Greg shared school duties with several cousins and a couple of mates. He was a good student, placing third in his class in the 1931 exams. It was said that he might have gained entrance to university, but for family responsibilities. But he was also game, and punched a bully who had picked on him on the walk home. This, by Greg's account, was the only time he was ever in a fight.

Greg told me many stories about these years, but one that stuck with me was the way that he claimed to have taken his shoes off on the walk to school. He did not want the poorer children to know the family was relatively comfortable. While the late October crash of the New York Stock Market in 1929 probably did not immediately affect the butchers of far-flung Junee, it is as convenient a date as any from which to date a period of struggle. Greg's shoes probably stayed on when he first went to school. It was the advent of the Great Depression when he was just shy of his tenth birthday which probably made him conscious of well-covered feet.

Unfortunately for Greg and his siblings, their father Horace drank too much and tended to gamble. I have a pair of First World War binoculars which Greg gave me that Horace apparently won playing cards. Horace certainly knew all the tricks and I absorbed many of them in my own childhood through the many family retellings. A favourite was a simple play on words. The day had to be just right, with heavy grey clouds and a downfall obviously imminent. It helped to initiate it at a drinking establishment.

'I'll bet you', Horace would tell the unsuspecting punter, 'that it won't rain for six weeks.'

When they took the bet, they would smugly wait for the rain. It would start falling and they would turn to Horace and ask to collect their bet.

'Not yet', he would tell them. 'I said it won't rain *for six weeks*', he would say, stressing the last three words, and beginning his own smug wait until the rain stopped.

Greg told me of a more dangerous encounter from about this time, or perhaps slightly later, which probably related in part to Horace's tricks. Apparently one night a mentally ill fellow came to the house with a gun, calling out and threatening Horace. The wild butcher, who was not so easily frightened, got dressed in his nightgown, grabbed his butcher's knife on the way out the door and confronted the would-be attacker.

'If you don't bugger off,' he yelled, or something rather similar, 'I'm going to cut you all up!'

And waving the knife he drove the stunned assailant back into the darkness. Not a shot was fired.

Although lacking further contextual details, this tale could illustrate the tensions of the period, pushing a person from stress to a disturbed mental state and acts of desperation. But, as David Potts argued in *The Myth of the Great Depression*, the economic crisis of the early 1930s did not produce unrelenting misery or starvation. While it certainly brought on hardship and budgetary stress, the presence of family networks of support, the newly implemented government dole, and public works schemes meant that there was less utter destitution than is often associated with the period.

It was undoubtedly a difficult time, particularly for those affected by the wider economic situation, but impact depended on the effect on savings and the source of income, as well as the price of consumables. Builders and contractors were among the first to feel the effects of a slowing economy, and butchers and other food retailers noticed the difference as people bought less meat or cheaper cuts. As unemployment rose to encompass somewhere between a quarter and a third of the male population, depending on how it is calculated, the working classes could particularly feel the squeeze and easily cascade into situations of destitution. Renters had trouble meeting their housing requirements, and some city areas in particular witnessed overcrowding, while other displaced persons would take to the roads with their swags. And while there were some spectacular cases of wealthy people losing their savings, it was perhaps more commonly the middle classes that felt the pinch of the depression, which threatened their standards of living. The numbers of the poor would swell, and economic distress was widely experienced, but the advent of the dole served at least to limit destitution so that the Great Depression was not really a great famine. Many people remembered hard but happy times, perhaps refracted through the lens of childhood, but nonetheless highlighting that happiness was not impossible.

But some simply bought their happiness in liquid form, and this in particular caused problems for families. In mid June 1931 two cars near Junee 'came into collision'—as a newspaperman politely put it. 'Both cars were knocked about, the side being torn off one, and a wheel knocked off the other.' There was 'other damage', which also included a head wound to a female passenger in the oncoming car. Horace Duck was fined £10 for drink driving.

As well as being a bit of a gambler and drinker, Horace did not have a good head for business, especially in the hard times of the Depression. He was a very likable fellow, especially among the children around town, for whom his quick wit and pleasant personality proved to be well remembered. Yet his affable nature got the best of him where it perhaps should not have done. It was later said of him that he would say, 'No money, no meat', but, with a hard-luck story from a desperate customer or two, it was Horace who could end a day in his butchery with no money, no meat. He would extend credit in acts of human kindness, but the business suffered, and with it, his family.

'They did well for a while,' Greg later said of his father's business, 'but the Depression came and like everyone else they went broke.' Horace 'kept the butchering business going, of course broke all the time. Everyone was broke. He knew they weren't going to pay him'.

And eventually Horace had to stop paying other people. One day, rummaging through Pa's old documents, I found three old cheques. They were all printed on well-worn and oft-folded speckled green paper and were from The Commercial Bank of Australia Ltd. The first was a payment of £2, dated 29 October 1935 and signed by H. Duck. Why it had been kept, I will never know for sure. But the reason the following two were kept was a bit clearer. They were also signed by Horace and were dated 5 March and 13 March respectively, both from 1936. The first was for £10. On the reverse side was some writing in another hand: 'Present Again'. This was then struck through with a red coloured pen, and in the same red was added: 'Refer to Drawer'. The second cheque, for £12, had a similar grouping of notes written on the back, this time in three differently coloured pens: 'Post Dated', struck through; 'Present Again', also struck through; and then 'Refer to Drawer'. Horace, as these tattered old relics of the 1930s revealed, was writing cheques that bounced.

And then, things got worse. Two documented events from December 1938 reveal the essentials. Horace was reported 'very ill in a city hospital'. Two days later some rates were gazetted as overdue on land that Horace jointly owned with other locals. Financial ruin and the loss of the main breadwinner both loomed after years of hardship within the whole community. Except, that is, that Greg left school and went into business, eventually taking the leading role in running the butchery.

'I left school early to go work for five bob a week', he said. Greg was one of a number of people interviewed by the shire council in the early 2000s, and his contributions to *Junee Speaking of the Past*, added to what he told me himself, enabled me to hear his idiom clearly: 'Nobody had any money in the Depression. You had to go through it to realise.' Many other contributors echoed his sentiments.

Greg always said it was because he had to support the family that he went into butchering. While he later had a natural professional interest in the trade—and had the uncanny and unsettling ability to judge a person's weight by look and a quick feel of the muscle and fat content of their forearm, as well as an eye for a good steak—there were two areas of the business that most interested him: people and bookkeeping. He knew that chatting to people, turning the business into a personal encounter, was a good strategy. When he started working, the town was always busy, because people from the surrounding district would travel in by horse and sulky to shop and do business. The art of a good chat he may well have learned from his seemingly affable father. But it was in the bookkeeping that he excelled, where his father apparently could not. Greg was still kind to his customers, but he did it in ways that protected his family. And he must have done a good enough job of it, because he can remember families that lost their properties to debt. His own grandfather, Billy Duck, was apparently only saved from penury by selling off much of his land.

With a natural head for numbers, Greg pulled the family business out of crisis. Even before Horace had written those dodgy cheques, Greg was undertaking financial precautions. He joined the Australian Mutual Provident Society in 1934. And he kept his original certificate, which I later rediscovered among his things. For twenty-four pence each week, he invested for his own future benefit and, to some extent, insured his family in the event of an early death. It was another documentary relic of a financially troubled age and told its own story of the differing mindsets of son compared with father.

Greg had many memories of the Great Depression, but some, like the shoe thing, particularly stand out. He recalled his mother Frances giving aid to the poor swagmen who came to their house seeking food. One of Greg's younger sisters, Joyce, remembered one time when their mother put a sick pauper in their shed and fed and nursed him until well. As such, while the Depression was a time of hardship, it was also a time of community cohesion, at least through their eyes. The name can be a little misleading.

The Depression was certainly a hard time, often a terribly harsh one, but it was not unremittingly miserable for all. People could still be happy.

The other main memories Greg shared often seemed to be food-related. He was friendly with the Chinese gardener George Ah Yeck, who delivered vegetables around town. 'Every Christmas we used to get a bit of ginger off him', Greg recalled, and I know he had a lifelong fondness for that particular spice. He also had a particular love of Chinese food, later fascinated by the way that stir-fried meat could be made so tender, so much so that he investigated the matter with the local Chinese chef.

But mostly their food was simple fair. Bread and dripping—animal grease spread on bread—seems a stereotype of the Great Depression. Yet all my relatives were adamant that it was a common, basic, and cheap meal, consumed often. And being butchers, the Ducks would have had ready access to the dripping, and the O'Rafferty's, being bakers, had the bread. And by the early 1930s their businesses were just across the road from each other.

The O'Raffertys had moved from Henty to Junee, enabling young Eileen to spend part of 1933 staying with a family friend at Lake Albert on Wagga's outskirts, some 40 kilometres from Junee. Highlighting Junee's regional prominence, the O'Raffertys advertised the bakery in the widely distributed Catholic *Freeman's Journal* from mid 1934, which regularly appeared over subsequent months and years. It said, 'E. O'Rafferty, Bakers. Crown Bakery, Junee. Bread, Pastry, Cakes. We Deliver. Junee—Broadway, Park End'.

This advertisement is interesting for a range of reasons. It showed yet another family association with that particular publication that Jimmy Kiss had read in the previous century. It helped confirm recollections of where the bakery was: basically diagonally opposite the very wide street known as Broadway from the sometime location of the Duck butchery. And its name, 'Crown Bakery', pointed to it still being quite a loyalist era at that time, despite the influx of French and American culture. But the thing that most piqued my interest was the first letter: 'E'. 'E. O'Rafferty'. Emma seemed to be the one running the business.

When diagonally opposite each other, the two shops certainly interacted. I have been told that the O'Raffertys sold 'very good pies', and they almost certainly contained meat from Duck's butchery, which might explain how two Duck boys came to know and later marry two O'Rafferty girls. One of the pairs was Greg and Eileen, Pa and Nanny. And so, it seems, I could ultimately be a product stemming from a union brought about by the crust and filling of a very tasty meat pie.

The documentary record from this period for the next generation of Brisbane Hileys down from the socialite seniors is quite slight. For them the Depression years also brought on hardship, although Ernest Hiley was fortunate to be regularly employed as a clerk. In the 1930s they were in the Brisbane suburb of Wooloowin. While the senior Hileys were certainly far from poor, it was really their long occupation of their property that had placed them in the leafy inner-city suburbs. But, as in Junee, the Depression did not wipe away normal suburban activities. In 1930, for instance, young Daphne Hiley was 'outstanding player for the winners' in a 36 to 4 win by Wooloowin over Chermside in basketball.

With her seemingly dilettante grandparents and white-collar parents, Daphne moved in a strange spectrum of circles. She remembered seeing old Fred Hiley, always well dressed, often with a carnation on his lapel, and generally carrying a 'swagger cane'. This image strikes me as being almost the embodiment of the comfortable 1920s. But first Elizabeth and then Fred died during the 1930s. Agnes, Daphne's mother, rarely spoke of her own family. The hard-drinking Anderson Dobson, Daphne's maternal grandfather, was never mentioned. Daphne could not recall having even met him, although I did find some records suggesting at least one family trip to Toowoomba when she was young. So this Hiley family kept in some touch with the wider relatives and had a particular attachment to the Hiley grandparents, but mostly it was a suburban, working existence. They had employment and food and were content with that. Many were far worse off.

The children were clearly very at ease with their situation, illustrated by Daphne herself, who wrote to Brisbane's *Sunday Mail* in February 1933. She was the winner of the paper's weekly literary competition for 26 February on the topic of 'Peaceful Development'. In the immediate decades after the First World War, it is remarkable that a child would write how Australia 'became great not by war, but by the hard work of her people'. It highlights that the immense significance sometimes attached to the First World War as so centrally nation-defining was a much later construction. Yet with the benefit of hindsight and a greater knowledge of Australia's early past, I have to disagree in part with the general premise of Daphne's letter, because she did not mention any conflict with Aborigines. But this is precisely what a child in 1933 was taught, and so I cannot hold that against her.

Daphne won a few of these competitions, so I could see her early thoughts on a range of issues. One was comparisons between the English and Australian landscapes. Her idea of the 'typical Australian landscape' was 'a rolling plain dotted with trees, and peaceful, grazing cattle. In the good season this land is covered with green grasses, wattle trees often forming a mass of gold on the wide expanse of green. The warm sun beats down on this scene, and here and there a solitary homestead stands with outlying sheds, in the shadow of the great gums'. There were, I think, strong echoes of Elizabeth Hiley's view of her Truman childhood in Daphne's perception of her own country. Yet Daphne's recollections also have the touch of the harder times which Australia then knew. Her typical plains 'sometimes become arid under the relentless rays of the sun, and the sky seems to be of molten lead. The once green grass is dry, and rustles as the hot wind blows through it. The creeks have all dried up and only an empty bed is left where once the water flowed'.

Another of Daphne's junior literary prize-winning letters was on 'The Dignity of Labour' and is another revelation of how Australians saw themselves and their nation in 1933. Labour was, Daphne argued, 'continually endeavouring to raise the standard of living and to increase the general happiness of the community'. She went on to point to infrastructure, industry, and workmanship, and stated that it was 'by labour that Australia became the prosperous nation she is today'. The letter was, I noticed, written in a poignant context. Ideological divisions about capital and labour were in some quarters extremely topical. Daphne's letter came after a period of major public works like the Sydney Harbour Bridge, which seemed to herald a new era of public infrastructure. Yet the Depression was still going on, the continued experience of which was in many ways facilitated by conservative monetary policies.

Daphne's letter, like the others, was in a section of the paper 'for the boys and girls'. This section seemed to be frequently devoted to teaching Australian children about the wonders of the British Empire. A picture of the King was prominent, because Empire Day was around the corner. A Buddhist temple was also pictured, and the children were informed that it was ensconced in 'a little pendant called Ceylon' which dangled geographically off the subcontinent of India. Sri Lanka had often been called the Jewel of India, but the phrasing suggested it was a bit of British jewellery.

Underscoring this attitude, the children were able to read that the British ruled 'about one-fourth of all the world's land'.

These projected images of Australia and its place in the world, as revealed by a child's letters, had a complement in a young man's photographs. Gordon Brodie, Alexander's second son, was a keen amateur photographer. The family still has one of his old photo albums from the 1930s.

The first pages were mostly filled with holiday pictures of fishing, swimming, and horseriding at places like Tuggerah, Kanoona, and Broulee. Gordon's distinct handwriting captioned many of the images in faded ink. There was a little hut called 'Allawah' which seemed to go with the Kanoona images, probably one of Alexander's investment properties. Apparently, Gordon told me, Alexander bought some properties for two of the boys that wanted to be farmers. 'Yootha' was certainly one of these, because it has left a bit of a documentary trail, and later photos in the album relate to it.

During the Depression years Alexander based his dentistry business part-time in his Cheltenham home. Apparently dental care was one of those things that people reduced during the hard times, with a knock-on effect for the dentists. Within a few years, coronary artery trouble encouraged him into his early retirement. He continued to play bowls regularly, including in the local doctors versus dentists games, played golf and learned how to paint. And, it seems, he enjoyed travelling with his family through a recognisably Australian landscape.

In Gordon's 1930s album there is a page labelled 'Taking the Rover to Lex 1933', which shows snapshots of an old soft-top car's progress across the land, charting an adventure once enjoyed. The picture of 'Crossing the Talbragar' shows the car entering a fast-flowing waterway; there appears to be repairs under the bonnet underway in another; and a third is simply labelled 'Arrived "Bunnydoon"'.

Gordon would often travel up into the country to spend time with his brothers on the land as they struggled to make a go of farming in those dreadful years. Pictures of horse-drawn carts carrying hay, tractors pulling ploughing equipment, rabbit fences, rabbit corpses, iron water tanks, wooden fences, and many other similar images are all so typical of country Australia in the 1930s it is almost hard to believe they were taken by a person I know well. Again they reveal some happy memories from the

Depression era. If the city was bustling with progress, the country was filled with hard work and smiles. Life was hard, but there was clearly something good about it.

And there must have been good humour, because there are a few very strange-looking photos labelled 'Water Divining', including some of 'Mum', Ellen Brodie with arms outstretched and palms upturned, in a floral dress with a giant hat, looking rather un-Scots Presbyterian. It is hard not to wonder what her father Reverend Dill-Macky would have thought. At Yootha they were in the hilly and scrubby country of the Warrumbungles, and most of the photos look extremely Australian.

The land captured in these images is one of eucalyptus trees, ragged ridges, plains, and creeks. The Australia of my grandparents' childhood was tough, but it is also recognisable to me. Whether in the bush, or in the built environment, the domestic routines, and the social activities, it is all very familiar, in every sense of that word. Members of my family, known to me, lived in this world. Stories they have told, objects they owned, pictures they had taken, and words they had written all linked their world to mine.

And other factors increased this sense of connectedness. Partly this was technological and social change, which made their world like mine. With movies, universal suffrage, and radio, this was not the pioneer world anymore. Yet elements of the past persisted in ways that have transcended epochal divisions, such as through the playing of sport, parts of the domestic diet, and even some aspects of the wider economic model of the country, town, nation, and globe.

Of their precise historical moment, Gordon's photos did not record the stresses of financial ruin, the hunger people often felt, or the families which were ripped apart. My respective families all got through the hard times, were forever marked by the experience and were grateful they had gone. But even as things were again improving, there were some hints of another lurking danger. I tried to ask Gordon about some of his oldest photos, but he could not really remember many details. He was ninety-nine years old, and they were taken a long time ago. I pointed to a photo and asked him why it was there.

'That's of the university regiment', he said.

It was labelled 'Instructing in the lewis gun', and depicted uniformed men, some just boys really, and a machine gun.

Gordon went to Sydney University and studied medicine, and while there he joined the university regiment. There are other photos in the album from his university regiment days, including one of boys in uniform standing at attention with rifles against their shoulders. It is labelled a touch jokingly as 'The Guard'. But the truth was those guards would soon be needed. An Australia recognisably my own was about to come under direct attack.

CHAPTER SEVENTEEN

FORTRESS AUSTRALIA 1940

ON 12 AUGUST 1940, having travelled to Sydney for the purpose, it seems, John O'Rafferty enlisted in the Australian army for the second time in his life, to serve in a second global war. In Europe, France had been invaded, and Britain was beginning to experience the aerial assault known as the Battle of Britain. Yet in 1940, while London burned, the minutiae of municipal government in Australia rolled on. In July 1940, for instance, Greg Duck renewed the licence for the slaughter yards on the edge of Junee. It was an everyday act, a proof that although Australia was a combatant nation its routines could and would continue.

When another war in Europe commenced in 1939 it had caught at least one resident of Junee by surprise. Newspapers reported that there was 'a lady in Junee … who possesses an almost uncanny knack of foretelling the future'. She had supposedly picked when people were going to die, identified a Pope in advance and knew when a drought would end and the next heatwave start. She reportedly firmly said, 'I'll eat my hat if there is war'. I first spotted this report of her prediction in the *Grenfell Record and Lachlan District Advertiser*, dated 31 August 1939. The next day Germany invaded Poland. Her litany of success had come to an embarrassing end.

The local response to the new and distant conflict is nicely captured, I think, by editorial distress. Apparently, an editor noted, a public meeting 'to form a dog-racing venture' in Junee in November attracted 100 people, while 'only 13 persons were present' at a meeting to form a 'Junee Mayor's Patriotic and War fund'. The people were arithmetically 7.69 times more interested in real dogs than they were in the proverbial dogs of war. People, the editor may not have fully appreciated, were war-weary. And while the federal government had quickly followed Britain into war, during the first months of conflict, sometimes known as the 'phoney war', the average Australian citizen's life went on much as it had been.

This is well exemplified by the Ducks in Junee. Horace Duck had only returned to Junee in March 1939 after a few months in hospital in Sydney with a chronic illness. This was certainly the final straw in any meaningful role in his management of the butchery. He continued to work, but his son Greg was by now firmly in charge. I have a wonderful photo of Greg about this time, grinning by one of the butchery doors, and another of him leaning casually within a group, looking rather like a movie star. He was fit, strong, and handsome. Like his father in a previous conflict, he did not join the military. In fact Greg was considered essential services and thus ineligible for the armed forces. The people of Australia had to eat. Despite killing things for a living, he was a fairly gentle-minded soul, so I doubt he would have longed desperately to go to war anyway. And by then, as his sister later remembered, the family was depending on him.

At fifty-two years of age, John O'Rafferty was hardly ready for frontline service. Emma's capable running of the bakery may have facilitated his enlistment, helped by his prior service. Family tradition has it that he worked as a driver as he had during 1919—doing what precisely, nobody knew. John's 'Service and Casualty Form' from his Second World War engagement is in the same folder at the National Archives of Australia as his First World

War service record. It is a simple little card, with neat typed details. His eyes were still blue, but his hair was now turned from 'brown' to 'grey'. On a brighter side, the military measured him at 5 feet 8 inches, a full inch and a half taller than in 1916.

Once again, John was 'Taken on strength', but this time it was at the 'Show Ground Int. Camp. Hay' with the 16th Garrison Battalion. The abbreviation revealed John's role in part of Australia's military tradition often neglected in favour of frontline exploits. Expanded, it becomes 'Internment Camp'.

Australia had interned 'enemy aliens' in the First World War, effectively incarcerating them, and proceeded to do similarly in the Second World War. People born overseas were suspected of being threats to national security and many were arrested and interned for the duration of the war, often on quite specious grounds. The Hay camp was built in July 1940 and it was partly anticipated that it would receive prisoners of war, specifically Italian prisoners in the wake of Italy joining the conflict on Germany's side in June 1940. But it was soon filling with Italian internees, many of them civilians in Australia who happened to be of Italian origin. Many Italians had come to Australia over the preceding decades, despite the widespread political narrative of a White Australia of British stock.

The site was chosen because of its isolation. Hay sits in a wide, flat land, a considerable distance from any nearby population centres, and in summer it is hot, dry, and dusty. The Cobb and Co. coachman Bob Dean used to work part of this terrain when the railways had pushed him west, and one of the coaches he drove still takes pride of place in central Hay. The town is roughly twice as far from the nearest coast as Italy is wide, but by then the railway had been connected and Bob Dean was gone. The trains which carried the prisoners branched off from the Sydney to Melbourne line at Junee and chugged past Duck's butchery and along the railway line that ran in front of the little Duck house on Junction Street.

When John O'Rafferty arrived in August, Hay was about to receive its first major cohort of internees, giving the camp a certain historical notoriety. A boatload of Germans were shipped from England on the *Dunera* and eventually deposited in the camp. They had experienced a dreadfully bad trip in horrendous conditions and would not have been in great shape. And what was worse than their horrendous boat ride, followed by their immediate internment in an isolated and difficult landscape, was the fact that many were actually refugees from Germany. Many of them were Jewish.

It is my own sad link with the Holocaust: a railway and a camp in the Australian outback.

Fortunately the '*Dunera* boys', as this group were called, did not reside for long in the camp before being released, and they received significantly better treatment in Australia than they had in and en route from England. Then, as 1940 went on, the various camps that made up the Hay interment complex continued to fill with Italian civil internees. They were joined by Japanese internees from northern Australia in late 1941, and later on prisoners of war from both Italy and Japan were also held in Hay. The Hay Historical Society's *Haywire: The War-time Camps at Hay* provides a detailed survey of the story of the camps, and particularly the conditions the internees experienced, as well as documenting the experience through some fascinating artworks that internees produced.

John's own war service record does not give much in the way of details. He was promoted to 'L/Corporal' in October 1940 and was transferred between the various compounds within the Hay Camp. But a sense of the camp's essential functions is captured by a file on the camp in the National Archives of Australia. It is filled with letter copies, reports, and other bits of official paper. In one report, dated 1941, a particular section concerned 'P.O.W. Labor. Present Use And Future Plans'. It reveals that the internees were basically gardening, with '22 acres of irrigated land' being worked. They were clearly being put to work 'digging channels, making roads and culverts and tree planting'. And there was a list of ideas for future work: 'Road making, Carpentry & Building, Bread-making, Market gardening, Fodder growing, Poultry farming, Tailoring and bootmaking, Mail-bag making, Pig-farming, Canal making for irrigation, Dairy farming, Brick making, Forestry, Low-level weir across Murrumbidgee river below Hay.' And much of this was carried out, even if some of it was perhaps a bit optimistic.

Housed behind barbed wire fences, overlooked by watchtowers, and apparently having a problem with the removal of 'night soil' because of a lack of sewage, and 'vermin' in some of the sleeping areas, the internees could not have found the experience a welcome one, nor could their guards. But many made the best of it. Italians socialised, gardened, attended English schools, played music and generally tried to distract themselves from the situation they were in. John, meanwhile, presumably drove between the camps and about the country.

In Brisbane, Daphne Hiley had been working as a clerk. She also performed amateur theatre. In the Brisbane newspapers there are several references to her acting from 1938 through to 1940. She was a member of the Twelfth Night Theatre group, and details of its performances provide a good insight into the local entertainment scene. In September 1939, when the war in Europe was only a few days old, Daphne performed in the play *Grumpy*, which the *Courier Mail* described as being about 'an aged criminal lawyer who turns private detective when a diamond robber enters his home'. It was already an oldish play by then, written in 1913 for Broadway, and had even been made into a silent film in 1923. Apparently, the *Courier Mail* asserted, 'Daphne Hiley created a charming personality for the part of Virginia Bullivant, the heroine'.

In 1940 Daphne continued with the group. 'Full marks to Daphne Hiley for the sweet frock she wore', the *Sunday Mail* boasted of her March performance of *Dear Octopus*. In May she was in a more militaristically themed play, *Soldadera*, which was a 'drama of a Mexican revolution'. I cannot quite picture Grandma participating in a Mexican revolution, but apparently she did, even if only playing at it. And then in June 1940 the proceeds of yet another performance were intended to 'be used to purchase a war savings certificate'. The thespians were now aiding the war effort.

The immediacy of the war, and its life-changing capacity, was often brought home to me by my grandparents. When undertaking a school project researching the Second World War in the 1990s I decided to interview my Brodie grandparents. When I rang up, Daphne answered the phone. I had a cassette recorder wired in so that I could record the conversations. She was, however, relatively reticent. She certainly never mentioned the acting.

'Well, I was first of all in the VAD, a Voluntary Aid Detachment,' she said, 'then in the army as VA.'

I had seen pictures of her in nursing and army uniforms at her house and knew that she had served. Daphne pointed out to me that the women joined up 'to relieve the men of camp duties and so on, the administrative work and so on, and the women did the work at the base hospitals and so on'. Their role, as she saw it, was to free up the fighting men for overseas service. This mobilisation of the feminine resources of the nation, while still expressed in conservative terms, was a major development between the first and second world wars in Australia. It reflected that broadening of women's economic impact and a better acceptance of them as persons capable of contributing to society in ways that extended beyond spouses and mothers.

It might not have marked the end of that process, but it was a significant step forward.

'I served up and down the east coast of Australia with various army units,' she continued, 'and I did clerical work, VA—nursing work first of all, then clerical work—and was eventually an officer in charge of the girls at the hospital.'

When I asked her again more recently, she simply wished to suggest that she had made good friends during the war and regretted not having kept in touch with them afterwards. But back in the 1990s Gordon had come on the line soon afterwards and was much more forthcoming.

'I was a medical officer and I was attached mostly to field ambulances,' he said, 'which is a mobile unit supporting the fighting units and everybody else. I was in various units.'

Fortunately for me, Gordon Brodie's war is relatively well documented. Apart from his service records, he also wrote his own account of the war for the family, spoke of it at length to me in that 1990s interview, and kept a photo album. I also recently interviewed him again, hoping to follow up some of the details. I was visiting and staying with them in Picton for a few days. He and I were sitting in what used to be the waiting room of his surgery. He practised as a general practitioner for many years, with a section of the family home given over to the sick of Picton. It gets warmer there and, at ninety-nine years old, he liked the warmest spot to sit.

Immediately after his graduation, he was working long days at the Royal North Shore Hospital in Sydney. With a shortage of doctors because of the war, Gordon and other new graduates had to work exceedingly long hours, gaining little rest and sleeping mainly at the hospital. He could, he later claimed, see 'up to 120 patients per day'.

'I went down to join up and they told me to go back to hospital. They didn't need me so urgently at that stage and they put me in uniform and gave me an N number,' he said, 'and I did about another three months at hospital and they called me up then and I got my NX number.'

His official war service record places his enlistment as 12 May 1941. There is a pair of photographs of him, face-on and in profile, with his NX service number printed on them. He was attached to the 18th Field Ambulance, and before the year was out he had been appointed a captain. Otherwise, military officialdom simply recorded his various movements in and out of units. It is a familiar litany of complicated abbreviations and military jargon.

Gordon's own words proved more immediately helpful. After enlisting he 'camped in the chook pavilion of the showgrounds' in Sydney. He was posted soon thereafter and was on the move. They travelled, as he said, 'via train to Melbourne, then Adelaide, and up to Alice Springs, then we got on trucks and trains and all sorts of things and very slowly made our way up to Darwin'.

Meanwhile, on 1 August 1941, Daphne Hiley had enlisted with the Voluntary Aid Detachment. I had to have her service record ordered and digitised by the National Archives of Australia, because only the serving men's records seem to be commonly open for access and already available. It is, I supposed, a reflection of the greater historical interest in the fighting than the support structures and the home front. On her form, Daphne gave her father as her next of kin, also giving her address as the same as his. She was still living at home, but working as a clerk, at the time of enlistment. Like Gordon, her photo was taken, and attached to the records.

Also like Gordon, Daphne's record was filled with scrawled dates and acronyms. She was the first female in my family to have the now-familiar words 'Taken on Strength' written on a service record. And soon she was 'attached for duty' with the Australian Army Nursing Service. But her skills at bookkeeping must have been spotted, because by the middle of 1942 Daphne had been 'Classified as Clerk T.G.II (Senior)' and was on a different military career trajectory.

As Gordon travelled the long route to Darwin in late December 1941, the soldiers were no doubt aware of the great events playing out in the new Pacific War. Japan attacked British Malaya on 8 December 1941. This was a few hours before Pearl Harbor was bombed in Hawaii on 7 December 1941, but due to the location of the global date line the American date lives in infamy. In actuality, though, the bombing of Pearl Harbor was the second of these two Japanese attacks to take place.

Arriving in Darwin, Gordon 'joined the 2/12 Fd. Amb., situated a few miles down the road from Darwin town'. He did not stay there terribly long, however, before being moved. He once told me of his irritation that his service record failed to capture the many little moves and temporary attachments to other units he experienced. The broad sweep of his formal record seems to bear this out, showing lengthy gaps between moves and other obvious lacunae. Yet, often enough, its omissions sometimes confirm bits that he filled in, and his next move was one of these.

'After a few weeks', he said, 'I was seconded to the 14th Anti Aircraft Battery and was quartered at their section of four 3.7 inch guns on Darwin Oval, which was right on the Harbour edge.' It was, he said, 'a truly magnificent spot'.

1942

As I sat with Gordon in Picton, I flicked through his war photos with him. Unlike the previous war, or even the broad inter-war period, the story of my family's activities during the Second World War firmly leaves the realm of purely documentary history and becomes vividly lived. All my grandparents were adults in the war and their memories, the tangible relics they have of the conflict, and their documented activities all overlap. It is a firm and datable period, 'the war', rather than their vaguer memories of childhood and adolescence. The war sharpened their senses, providing them with clearer impressions of the historian's perennial questions of when, where, who, what, why, how, and with what effect.

Gordon's war album is unusual, mostly because he has one. Only three cameras were allowed per battalion, he told me. Because he was a keen photographer and was friendly with one of his commanding officers he managed to get one of the three. The CO and the intelligence officer each got the others. As he moved postings Gordon took the camera with him. Because of this, there is a good collection of pictures by and of him at this time. He was relatively short, and slightly built, and he sported a thin little moustache.

In the breakfast room of his house is a portrait, drawn by the war artist Roy Hodgkinson, that was apparently done over a few minutes in their barracks one day. It is an amazing likeness of Gordon wearing his round tin helmet, staring into the distance with bright blue eyes. Gordon's resemblance to this portrait was still strong, as were his memories. I interviewed him twice, more than fifteen years apart, and the details he remembered were truly remarkable for their exactitude and similarity, especially those about

19 February 1942. This was only a few days after the fall of Singapore to the Japanese army. Australians felt threatened and relatively defenceless.

He got up and got to work that morning, not knowing what his day would bring.

At 9:30 in the morning on an unusually clear day, Gordon recalled that he 'was doing a sick parade sitting in a little hut made of bamboo and stuff'. The men came in and out for their inspection. Such were the daily duties of a medical officer. Then, about half an hour later 'the alarm went off'.

It was not exactly high-tech. He said that it 'usually consisted of somebody belting a hanging bit of metal with another thing'. And it was being sounded 'fairly often at that stage', and always turned out to be a false alarm, so their attitude was cautious, but drifting towards casual.

But 'this was really belting hard this time,' he noticed, 'so I decided to go and have a look. I put on my tin hat and gas breaker, gas mask, and then I told the blokes that were sick' to get into cover. 'It looked to be reasonably safe' for the patients, so he went to investigate. The hut was on the edge of the oval. Wanting a better view, he 'wandered slowly, expecting nothing' out into open space.

He spotted his friend Mick, who was a 'section commander of 3.7 inch anti-aircraft guns'. Mick was 'standing and looking up at the sky', so Gordon walked over to him.

'Well, what is it this morning, Mick?' Gordon asked.

'I dunno, but look', Mick replied, and pointed to a formation of nine planes in a V heading towards them from the south. And as they looked, eyes adjusting to the brightness, they noticed further V formations, one after the other, crowding the sky.

'Now whose are they?' Gordon wondered out loud. 'Yanks I suppose?'

'Yeah,' Mick said, 'I suppose they are. The Yanks don't notify us often. They should, but they don't. And it's coming from the south, so it's most likely Yanks.'

As the men talked, the planes continued to come. They were soon almost overhead. Gordon and Mick, craning their necks upwards, caught sight of 'little white things, shiny things reflecting the sun' which were falling underneath the planes. As their eyes caught the sunlight reflecting off the metal, their brains made the connection. They were bombs.

The carrier fleet that had attacked Pearl Harbor had launched 188 fighters and bombers, and Darwin was their target. The Japanese formation had now commenced its bombing run. Australia was under attack.

Gordon and Mick dived for cover. Scrambling to a sandbagged wall a few feet from a nearby hut, they huddled down. Explosions ripped apart the oval all around them.

With calculated efficiency, the large V formations ensured that a wide area was exposed to the bombing. Anti-aircraft guns roared into action, but proved ineffective. The Australians had not trained sufficiently with live rounds to realise that the timing mechanisms were improperly calibrated for the tropical environment.

In the harbour the ships that could move—and had realised what was happening—tried to. Anti-aircraft weaponry and machine guns blazed at the skies. Of the Allied aircraft, only one American Kittyhawk fighter plane survived the initial attack. The rest were shot down in seconds by Japanese Zeros. The Australian Wirraways were inert and useless on the ground. The Japanese had the advantages of surprise and experience. Darwin did not stand a chance.

Huddling behind a sandbag wall, Gordon and Mick kept still as the Japanese dominated the Australian skies.

'They flew over the top of us with fighter planes firing the occasional burst of machine gun fire,' he recalled', 'so we stayed there for a while and none of us got hit.' Others were not so lucky. Hundreds were killed, including many civilians. Lots of people were wounded. Buildings were damaged. Ships were sinking. Oil had leaked into the harbour, parts of which were now on fire.

Lasting about three-quarters of an hour, the first attack on the Commonwealth of Australia was a military triumph for the Empire of Japan.

When the planes were finally gone, Gordon attended to the wounded. He was 'called out to some place near the airport where some bloke was injured'. It was one of the anti-aircraft gunners stationed over there. Gordon had a utility vehicle and a driver, so they set off, getting a view of the damage on the way. 'That drive itself', he later said, 'was quite an adventure.' They could see smoke from the ships and fires in the harbour billowing thickly into the sky. So too, probably, could the next wave of Japanese bombers.

Arriving at the airport, Gordon discovered that the wounded man had already been moved, probably by Royal Australian Air Force medical staff. There was considerable damage to the base, he noticed. Driving past the aerodrome back towards the oval he could see that 'the buildings were all alight'. The field was scarred from 'daisy cutters', bombs designed to damage large areas and concentrations of people. Gordon could hear a sound like a series of firecrackers. Much of the small ammunition in the burning area was exploding.

As he got back to the oval Gordon noticed that the yellow flag, the warning sign that planes were overhead, was flying again. Stopping at the gate, he turned and looked at the harbour. He saw that 'ships were alight, oil was all over the place, and the American destroyer the *Peary* was sinking'. The hospital ship *Manunda* appeared to be hit. People and ships were scrambling to effect what rescues they could. It was the worst possible moment for another raid.

While the initial attack had targeted practically everything, if particularly the harbour, the second raid proved to be a deliberate assault on the airport. The damage was horrific. And coming so soon after the first, it triggered a mass evacuation of Darwin. In one day, 242 enemy aircraft had utterly dominated the sky over an Australian city. Large parts of the town had been reduced to rubble—and its people to panic.

Sitting and listening to Gordon tell me this story I noticed how he sometimes slipped into the present tense. 'When they got organised they took off for the south', he said at one point, but added, 'my job was here.' But 'here' was a warm room on a nice day in Picton. He seemed to re-live that day more than any other of his life, almost inhabiting it perpetually sometimes, such was its effect on those who experienced it. And like many others, he wanted to know why and how. Proof of this was on a shelf of books behind me, several of which explicitly dealt with the attack on Darwin. He told me that he thought Peter Grose's book *An Awkward Truth* was a good account of the raid and the ridiculous aftermath. In fact I had already read it and quite agreed. But I was interested in hearing more of his personal experience of the attack and what followed.

He spoke of being 'exhausted' that night, and going to sleep on the little metal-framed army bed. But he was woken about 10 pm.

'Come on sir,' somebody said, waking him, 'you're wanted up there, there's been an accident'.

The heads of the anti-aircraft gun emplacements had had a meeting about why they failed to shoot down the enemy. Apparently one of them was returning to their unit in a utility vehicle afterwards when they had a front-on collision with an American one. Everyone was driving without lights because of the blackout, as a precaution against a night raid. But this was not the cause of the collision, Gordon told me. Rather, he thought it was 'because the Americans were driving on the wrong side of the road.'

‘So I picked up one cove of ours pretty badly hurt’, he told me, and ‘took him along to the hospital. It was a shemozzle the hospital. They were evacuating.’

And over the next few days he witnessed the evacuation. It was, he said, ‘utter shemozzle. Hundreds of trucks, people were going south on sanitary vans. Some walking. Cars. The town itself was a shemozzle. Men, women, kids. We watched them go by’. A local dog, one of many left by fleeing people, adopted Gordon, and so he kept it and named it Flopsy.

There is a photo of Flopsy in his photo album, taken by someone else. It shows Gordon, pipe in mouth, looking down at Flopsy, who looks like a blue healer. The dog in turn is gazing up at Gordon. But there are also photos of damage to the town. Most of these were taken by Gordon during subsequent days, weeks, and months. He ‘remained with the A.A. Bty’, as he recorded in his brief account of his war, ‘for some months during which there were many raids’. His photo album contains images he took of the damage of the first and later raids and some of the action of subsequent ones.

There are photos of bombed-out buildings, ‘A.A. Guns in Action’ on the oval, trenches, spotters, machine gunners, and one carefully posed image of the sky, which he always becomes irritated by, because it was supposed to capture the perfect V of incoming Japanese planes. The sky must have been too bright and overexposed it. Several of them have been published, although the original provenance has become confused with time. One that is often used as an image of a machine gunner in action is actually of the painter Roy Hodgkinson painting the gunner. Only once Gordon pointed this out to me did I see what the second figure in the picture was obviously doing, and it was not loading ammunition. There are also more everyday activities, bush pictures capturing the landscape and local conditions, Aborigines from the Daly River, and many soldiers.

Most of these uniformed men, he told me, died when the hospital ship *Centaur* was torpedoed by a Japanese submarine off the Australian coast in May 1943. It was carrying his original unit, the 2/12 Field Ambulance. Gordon had been detached from them when they were removed south from Darwin because he had not been there all that long and was instead attached to the 2/4 Infantry Battalion. It is one of those little blips in Gordon’s service record, hastily scrawled in pencil, for which his own memories fortunately provided a bit of context. And it is a move that undoubtedly saved his life, even if he did not know it at the time.

When Japan entered the war so dramatically in December 1941, one of the Australian government's first responses was to send Japanese people resident in Broome and surrounding areas to the Hay internment camp. Many of these people had lived and worked in Australia's northern waters as pearl divers, but, as with Italians and Germans, they were labelled as enemy aliens. Apparently, it was not clear to the authorities at the time that the successful near-destruction of Darwin was achieved without any obvious domestic aid and the effort taken in transporting Japanese people south may have been better spent.

As noted, John O'Rafferty's particular activities at Hay mostly concerned driving, probably things like taking some prisoners out from the camps to work. Italians were utilised for chopping firewood, for example. But there is a little note that says he was admitted to the camp hospital in May 1942 with a 'Scalded hand'. I can only guess at the cause. Perhaps it was a cooking accident, or maybe a radiator malfunction and an attempted fix that went wrong. Either way, he hurt his hand and ended up in the camp hospital, which at the time was the original colonial-era town gaol. It must have been a nasty burn, because he was in hospital for two weeks.

Some of John's sons signed up to serve in different capacities. George joined the navy and Ted joined the army. So during the course of the war the O'Rafferty presence in Junee was a bit diminished. And during the month that John was nursing a scalded hand, another government response to the war affected his and my civilian relatives in Junee with the commencement of rationing.

In another high school history project, I asked Greg Duck about the home front. To my surprise, he took me out the back and ferreted around a bit, until he pulled out some sheets of reddish coloured paper. They were ration coupons. Each sheet was perforated, like postage stamps, and had identical text printed in every little box. He had a surprising amount of them. The main things subject to rationing were food and clothing and, because he was a butcher, Greg got to see a lot of ration coupons during the war. People would be allocated a certain quantity of the rationed item and the coupons helped to regulate it. But, as the large sheets that Greg retained suggested, not all worked quite as the government had hoped.

The needs of the war, as well as rationing, certainly created some shortages. Perhaps in a small way because of the need to print large numbers of ration coupons, paper was something that the butchers were often short of. 'During the war', Greg later said, 'it was pretty hard to get any sort of paper and a lot of people used to bring their own saucepans or basins to carry the meat home.'

But rather than diminish his business, the war kept Greg busier than usual. To cope with the increased demand on the railway network, the railway line was being duplicated north of Junee. With two lines, trains could consistently run up and down towards Sydney without the need to wait at sidings for trains coming from the opposite direction to pass. It was a major infrastructure programme and employed large numbers of men living in a temporary camp built in the Junee triangle. This was a section of land at the inner angle of the main north–south railway line and the branch line to the western Riverina. Some of the men had families living with them in tents and huts, and I have been told that some Italians also worked on the line, although no doubt under a watchful eye. They used to attend Sunday Mass in a group at the Catholic Church. So, with a large number of hungry labouring men near to, and being serviced by, Ducks' butchery, Greg really was an essential war service.

But he had his mind on other things. He had his eye on John O'Rafferty's daughter Eileen.

Down the road from the butchery and across the track from the Junee Railway Camp was the Red Cow Hotel. It is a single-storey hotel on a corner, with a verandah that sweeps around both sides. Being on Junction Street, it is only several doors along from the old Duck residence, and Greg likely walked by it on his way to and from home and no doubt stopped in often enough, even if only for meat deliveries. Working there as a cook was Eileen O'Rafferty. I can vouch that she was an excellent cook and Mum in fact still has her recipe book. The fantastic Christmas pudding we enjoy each year is Eileen's recipe. But because she was ever afterwards a very private woman and she died when I was young, I do not really know a great deal about her early life. Apparently one of her recollections of the war period was of Italian men who were put to work on various nearby farms, presumably as supplementary labour.

Eileen came from a large family and had left home by the time she was working at the Red Cow Hotel. She was living by herself as a boarder at the Loftus Hotel, where she also worked as a waitress. The Loftus is a magnificent building that overlooks the railway station and is another of Junee's several establishments from the days when it was a busy railway centre, with people constantly coming and going. Two storeys high, with big wide verandahs trimmed with wrought iron, the Loftus looks like a typically wonderful Australian hotel.

As with old buildings, it can sometimes be hard to picture people in their youth. A photo can perhaps give some hint of a personality, but the complex reality of a person cannot be reduced to a smile or a single facial expression locked by the flash of a bulb and the click of a shutter. But sometimes the nuanced complexity of people in their youth can come out through their stories. And one day Greg surprised some of the family by talking about a time when he and Eileen were young lovers.

Greg spoke of how he could remember the wonderful feeling he had walking home in the early hours one morning. The sun had not yet come up and the air was cold. He had to get home to get ready for work. He had just spent the night at the Loftus.

In a world where they had brothers and sisters at war, work had its stresses, and there was the nuisance of rationing, Greg and Eileen had a wonderfully illicit relationship. It was a little secret they kept to themselves for decades afterwards. The rich memory kept for many years and only ever told in a few quick lines.

That sense of perfect contentedness in the company of another person, of brief moments spent together in busy lives, was given formal recognition on 7 September 1942. Greg and Eileen boarded the southbound train in Junee. The train chugged down through Harefield, past Bomen and across the Murrumbidgee River. The couple got off at Wagga, where they went to St Michael's Cathedral and were married before a small handful of witnesses. Eileen did not even buy a wedding dress. She did not want her parents to waste their money on one, or on a big reception. They went to one of the nearby cafes for a celebratory meal of toasted cheese sandwiches instead and caught the afternoon train back to Junee. Greg even went back to work that afternoon. Wartime was no time for a honeymoon.

By November 1942 Gordon's war was a bit of a routine. During this period he suffered a bout of dengue fever, but otherwise managed to escape serious harm. The Japanese raided Darwin often enough and sometimes he was called out to tend the wounded. At night he would frequently hear the humming sounds of planes flying nearby and learned to distinguish between the various types. Some nights it was American patrols; other nights he could hear Japanese planes doing reconnaissance.

Then one day, he was ordered to report to the wharves.

The 2/4 Infantry Battalion, it turned out, was heading to Timor. As an RMO, a regimental medical officer, Gordon was going as well. Their specific target was Beltano Beach, and their objective was to rescue wounded Australian commandos and sick and injured Portuguese civilians. They were also under orders to blow up HMAS *Voyager*, a destroyer which had been the Timor commandos' usual supply ship, but which had run aground. It was hoped to get the whole thing done without the Japanese even knowing. Speed and stealth were crucial, but none of the really fast ships were available.

So Gordon boarded the corvette *Castlemaine*. Its role was primarily concerned with the evacuees. It was 'armed, but not very heavily', Gordon said. Also heading to Beltano was the *Armidale*, with a force of Javanese commandos on board. Darwin was being used as a staging ground for Australian operations, just as the Japanese had feared it would be. The ships were to leave Darwin Harbour and then rendezvous in the darkness at Beltano. They were supposed to guide themselves to the right location by fires lit by the Australian commandos already on the beach.

As the *Castlemaine* got underway and passed the boom gates of Darwin Harbour, the dreaded yellow flags were flying. Enemy aircraft had been spotted in the area, almost certainly reconnaissance aircraft. What the Australians did not know was that the Japanese now had land-based aircraft, capable of launching from Dili airport. Aerial discovery had become much more likely, and swift Japanese attacks on identified targets were therefore easier.

Early in the voyage, only a few hours out of Darwin, a Japanese plane spotted the *Castlemaine*. Soon thereafter the ship was attacked. The *Castlemaine* commenced defensive manoeuvring, twisting and turning in the sea to make it harder for the Japanese pilots to line up their target. The ship's gun crews scrambled to their stations.

The *Castlemaine* carried a 4-inch gun up front and had several machine gun posts. Gordon was technically a non-combatant, but somebody threw him a 303 rifle, and so, with the chief engineer of the ship, he ran to the stern. There they took cover among the structures at the ship's rear as best they could.

Bombs fell from the attacking Japanese aircraft, but landed in the water. The ship's guns flared in response as the planes continued overhead.

Gordon saw another plane approaching. 'I thought he was signalling to us', he recalled. 'There were flashing lights and things, but then I realised they were gunshots and he was firing madly at us, you see. So everybody on the ship fired back at him, including me. We didn't hit him—at least he didn't fall.' Gordon's 303 rifle was ineffective against the Japanese Zero strafing the ship. 'I didn't bring it down', he said.

Radio silence was now redundant, so the ship contacted Darwin for help and further instructions. They were ordered to continue onwards, and a Beaufighter aircraft was sent from Darwin to shadow the ship.

Delayed by the attack, the *Castlemaine* arrived late at the Timor coastline. They could not see any guiding fires. The commandos, fearing discovery by the Japanese if they stayed too long, had already extinguished them and returned to the relative safety of the less exposed jungle. Gordon was on the bridge, and the captain asked him, 'Can you see the destroyer?' But they could not, it seems. At a loss as to what to do, the captain turned the ship back towards Darwin and asked for further instructions.

Fortunately, they were able to meet the *Kuru*, a motorised landing craft which had the evacuees on board ready to be transferred. The *Castlemaine* 'took on some wounded Australians and Portuguese sick', which Gordon 'then had to look after'. As the *Castlemaine* made its return trip to Darwin, Gordon was busy with the bloody mess of tending the wounded.

Meanwhile the *Armidale* was ordered to land the Portuguese commandos, so it headed towards the Timor shore. But the Japanese were now on to the Allied operations and land-based aircraft soon sank it. As Gordon recounted this story to me, he described how the *Armidale* was sunk 'with nearly all the crew, and almost all the Javanese commandos sunk. They had a very epic journey, the survivors. After many days and many deaths they were eventually picked up. And our government unfortunately kept very quiet about it'.

This was a poignant reflection of the way that wartime propaganda affected how Australia's Pacific War has been remembered. The notion that Australia was fighting for its own survival in 1942 has continued to persist and in a way misses a bigger point. After the first raid on Darwin, there were subsequent attacks on other towns like Broome, whose first attack Ian Shaw detailed in *The Ghosts of Roebuck Bay*, and there were lots of other repeated strikes throughout Australia's north. But although the Australian government used these attacks as propaganda to manage morale, foster recruitment, and encourage widespread cooperation with government plans and policies, it was relatively clear that Japan's interests and intentions lay elsewhere, primarily the oilfields near Java. As Peter Stanley's *Invading Australia* effectively demonstrated, Australia was not under serious threat of invasion. The Japanese had decided against even trying it. They did not want land; they needed oil.

And Japanese operations against Australia bear this out. They were concerned with the way Australia could act as a useful military staging post, precisely as the British had first hoped to use it in 1788. But the fact is that by 1942 Australia was more than just a base. It was actively using its own resources to help other people fight for their countries, and it was one of the key parts of offensive warfare in retaliation against the Japanese Empire. Japan knew this, which is why it bombed northern Australia in the first place. And the continued harrying actions of the Australian forces were what led to a Japanese cruiser chasing the *Castlemaine* back towards Darwin. It was only thwarted in running down its slower and smaller prey by the timely intervention of 'some R.A.A.F. people that had been sent out to attack the cruiser', as Gordon put it.

Throughout 1941 and 1942, Daphne Hiley had mostly stayed in Brisbane. But about the time Gordon was running to and from Timor, she was moved to Toowoomba. It was still home territory, but it was the beginning of a major shift for her, and for the Australian volunteer women. In early 1943 there was a rush of scribbled activity on her record. Promoted to 'A/SGT', acting sergeant, she then 'M/OUT', marched out, to the acronym 'A.A.M.W.S.', Australian Army Medical Woman's Service. In March she was sent to 'Officers School Melbourne' and by June had been confirmed as a sergeant. In July she was promoted to lieutenant.

Another form in her file followed all this. It was A. Form B.199(a), which detailed the 'Officer's Record of Service'. She was given a personal number, which had to be changed in November 1943. It is crossed out, with a replacement written above. Her record explains why in the curt pencilled scrawl: 'Volunteered & accepted for service in AIF & allotted personal No. QFX59244.' Grandma had just joined the army.

Like Daphne, Gordon had travelled south towards Melbourne during 1943. After the excitement of late 1942, Gordon was attached to the 27th Australian Infantry Battalion and was able to head south with them 'for a spot of leave', as he said. 'Then we went up to Northern Queensland', he told me.

'I was at Townsville for about six months', he said. While there, the 27th was 'loading bombs, including mustard gas'.

And so Gordon got to see and deal with the effects of mustard gas on Australian troops on home soil. Not from enemy attack, but from 'leaking bombs'.

I was surprised to hear this, not having realised that Australia had chemical weapons. Gordon's own brief written account of his war also mentioned this incident, and went one further: 'I flew then for a week to Heidelberg, near Melbourne, for a gas warfare school.' He was aware that he had glanced by a dark chapter in Australia's military history. This has only recently been given greater attention, including by Geoff Plunkett in *Death by Mustard Gas*, which detailed some of the shocking realities of chemical warfare agents present in Australia during the Second World War, and their harming of civilian wharfies tasked with unloading some of them.

After Townsville, Gordon was sent to the Atherton Tablelands in Queensland for further training. His photo album records parts of his time in Queensland and has a series of pictures of Magnetic Island, and of his mates at Atherton. Daphne has a smaller collection of photos, which also show her and her friends moving up and down Queensland, the locations sometimes recorded, like one of Trinity Bay, Cairns. Hers most likely date to a slightly later period, but they reflect the general experiences of camp life and the pleasure those in the military forces obviously took in picnicking in the bush whenever they could. The war gave many of them opportunities to explore wide sweeps of the continent that they may otherwise never have visited.

Yet in recording the general sense of good company, there is also sadness. With the loss of the *Centaur* in May 1943 many of Gordon's photos of his friends were probably among the last pictures taken of these fellows. They suddenly became pictures of dead mates.

Even Daphne's photos, which contain a few snaps of army camps, show uniformed men in formation, many of whom were likely to have soon been deployed overseas. A great push against the Japanese front was underway. And soon enough Gordon's turn came. In May 1944 he boarded the *Duntroon* in Cairns at about 3 am one morning and was carried north to the island of New Guinea.

1944

Like many other parents, Gordon's parents Alexander and Ellen would have followed the war as closely as they could. But things had changed since the days when Alexander's contemporaries wrote brutally blunt letters home about their experiences in the South African Traansvaal which were published for all to see in the local newspapers. Censorship was better at keeping civilians and war at a discrete remove, and the new technologies of radio and cinema were better deployed by governments to control the message of the war's progress. But media coverage would no doubt have made Gordon's general experiences at Darwin familiar to them, nonetheless, and his imminent departure from Australia's soil would have been a cause of great anxiety. Alexander painted a postcard-sized picture of their house at Cheltenham and posted it to his son. On the back were written a few lines: 'Would you like this little picture/ As still from us you roam /There are loving hearts awaiting you/ At home sweet home'.

Later in 1944 Alexander and Ellen would welcome home another of their children, who stayed with them for a few weeks. Gordon's brother Arthur had enlisted in 1941 and been sent to the Middle East. Like Gordon, he later wrote a record of his experiences in the conflict, and the names of places alone resonate strongly in Australian military tradition: Egypt, Palestine, Syria, Lebanon, and El Alamein. Fortunately, by the time Gordon was leaving Australia Arthur was back safely on Australian soil, so the parents had one less major worry.

But being in Australia did not guarantee safety. Arthur had to contend with a bout of malaria, which he successfully overcame. And in the Hay internment camp, only two days after Gordon had left Cairns, John O'Rafferty contracted myocarditis. He was put in the camp hospital, the old colonial gaol, the coolest spot the authorities could find. John never recovered sufficiently to return to active service and was discharged as 'medically unfit for further military service' later that year. It was just as well, perhaps, because in July some of the Italians in the camp turned violent, sick of their incarceration. And in August a major breakout of Japanese prisoners of war at the Cowra camp occurred, causing mayhem, injuries, deaths, civilian fear, and a rearrangement of the camp structures. Many of the Cowra survivors were moved to Hay.

Horace Duck, still sometimes working at the butchery in Junee, was adjusting to life with one less finger. The year beforehand, in June 1943, he had got a splinter in one of his fingers on his right hand. It became badly infected and hospitalised him for quite some time. By December, with medical staff despairing of a spreading infection, the finger had to be amputated. He had experienced six months of agony, and probably some embarrassment, but such was the state of medicine at the time. The slightest infection could kill and he was quite lucky to lose only a finger. At least he took it in relatively good humour and later joked to customers that the missing digit was in the sausage meat somewhere.

On arriving at Lae, in New Guinea, Gordon discovered a friend of his, 'one Will McLaren, of Kokoda track experience, who was then running a native hospital and training school'. Having held the Japanese advance, Allied forces were now pushing back. For the army's medical staff, this meant their concerns broadly encompassed the civilian population as well as their brothers in arms. McLaren went into the highlands to investigate a dysentery outbreak, and Gordon was asked 'to look after the hospital in his absence'. It was while there that he encountered a new drug—penicillin. 'We had none of course,' he said, the drug still largely being an American war secret, 'but one of the medical orderlies knew someone at the Lae AGH [American General Hospital] and he thoughtfully stole some for me. It certainly saved the life of a native with pneumonia.'

The photos that Gordon took of the Papuans have fascinated me since I first saw them. They are one of the most amazing parts of the war experience he depicted, helping to capture aspects of how Islander peoples experienced the war. They are a reminder that the war was fought on other peoples' lands, in part for those people and for those lands, against a common enemy. The notion of men fighting in foreign jungles simply to defend Australia has always struck me as a naively selfish interpretation of events, which does a disservice to the men who experienced it. As Lachlan Grant's *Australian Soldiers in Asia-Pacific* reveals, the relationships between soldiers and the people they met were varied and complex and tend to complicate narratives that are inclined to focus on Australia as just a British outpost. Gordon's grey photographs are stark proofs of how complex history really is. It was anything but black and white.

A number of the photographs belong to Gordon's time at Lae, including a series of images of the 'Native Hospital Lae 1944'. Here the sick and wounded locals were treated for a range of conditions. Other photographs document everyday activities like husking coconuts, building hut roofs out of palm leaves, boating, and cooking captured fish. Life in the islands did not simply stop for the war, whatever the interruptions, and he therefore has a veritable pictorial anthropology of sorts. But more than simply documenting their lives, the pictures show that Gordon was interested in their lives.

After Lae Gordon was stationed at Wau, where, he later wryly said, he 'played a lot of chess'. Mostly they were engaged in training, because the fighting had moved on from that sector. But he was clearly busy with his camera, because photographs of 'Police Boys', a single Papuan smoking a pipe, and various images of Papuan huts all speak to ready engagement with the local people. And he must have done some difficult rounds of the territory as one photograph of his driver beating a way through the jungle indicates. If I did not know the provenance, I would assume it was a Kokoda Track picture. When I asked him at greater length about it, he responded, 'Oh, there I was just doing sick parades and checking people. There was no activity in that island'. But the peace did not entirely last. 'In some of the other ones', he said, 'I had to go out and bring blokes in, that sort of thing.' Of these encounters, he simply did not give much detail, and I did not like to press him.

Over the following months Gordon was moved around nearby islands, roughly comparable with some of Captain Neil's old trading territory. He was next at Nissan, a small coral island north of Bougainville, where the Americans instructed him in the art of waterskiing behind a Patrol Torpedo boat. From here he took numerous trips to nearby locations, generally for the purposes of assessing and assisting Islanders after the Japanese had departed. 'They were not in very good shape', he said simply and ominously of the Feni Islanders. So with the aid of fellow military medics from New Zealand and America, Gordon 'flew in a Catalina flying boat back to Feni' with a supply of penicillin donated by the Americans.

Another mission involved visiting Tanga, where there was a Christian mission. One of his photographs shows the church from the inside.

He pointed it out to me, telling me to note 'the roof of it with holes all through it, sunlight shining through'. They were 'bullet wounds', he said. Other photographs show him and others inoculating Islander children against disease. By and large he recalled that the Islanders had generally 'been knocked about pretty badly'.

On Bougainville he photographed a downed Japanese Zero, and it was on this island that he came closest to the fighting front, having been transferred to the 11th Australian Field Ambulance. Apparently he got seasick on the landing barge on the way in to shore. But despite disliking the actual trip, he was still fascinated by these odd boats and captured some photographs of the manoeuvres that were required to right them. Large numbers of Islanders would assist to free the boats after they got jammed on the sand. Pulling long ropes left and then right, they would gradually wiggle the boats free, so that they could return for more troops.

The photograph of the downed Zero was not proof of a past threat—rather, it was evidence of a present reality. On the very next page of his album are two amazing pictures. One is of a group of women and children walking in a hurried fashion, carrying luggage and infants. It is labelled beneath with one simple word: 'Refugees'.

The other photograph on that page was of a wounded Australian soldier being carried in a basic stretcher by several Islanders. These are the men that Gordon regularly worked with as a medic. He knew some of the famous 'Fuzzy Wuzzy Angels' by name.

And sometimes, he got a little too close to the fighting for comfort.

One day by the Puriata River, the day after the Australians had pulled out of camp, Gordon recalls a sense of shock when the Japanese 'came in and blew up the bridge just where we were camped'. Such determined resistance, even so late in the conflict, was impressive, yet also gave cause for great concern. Because of the destroyed bridge, Gordon said, 'we had to cross, driving the vehicles into the river, which is about mid-thigh deep, running very swiftly and very rocky'. Naturally, he took some photos of the scene.

Crossing the same river on another occasion, Gordon was heading out with 'half a dozen' Islanders to bring in a wounded soldier on a 'bush-made stretcher'. But continued Japanese operations in the area had the Islanders a bit concerned. Gordon recalled that 'no way were they going to show me the way—not unless I went in front—so I ended up crossing a ruddy river, exposed to hundreds of yards on either bank, feeling very uncomfortable because they wouldn't go unless I went first, so I went first'. Nervously watching the jungle, feeling his way across a rocky river one slippery stone at a time, he heard a flitting sound interrupt the river's usual swoosh and gurgle.

'I had my revolver in my hand before I knew, ready to shoot,' he said, 'but it was just a bird.'

The party continued into the jungle and retrieved the wounded soldier.

Gordon only told me of one other really dangerous encounter, again operating in the Puriata River area.

'I went up at one stage with another RMO, with a battalion in front of me,' he said, 'and the battalion was going to put on a bayonet attack, clearing up some Japs. And I went up with him. It was something of a shemozzle. I didn't know, of course, where I was; you couldn't see anything. It was jungle everywhere. And we started, and I jumped into a very tiny slit trench with another bloke and all the leaves were falling down around us from gunfire. But I didn't see anything of any of them then.' He could never see why that particular bayonet charge was deemed necessary. I suspect that as a medic, he had a particular dislike for the cut and thrust of close quarters combat.

Soon enough he was out of the action. In his service record is a confidential report, assessing Captain Gordon Brodie. In the general remarks section, it said: 'Good type. Enthusiastic. Fair Command. Has had practical experience.' It was, I thought, not a bad assessment of his war. But I know that he would want at least one word added: Lucky.

While awaiting transport back to Australia for a period of leave, word came through on the radio that the war in Europe was over. But he was not going back to home as he knew it. His military record notes in sad specificity one of his life's worst moments: 'Change of Next of Kin, Father: Deceased. Next of Kin: Mother'. His father had died while he was on duty; the house Alexander had painted had one less occupant.

Fortunately the final lines of Daphne Hiley's service record recorded a happier moment, written in the same terse style: 'Officer married, name now Lt D. J. Brodie'. During 1945 Gordon had remained on Australian soil, working in northern Queensland, among other duties. Eventually their paths had crossed at a military medical facility out of Sydney, and it had stayed crossed. After Japan surrendered in August 1945, the Australian military commenced the complex process of demobilisation. Gordon and Daphne's engagement, with a photograph of Lieutenant Hiley, was announced in the Brisbane *Sunday Mail*'s social pages, perhaps the first hint of a return to civilian life.

Gordon took up residence as a local general practitioner in Picton, just south-west of Sydney, with Daphne continuing her administrative career by running the practice. Gordon was appointed to be one of the local repatriation medical officers, assisting in getting the soldiery back to normality. He had many adventures serving the district and was still working into the period when I was first visiting. He still wore his war greatcoat with considerable regularity until sometime in the 2000s, when Grandma finally won out and got him to stop wearing it.

Rather appropriately, the final photograph in Gordon's war album was of 'Lieut. D. Hiley farewelling AAMWS Contingent Force for BCOF Japan 1946 Before leaving Australia'. I became quite fascinated by the British Commonwealth Occupation Force after reading Robin Gerster's book *Travels in Atomic Sunshine: Australia and the Occupation of Japan*. And in exploring the family's war, I discovered that Corporal Ted O'Rafferty, John's son and Eileen's brother, was part of this post-war occupation force of Australian soldiers. And what is more, he too had a few photos that he had given to his sister Eileen, including one immediately recognisable as Hiroshima. On the back, for the benefit of his family, he wrote: 'The atomic Bomb exploded right over the top of the Building in the rear.' In the foreground, no doubt capitalising on the soldier-tourists, was a shop with an English sign: 'Bookseller Atom', it was called.

Ted also had pictures of Japanese children, brought home to show his family. One of the boys was wearing thongs. It was as if the pictures could convey what words could not quite express. These were people, not monsters. They were 'Shoe Shine Boys', and 'My Caddy'. They were people, with jobs, with families, with smiles. It was like the photos of Islanders in Gordon's war album, including two boys, just schoolchildren, labelled as 'Peto and Conerad'. They had names.

The Second World War broadened Australia's outlook. Other military engagements would follow in the subsequent century, from Japanese occupation, through the Malayan emergency, Indonesian Confrontation, Korea, Vietnam, Iraq, Timor, Afghanistan, and so on. So too would a broader economic and cultural gaze grow, especially as Australia began to take a greater regional responsibility—rather than operating primarily as a British naval base and prison facility at the corner of the Southern, Indian, and Pacific oceans, as it had been when Thomas Kennedy first arrived in 1797.

The war in Europe also had a great impact, drawing refugees to the southern continent, continuing and greatly expanding a tradition of cultural and ethnic plurality that the White Australia Policy had rather vainly tried to suppress, and leading eventually to a modern and largely happily multicultural Australia. Japanese and Italian people had not been interned in Hay because that ideology was a roaring success—for if it had been, many of them would not have been in Australia in the first place. And widespread concerns about American troops, particularly African American ones like some of the American doctors Gordon photographed, forced some aficionados for a 'white Australia' to face up to the new global realities.

There are many intricate strings of causes and effects linked to 'the war'. It helped embarrass Australian governments into dropping its unhelpful obsessions with race, with profound effects in particular for Aboriginal peoples, many of whom had served during the war. Eventually a nationwide referendum in 1967 showed the Australian people repudiating the official racism of the Federation as constituted in 1901.

The war also helped Australia strategically, by encouraging it to look further afield than the Commonwealth, and to recognise America as a cultural and military ally. However, some members of its government still felt the attraction of empire, and slavishly allowed atomic weapons testing in Australia's interior by the British, irradiating Australian servicemen and once again displacing Aborigines. The radioactive clouds these tests produced floated across the continent, including over the densely populated east coast, and were tracked by scientists even as they passed over the heads of a largely unaware public. Among the participants at the Montebello Islands testing site off Western Australia's coast was the ship HMAS *Junee*, whose bell and diving suit are displayed in the Junee Council Chambers, a little relic of the Cold War in country Australia.

Yet despite some such setbacks and regressions in following decades, the war charged Australia's economy and fostered a strong sense of nationhood. It also set up the new global political struggles of the future, with Australia a serious participant in moves for international governance. There are lots of elements of Australia's development that can be linked to the war, but the most significant is the simplest, one common to many Australians: the war saw both sets of my grandparents brought together.

CHAPTER EIGHTEEN

THE PAST HAS NO CONCLUSION
2015

MY MUM AND DAD were both born in the 1950s, became teachers, met in Junee, married, and had me in 1981. The process was simple enough, even if their stories encompass a period of great social change. Their stories, like those of my younger siblings, like mine, and like Australia's, are still being written. What records we will leave remains to be seen.

Towards the end of my research for this book I found a little funeral prayer card for my great grandfather, John Thomas O'Rafferty, among Pa's stuff. At the top was a small quotation from St Ambrose: 'We have loved him in life, let us not forget him in death.' It seemed to me a reasonable reflection on my journey in writing this story of my ancestors. Many of these people had been forgotten by the family, and it reminded me that if we do not stop and reflect on the past, then we run the danger of losing it.

Also among Pa's papers was an envelope containing some old letters. My great aunty Joyce had written to him, giving him some of their 'Mum's letters'. Joyce had left home to become a nun and Frances Duck had written to her in the convent. There were two letters inside. Each was undated, but datable to the 1940s because of the content. They reveal some ordinary moments for the family, of a sort that I had not really uncovered much during the course of my wider quest for family members and their stories. These everyday conversations reveal that Frances Duck's children would often visit her, most particularly Greg. 'All the boys are so very kind & say such nice things to me', she wrote. 'Greg comes in for awhile about 8.30 pm nightly & is a real soothing tonic for me, he said he will always see that Ann is well looked after & happy & told me to tell you that if ever you want anything to let him know.' It was, I thought, a wonderful testament to Pa's character. I knew well what he thought of his mother, 'Saint Frances', but this gave me an insight into what she thought of him. Frances went on to tell her daughter that 'although he doesn't write he is always there if you need him & I know he is'. Frances had been suffering from a condition of the stomach for a long time. As these letters hint, she might have seen her own end was not too far off and was very glad that Greg would continue to take care of the family.

Other family members clearly visited while the letters were being written, including Eileen, who was mentioned as having 'just come in'. The visit most likely involved the sharing of a pot of tea and perhaps some baked treats. When Eileen had left, Frances continued writing the letter. She wrote about normal parts of her life. There was a mention of dogs, which 'are never allowed inside', a cake, which she thought 'should be moist', and Greg's new car, which was 'a single seater with a little dickie seat' and made him laugh a lot.

'Well how am I?' Frances asked, before saying that 'the last two weeks I haven't been so hot'. Despite regular injections from the doctor, she was 'still very sick on the stomach' and found it 'very hard to eat'. Food and medication, she was convinced, 'keeps my tummy sore'. She explained how she planned 'to just quietly knock it off' to see if she improved without the medication. If she did not get any better, then she thought she might 'ask Dr how about going into that hospital in Wagga that's run by the nuns', although, she said, 'I can't think of the name'.

Frances died in 1948. In the terse language of a newspaper report she was 'a sufferer for six years.' I was glad of the letter, which helped me to get a bit more insight into my great-grandmother and the world that she inhabited. It helped me to realise that I had only really scratched the surface of my family's stories, or even of my country. These everyday interactions of family and friends rarely pass intact into historical memory. But sometimes with the tiniest of hints it is possible to realise and build up an understanding of the past and to make connections between peoples and places, even across time. I realised that Frances was referring to Calvary Hospital in Wagga, where, much later, I was born.

Unpicking the detail of an expansive family tree and using that to write a history of Australia seemed at the outset to be a straightforward task. I have ended up with a more nuanced demographic profile in this history than is usually produced by many standard historical methods. In the past, as in the present, children, adults, and the elderly, men and women, all lived side by side, their stories interacting and their lives overlapping. By capturing this my aim has been to provide a sense of continuity that is lacking in traditional histories that divide time into neat periods and tend to deal mainly with adults, relegating children, the elderly, and often enough women, to separate chapters.

But I have also strived through this to produce a national story. Naturally, the experience of my family has determined the main topics and issues I have covered, and I make no pretence of having covered everything that ever happened in Australia. Indeed, if any argument about the nature of Australia's past can be offered on the basis of this extensive research exercise, then it can be reduced to a simple formula: Australia's history is complex.

Australia became my home by an accident of birth, the end product of many generations of movement and child-bearing. In an unimaginably ancient past, this continent was home to algae, then reptiles, dinosaurs, birds, and mammals. Some of the oldest evidence of life itself is found in Australia.

Sometime around 45,000 years ago, the last hominid species to spread out from Africa finally made its way to Australia, at that time joined to Papua and Tasmania by land bridges in a supercontinent we call Sahul. These people had to cross a body of water over which they could not see their destination. Drawn perhaps by smoke or birds, they followed their intuition, establishing themselves and their descendents in a previously unpeopled land. This migration is, by inference, among the earliest evidence of complex watercraft, and therefore of the main tool necessary to build complex watercraft: language.

Over millennia Aboriginal peoples adapted to their new homeland, altering parts of it. The shift from the Pleistocene to the Holocene epochs about 10,000 years ago marked a global settling down as the world's climate stabilised. People in Africa, Europe, Asia, and Australia gradually formed into relatively distinct cultural entities, although these naturally shifted and changed over the centuries. Eventually one of those broad cultural groups, 'the British', began to colonise large parts of the globe, including Australia.

In the relatively short term, I am mostly a British Isles mongrel. The longer term, however, is more complex. By participating in the National Genographic Project 2.0, a worldwide genetic study partnered with the National Geographic Society, I can chart some of my ancestral movements in the very distant past. Some of my forebears were among the first of the species *Homo sapiens* to leave Africa. But I am an amalgam of hominid species. Part Neanderthal and part Denovisian, I have a complicated family story. Even my recent European lines reveal that I have some Northern Asian heritage, probably transmitted by the Sami people from east to west across the Arctic tundra, where mammoth once roamed. And, among other things, I have a reasonable proportion of Mediterranean gene markers, intensely satisfying my Classical inclinations. Technically, and amazingly, I am related to you, whoever you are. We are all kin somehow.

And that is the ultimate message Australia offers the world. The who, what, when, where, why, how, and with what effect of historical writing all fade into insignificance in the face of the simple fact that we are here, and this is our home: continent, nation, and family rolled into one. Australia should be a place where people come together.

As an exercise in historiography a familial history of this familiar place has much to offer beyond providing demographic nuance, indulging individual curiosity, or providing a weighty argument against any potential accusations of my being 'un-Australian'. Behind the story of a handsome baby in a red jumpsuit, who grows into a skinny boy with snowy blonde hair in yellow gumboots, who then shot up into a gangly darker-haired teenager, before entering what is technically referred to as adulthood, is a historical method of some power: you can choose your friends and historical subjects, but not your family. And by being forced to engage with them and their worlds, the tendency to turn the past to your own ends is more limited than when one can pick and choose what to research and write about.

Allowing my family to chart the narrative of Australia has enabled me to get past some of the preoccupations of academics, folklorists, and political commentators, while bringing together the advantages of research undertaken at levels personal, local, national, and international through an extensive primary research exercise. By focusing on the stories of my many people, I ended up with a history of the continent and nation. And by doing this, the story is in some ways very different from those that have tended to dominate the way Australia's national story is recalled and recorded. It is a story which finally transcends the tired myopia of Australian exceptionalism, where everything has to be uniquely or 'quintessentially' Australian. And it is a story that does not subject us to that banal metaphor where events 'forge' identities.

In particular this personal perspective helps mitigate the obsessive drive to revisit the politics of the present upon the past which has infected Australian historical writing throughout the past half-century. Australian history has become a political football, as shown by repeated arguments over school curricula, surveillance given to presentations of the past in public institutions, and the commodification of various little bits of it.

Although regularly used as terms by historians, or to describe historical writing, 'right wing' and 'left wing' are almost pointlessly broad characterisations. The terms derived from a physical way of determining sides on particular questions, with one group gathering on the right of a room and the opposing group on the left, before the moderator counted the results. But it has come to stand for packages of ideas. And so individual thoughts on particular issues are forcibly subsumed in the collective, much like big histories can mute individuals by constantly addressing groups: Labour, Liberal, National, Green, princes, merchants, peasants, convicts, Aborigines, women, upper classes, middle classes, lower classes, etcetera, ad nauseam. We seem to have forgotten that the winged metaphor serves solely to affirm the irreconcilability of ideas, ideologies, and people, and the parties to which they are ascribed, and to map human history as a mostly binary perpetual struggle, each side variously flapping up and down, vigorously going nowhere.

Real life for real people is just not lived in a state of permanent political struggle, or as some sort of distillation process for identity formation, and rarely has it been. The goldfields were of far greater importance to individual Australian people and families than they ever were for Australian democracy, for example, so it is time to let go of Eureka a bit and discover again the bigger picture of which it was a part. The gold fever variously made Australia's people sick, angry, strong, rich, and poor, and much else besides. But to turn it into the background for a 'defining' moment of our democracy, to treat that as a uniquely and exclusively Australian event, and, in doing so, to leave out everything else from the story, is demonstrably misguided. We cannot corral the complexities of the past into a single word or an associated iconographical amalgam of ideas that take their shape in flag form. It is like the tired habit of reducing the entirety of the First World War to the words 'Anzac' and 'Gallipoli', or to think our convict legacy is little more than the First Fleet. They are all interesting stories, and they are important stories, but they are not the totality of our story, our experience, or our heritage. We are bigger than that. It is time we reached out for our identity on our own terms.

Similarly, another significant area a familial approach to history helps redress is Australia's complex racial history, still often subject to the broad characterisations by which it has repeatedly been bound. Approaches that have largely dealt in binaries have often enough simply proved binarising. Contrary to narratives focused on abstractions, imaginary universals, and unhelpfully broad collectives of often arbitrarily grouped people, a familial approach helps bring in some much-needed nuance. The fact of frontier wars is something that my people lived with, even though few had any potential to have participated in, or lived through, such conflicts. More than discord, my family reveals some of the diverse regularity of real engagements that settlers and their children had with Indigenous peoples throughout the whole sweep of our story, highlighting the presence of a wide range of people and interactions in our shared past. While not necessarily the full story, these interactions reveal that relationships continued past the moments of first contact and intense conflict and often operated at more personal levels than is often allowed in Australia's previous social histories. Whether it is Dill-Macky's charitable drive, Neil Brodie's employment of and conflict with various Islander peoples, Joshua Higgs' conversations with Aborigines on the frontier, the Kiss boys racing alongside Charlie, or even more pointedly William Kiss's mysterious Hawkesbury mother, we need simply to admit that the story is complex. Let us finally recognise that ours is not a story of two irreconcilable sides, revealed all too often in Australian histories by a slightly embarrassed and prefatory chapter on 'Aborigines' before the real business of 'history' begins.

Allowing the real lives and inter-generational activities and connections of my people to unfold has also enabled me to better chart the process of modernisation itself, and to situate Australia in wider geographical and longer chronological contexts that are more sensitive to continuities and changes across time and space. The Industrial Revolution, for example, was not dumped on Australia. Much of it happened in Australia, in tandem with wider developments. Universal suffrage advanced in Australia in parallel with other parts of the globe, and it is no accident that women gradually gain in prominence as the narrative advances. And like these structural developments, accretions of cultural artefacts came to form a collective of Australia's multi-culture. Enjoyment of *The Man From Snowy River* did not stop Australians from engaging with wider cultural horizons, whether the neo-gothic re-imagining of the European past, French-inspired architecture, Italian coffee culture, Chinese cuisine, or the jazz and movies of America.

Until relatively recently many of our historians have had a relatively narrow ethnic and cultural outlook. Yet the presence of Americans, Chinese, Pacific Islanders, Central Europeans, and more, is demonstrable in Australia from the earliest days of settlement. From the Makassans who fished for Trepang in northern Australia in the eighteenth century, to the Saunders' German wine-making neighbours, to the Chinese fellows who wanted a drink in the hill country, to Pedre Hansen, the Danish boat builder of Balmain, Australia's is not a bi-cultural or monocultural story. Even my relatively stereotypical family tree crossed paths with diverse situations with considerable regularity.

Family also brings out the complexities of cultural identity. Whether having a strong sense of Irish, Scottish, or Yorkshire extraction, my family regularly married and interacted across what are sometimes treated as if they were absolute cultural divides. Even sectarianism and prejudice, while clearly present throughout Australia's past, serve to highlight that we have never been the nation of anti-religious or apathetic neo-secularists that some historians have tried to suggest we are. Australians have tended to treat their beliefs with seriousness, whether they are Christian, Jewish, Muslim, Daoist, Confucian, Buddhist, Hindu, Animist, atheist, or any other of humanity's ways of understanding our place in the universe. And although there are notable exceptions, generally we have treated other Australians' faiths with respect also, and complaints against our own with good humour. The churches, synagogues, mosques, and temples that dot our built landscape are all tributes to our shared history of promoting tolerance and a functional civil society. Our tradition of secular government fostered a sense of all religions and beliefs being treated fairly in the public sphere, not being ejected from it.

A family history filled with ordinary people refocuses both biographical and social histories to better interact with each other. A social history of certain groups or classes would exclude some members of my family, in some instances arbitrarily separating spouses from each other, or children from parents. Yet class does come through as an important divisive element of Australian society. Our past was clearly less egalitarian than many of us think it was, but this points out to us the source of that treasured Australian aspiration: the way it should be must be better than the way it was. Knowing the 'was' helps us stay on track. In contrast, detailed biographies of ordinary people also allow us to break from a common biographical model, where historian after historian publishes books charting the lives of individuals who are suspiciously frequently lone men of genius, often misunderstood in their own times, driving history forwards. With some extremely rare exceptions, human history has not really worked like this: it is rather a comment on emotional trends within the historical profession. A history of ordinary Australians should remind us to value our own lives and our own contributions to our society and our times. We are all important. Frances's letter about her family, detailing how they were good to each other, is the best legacy we could leave to posterity, whether it gets documented or not.

So, through these and other ways, looking at Australia through a family-history lens reveals the overwhelmingly complex nature of our past. It is not a simple narrative of sequential developments. It is not a story of good people versus bad people. It is not the story of an ideological struggle between left and right, upper and lower classes, or other sections of the community. It is, like a family, a messy thing, that still somehow strives to make and maintain a sense and bond of unity. Australia's is the story of people, dissimilar in many respects, but still linked to each other in a relationship that links place and people in the past, present, and future. Relaxing our approach to our past, forgiving if not forgetting, accepting it on its own terms, helps us to take pride in the story not simply of Australian character, but also of character development. Rather than a pride-filled march through time of some immutable 'Australian spirit' where everyone sang the same tune, looking closely at our past reveals our diversity. Like cicadas in the eucalyptus trees, it is at once a beautiful and wondrously cacophonous thing.

And there are more songs out there than those captured in this book, so our challenge is to find them. Australia's is not a story of three acts: Aboriginal, colonial, and national periods. Nor is it just a series of unconnected or interconnected identity-forming events like the First Fleet, Eureka Stockade, Ned Kelly, Federation, First World War, Depression, and Second World War. Rather, ours is the story of many millions of stories, and a family history charts continuities and connections that weave through and sometimes past those events. Australians do not always agree on everything, even perhaps about what we stand for. Brothers and sisters quarrel as well as play. Sometimes, members of our group disappoint us, and we split into political factions seemingly determined to amplify the disappointing effect. But children can grow up and mature. Occasionally some of us are hostile to outsiders and become selfish about small sections of our family, perhaps liking the way things are, or misunderstanding the way things were, certainly worried that life will change. But the idea of the 'good old days', as Pa often told me, 'is a load of shit'. So as we look back at our own familiar paths and pasts we will be faced with the immutable truth that Australia has never been static. Neither the continent's original inhabitants, nor those who have come after them, have ever been, or ever will be, an unchanging people in an unchanging land.

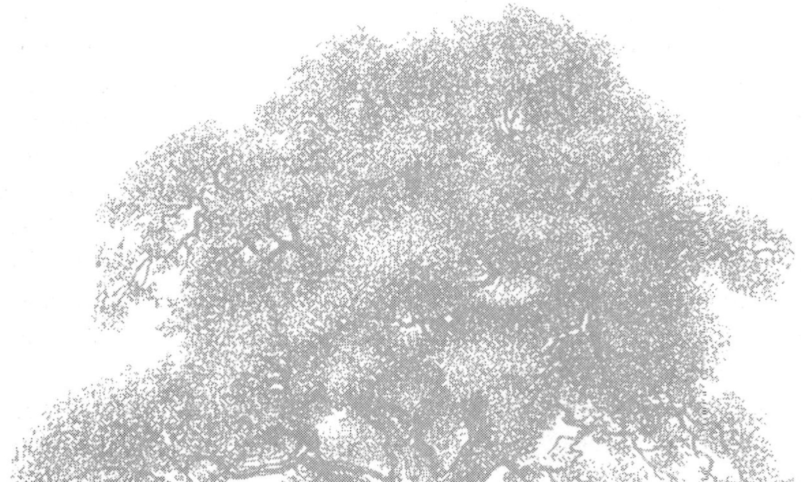

THE KEN OF KIN

NORMALLY, THIS IS where a bibliography and list of source material goes. I have, however, written this with an eye to the process of research, as well as the product, so a long list of items will be of limited benefit for the sake of dramatically increasing the size of an already large book. The expert or enthusiast should be able to source my stories with a sensible reading of the context, and everyone else can take it on trust. I have mentioned some historians in the text where appropriate, generally striving for currency and immediacy of relevance, but there are necessarily omissions in a work of this size. Readers are increasingly well served with quality research on Australian topics and should be able to further explore issues and themes with relative ease should they so desire.

I would, however, like to draw attention to some of the main research tools that have informed this book. Firstly, my immediate family have been a source of much knowledge, and I thank them for enabling me to share their stories. I am no linguist, but I suspect the similarity between the words ken (meaning knowing) and kin (meaning family) is no great mystery. My family members living and dead have all made this possible.

Secondly, I have made extensive use of Ancestry.com for tracking and accessing materials, particularly those on the British Isles side of the great migration. They do a marvellous job, especially of coordinating electronic versions of manuscript materials held in public institutions around the world.

Thirdly, I acknowledge and thank the libraries, archives, and museums that are our formal sites of institutional memory, particularly, in the case of my family, the National Library of Australia, State Records Authority of New South Wales, State Library of New South Wales, Mitchell Library, Public Record Office of Victoria, State Library of Victoria, Tasmanian Archive and Heritage Office, Queensland State Archives, State Library of Queensland, National Archives of Australia, Australian War Memorial, and the registries of births, deaths, and marriages in New South Wales, Victoria, and Queensland. I have also utilised other state, national, and international archives, museums, and art galleries. I wish them all a continued existence for the wonderful service they provide humanity, and for so often enabling me to indulge my curiosity about the past, especially in this great age of austerity that sometimes seems a deliberate attempt to bring on a modern sequel to the 'dark ages' of late antiquity and early medieval times.

The National Library of Australia's 'Trove' deserves a special mention all of its own for providing electronic access to Australia's historical newspapers. Without this, we would still be in the dizzying and pitiful hell of the microfilm reader. It is, to my mind, the best research tool in the world.

Finally, I would encourage Australians to discover their own connections with our past, whether that be through their own family stories or the places where they have chosen to live. Whether you or your family arrived here 45,000 years ago or yesterday makes no difference. If you are here, you are one of us.

ACKNOWLEDGEMENTS

CONVENTION CAN OFTEN trump conviction, as with Thomas Kennedy's petition to the governor mentioned a few hundred pages back, so one must be wary in reading any given text too literally if it follows a regular format. But historians of the future should rest assured that these following acknowledgements of aid and amiable service are genuine and heartfelt, for without these people, this book simply would not have happened.

First thanks must go to Rose Michael, who recognised and helped form a story. I will be forever grateful. From this, a cohort of people helped bring this book to completion including a range of wonderful people at Hardie Grant. Like the folk described in this book, a publisher's staff are undoubtedly busy and essential but are not always specifically documented. I hope they will recognise that KIN is a tribute to their work and the sorts of people often working behind the scenes of recorded history. Another individual who should be singled out, however, is Pam Brewster. Pam has guided this project throughout its journey to completion, and I could not have had a better publishing Jedi-master to watch over my progress. Just as I opened or signed off so many emails, I again write: Thanks Pam!

I am also extremely grateful to Marg Bowman, my copyeditor. Great fixer of mistakes, adder and remover of commas, polisher of text, huntswoman extraordinary of any odd ambiguity, Marg is also a genuinely intelligent reader who got me to think a bit more and push a little further, improving not only the writing, but also the analysis and argumentation.

Fairly uniquely, KIN proves that sometimes even authors judge books by covers. When I saw the design by Nada Backovic I was awestruck, and as I worked on completing the book that brilliant image was often in my mind, which captured the essence of a text even as it was being finalised.

Although I have pointed to the institutional repositories of fact (and some fictions) I want to particularly thank the staff of the various libraries and archives that I visited, corresponded with, and used. In many archives there is a familiar tension between the needs of professional and genealogical researchers, and I am glad to say I was served well in both capacities. I also wish to draw attention and thanks to the administrators of our electronic access, particularly to the National Library of Australia's great treasure, Trove. A significant factor in facilitating modern research is not just technology, but also technicians.

My friends and family listened to me, tolerated me, and undoubtedly supported me. I will not name them all, but they know who they are. Among a few exceptions I will name are my grandparents. Nanny, who I only knew ever so briefly but who gave me a lifelong love of tea and cake. Pa, who would have loved this book, and gave everyone the impression they were his favourite even though it really was me. Grandma and Grampy, who allowed me to quiz them for this book and to delve into their stories. I hope they will enjoy reading it. So too Dad deserves a mention, for coming on some of the journeys to obscure places mentioned in the book, and acting in a small way as research assistant. And I can honestly say that Mum does more than even this big book could contain. As the Australian university sector collapsed, my Mum stepped in, and I cannot thank her enough.

Last, but also there from the first, is Kristyn Harman. Companion to the Tambo River, Hay, Bega, and beyond, Kris is compassionate and critical in the right sort of way, and I am proud to have had her by my side throughout this journey.